THE WORK OF THE BRITISH LAW COMMISSIONS

The Law Commission (of England and Wales) and the Scottish Law Commission were both established in 1965 to promote the reform of the laws of their respective jurisdictions. Since then, they have each produced hundreds of reports across many areas of law. They are independent of government yet rely on governmental funding and governmental approval of their proposed projects. They also rely on both government and Parliament (and, occasionally, the courts or other bodies) to implement their proposals.

This book examines the tension between independence and implementation and recommends how a balance can best be struck. It proposes how the Commissions should choose their projects given that their duties outweigh their resources, and how we should assess the success, or otherwise, of their output.

Countries around the world have created law reform bodies in the Commissions' image. They may wish to reflect on the GB Commissions' responses to the changes and challenges they have faced to reappraise their own law reform machinery. Equally, the GB Commissions may seek inspiration from other commissions' experiences. The world the GB Commissions inhabit now is very different from when they were established. They have evolved to remain relevant in the face of devolution, the UK's changing relationship with the European Union, increasing pressure for accountability and decreasing funding. Further changes to secure the future of independent law reform are advanced in this book.

The Work of the British Law Commissions

Law Reform… Now?

Shona Wilson Stark

•HART•
PUBLISHING
OXFORD AND PORTLAND, OREGON
2017

Hart Publishing
An imprint of Bloomsbury Publishing Plc

Hart Publishing Ltd
Kemp House
Chawley Park
Cumnor Hill
Oxford OX2 9PH
UK

Bloomsbury Publishing Plc
50 Bedford Square
London
WC1B 3DP
UK

www.hartpub.co.uk
www.bloomsbury.com

Published in North America (US and Canada) by
Hart Publishing
c/o International Specialized Book Services
920 NE 58th Avenue, Suite 300
Portland, OR 97213-3786
USA

www.isbs.com

First published 2017

British Library Cataloguing-in-Publication Data
A catalogue record for this book is available from the British Library.

ISBN: HB: 978-1-50990-691-8
ePDF: 978-1-50990-693-2
ePub: 978-1-50990-692-5

Library of Congress Cataloging-in-Publication Data

Names: Stark, Shona Wilson, author.

Title: The work of the British Law Commissions : law reform... now? / Shona Wilson Stark.

Description: Portland, Oregon : Hart Publishing, 2017. | Includes bibliographical references and index. | Description based on print version record and CIP data provided by publisher; resource not viewed.

Identifiers: LCCN 2017008372 (print) | LCCN 2017012712 (ebook) | ISBN 9781509906925 (Epub) | ISBN 9781509906918 (hardback : alk. paper)

Subjects: LCSH: Law reform—Great Britain. | Great Britain. Law Commission.

Classification: LCC KD654 (ebook) | LCC KD654 .W56 2017 (print) | DDC 340/.30941—dc23

LC record available at https://lccn.loc.gov/2017008372

Typeset by Compuscript Ltd, Shannon

ACKNOWLEDGEMENTS

The idea for this study emerged during a year spent as Legal Assistant at the Scottish Law Commission from 2010 to 2011. For their encouragement in those early stages and beyond, I would like to thank Fiona Leverick, James Chalmers, Sharon Cowan and George Gretton.

This book developed from a doctoral thesis undertaken at the University of Cambridge. I am grateful for the generous financial support I received during my studies from the Cambridge Home and EU Scholarship Scheme, the Girton College Pfeiffer Scholarship, the Clark Foundation for Legal Education, the Girton College Pillman Fund and the University of Cambridge Faculty of Law Yorke Fund. I am equally grateful for the doctoral supervision I received during that time, first from John Ford and latterly from John Allison. I am also indebted to Stuart Bridge for being my advisor, and to Hugh Beale and Kenneth Reid for examining my dissertation. I learnt many valuable lessons from each of them, which I have carried with me during the transition from dissertation to book.

For assistance with archival work, and for permission to publish the results of that work, I am grateful to the BBC Archives, the Churchill Archives Centre, the National Records of Scotland and the National Archives.

This project would have been impossible without the support and enthusiasm of staff and Commissioners of both the Scottish Law Commission and the Law Commission. I would like to thank them for providing me with access to materials and for discussing my research with me as it progressed. Particular thanks are due to Lord Pentland, Andrew Steven, Michael Hallissey, Sir David Lloyd Jones, Adrian Hogarth, Elaine Lorimer, Phil Golding, Elizabeth Cooke, Catherine Vine and Dan Leighton. A special thank you to Malcolm McMillan for tolerating my persistent correspondence with his characteristic candour and good humour. Hector MacQueen is also due particular thanks for his enthusiasm and support from the inception of this project and, crucially, for his most constructive review of my draft manuscript.

I am indebted to those with an interest in law reform, including many former law reformers, who read or listened to my papers and indulged me in conversations about the Commissions over the last few years. Special thanks are due to: David Nichols, Gerry Maher, Neil Faris, Sir Roger Toulson, James Crawford, Sir Kenneth Keith, Sir Henry Brooke, Jeremy Horder, Andrew Burrows, Sir Stephen Silber, Charles Harpum, Michael Sayers, Dame Mary Arden, James Lee, Matthew Dyson, Joanna Miles, Julia Bargenda, Annet Oguttu and Dellene Clark. I also thank the delegates of various conferences and seminars at which I have presented my work: the Girton College Graduate Research Seminar (Cambridge, May 2012); the Scots Law Research Conference (Edinburgh, June 2012); the Society of Legal Scholars Annual Conference (Edinburgh, September 2013); the Centre for Public Law Seminar (Cambridge, November 2013); 'Fifty Years of the Law Commissions: The Dynamics of Law Reform Now, Then and Next' (an international conference to mark the Commissions' fiftieth anniversaries) (London, July 2015); the Glasgow Forum for Scots Law (Glasgow, September 2015); and the Royal Society of Edinburgh Evidence Workshop (Glasgow, June 2016).

Thanks are also due to Christ's College for the sabbatical term which allowed me to complete this work and in particular to Richard Williams, Dominic de Cogan and Rumiana Yotova for relieving me of various teaching and administrative commitments.

I am most grateful to Hart Publishing for their assistance throughout the editing and publishing process. Particular thanks are due to Bill Asquith, Francesca Sancarlo, Tom Adams, Anne Flegel and Anne Bevan.

Finally, thank you to Findlay Stark for his unwavering support throughout the progress of this project. It is no exaggeration to say that without him this book would not exist, because without his encouragement I would not have embarked on this project. He was there from my very first research proposal until the finalisation of this manuscript. For that support, and for so much more, this book is dedicated to him.

SWS
Cambridge, December 2016

TABLE OF CONTENTS

TABLE OF CASES

United Kingdom Courts

Non-United Kingdom Courts

TABLE OF LEGISLATION

United Kingdom

Non-United Kingdom

TABLE OF GB COMMISSION MATERIAL

Scottish Law Commission

Annual Reports

Programmes

Discussion Papers

Reports

Miscellaneous

Law Commission

Annual Reports

Programmes

Consultation Papers

Reports

Miscellaneous

Collaborative Projects

1

Introduction

Many of us interact with the work of the Law Commissions on a regular basis. We may interact directly, such as when we consult a Commission report, or when we respond to a consultation. Or we may interact indirectly, and even unknowingly, when we make use of a law which resulted from a Commission proposal. We may interact as lawyers or, for example, as bankers, Land Registry workers, police officers, shopkeepers, landlords or company directors. We may even interact as individual citizens, usually without realising it, when we benefit from a law proposed by the Commissions, such as in the field of consumer or tenants' rights. But how many of us stop to consider why the Commissions exist, how they choose their projects, how they craft their proposals and how their reforms end up on the statute book—or why they do not? This book addresses those questions. It does so shortly after the Commissions celebrated their golden anniversaries in June 2015. Such a landmark signalled an appropriate time to look back and consider the achievements of the Commissions, as well as whether there is room for improvement. In particular, after 50 years, are there any changes that need to be made to ensure that the Commissions remain relevant? The main reason for the Commissions' existence is that the law cannot stand still—neither, it will be argued, can our law reform machinery.

In examining the work of the Law Commission for England and Wales (LCEW) and the Scottish Law Commission (SLC; together the Commissions) this book first details the Commissions' formation on the premise that, as Winston Churchill once said, 'the longer you can look back, the further you can look forward'.[1] In other words, before we can ascertain what the proper role of the Commissions is today, it is important to consider what their role was intended to be at the outset. The Commissions were established by the Law Commissions Act 1965 (the 1965 Act). It is argued in this book that the 1965 Act should be both clarified and updated. Certain of its provisions have caused a lack of clarity from the outset, such as the Commissions' duty to 'take and keep under review all the law',[2] a duty which

[1] See SW Stark, 'The Longer You Can Look Back, the Further You Can Look Forward: The Origins of the Scottish Law Commission' (2014) 18 *Edinburgh Law Review* 59 ('The Longer You Can Look Back').

[2] 1965 Act, s 3(1).

has been described as 'mission impossible'.[3] Because of their limited resources, the Commissions cannot possibly examine 'all the law', and the 1965 Act gives no guidance to the Commissions as to what they should prioritise. Contrary to what may be expected by those familiar with the Commissions' more technical work, the Act does not give any priority to so-called 'lawyers' law'.[4] The proper scope of the Commissions' activity (how the use of their resources should be prioritised) therefore remains unclear from the face of their founding statute. 'The challenge', as Lady Hale has put it, 'is to work out the most valuable tasks the Commission[s] can accomplish'.[5] The Commissions have tried to meet that challenge by structuring their exercise of discretion according to non-statutory project-selection criteria. A way of determining the appropriate scope of their activity through the development and increased use of those criteria is advanced in this book.

Many changes occurred during the Commissions' first five decades. Certain changes have been internal (such as the changing personalities of the Commissioners and other staff) and others have been external (such as devolution, the UK's changing relationship with the European Union (EU), increasing calls for transparency, reduced governmental funding and the changed role of the Lord Chancellor). This book considers how those changes have affected (or should affect) the role the Commissions play today. New developments pose new challenges for the Commissions and force us to re-evaluate our expectations of them as law reform bodies. For example, the 1965 Act directs the Commissions to work towards the codification of the law.[6] Codification and harmonisation were high on the agenda in the 1960s due to the UK's impending entry into what is now the EU. For various reasons advanced in this book, including the fact that EU membership is probably no longer a relevant concern, codification should no longer be one of the Commissions' aims. Additionally, the Commissions now face the challenge of working in an increasingly devolved and fragmented UK. We should not expect the same of our Commissions as we did in 1965.

It is not, therefore, just the Commissions which must change, but also our perceptions of them. Such change needs to occur not only in the types of projects we expect our Commissions to undertake (ie, not just 'lawyers' law'), but also in the evaluation of the success (or otherwise) of a Commission project. Given that it is the usual desired outcome of a project, we may have a tendency to equate the success of a Commission project with its legislative implementation. Legislative implementation cannot be ignored, but we must give more consideration to what

[3] B Hale, 'Fifty Years of the Law Commissions: The Dynamics of Law Reform Now, Then and Next' in M Dyson, J Lee and SW Stark (eds), *Fifty Years of the Law Commissions: The Dynamics of Law Reform* (Oxford, Hart Publishing, 2016) 19 ('The Dynamics of Law Reform'; and Dyson, Lee and Stark, *Fifty Years of the Law Commissions*).

[4] See E Clive, 'Law Reform and Social Policy' in Dyson, Lee and Stark, *Fifty Years of the Law Commissions*, 66.

[5] Hale, 'The Dynamics of Law Reform' 19.

[6] 1965 Act, s 3(1).

it means for a proposal to be 'implemented', especially in the light of increasing use of methods other than primary legislation (for example, secondary legislation, court rules or judicial decisions). Furthermore, overconcentration on legislative implementation as the sole or main measure of success naturally increases the probability of attempts to improve implementation rates. This book details such attempts, many of which have been noble efforts to raise the Commissions' profiles. Certain efforts can, however, jeopardise the Commissions' independence from government. For example, projects may be chosen according to their likelihood of implementation rather than proper consideration of the non-statutory project-selection criteria. This book advances a more sophisticated method of evaluating the outcome of a Commission project which can consequently better protect the Commissions' independence—the benefits of which are advanced in this book.[7]

The Commissions are technically independent from government, yet they rely on government for their funding and for approval of their proposed projects. In addition, governmental approval of Commission recommendations is the main route to their implementation.[8] A tension between independence and implementation is therefore inevitable to a certain degree. But the heat behind that tension must be carefully controlled. By both clarifying and updating the 1965 Act, the Commissions' position could be improved, thereby securing the future of independent law reform in Great Britain.

I. Lifting the Law Reform Bonnet

Comparatively little has been written about the machinery of the Commissions compared with the ink that has been spilled over their specific proposals. George Gretton, a former SLC Commissioner, has remarked that a lot of Commission work is of an 'under the bonnet' type—dealing with the laws that most people take for granted and only notice when they are in need of repair.[9] The same can be said about the Commissions themselves, separate from their individual projects. We arguably take their work for granted, not stopping to consider why they exist, how they function, why they have chosen a specific project, or why they have drafted a specific proposal. This book lifts the bonnet on the Commissions to probe deeper into the machinery of law reform. The Commissions' working methods are not

[7] For a robust defence of the need for independence in a law reform body, see W Binchy, 'Law Commissions, Courts and Society: A Sceptical View' in Dyson, Lee and Stark, *Fifty Years of the Law Commissions*, ch 16.

[8] Other routes include, eg, implementation by Private Members' Bills, court rules or judicial decisions.

[9] G Gretton, 'Of Law Commissioning' (2013) 17 *Edinburgh Law Review* 119, 127 ('Of Law Commissioning').

a complete mystery, but many accounts of their work are outdated.[10] A growing field of legal scholarship, a large amount of which is written by previous Commissioners or staff, examines the machinery of law reform.[11] This book contributes to that field by providing a current analysis of both the LCEW and the SLC from an external perspective. As one former LCEW Commissioner has noted, a 'degree of disinterestedness' is needed to properly assess the 'strengths and weaknesses, successes and failures' of the Commissions.[12]

Because the Commissions have not been studied in much depth so far in their 50-year existences, the appropriate scope of their activity remains unclear to outsiders. The Commissions have been criticised for acting, or failing to act, in certain areas.[13] At the Commissions' outset, certain views were expressed that they were best suited to examining so-called 'lawyers' law'.[14] If that view persists today it would fundamentally misunderstand the Commissions' role because they also work (frequently and successfully) in more obviously controversial areas, such as criminal law or family law. This book answers such criticisms and alleviates such misunderstandings by clarifying the Commissions' proper scope of activity. Such clarification is important if we are to properly engage with the Commissions by, for example, suggesting appropriate projects for them to study in their *Programmes of Law Reform*.[15]

[10] eg, JH Farrar, *Law Reform and the Law Commission* (London, Sweet & Maxwell, 1974); WH Hurlburt, *Law Reform Commissions in the United Kingdom, Australia and Canada* (Edmonton, Juriliber, 1986); and G Zellick (ed), *The Law Commission and Law Reform* (London, Sweet & Maxwell, 1988).

[11] See, eg, over the past decade alone: T Etherton, 'Law Reform in England and Wales: A Shattered Dream or Triumph of Political Vision?' (Bar Law Reform Committee Lecture, 2007); N Brotchie, 'The Scottish Law Commission: Promoting Law Reform in Scotland' (2009) 9 *Legal Information Management* 30; L Blom-Cooper, 'Reform? Reform? Aren't Things Bad Enough Already?' [2010] *PL* 441; M McMillan, 'The Role of Law Reform in Constitutionalism, Rule of Law and Democratic Governance: Reflections by the Scottish Law Commission' (Association of Law Reform Agencies of Eastern and Southern Africa Lecture, 2011); J Munby, 'Shaping the Law—The Law Commission at the Crossroads' (Denning Lecture, 2011); L Clark, 'Law Reform and the Work of the Scottish Law Commission' (lecture at the Annual General Meeting of the Scottish Legal Action Group, 2012); B Dempsey, 'Law Reform and Devolution: Consultation Processes and Divorce Law in Scotland' (2012) 63 *Northern Ireland Legal Quarterly* 227; J Horder, *Homicide and the Politics of Law Reform* (Oxford, OUP, 2012); Gretton, 'Of Law Commissioning'; D Lloyd Jones, 'The Law Commission and Law Reform in a Devolved Wales' (Wales Governance Centre Annual Lecture, 2013); E Cooke and HL MacQueen, 'Law Reform in a Political Environment: The Work of the Law Commissions' in D Feldman (ed), *Law in Politics, Politics in Law* (Oxford, Hart Publishing, 2013); G Maher, 'Principles and Politics in Law Reform: Sexual Offences in Scots Law' 2013 *Juridical Review* 563; S Wilson, 'Reforming the Law (Commission): A Crisis of Identity?' [2013] *PL* 20; Stark, 'The Longer You Can Look Back'; G Palmer, 'The Law Reform Enterprise: Evaluating the Past and Charting the Future' (2015) 131 *LQR* 402 ('The Law Reform Enterprise'); Lord Carloway, 'To "Mend the Laws, That Neids Mendement": A Scottish Perspective on Lawyers as Law Reformers' (speech at the Commonwealth Association of Law Reform Agencies Conference, Edinburgh, 2015); Dyson, Lee and Stark, *Fifty Years of the Law Commissions*; and Lord Pentland, 'The Scottish Law Commission and the Future of Law Reform in Scotland' 2016 *Juridical Review* 169.

[12] P North, 'Law Reform: Processes and Problems' (1985) 101 *LQR* 338, 338.

[13] See, eg, GJ Borrie, 'Law Reform: A Damp Squib?' (Inaugural Lecture, University of Birmingham, 1970).

[14] See, eg, HL Deb vol 264 col 1160 (1 April 1965) (Viscount Dilhorne).

[15] And such suggestions are actively sought by both Commissions in consultations to those programmes.

When forced to reflect on our views of the Commissions as institutions, separate from any praise for, or criticism of, particular projects, reactions are overwhelmingly positive. Such reactions can be seen, for example, from the respondents to the first *Triennial Review* of the LCEW who unanimously expressed 'extremely strong support for the functions of the Law Commission to continue'.[16] There were, however, only 46 respondents to that review. Although that is not a trivial number (and it included many eminent names and groups)[17] it is a fraction of the number of people who interact with the Commissions or their work. If we view the Commissions as positive additions to our law reform machinery, we should not take them for granted. And if we have criticisms to make, those are equally important. The Commissions, being government-funded bodies, have had to struggle to justify their existence in times of austerity. The LCEW was one of the bodies at risk of abolition in the Coalition Government's so-called 'bonfire of the quangos' in the Public Bodies Act 2011.[18] The LCEW survived, but the Commissions now operate with increasingly tight funding and under closer scrutiny. For example, the funding received by the LCEW in 2015–16 had not increased in real terms from the amount it received 20 years earlier.[19] The LCEW is also now scrutinised regularly by way of triennial review by the Ministry of Justice as part of the greater accountability of the public bodies that survived the Public Bodies Act. The Commissions therefore need our support to survive, both in the form of interaction with their work, and in understanding how and why they operate in order to maximise such interaction.

The SLC and the LCEW were established by the same legislation, but have always operated slightly differently. Changes made over the years, particularly the enactment of the Law Commission Act 2009, which only applies to the LCEW, have exacerbated such differences. We will see in chapter two that the SLC would not have been created were it not for the establishment of the LCEW. The bodies have had different experiences, particularly with regard to their relationships with government. Those different relationships have resulted, for example, in different responses to pressure caused by falling implementation rates of Commission proposals. Despite both structural and jurisdictional differences, the Commissions have a duty to act in consultation with one another under the 1965 Act.[20] By comparing the two Commissions, this book, like the Commissions themselves, promotes the sharing of valuable lessons between jurisdictions.

[16] Ministry of Justice, *Triennial Review: Law Commission, Report of Stage One* (2013) para 115.

[17] ibid app B.

[18] Public Bodies Bill as introduced, sch 7.

[19] £4.5 million in 1995 and £4.6 million in 2015–16: LCEW, *Thirtieth Annual Report: 1995* (Law Com No 239 (1996)) app 5 and *Annual Report 2015–16* (Law Com No 367 (2016)) app B respectively.

[20] 1965 Act, s 3(4).

II. Beyond Great Britain

The sharing of lessons between jurisdictions applies beyond Great Britain. The Commissions were inspired by, and have inspired, other law reform bodies around the world. The Commissions' predecessors, as well as previous domestic bodies, include the New York State Law Revision Commission (established in 1934) and the Louisiana State Law Institute (established in 1938). Law reform bodies modelled on the LCEW and the SLC include the South African Law Reform Commission (established in 1973),[21] the Australian Law Reform Commission (established in 1975),[22] the Law Reform Commission of Ireland (also established in 1975), the New Zealand Law Commission (established in 1986) and the Northern Ireland Law Commission (NILC; established in 2008). Many other law reform bodies across the world pre- and post-date the Commissions. In total, there are at least 30 law commissions, in almost every corner of the world, including, in particular, in Africa, the Caribbean, the Indian subcontinent and the Pacific.[23] Certain aspects of different law reform bodies' experiences are mentioned in this book, where appropriate, to show similarities to, or contrasts with, the LCEW and the SLC. Questions of resources and priorities, as well as commission structure and size, may be very different across the world. The commission model, which has spread (mainly across the Commonwealth), has been adapted from country to country. The Australian Law Reform Commission, for example, has no power to choose its own projects, and faces the challenge of being a federal commission operating alongside regional law reform bodies.[24] In New Zealand, Sir Geoffrey Palmer is both former Prime Minister and former President of the New Zealand Law Commission—a career path one would not expect to see in the UK. Furthermore, the typical projects undertaken by a commission are likely to vary from country to country. For example, the Malawi Law Commission's *Annual Work Programme* for 2012 listed ongoing projects on the review of statutes relating to witchcraft and to traditional leaders ('chiefs').[25] In smaller jurisdictions or provinces, part-time solutions may be preferred, such as in Northern Ireland,[26] or 'unique'

[21] Originally called the South African Law Commission.

[22] Originally called the Law Reform Commission.

[23] Palmer, 'The Law Reform Enterprise' 402. The Commonwealth Association of Law Reform Agencies lists 35 commissions, including provincial commissions in Canada and Australia, as members or associated bodies: www.calras.org/Membership/current.htm. The website also notes, however, that there are 'more than 60 law reform commissions and other permanent law reform agencies' worldwide: 'Background, History and Support' www.calras.org/About/history.html.

[24] See K Cronin, 'Working on the Larger Canvas—Law Reform in a Federal System: Thoughts on Forty Years of the Australian Law Reform Commission' in Dyson, Lee and Stark, *Fifty Years of the Law Commissions*, ch 6.

[25] Malawi Law Commission, *Annual Work Programme* (2012) para 1.2. Although it must be noted that the same programme contains projects on, eg, sentencing guidelines (para 1.1) and patents (para 1.2).

[26] On the pros and cons of part-time commissions, see SW Stark and N Faris, 'Law Reform in Northern Ireland: Cheshire Cat or Potemkin Commission?' [2016] *PL* 651, 664.

structures may be found, such as in Alberta.[27] Certain countries will have to strive harder than others to ensure that all their people are represented. For example, the federal Law Commission of Canada, now abolished, had a particularly difficult task to ensure that it was 'broadly representative of the socio-economic and cultural diversity of Canada, represent[ed] various disciplines and reflect[ed] knowledge of the common law and civil law systems'.[28] That meant recruiting Commissioners from different regions of Canada; Francophones, Anglophones and Indigenous Canadians; and common lawyers and civil lawyers; in addition to the usual task of trying to secure a gender balance and representation from various areas of law and branches of the legal profession.[29]

Despite various differences, given the shared roots from which many law reform bodies stem it may be that other jurisdictions will find material in this book that is familiar or helpful to them. It may even be that countries seeking to establish a new law reform body may find inspiration within these pages for techniques to employ, and those to avoid. It has even been suggested that the Commissions' 'method' could be employed by other bodies such as the EU.[30] It may be, therefore, that this book can inspire other bodies which seek to mimic the Commissions' approach. And of course, there may be elements from other jurisdictions which can be adopted by, or adapted for, the GB Commissions.

III. Overview

Understanding the reasons for the Commissions' establishment is important in order to ascertain whether those reasons still endure today. If not, it follows that we might expect the present-day Commissions to function differently from how they did in 1965. In chapter two, therefore, archival material is used to trace the background to the Commissions' formation.

The legislation which established the Commissions, the 1965 Act, is vague and lacks definition. For example, the 1965 Act leaves the scope of the Commissions' activity unclear by mandating that they should 'take and keep under review all the law'.[31] Because of the size of the Commissions, they must select only certain areas of law to examine.[32] As the Law Commissions Bill progressed through

[27] M Kirby, 'Forty Years of the Alberta Law Reform Institute—Past, Present, Future' (2008–09) 46 *Alberta Law Review* 831, 845.

[28] Law Commission of Canada Act 1996, s 7(3).

[29] Y Le Bouthillier, 'The Former Law Commission of Canada: The Road Less Travelled' in Dyson, Lee and Stark, *Fifty Years of the Law Commissions*, 102.

[30] H Beale, 'The Law Commission Method: Exportable to the EU?' in Dyson, Lee and Stark, *Fifty Years of the Law Commissions*, ch 24.

[31] 1965 Act, s 3(1).

[32] Each Commission consists of five Commissioners (including the Chairman) and supporting staff. The smaller number of SLC supporting staff is considered in ch 6.

Parliament, concerns were raised about other issues not dealt with in the legislation. It was unclear, for example, how parliamentary time would be found for the Commissions' proposals,[33] or how they would manage to codify the law.[34] Concern had also been expressed, particularly in Scotland, as to what the purpose of the Commissions' duty to cooperate was,[35] and whether Scots law would be completely harmonised with English law.[36] Because the 1965 Act still provides the Commissions' basis, the questions it did not address remain unanswered to this day. Answers to those questions are proposed in the remainder of the book.

The first ambiguity which must be resolved is the proper scope of the Commissions' activity, and the 1965 Act's broad duty to 'take and keep under review all the law' is our starting point.[37] The Commissions, the Ministers[38] and government have discretion to select, approve or refer suitable projects for the Commissions' examination. Such discretion is essential because the Commissions cannot, due to their limited resources, examine all the law at any given time. Commission, ministerial and governmental discretion must, however, be properly structured and exercised in order to target the Commissions' resources to the most deserving projects. To address the fact that the 1965 Act leaves the Commissions' scope of activity extremely broad, the Commissions have developed their own methods of attempting to ensure that the most deserving projects are embarked on. Since 1997, in an attempt to structure its exercise of discretion, the LCEW has used three criteria when selecting a project: availability of resources; suitability of the project; and importance of the project.[39] The same criteria were adopted by the SLC in 2005.[40] Chapter three demonstrates how those criteria should be developed in both their content and their use. The discretion enjoyed by Commissioners, Ministers and government can be controlled to improve the Commissions' output and the assessment of that output. Properly developed, the criteria provide a way of securing the scope of the Commissions' activity to protect them from arbitrary control (whether by the Ministers, the rest of government or their own Commissioners). Careful application of the criteria would ensure that the Commissions' limited resources are allocated wisely, and transparent project selection would protect them from criticism for acting, or failing to act, in certain areas. The project-selection criteria are central to this book and further reasons for their importance are advanced in subsequent chapters.

Implementation by legislation has historically been the main measure of a Commission project's success. Lord Scarman, the LCEW's first Chairman, said

[33] eg, HC Deb vol 706 cols 60, 64–65 (8 February 1965) (Sir John Hobson); col 88 (Sir David Renton).

[34] 1965 Act, s 3(1); eg, HC Deb vol 706 col 146 (8 February 1965) (Norman Wylie).

[35] 1965 Act, s 3(4).

[36] eg, 'No Complete Assimilation with English Law: Mr Ross Gives Assurance' *The Scotsman* (9 February 1965).

[37] 1965 Act, s 3(1).

[38] The Lord Chancellor for the LCEW and Scottish Ministers for the SLC: 1965 Act, s 6(2).

[39] LCEW, *Thirty-First Annual Report: 1996* (Law Com No 244 (1997)) app A.

[40] SLC, *Seventh Programme of Law Reform* (Scot Law Com No 198 (2005)) para 1.2.

that the LCEW's reputation would 'stand or fall by the contributions it makes to enacted law'.[41] Although implementation cannot be ignored, it is misguided and dangerous to equate it with success for three reasons. First, concentrating solely on implementation risks usurping chapter three's project-selection criteria, which have been designed specifically to ensure that the most deserving projects are embarked on. A project selected according to proper consideration of those criteria should not be vetoed simply because its eventual implementation is an uncertain prospect. Second, too much emphasis on implementation risks reduction of the Commissions' independence by making it possible that they will pander to government in both the projects they select and the substantive reforms they propose. One of the project-selection criteria, the suitability of the project, involves considering the likelihood that the Commissions are the only bodies able or willing to examine an area of the law. One consequence of a loss of independence is, therefore, that the reform of such areas of law would be neglected. Third and finally, implementation gives no indication of the quality of the proposed reforms. Commission recommendations are not always uncontroversial and cannot always be assumed to be good.[42] Furthermore, overconcentration on implementation puts the quality of the Commissions' recommendations at risk. They may be tailored to suit the government, rather than being based on the 'careful research and wide consultation' the Commissions are often admired for.[43] Because of an increasing focus on providing value for money, the Commissions perceive governmental pressure to measure their achievements by demonstrating the implementation of their proposals as legislation, as even a glance at any recent Commission annual report reveals. If the Commissions are not seen to score quick implementation points, they may be vulnerable to abolition.[44] Governments do not see any value in 'fine academic analyses of a theoretical nature if none of the work reaches the statute book'.[45] This book therefore addresses the question of how to balance independence and implementation satisfactorily by providing a more sophisticated way of assessing the outcome of Commission proposals than merely equating legislative implementation with success. In this book, 'implementation' is understood in its full, ordinary meaning, to include not only projects implemented (fully, substantially or partially) by primary legislation, but also by less usual means such as secondary legislation and judicial decision.

Three arguments to alter the way implementation is viewed are advanced in chapter four. First, it is argued that the broad interpretation of implementation (which includes, for example, proposals which have helped to shape the common law),

[41] L Scarman, *Law Reform: The New Pattern (The Lindsay Memorial Lectures)* (London, Routledge & Kegan Paul, 1968) 17. *cf* Palmer, 'The Law Reform Enterprise' 407.

[42] See, eg, ch 4, section V.

[43] LCEW, *Thirtieth Annual Report: 1995* (Law Com No 239 (1996)) para 1.2, quoting Lord Mackay when he was Lord Chancellor.

[44] Abolition of law commissions is not unheard of. For example, the federal Law Commission in Canada has been abolished twice, once in 1993 and once in 2006. The recent Northern Irish experience is discussed in ch 6, section III.C.

[45] Palmer, 'The Law Reform Enterprise' 407.

to a certain extent already used by the Commissions, should be more transparent. This interpretation better reflects the impact the Commissions have actually had on the law than slavish adherence to enacted law. Second, to reduce the expectation of immediate implementation, it is recommended that government should be obliged periodically to reconsider, and make public, its position regarding rejected Commission proposals. Third and finally, it is proposed that the Commissions' output should be viewed as a whole to reflect the fact that the selection criteria often pull in different directions. In particular, certain projects might be sufficiently important that their examination can be justified, notwithstanding the fact that immediate implementation is uncertain.

As already mentioned, one of the Commissions' specific tasks is to strive for the codification of the law.[46] Despite codification being a divisive topic in the British jurisdictions, it was made one of the Commissions' tasks due to dissatisfaction with the law in 1965—both the common law and the cluttered statute book—and a desire to harmonise and codify UK law for entry into what is now the EU.[47] In chapter five, it is argued that codification projects are less likely than certain other projects to satisfy the chapter three project-selection criteria. Because of their limited resources, the Commissions have achieved little by way of codification to date. They have discovered that reform and codification cannot happen simultaneously and now therefore prioritise reform, with a view to returning to codify the law at a later stage. The second, codificatory stage of such projects is less likely to satisfy the 'importance' project-selection criterion than projects proposing substantive reform. It is therefore entirely proper that the Commissions tend to dedicate their limited resources to projects not designed to codify the law immediately. Furthermore, certain developments have restored the reputation of the common law and its capacity to be a tool of law reform, reduced the need for decluttering the statute book, and entry into (and now likely exit from) the EU took place successfully without codification. In addition, the term 'codification' has been used inconsistently by the Commissions because it has no precise meaning. Removal of the specific codification duty would remove the confusion caused by the term, as well as the unrealistic pressure to codify, thereby silencing critics of the Commissions 'disastrous' codification record.[48]

Examination of the changing constitutional landscape within which the Commissions operate reveals further reasons why development of chapter three's project-selection criteria is needed. In 1965, the Commissions were actively encouraged by government to harmonise the laws of England and Scotland 'wherever possible'.[49] The motivation for such harmonisation was impeding entry into the EU and the desirability of the UK being perceived as 'one unit'.[50]

[46] 1965 Act, s 3(1).

[47] See ch 5, section II.

[48] F Bennion, 'Additional Comments' in G Zellick (ed), *The Law Commission and Law Reform* (London, Sweet & Maxwell, 1988) 63.

[49] AG Brand (SLC) to HHA Whitworth (Scottish Office), 'Full-time Commissioner', 29 September 1967, National Records of Scotland (NRS) HH83/702.

[50] LCB Gower, 'A Comment' (1967) 30 *MLR* 259, 260.

Since the turn of the twenty-first century, devolution signalled a new era for Scotland, Wales and Northern Ireland. Not only has devolution made the prospect of a harmonised 'British' law less likely (with the result that a project's potential to harmonise the law is less important when deciding its viability), but it has also posed new practical challenges. For example, Welsh devolution has resulted in the LCEW having to adapt in order to effectively promote law reform in both England and Wales. The Wales Act 2014 has made significant changes to the 1965 Act to increase Welsh input into the LCEW. Since devolution, a greater number of governmental parties may interact with the Commissions, necessitating urgent adoption of clear project-selection criteria in order that the most appropriate Commission projects are selected, approved and referred.

The Commissions have a duty to 'act in consultation with each other',[51] which sometimes leads to collaborative Commission projects. Tripartite projects with the establishment of the NILC in 2008 raised new challenges,[52] although the fate of the NILC is presently uncertain, it having had its funds withdrawn in April 2015.[53] Collaborative projects raise difficulties, not only due to the legal differences between the jurisdictions, but also due to the practical problem of coordinating the Commissions. It is argued in chapter six that the project-selection criteria are essential in ensuring that the most valuable collaborative projects are embarked on. In fact, they are needed more than ever to ensure that both (or all three) Commissions are clear about which projects deserve the use of their limited resources.

IV. Some Final Preliminaries

To conclude this introductory chapter, a few short words on abbreviations and other practicalities are necessary. References to England and English law include Wales, except where specified. As noted above, the Law Commission for England and Wales is abbreviated as 'LCEW' in this book, although its official title is simply the 'Law Commission', something which agitated certain Scots during its creation.[54] The Scottish Law Commission is abbreviated as 'SLC'. Any reference to 'the Commissions' or 'Commission' in the sense of, for example, 'Commission work' or 'Commission proposals' applies to both the LCEW and the SLC equally unless specified. The term 'GB Commissions' is used to refer to both the LCEW and the SLC where discussion of international bodies could cause any confusion.

Except where otherwise provided, the law is stated as at 31 December 2016.

[51] 1965 Act, s 3(4).

[52] 1965 Act, s 3(4) as amended by the Justice (Northern Ireland) Act 2002, sch 12, para 9.

[53] See further ch 6, section III.C; and SW Stark and N Faris, 'Law Reform in Northern Ireland: Cheshire Cat or Potemkin Commission?' [2016] *PL* 651.

[54] HL Deb vol 265 cols 399–400 (14 April 1965) (Earl of Selkirk).

2

The Origins of the Law Commissions

Before we can examine the role of the modern-day Commissions, it is essential to consider their origins. Indeed, we need to look further back than 1965 to consider previous attempts to set up law reform bodies, because those bodies, although less successful than the Commissions, paved the way for the Commissions' arrival.[1] In this chapter, we will discover the reasons for the Commissions' establishment in 1965 and why they were more successful than previous similar attempts. Although both Commissions were established by the same legislation and are similar, fundamental differences between them will begin to emerge. The Scottish Law Commission (SLC) would not exist were it not for the Law Commission for England and Wales (LCEW), but the bodies have continued to diverge over the years. The Law Commissions Act 1965 (the 1965 Act) is the focus of the second half of this chapter: the pre-parliamentary discussions, the Bill's passage through Parliament and the legislation as enacted. The 1965 Act still provides the Commissions' foundations, and an assessment of it uncovers consequent issues that are addressed in the rest of this book.

I. Pre-1965

Certain events prior to 1965 contributed to the Commissions' establishment. Such events include the establishment of previous law reform bodies, and the publication of the book *Law Reform Now*.[2]

A. Previous Law Reform Bodies

i. England

Law reform bodies were not a new concept in England. Attempts had been made to tidy the statute book as far back as 1593,[3] and Sir Matthew

[1] R Chorley and G Dworkin, 'The Law Commissions Act, 1965' (1965) 28 *MLR* 675, 678 ('The Law Commissions Act, 1965').

[2] G Gardiner and A Martin (eds), *Law Reform Now* (London, Victor Gollancz, 1963) (*Law Reform Now*).

[3] For a summary of previous English law reform bodies, see M Kerr, 'Law Reform in Changing Times' (1980) 96 *LQR* 515, 518–21.

Hale's seventeenth-century Commission has been described as 'the first law commission'.[4] The pressure for systematic law reform picked up pace in the nineteenth century. Jeremy Bentham, among others, advocated the creation of a Ministry of Justice responsible for law reform in his unfinished *Constitutional Code* of 1822–32.[5] Two years before he became Lord Chancellor in 1830, Henry Brougham spoke in Parliament for six hours on the need for reform of the common law, necessitating 'a Commission for inquiring into the defects, occasioned by time and otherwise, in the Laws of this realm of England'.[6] This speech was referenced by Lord Chancellor Gardiner during the second reading of the Law Commissions Bill in the House of Lords in 1965, when he noted that to detail everything presently wrong with English law would take 'rather longer than [six hours]'.[7] Another previous Lord Chancellor, Lord Cranworth, wrote a letter to the Chancellor of the Exchequer in 1853 to request the appointment of five Commissioners to examine the current statutory law. Gardiner also referenced this request during his introduction of the Law Commissions Bill in the House of Lords, carrying with him a 'photostat' (photocopy) of the letter itself for reference.[8] Shortly before he became Lord Chancellor, Richard Bethell (later Lord Westbury) argued for the creation of a Ministry of Justice and the importance of codification, and described what sounds like a law commission in 1859, when he wondered:

> Why is there not a body of men in this country, whose duty it is to … see how far the law is fitted to the exigencies of society, the necessities of the times, the growth of wealth and the progress of mankind?[9]

Nothing much came of these nineteenth-century requests, save for various bodies that had the more limited role of consolidating and repealing the existing law.[10] The time was not yet ripe for a more substantive law reform body.

The immediate predecessors of the LCEW were the Lord Chancellor's Law Reform Committee (established in 1952 to replace the Law Revision Committee, which operated from 1934 until the outbreak of the Second World War), the Private International Law Committee (also established by the Lord Chancellor

[4] S Sedley, *Lions under the Throne: Essays on the History of English Public Law* (Cambridge, CUP, 2015) 92.

[5] Bentham's exact recommendations were more complex, because he advocated the creation of both a Ministry of Justice and a Ministry of Legislation: see J Bentham (published under the superintendence of his executor, J Bowring), *The Works of Jeremy Bentham*, vol IX (Edinburgh, William Tait, 1843); and H Beynon, 'Mighty Bentham' (1981) 2 *Journal of Legal History* 62, 67.

[6] HC Deb vol 18 col 246 (7 February 1828).

[7] HL Deb vol 264 col 1140 (1 April 1965).

[8] HL Deb vol 264 col 1218 (1 April 1965).

[9] R Bethell, 'Address on Vacating the Office of President of the Society, at the Anniversary Meeting, 21st February, 1859' (1859) 2 *Juridical Society Papers* 129, 132.

[10] Many such bodies were set up and disbanded in the nineteenth century, with varying degrees of success. For an overview, see LCEW website, 'Statute Law Repeals at the Law Commission: A Review of Our Work 1965–2010' www.lawcom.gov.uk/wp-content/uploads/2015/03/slr_review.pdf. Brougham's speech also resulted in Her Majesty's Commissioners of Criminal Law being established in 1831, which produced several reports, but with little success.

in 1952) and the Home Secretary's Criminal Law Revision Committee (established in 1959). These bodies could only achieve moderate success because their members worked on a voluntary, part-time basis as they had other full-time jobs. One of the members of the Law Reform Committee, from 1952 until 1963, was Gerald Gardiner. Gardiner, as will become clear, was a fervent supporter of law reform. He was, however, candid about these part-time bodies' contribution, saying, 'you can't keep the law up to date by a body of gentlemen, however distinguished, meeting about once a quarter for an hour and three quarters after a full day's work. It's only scratching the surface'.[11] His frustration with the slow pace of reform was one of the reasons he gave for resigning from the Law Reform Committee.[12] Even those who, unlike Gardiner, did not think that English law was in dire need of reform, agreed that these bodies were inadequate—their pace of reform was too slow, they could not undertake a comprehensive review of the law, and there was not enough space in the legislative programme for their work, resulting in their recommendations not always being implemented as legislation by Parliament.[13] Furthermore, these law reform bodies had no autonomy to decide which areas of the law to examine—their projects had to be referred to them by government.[14]

ii. Scotland

Law reform bodies have at least as long a history in Scotland as in England. As long ago as 1425, an Act sought to appoint a commission of six 'wise and discreet' men to 'examyn the bukis of law of this realme'.[15] In the event, this early commission was 'fruitless', and over the years many other similarly unsuccessful attempts were made.[16]

Latterly, moderate success was seen in the form of the Lord Advocate's Law Reform Committee for Scotland, established in 1954 (also set up to replace a pre-war 'Legal Reform Committee'). This body, however, suffered from the same problems as its English counterparts—its members only worked part-time and, although it achieved a little, it could not carry out large-scale reform.[17] Unlike its English counterparts, however, it did have the capacity to select its own projects.

[11] 'The Economist Interviews Lord Gardiner' *The Economist* (28 March 1964).

[12] HL Deb vol 258 col 1087 (11 June 1964) (Lord Gardiner).

[13] eg, HL Deb vol 258 cols 1037–38 (11 June 1964) (Viscount Colville of Culross); Note by P Allen (Treasury), 'Machinery of Government Steering Group: Law Reform', 16 July 1964, National Archives (NA) T330/18.

[14] N Marsh, 'Law Reform in the United Kingdom: A New Institutional Approach' (1971) 13 *William & Mary Law Review* 263, 272 ('A New Institutional Approach').

[15] Statute Law Revision Act 1425 (APS II 10, c 10).

[16] HRM Macdonald, JC Mullin, TB Smith and JF Wallace, *The Laws of Scotland: Stair Memorial Encyclopaedia*, vol 22 (Edinburgh, Law Society of Scotland, 1987) para 627, and see paras 627–64 for a summary of the pre-1965 Scottish law reform bodies (*Stair Memorial Encyclopaedia*).

[17] For a summary of the Law Reform Committee's achievements, see ibid paras 650–64.

Both the English and Scottish part-time bodies, despite their failings, were able to analyse areas of law that might otherwise have gone unexamined. Gardiner, dissatisfied only by the slow progress of the Law Reform Committee's work, was of the view that such machinery simply needed to be on a larger scale. The advantages of independent law reform evident in the work of the Law Reform Committees were reasons to opt for the model eventually chosen for the Law Commissions. Indeed, the absence of a similar committee in Northern Ireland until 1989 may have been one reason why a law commission was not established there until some four decades after the GB Commissions.[18]

B. *Law Reform Now*

Law Reform Now was a book of essays edited by Gerald Gardiner and Andrew Martin, two left-leaning lawyers who pressed for law reform *now*, 'not tomorrow or the day after'.[19] Gardiner was instrumental in the establishment of the Commissions and the importance of *Law Reform Now* (and particularly its first chapter, authored by the editors, 'The Machinery of Law Reform') cannot be underestimated. Martin too played an important role, later becoming one of the first Commissioners of the LCEW.

Gardiner had been influenced by law reform bodies in the United States, and described himself as a 'humble student of the great Cardozo, particularly of his speeches that led to the formation of the New York Law Commission, to whose experience I owe so much'.[20] Benjamin Cardozo, apart from being a US Supreme Court Justice in the 1930s, helped to establish the New York State Law Revision Commission, which was set up in 1934 and is now 'the oldest continuous agency in the common-law world devoted to law reform through legislation'.[21] It was one of the bodies that helped to shape Gardiner's vision and formed the basis of his plan for a similar body for England.

Law Reform Now was not, however, an entirely new concept. It was the 'successor' to Glanville Williams' edited book, *The Reform of the Law*.[22] The preface to *Law Reform Now* explains that Williams had been asked to edit a second book on law reform, but was 'unable through pressure of work' to do so. The Commissions'

[18] SW Stark and N Faris, 'Law Reform in Northern Ireland: Cheshire Cat or Potemkin Commission?' [2016] *PL* 651, 654.

[19] Gardiner and Martin, *Law Reform Now*, ix. On the title page of the book, 'Now' is italicised to emphasise the urgency.

[20] G Gardiner, 'Comparative Law Reform' (1966) 52 *American Bar Association Journal* 1021, 1023 ('Comparative Law Reform'). Gardiner was not simply flattering his American audience: see HL Deb vol 264 col 1219 (1 April 1965) (Lord Chancellor (Gardiner)).

[21] New York State Law Revision Commission website, 'About the Commission' www.lawrevision.state.ny.us.

[22] G Williams, *The Reform of the Law* (London, Victor Gollancz Ltd, 1951) (*The Reform of the Law*); Gardiner and Martin, *Law Reform Now*, ix.

establishment owes much to Williams' unavailability. The fact that many of the substantive reforms advocated in Williams' 1951 book were repeated in *Law Reform Now* in 1963 only served to highlight the urgent need for reform.[23] One fundamental difference between *Law Reform Now* and its predecessors, however, was that, for the first time, a detailed plan was suggested for the setting up of a law commission. Chapter one of *Law Reform Now* set out a system that provided the inspiration for the 1965 Act. Williams, and many others before him, including Bentham, did not propose a law commission but rather a Ministry of Justice, which would oversee law reform.[24] Gardiner and Martin examined this proposal that had been suggested for 'well over a century ... time and again'.[25] They were not opposed to it in principle,[26] but preferred to strengthen the Lord Chancellor's Office by fitting a new independent unit within it—the Law Commission.

The idea of a law reform body was not new—as established above, law reform bodies had existed before—but the crucial innovation was that Gardiner and Martin's Commission would function on a full-time basis, staffed by 'not less than five' Law Commissioners.[27] Gardiner and Martin chose the model for the Commissions after analysing the benefits and the shortcomings of each of the three existing parts of the law reform machinery: government departments; ad hoc committees; and permanent bodies. Government departments were vital for having overall responsibility for certain areas of law, but their machinery was 'not geared' towards systematic and comprehensive law reform.[28] Ad hoc committees had a good success rate of their proposals being implemented (at least historically), but operated 'in isolation' and only on discrete issues.[29] The Law Reform Committees provided a valuable and high-quality service, but were limited by their part-time nature, and by the potential lack of governmental interest in their proposals.[30] Gardiner and Martin's Law Commission would therefore fill the gap in the current law machinery by improving on the Law Reform Committee model. The Law Commission would be a full-time, permanent body, operating continuously and choosing projects independently of government, but with a link to government in order to improve the likelihood of its proposals being implemented. A certain degree of independence would be important so that the Commission could choose its own projects, being 'free to take up proposals originating from non-official and non-representative sources: voluntary organisations and learned societies of all kinds, the universities, learned authors and the Press in general'.[31]

[23] Chorley and Dworkin, 'The Law Commissions Act, 1965' 680, fn 26.

[24] Williams, *The Reform of the Law*, ch 1, and above n 5.

[25] G Gardiner and A Martin, 'The Machinery of Law Reform' in *Law Reform Now*, 7 ('The Machinery of Law Reform').

[26] Gardiner had, however, written a decade earlier that he did not necessarily advocate the creation of a Ministry of Justice: G Gardiner, 'The Machinery of Law Reform in England' (1953) 69 *LQR* 46.

[27] Gardiner and Martin, 'The Machinery of Law Reform' 8.

[28] ibid 6.

[29] ibid.

[30] ibid.

[31] ibid 9.

Gardiner and Martin felt that English law was in dire need of reform. Therefore, in tasking their proposed body with 'law reform', they intended it to oversee a systematic overhaul of every part of the law, giving the Law Commission a very wide remit. Gardiner and Martin proposed that the Commissioners would be led by a 'Vice-Chancellor', a Minister of State who would represent the Commission in the House of Commons. The Commission would embark on its own choice of law reform projects and report its findings back to the Lord Chancellor, who would then place them before Parliament. In theory, it was already the duty of the Lord Chancellor and the Home Secretary to carry out law reform. Gardiner, however, was vocal about the fact that their roles comprised too many other duties for them to be able to deal with such a mammoth task.[32] Gardiner experienced the Lord Chancellor's heavy workload first hand when he held the position himself.[33] Gardiner's appointment as Lord Chancellor was one of a number of factors that contributed to the Commissions' establishment.

II. How Soon is 'Now': Why 1965?

A new era of law reform dawned, more brightly than ever before, in the 1960s. As we have seen, law reform bodies have a long, but not hugely successful, history in both England and Scotland. Pressure for systematic law reform was nothing new. In the 1960s, however, something changed in the reception of law reform, leading Gardiner to conclude shortly after the Commissions' establishment that '[n]ow law reform is popular, even among lawyers'.[34] Senior members of the legal profession's distaste for law reform had caused the failure of previous law reform attempts.[35] The change of heart in the 1960s occurred for various reasons. Farrar has explained that:

> The greater the population grows, the more urbanised society becomes and the more sophisticated and complex it is, the more crudity, obsolescence and inhumanity in the law become apparent and, in an open society, criticised. There develops a need to keep

[32] 'The Economist Interviews Lord Gardiner' *The Economist* (28 March 1964). See also Gardiner, 'Comparative Law Reform' 1023.

[33] His average working hours when he held the role were 09.15 until 02.00 and he noted: 'It would of course have been quite impossible for me to have devoted to law reform the time which it needs', although he observed that overseeing the LCEW added to his workload: G Gardiner, 'The Trials of a Lord Chancellor', Being the Presidential Address of the Rt Hon Lord Gardiner, Lord Chancellor, President of the Holdsworth Club of the Faculty of Law in the University of Birmingham 1967–68 (Birmingham, Holdsworth Club, 1968) 4 and 8.

[34] Gardiner, 'Comparative Law Reform' 1023. No consensus, however, as to the meaning of 'law reform' existed. See, eg, G Coldstream (Lord Chancellor's Office) to Treasury, 14 July 1964: '[N]one of the leading members of the judiciary, nor the responsible people at the Bar or in the Law Society, would agree with Gardiner that a "root and branch" operation [of law reform] is either necessary or desirable' NA T330/18, and section IV.A below.

[35] Marsh, 'A New Institutional Approach' 264.

> the law up to date with the changing facts and *mores* of society—a need in short for law reform and law reform bodies.[36]

This explanation portrays accurately British society in the 1960s—a society now becoming less passive, after being 'docile' and 'used to doing what they were told to do' during the wars.[37] There was a growing 'baby boom' population, and society was becoming more technological, more liberal and better educated through increased opportunities and media outlets. Systematic law reform became increasingly required to 'respond to philosophical and moral developments, to new social habits and patterns, to scientific and technological changes, to more complex commercial relationships'.[38] Pressure for law reform certainly existed in the early 1960s, but such pressure had existed before, for example, during the nineteenth century as noted above. Certain reasons, however, contributed to the successful establishment of the Commissions in 1965. The reasons for the Commissions' creation can be grouped into three related categories: social; legal; and political.

A. Social Reasons

Gardiner mooted that there were 'six aspects of the highly developed society' of the 1960s which necessitated either the creation of new laws or the reform of existing laws and, in his view, the establishment of the Commissions.[39] The social change seen in the 1960s was important in paving the way for the legal and political changes that followed.

First, new technology brought new dangers, for example, factory machinery, motor cars and nuclear radiation, and created a consequent need to legislate to regulate those new areas to protect citizens from harm. Gardiner described how the law had to strike a balance between guarding against risk and not stifling technological advancement.[40] The world was changing rapidly in the 1960s and, for reasons advanced later in this chapter, the current law reform machinery was unable to keep pace. Gardiner's first reason, however, is not necessarily an argument for a law commission specifically, as opposed to any other method of law reform. Indeed, reform in quickly developing areas may require expertise beyond a body

[36] JH Farrar, *Law Reform and the Law Commission* (London, Sweet & Maxwell, 1974) ix (*Law Reform and the Law Commission*).

[37] D Hope, 'Do We Still Need a Scottish Law Commission?' (2006) 10 *Edinburgh Law Review* 10, 23 ('Do We Still Need a Scottish Law Commission?'). See also Schwartz and Wade who noted, in the context of administrative law, that there was a 'spirit of abnegation and sacrifice' in the 1940s and 1950s: B Schwartz and HWR Wade, *Legal Control of Government: Administrative Law in Britain and the United States* (Oxford, Clarendon Press, 1972) 320.

[38] *Stair Memorial Encyclopaedia*, para 623.

[39] G Gardiner, 'Towards the Unity of European Law' [1968] *Nederlands Juristenblad* 5, 5 ('Towards the Unity of European Law').

[40] ibid 6.

consisting solely of lawyers so as not to, as Gardiner noted, stifle technological advancement.

Second, the population had become more mobile. Gardiner claimed in the late 1960s that houses changed ownership once every six years, and that people were no longer 'anchored to the ground'.[41] One consequence of such mobility was the need for a modern and efficient system of conveyancing. Another was the need for new remedies when debtors abscond. Reforms in such areas were (and still are) ideal tasks for the Commissions to deal with. They are technical reforms which arise from social development and which may rarely be noticed by the majority of the public. They are exactly the sort of 'under the bonnet' work for which the Commissions are now praised.[42]

Third, the population was becoming larger and increasingly concentrated in urban areas. A larger population necessitated new laws regulating the control of the use of land—for example, compulsory purchase, protection for tenants and regulation of nuisance. In Gardiner's words, an Englishman's home might be his castle, but 'the use of the castle has to be restrained in numberless ways for fear of interfering with the comfort of the owner of the castle next door'.[43] It is not convincing, however, to suggest that the need for regulating the use of land was peculiar to the 1960s—even the Romans concerned themselves with restrictions on property use in the interests of their neighbours.[44]

Fourth, citizens' private and family lives were increasingly under threat of being interfered with, particularly by the state. Gardiner was notoriously wary of 'bugging' and 'tapping' in his own life.[45] Because of technological advances in this area, the law needed to provide new protections to citizens in areas where it had 'not hitherto been much concerned'.[46] The concept of privacy, however, is still very much undeveloped in the UK, even post-Human Rights Act 1998.[47]

Fifth, sections of society were becoming more economically integrated and interdependent. As a result of a greater ability to travel, more industries and modern developments, more links were introduced into chains of operation necessary for everyday life. Consequently, there were more potential opportunities for things to go wrong. The law therefore, according to Gardiner, needed to ensure against 'excessive strains' to allow these chains to operate smoothly.[48] It is not entirely clear, however, what role the Commissions could play in this area, particularly when Gardiner concluded that what was needed most was control and restraint

[41] ibid 8.
[42] See below n 54.
[43] Gardiner, 'Towards the Unity of European Law' 8–9.
[44] See, eg, Gaius, *Institutes*, 2.14.
[45] During a debate on the British Telecommunications Bill, Gardiner regaled the House of Lords with the anecdote that, while Lord Chancellor, he conducted business in his chauffeur driven car, as he believed it to be the only safe place for a confidential conversation: HL Deb vol 420 cols 857–60 (19 May 1981).
[46] Gardiner, 'Towards the Unity of European Law' 9.
[47] See ch 4, section III.B.ii.
[48] Gardiner, 'Towards the Unity of European Law' 9.

of 'that potentially most powerful organisation of all, the executive of the State itself'.[49]

Sixth and finally, citizens were ever more aware of what was going on at home and abroad. Increasing travel opportunities and media outlets led to people being more informed about current affairs and developments all over the world. Technological advancements in communication techniques and travel also made it easier for like-minded individuals to get together and form pressure groups. As Gardiner put it, '[r]ough and ready justice is no longer acceptable'.[50] In the decades leading up to the 1960s, the public contributed increasingly to law reform by suggesting changes—a 'joint action of government and community'.[51] The areas of law however, where the public sought change, were not the sorts of areas that were suitable for the Commissions' examination. As will be established below, although not everything the Commissions deal with is entirely technical, they do not deal with political issues of the sort certain pockets of the British public sought reform of in the 1960s.[52] Even Gardiner admitted elsewhere that 'the public at large takes the law for granted' and does not clamour for law reform.[53] Gardiner justified the public's apparent satisfaction with the law, however, on the basis that '[p]eople do not campaign for changing that which to them is unknown'.[54]

The social reasons Gardiner advanced to necessitate the establishment of the Commissions were not consistently persuasive, but were nevertheless an influential response to the perceived pace and breadth of social change in the 1960s.

B. Legal Reasons

Not only was society in general changing in the 1960s, but so was the legal profession. As a result of the dissatisfaction with the state of the law for the reasons advanced above, a growth in critical legal literature began in the mid-twentieth century. Increasingly, writers did not just state the law, but criticised it. They 'identified problems and propounded solutions for the rationalisation and improvement of the law'.[55] Such criticism of the law highlighted the need for an efficient system of law reform.

[49] ibid 10.

[50] ibid 12.

[51] H Cam, *Law as it Looks to a Historian: Founders' Memorial Lecture, Girton College* (Cambridge, W Heffer & Sons Ltd, 1956) 6.

[52] Such as the abolition of the death penalty (see below n 89), the legalisation of abortion (Abortion Act 1967) or the decriminalisation of homosexuality (Sexual Offences Act 1967. Homosexuality was not decriminalised in Scotland until the Criminal Justice (Scotland) Act 1980).

[53] Gardiner and Martin, 'The Machinery of Law Reform' 1.

[54] ibid. More recently, Gretton has likened the Commissions to doing 'under the bonnet' or 'under the street' work: 'People know vaguely that under city streets are various pipes and cables but they are unlikely to have views about their construction, so long as the power supply, the water supply, the drainage and so on work': G Gretton, 'Of Law Commissioning' (2013) 17 *Edinburgh Law Review* 119, 127.

[55] *Stair Memorial Encyclopaedia*, para 623.

The growth in legal criticism also partly resulted from recent changes to the teaching of law at British universities—itself a product of increased ability to look to how law was taught elsewhere.[56] Previously in Scotland, subjects were more frequently taught by 'practitioners, contributing part-time to the not very exacting courses … which gave one the qualification that was needed to enter practice but did not stretch the imagination'.[57] As university teaching became more academic, honours-level courses (for those who took them) became more probing and critical, which had a 'profound influence on our way of life for the rest of the century and into the next'.[58] Similar changes were afoot in English universities.[59] Lord Hope has also noted that the legal profession was becoming larger and more diverse, moving (albeit slowly) away from its previous reputation for having members 'drawn from a relatively narrow, and relatively prosperous, segment of society'.[60] The law was now being applied by people with more diverse life experiences and by those who, because of their more probing legal education as well as their own backgrounds, were less likely to accept unreflectively the status quo.

Another reason for the establishment of the Commissions in 1965 has been advanced by the first LCEW Chairman, Lord Scarman, and by one of its first Commissioners, Norman Marsh. Scarman noted in 1966 that the common law 'stands little chance of survival to-day. Speed, accessibility, and convenience are … powerfully demanded of the law'.[61] Scarman also felt that 'law made by lawyers', was no longer acceptable because modern society had a 'wide-ranging social structure' for which judges could no longer speak.[62] If judge-made law was no longer seen as satisfactory by certain critics, then legislation would be seen by them as a superior source of law. Bodies like the Commissions, which, despite being staffed by lawyers, merely suggest potential reforms to government, therefore seemed attractive.

In 1971, Marsh spoke in similar terms about the dissatisfaction with judge-made law that had developed in the preceding decades. He stated that the decline of judge-made law led to Britain no longer being able to 'rely on that system as the main instrument of law reform'.[63] He gave five reasons why judge-made law was no longer satisfactory.[64] First, it was neither possible nor desirable for judges to

[56] See, eg, ID Willock, 'Impressions of Legal Education in the USA' 1959 *Scots Law Times (News)* 71.

[57] Hope, 'Do We Still Need a Scottish Law Commission?' 23.

[58] ibid 23–24. On the changes to legal education in Scotland, see, eg: Willock, 'Impressions of Legal Education in the USA'; JDB Mitchell, 'First Principles First' 1959 *Scots Law Times (News)* 1; DM Walker, 'Legal Education and Training' 1960 *Scots Law Times (News)* 41.

[59] For an overview, see A Boon and J Webb, 'Legal Education and Training in England and Wales: Back to the Future?' (2008) 58 *Journal of Legal Education* 79, 86–87. See also Farrar, *Law Reform and the Law Commission*, 1–2.

[60] Hope, 'Do We Still Need a Scottish Law Commission?' 23.

[61] L Scarman, 'Codification and Judge-made Law: A Problem of Co-Existence' (University of Birmingham Lecture, 1966) 2.

[62] ibid 18.

[63] Marsh, 'A New Institutional Approach' 266.

[64] ibid 266–70.

continue to make 'bold assumptions'[65] about the life of people in modern society for two reasons: (1) values were more diverse and were changing rapidly; and (2) changes to the judiciary led to modern judges lacking the 'charismatic authority' of their predecessors (for example, their salaries were lower and there were more of them).[66] Judicial decisions were therefore held in less high regard. Second, the common law was seen as unfair by those who were no longer prepared to wait for the 'chance element' of a case coming before a court.[67] It was also no longer acceptable that many parties could not afford access to the courts in order to cure the effects of bad law. Third, Marsh, like many others, felt that judge-made law resulted in a body of law which was 'unsystematic, incoherent and … uncertain'.[68] Fourth, judicial decisions which reformed the law, although 'welcomed by the critical academic lawyer', were 'unjust to the unsuccessful party' who was a 'victim in a case of retrospective law-making' where the law was changed by her case.[69] Finally, the House of Lords' inability to depart from its own precedents made it unsuitable as a tool of law reform.[70] As we will see later, complaints were also being heard about enacted law, and especially about the number of separate (and often obsolete) enactments.

In the 1960s, therefore, Gardiner and Martin argued persuasively that 'the overwhelming part of the legal profession' clamoured for law reform, making their dissatisfaction for the current law known through 'leading articles and correspondence columns of the daily press, in practically all the trade, trade union, and professional journals and—an almost daily occurrence—in the arguments submitted to and the judgments handed down by our courts'.[71] The idea of a body suggesting systematic law reform by legislation, and even potentially codification, consequently became popular.[72]

C. Political Reasons

Gardiner's association with the Labour Party, and his synergy with Harold Wilson, the Prime Minister, in particular, undoubtedly contributed to his success in establishing the Commissions. Gardiner claimed that the Conservative Government preceding Wilson actively opposed the creation of a full-time Law Commission.[73] The Conservatives cannot, however, have opposed the idea of law reform bodies entirely—the part-time committees discussed above had all been formed under Conservative governments.

65 ibid 266.
66 ibid.
67 ibid 267.
68 ibid 268.
69 ibid 269.
70 For discussion of the change to this rule, see ch 5, section IV.A.
71 Gardiner and Martin, 'The Machinery of Law Reform' 1.
72 Changing attitudes to judge-made law and codification are examined in detail in ch 5, section IV.
73 G Gardiner, 'Law Reform—Not Now?' (1974) 71 *Law Society's Gazette* 1065, 1065.

Reform was Wilson's goal for his government, spelled out in a manifesto full of plans for modernisation.[74] His plans proved popular with voters craving such change. The manifesto also reiterated, as noted above, that the 1960s were 'an age of unparalleled advance in human knowledge' and confirmed the government's intention to review 'the Statute Book with its encrusted laws'. Such a review suggests law reform, but in a narrower sense than Gardiner's vision, with more of an emphasis on tidying up the existing enacted laws, rather than making new ones, or examining the common law. Nevertheless, the Commissions' goal for the modernisation of the law left it well suited to the 'prevailing political landscape' at the time.[75]

Wilson's appointment of Gardiner as Lord Chancellor in 1964 paved the way for the Commissions' establishment. The role of Lord Chancellor was a powerful one for Gardiner, and he admitted it was 'the key position' for implementing the changes he had advocated in *Law Reform Now*.[76] Gardiner, however, did not leap at the chance of this appointment. When asked by Wilson in 1963 whether he wanted to be made a peer—specifically to line him up for the Lord Chancellor's role—Gardiner was uncertain, both about accepting the peerage and the later promise of being Lord Chancellor.[77] Gardiner eventually accepted the peerage, largely thinking about 'the chance to initiate some law reform',[78] and in due course Wilson became Prime Minister. The day after polling day, Wilson called Gardiner to Downing Street to ask him to become Lord Chancellor.[79]

It is rumoured that Gardiner made the implementation of his *Law Reform Now* proposal a condition of his acceptance of the post of Lord Chancellor,[80] although extensive archival research has found no documentary evidence to confirm this rumour. It is certainly possible that a verbal deal was struck, or that documentation was destroyed,[81] but no mention of such a condition is made in Gardiner's biography,[82] Wilson's personal account of the time,[83] archival papers relating to

[74] Labour Party, *The New Britain* (1964 manifesto).

[75] P Mitchell, 'Strategies of the Early Law Commission' in M Dyson, J Lee and SW Stark (eds), *Fifty Years of the Law Commissions: The Dynamics of Law Reform* (Oxford, Hart Publishing, 2016) 33 (Dyson, Lee and Stark, *Fifty Years of the Law Commissions*).

[76] BBC2 Television transcript, 'The Man Alive Profile: Lord Gardiner' interviewed by Desmond Wilcox (transmission date 25 March 1976) Churchill Archives Centre GBR/0014/GARD ('The Man Alive Profile').

[77] M Box, *Rebel Advocate* (London, Victor Gollancz Ltd, 1983) 141–44 (*Rebel Advocate*); H Wilson, *The Labour Government 1964–70* (Harmondsworth, Penguin Books Ltd, 1974) 89 (*The Labour Government*).

[78] Box, ibid 144.

[79] ibid 170.

[80] Chorley and Dworkin, 'The Law Commissions Act, 1965' 679; RT Oerton, *A Lament for the Law Commission* (Chichester, Countrywise Press, 1987) 7; M Zander, *The Law-Making Process*, 7th edn (Oxford, Hart Publishing, 2015) 446; M Kerr, *As Far as I Remember* (Oxford, Hart Publishing, 2006) 291; B Hale, 'Fifty Years of the Law Commissions: The Dynamics of Law Reform Now, Then and Next' in Dyson, Lee and Stark, *Fifty Years of the Law Commissions*, 18.

[81] Apparently Gardiner destroyed a lot of personal correspondence: Box, *Rebel Advocate*, 227.

[82] ibid. The text was written while Gardiner was still alive, in order that Box (his wife) could consult with him on its veracity (233).

[83] Wilson, *The Labour Government*. Wilson said his main motivation for selecting Gardiner was his stance on the abolition of the death penalty (89).

the establishment of the LCEW,[84] or Gardiner's surviving personal papers.[85] In any event, it would have been obvious to Wilson that Gardiner would want to make certain radical reforms, including the establishment of the Commissions in particular. Indeed, Wilson had publicly committed his government to set up the Commissions if Labour won the general election,[86] and, once in power, the proposal to create law reform bodies was made in the Queen's Speech.[87] On becoming Lord Chancellor, the first piece of legislation Gardiner invited Parliament to pass was the 1965 Act. On more than one occasion, Gardiner described the Commissions as 'the main thing that I achieved'.[88] Gardiner was also part of a government which achieved other huge reforms of the law—notably the abolition of capital punishment for murder.[89] It is striking that it was the Commissions of which he was most proud. He accepted that he was 'very lucky about law reform' in terms of timing.[90] It was generally felt that reform was needed by many in the legal profession (including the judiciary) and, most importantly, 'the Prime Minister in particular'.[91] Gardiner clearly believed that the successful realisation of his law reform plan was partly due to Wilson. Of course, it cannot be known whether a different Prime Minister might also have supported Gardiner's plans. It was important, however, that that Prime Minister should be a Labour one in order for Gardiner to be made Lord Chancellor and for him to be in the position to put his plan for the Commissions into action. Gardiner was indeed lucky that his plan coincided with the 'rare event' of law reform being on the political agenda.[92]

III. Pressures for a Scottish Law Commission

A. 'English Circumstances and English Pressures'

It is fair to say that it was 'English circumstances and English pressures'[93] which led to the 1965 Act, with the provisions for Scotland 'tacked' on.[94] Gardiner had

[84] See, in particular, National Archives BA25/24, BT299/81, CAB21/6073, CAB130/214, HO307/106, LC02/7423, LC02/7424, T330/18, T330/40, TS58/754.

[85] The Papers of Lord Gardiner, Churchill Archives Centre, GBR/0014/GARD.

[86] At a public meeting at the Society of Labour Lawyers, 20 April 1964, reported in the press: 'Wilson Hint of Annual Law Reform Bill' *The Times* (21 April 1964); and 'Mr Wilson Plans Law Reform' *The Guardian* (21 April 1964).

[87] HC Deb vol 701 col 41 (3 November 1964).

[88] 'The Man Alive Profile'. See also Box, *Rebel Advocate*, 178.

[89] Albeit by a Private Member's Bill: Murder (Abolition of Death Penalty) Act 1965. Capital punishment was a subject which was also close to Gardiner's heart: G Gardiner, *Capital Punishment as a Deterrent: And the Alternative* (London, Victor Gollancz, 1956); Box, *Rebel Advocate*, 178–79.

[90] 'The Man Alive Profile'.

[91] ibid.

[92] A Beith, 'Introduction' in Dyson, Lee and Stark, *Fifty Years of the Law Commissions*, 75.

[93] WH Hurlburt, *Law Reform Commissions in the United Kingdom, Australia and Canada* (Edmonton, Juriliber, 1986) 86 (*Law Reform Commissions*).

[94] HL Deb vol 264 col 1190 (1 April 1965) (Earl of Selkirk).

no plans for a separate Scottish Commission initially. On the second reading of the Law Commissions Bill in the House of Lords, he admitted that he 'had thought that perhaps it might be wise to start with England; but Scotsmen know a good thing when they see one and they were not going to be left out'.[95] Scots law was generally believed to be in less need of reform than English law, due in particular to its partially civilian heritage and restatement of the civil law by Stair, albeit that that took place in the seventeenth century.[96] Passages from Hansard as the Law Commissions Bill progressed described the belief that 'English lawyers can profit from the experience and wisdom of Scots law'.[97] Gardiner declared that he had been 'brought up to believe that Scottish law is better than English law'.[98] *Law Reform Now* also made references to the better solutions to certain legal problems contained in Scots law.[99] The lack of a plan for a Scottish Law Commission was, therefore, not an Anglocentric oversight, but the result of an assumption that one was simply not needed.[100] The fact that provision for Scotland was made at all has been credited to one of the first Commissioners of the SLC, TB Smith.[101] Smith himself claimed that representations he made via the Scottish Universities Law Institute (SULI) helped to encourage the government to form a separate SLC.[102] Smith's contribution may, however, have been overstated.

B. Thomas Broun Smith

Smith, despite being known as a traditionalist,[103] was often involved in law reform. Apart from his appointment as a Commissioner, he became a member of the Law Reform Committee for Scotland in 1954, and often wrote on the subject of law reform. He admired Louisiana's State Law Institute, a law reform body,

[95] HL Deb vol 264 col 1156 (1 April 1965).

[96] HC Deb vol 706 cols 152–53 (8 February 1965) (William Ross).

[97] HC Deb vol 706 col 56 (8 February 1965) (Sir Eric Fletcher).

[98] HL Deb vol 265 col 400 (14 April 1965).

[99] Gardiner and Martin, *Law Reform Now*, 19, 45, 61, 78 and 163–64. Smith observed, however, that many of the admired practices were not being followed in Scotland, in deference to the supposedly inferior English rules: TB Smith, 'The Gardiner Plan has its Pitfalls' *The Scotsman* (15 January 1965) ('The Gardiner Plan').

[100] See N Brotchie, 'The Scottish Law Commission: Promoting Law Reform in Scotland' (2009) 9 *Legal Information Management* 30, 31.

[101] J Hunter, 'Thomas Broun Smith 1915–1988' (1993) 82 *Proceedings of the British Academy* 455, 466 ('Thomas Broun Smith').

[102] Hurlburt, *Law Reform Commissions*, 86, citing TB Smith, 'Reflections of a Would-be Law Reformer' (unpublished, 1982).

[103] Both the Scottish Office and the Lord Advocate's Department doubted Smith's appointment to the SLC on the basis that he was too much of a traditionalist to be a law reformer: REC Johnson (Lord Advocate's Department) to RH Law (Scottish Office), 17 March 1965, National Records of Scotland (NRS) HH41/1609; G Stott to REC Johnson, 22 March 1965, NRS HH41/2049; REC Johnson to Lord Advocate, Minister of State and Secretary of State, 'Scottish Law Commission', 24 March 1965, NRS HH41/1609.

and expressed the hope that a similar body could be established for Scotland.[104] He thought that the part-time English and Scottish law reform bodies[105] did 'valuable' work, but that it was problematic that there was no guarantee that their recommendations would be implemented by Parliament.[106] Smith was concerned by the dearth of Scottish legal writing, which he worried led to Scots lawyers looking to English texts for solutions and the subsequent infiltration of English law north of the border.[107] He observed with regret that the Carnegie Trust for the Universities of Scotland reported in 1961 that Scots law was in danger of decaying 'beyond hope of revival unless strenuous and far-sighted measures [were] taken … to restate Scots Law'.[108] To address such concerns, which had been rife for some time, Smith was instrumental in founding SULI (with Carnegie Trust funds) in 1960. SULI is a publishing enterprise that endeavours to restate Scots law through a series of textbooks, and that still operates today. One recurring theme of Smith's work is that of a staunch defence of Scots law against English influence, and he is usually described as a 'legal nationalist'.[109] It is unsurprising, therefore, that the creation of a Law Commission for England, without a corresponding one for Scotland, would have worried him. Lord Hunter credited Smith as being 'partly instrumental in inducing at a relatively late stage a Government change of mind' in adding Scotland to the 1965 Act.[110] It appears, however, that his contribution to the creation of the SLC may have been overstated.

There was no public mention of a separate Commission for Scotland until the White Paper and Law Commissions Bill were published on 20 January 1965. There had been much speculation in the press as to what the English Commission meant for Scotland. Concerns were rife that English and Scots law would be unified and it was unclear whether the new Commission was for Great Britain,[111] or whether Scotland would miss out and its law would 'lag behind its English counterpart'.[112] Smith published two newspaper articles calling for a separate Commission for

[104] TB Smith, *Studies Critical and Comparative* (Edinburgh, W Green & Son Ltd, 1962) xxi–xxii, 88 and 94. (*Studies Critical and Comparative*). The Louisiana State Law Institute was founded in 1938 and still operates today: Louisiana State Law Institute website, 'Foreword' www.lsli.org/foreword. In 1960, Smith was elected an honorary member of its council.

[105] Described at section I.A above.

[106] Smith, *Studies Critical and Comparative*, 235.

[107] TB Smith, 'The Scottish Universities Law Institute: The First Year' 1961 *Scots Law Times (News)* 97, 97.

[108] ibid.

[109] KGC Reid, 'While One Hundred Remain: TB Smith and the Progress of Scots Law' in E Reid and DL Carey Miller (eds), *A Mixed Legal System in Transition: TB Smith and the Progress of Scots Law* (Edinburgh, EUP, 2005) 16. *cf* Hunter, 'Thomas Broun Smith' 457 and GL Gretton, 'The Rational and the National: Thomas Broun Smith' in Reid and Carey Miller, ibid, who argues that this description is a 'caricature' of Smith (30).

[110] Hunter, 'Thomas Broun Smith' 466. See also Reid, ibid 4.

[111] 'One Law for England and Scotland?' *Glasgow Herald* (6 January 1965).

[112] 'Danger to Scottish Reforms: Law Officers Needed in Commons' *The Scotsman* (5 December 1964).

Scotland on 15 and 16 January 1965.[113] The English press had picked up on Smith saying that Scotland would 'resist' Anglicisation of Scots law by the LCEW.[114] Even without the benefit, however, of examining government background papers to the establishment of the Commissions, which became public in the 1990s,[115] it is clear, based on timing, that the introduction of a separate Commission for Scotland cannot be credited to Smith. In fact, as we will see in the next section, the discussions surrounding the introduction of a Scottish commission had been ongoing since late 1964. Nowhere in those discussions are Smith's or SULI's pleas cited explicitly, although it is possible that Smith's views were taken into account tacitly. By his own admission, the introduction of the Law Commissions Bill in January 1965 was the first Smith knew that the creation of a separate Scottish body was a certainty.[116]

Not only did Smith perhaps not contribute directly to the creation of the SLC, but the new Scottish law reform body deviated from Smith's ideology on two grounds. First, the SLC is not as large as the LCEW. Smith noted his displeasure at the discrepancy in resources immediately.[117] Second, far from Smith's request that Scots law be restated, the Commissions were seen by certain of their members as a way of harmonising (and codifying) British law, as a precursor to entry into what is now the European Union (EU).[118] Gardiner saw harmonisation as a goal in itself. For example, in relation to an ill-fated joint undertaking between the Commissions to harmonise and codify contract law,[119] Gardiner, clearly optimistic about the project, noted that 'in a small country like Britain it was silly having two laws of contract, north and south'.[120] Smith worried about the Anglicisation of Scots law if Scotland did not have a commission,[121] but did not know how the two Commissions were intended to interact. Moreover, considering the English praise for Scots law, it is not at all certain that harmonisation would have been achieved by importing English elements into Scots law, as opposed to vice versa.[122]

113 'The Gardiner Plan', and 'Little Sympathy for its Ideas' *The Scotsman* (16 January 1965) ('Little Sympathy').

114 'Scots Lawyers Loth to Give up Independence' *The Guardian* (8 January 1965).

115 Under the Public Records Act 1958, s 5(1) (as amended by the Public Records Act 1967, s 1) such records were only generally available to the public after 30 years. The Freedom of Information Act 2000 now provides a more general right of access to 'public authority' (as defined by sch 1) documents.

116 TB Smith, 'Legal Imperialism and Legal Parochialism' 1965 *Juridical Review* 39, 54.

117 TB Smith, 'Unification of Law in Britain: Problems of Co-Ordination' (1965–66) *Acta Juridica* 93, 111.

118 LCB Gower, 'A Comment' (1967) 30 *MLR* 259, 260 ('A Comment').

119 The Commissions embarked on this project shortly after their establishment, but abandoned it in the early 1970s.

120 Gardiner, 'Comparative Law Reform' 1024. The issue of codification is examined in ch 5; collaboration and harmonisation are returned to in ch 6.

121 Hunter, 'Thomas Broun Smith' 466.

122 Such an observation has also been made in relation to judicial law reform, citing *Donoghue v Stevenson* [1932] AC 562 as an example: A Paterson, *Final Judgment: The Last Law Lords and the Supreme Court* (Oxford, Hart Publishing, 2013) 235.

Although it may be an overstatement to credit Smith for the SLC's creation, he did help to shape it in its early years. Like those who were more instrumental in the SLC's creation, Smith felt that '[i]f there are to be Law Commissioners for England an equivalent body should be appointed in Scotland'.[123] He felt that it would be 'cowardly' for Scotland to 'fossilise' her laws by failing to acknowledge the new law reform machinery.[124] Despite the fact that Smith expressed the view that unification of Scots and English law by codification would be 'premature' and would pose 'formidable problems',[125] he went on to become the Commissioner responsible for the aforementioned contract code project. In so doing, he was able to protect Scots law from unwarranted Anglicisation.[126] Furthermore, although he acknowledged that it would be harder to find the requisite body of full-time Commissioners in the smaller jurisdiction,[127] Smith stressed that Scotland should not participate 'as a minority and on less than equal terms with English lawyers'.[128] The first SLC Commissioners, including Smith, were all appointed on a part-time basis.[129] Once he was appointed, Smith continued to be adamant that the SLC should be a full-time body.[130] He campaigned to become a full-time Commissioner, and succeeded in 1972.[131] Other full-time appointments had recently been made.[132]

Smith may not have been instrumental in the SLC's establishment, but he did shape it in its formative years by protecting it from being overwhelmed by the LCEW in terms of their respective sizes, and by defending Scots law against Anglicisation. Smith was not entirely happy with the initial constitution of the SLC, which can be more directly attributed to the Secretary of State for Scotland and the Lord Advocate.

C. The Secretary of State for Scotland and the Lord Advocate

The Scottish Office and the Lord Advocate's Department had been observing carefully the plans being made south of the border for a commission since October 1964. They knew that once a law reform body was assured in the Queen's Speech, the Secretary of State for Scotland would have to respond with how Scotland

123 Smith, 'Little Sympathy'.
124 Smith, 'The Gardiner Plan'.
125 ibid.
126 The contract code is discussed in detail in ch 5.
127 Smith, 'Little Sympathy'.
128 Smith, 'The Gardiner Plan'.
129 The judicial chairman was appointed on a full-time basis.
130 TB Smith to G Stott (Lord Advocate), 20 March 1965, NRS HH41/1609.
131 SLC, *Seventh Annual Report 1971–72* (Scot Law Com No 28 (1973)) para 1.
132 AM Johnston in 1968, who was replaced by EGF Stewart in 1971.

would be affected and, specifically, whether arrangements would also be made to keep Scots law under review.[133]

Gardiner had suggested that one Commission should be established for England and, if it was successful, the enterprise could be expanded to Scotland—either by way of a separate body or by having a 'Commission for Great Britain'.[134] The latter suggestion was quickly rebuffed by the then Secretary of State for Scotland, William Ross, who argued that separate Law Reform Committees had been established for a reason, and that one 'Great British' Commission would be unworkable.[135] The then Lord Advocate, Gordon Stott, agreed, adding that a separate SLC would be required not only because of the differences in the legal systems, but also because of 'prestige'.[136] Stott was, however, privately not enthused by the idea of the Commissions. He was not impressed by Gardiner or his plans,[137] and, apparently, neither was Ross.[138] In particular, Stott was not impressed by Gardiner's ideas for the LCEW, wondering whether he really had 'a clear idea of what he wants'.[139] Stott's criticism of Gardiner's ideas was undeserved, because *Law Reform Now* does quite clearly lay out Gardiner's plan in precise terms and strongly advocates law reform in a broad sense.[140] More deserving of attention were Stott's concerns that, without new parliamentary procedures, the Commissions could 'be a source of delay rather than expedition'.[141] The introduction of the Commissions would be 'useless' if mechanisms were not changed to make more parliamentary time.[142] Despite his concerns, Stott ultimately felt, however, that it was 'essential' to follow England's lead on the matter.[143]

The Secretary of State for Scotland and the Lord Advocate thereafter joined forces. They wrote to the Lord Chancellor's Office to ask that a separate law reform body be established for Scotland without waiting for the English Commission to be tested.[144] It was recommended that the Scottish body could be on a smaller

[133] Note of a Meeting held between the Secretary of State for Scotland et al, 30 October 1964, NRS HH41/2048 (Note of a Meeting).

[134] Cabinet Home Affairs Committee, 'Establishment of a Law Commission: Memorandum by the Lord Chancellor', 10 November 1964, NA CAB21/6073, para 14.

[135] W Ross (Secretary of State for Scotland) to J Callaghan (Chancellor of the Exchequer), 26 October 1964, NA BA25/24.

[136] Note of a Meeting. See also JH Gibson (Lord Advocate's Department) to G Coldstream (Lord Chancellor's Office), 'Proposed Law Commissions', 5 November 1964, NRS HH41/2048 ('Proposed Law Commissions').

[137] In his *Lord Advocate's Diary 1961–1966* (Aberdeen, AUP, 1991), Stott called Gardiner 'a cold fish' (139) with 'half-baked ideas' (146) (*Lord Advocate's Diary*).

[138] ibid 147.

[139] ibid 143.

[140] Hope, 'Do We Still Need a Scottish Law Commission?' 13.

[141] Stott, *Lord Advocate's Diary*, 144.

[142] G Stott to W Ross, 2 November 1964, NRS HH41/2048.

[143] ibid.

[144] Gibson to Coldstream, 'Proposed Law Commissions'; RH Law (Scottish Office) to G Coldstream (Lord Chancellor's Office), 'Law Reform', 11 November 1964, NRS HH41/2048; 'Scottish Law Reform Commission: Paper by the Secretary of State for Scotland and the Lord Advocate' (undated paper to Home Affairs Committee), NRS HH41/2048.

scale, because the Secretary of State for Scotland felt it would be impossible to find enough suitable candidates to fill the same number of roles as the LCEW (five full-time Commissioners).[145] The Lord Advocate was of the same opinion.[146]

Three convincing reasons were advanced for the immediate creation of a separate SLC.[147] First, although Scots law was not in a dire state, enough areas needed examination to justify something more than the part-time Law Reform Committee, which, it was acknowledged, had 'shortcomings'.[148] Second, because the SLC would be smaller than the LCEW and would therefore function differently from it, waiting to see how the LCEW fared could not be justified. Third and finally, because the LCEW would touch on areas that would affect Scots law, an equivalent body in Scotland would be required.

The SLC was created out of a sense of institutional necessity, rather than a burning desire for Scots law reform. Both the Scottish Office and the Lord Advocate observed that, after the creation of the LCEW, there would likely be calls for a similar body in Scotland, although there was presently 'little attention' on law reform in Scotland compared with Gardiner's crusade in England.[149] A few murmurings, however, drew attention to the need for the reform of Scots law. The Muir Society highlighted areas of law it thought were in need of review,[150] but did not have as strong a voice as its English equivalent, the Society of Labour Lawyers.[151] Furthermore, as we have already seen,[152] by the mid-twentieth century, academic writing increasingly analysed critically the law and argued for reform where it was perceived to be needed. This increase can be seen in Scots legal literature. For example, by the late 1950s, articles compared Scots and English law,[153] expressed dissatisfaction with decisions of the Scottish courts,[154] and suggested areas of law the Law Reform Committee for Scotland should examine.[155] Most writing of the time was still, however, descriptive rather than critical, and was mainly concerned with alerting practitioners to developments in the law. Not only was there no real

[145] Law Commissions Bill, 'Lobby Conference: Brief for Secretary of State', 20 January 1965, NRS HH41/1609; HL Deb vol 265 col 525 (27 April 1965) (Lord Gardiner, citing William Ross's views). See also Anon, 'The Law Commission Bill' 1965 *Scots Law Times (News)* 29, 30.

[146] Note of a Meeting.

[147] Gibson to Coldstream, 'Proposed Law Commissions'.

[148] JH Gibson (Lord Advocate's Department), 'Note on Arrangements for Law Reform Measures etc', 27 October 1964, NRS HH41/2048.

[149] RH Law (Scottish Office) to Secretary of State, 20 October 1964, NRS HH41/2048; RH Law, 'Notes of Meeting with JH Gibson and the Lord Chancellor's Office on Law Reform Commissioners', 27 October 1964, NRS HH41/2048.

[150] See, eg, 'Review of Scots Law' *Glasgow Herald* (16 November 1964).

[151] The Society of Labour Lawyers sponsored the publication of Gardiner and Martin, *Law Reform Now*.

[152] At section II.B.

[153] eg: G Gordon, 'New Evidence in Criminal Appeals' 1957 *Scots Law Times (News)* 125; TB Smith, 'Malice in Murderland' 1957 *Scots Law Times (News)* 129; N Gow, 'Delay in Divorce Cases' 1958 *Scots Law Times (News)* 125.

[154] eg, Anon, 'Corroboration of Evidence in Scottish Criminal Law' 1958 *Scots Law Times (News)* 137.

[155] eg, AE Anton, 'The Formal Validity of Wills' 1958 *Scots Law Times (News)* 217.

clamour for substantive law reform, no one was campaigning for new law reform machinery either, until such campaigning began south of the border.

According to Smith, however, Lord Cooper (who had a great influence on Smith), called for a law reform body with 'striking' similarity to Gardiner's plans in an address in 1953.[156] Elsewhere, Smith credited Cooper as being 'the pioneer of the idea of a permanent Law Commission'.[157] Cooper was indeed a strong proponent of reform, with many of his most notable works following that theme.[158] He had stressed the importance of comparative law and the need to look beyond Scotland for influence.[159] He commented on the ever-increasing amount of case law and how it clogged up the judicial machinery, and urged the establishment of a Ministry of Justice to aid the 'heart-breaking enterprise' of law reform.[160] He saw codification of certain areas of law as a favourable option, but thought there was 'little hope' of it being a workable solution in the short term.[161] It is an overstatement, however, to credit Lord Cooper with Gardiner's plan, because he merely reiterated a cry for a Ministry of Justice that, as we have already seen, had been made repeatedly since the nineteenth century. The address Smith referred to was given by Cooper to the Society of Public Teachers of Law (now the Society of Legal Scholars) at its 1953 annual general meeting in Sheffield and mainly concerned reform of the courts, with an incidental plea for a Ministry of Justice. The address was reported in Scotland as being 'unanimously regarded as one of the best that have been delivered at these meetings' and it was hoped that it would lead to 'an early and intensive study of the problems raised'.[162] The Ministry of Justice plea, however, went unanswered and no other Scottish voice advocated systematic law reform. Although Smith cited Cooper's argument with praise, their law reform visions were quite different. Whereas Smith idolised the Louisiana State Law Institute and created SULI as a method of protecting Scots law, Cooper saw law reform in a wider sense. Like Gardiner, he envisaged the increased use of comparative law and a complete overhaul, rather than simple restatement, of the law.[163]

By November 1964, the Lord Advocate and the Secretary of State for Scotland agreed that a Scottish Law Commission would be set up under their joint

[156] Smith, 'The Gardiner Plan', referring to 'Defects in the British Judicial Machine' in TM Cooper, *Selected Papers 1922–1954* (Edinburgh, Oliver and Boyd, 1957) 244 (*Selected Papers*).

[157] TB Smith to G Stott, 20 March 1965, NRS HH41/1609.

[158] Much of the work in *Selected Papers* followed a reform theme, for example: 'Legal Education in Scotland: A Criticism'; 'Trial by Jury in Scotland: Is There a Case for Reform?'; 'The Future of the Legal Profession'; and 'Defects in the British Judicial Machine'.

[159] Cooper, 'The Importance of Comparative Law in Scotland' in *Selected Papers*, 142–52.

[160] Cooper, 'Defects in the British Judicial Machine' in *Selected Papers*, 255.

[161] ibid 249.

[162] GCH Paton, 'Discere Docendo—III: An Account of the Thirty-ninth Annual General Meeting of the Society of Public Teachers of Law, 17th to 19th September 1953' 1953 *Scots Law Times (News)* 242, 244.

[163] Smith too had endorsed looking to other jurisdictions for guidance, but only those with a 'true affinity' with Scots law: TB Smith, 'The Scottish Universities Law Institute: The First Year' 1961 *Scots Law Times (News)* 97, 98.

control.[164] Scottish commentators were generally pleased that there would be a separate SLC.[165] Scots law would not 'tail along … in the wake of law reform in England'.[166] But the difference in size between the SLC and the LCEW did not prove popular. One critic summed up accurately the thinking behind the SLC when he said:

> It looks to me as if it is a case of 'Well, we are having a Law Reform Commission in England, and if we do not do something for Scotland, they will begin to complain about it; so let us give them a Commission but do not let us spend too much money on it'.[167]

And so two Commissions were to be established—one for England and Wales, and one for Scotland. Although the need for a Scottish law reform body had been almost entirely created by the creation of the English Commission, most commentators were pleased with the development. Without a separate commission, it was feared that Scots law would either be entirely subsumed by English reforms, or would look outmoded when compared with the newly reformed English law. The main remaining point of contention was the smaller size of the SLC. But whether or not Scotland would have its own Commission was not the only topic of debate before the Act was passed, or indeed before the Bill was drafted.

IV. The Law Commissions Act 1965

When the background papers to the 1965 Act were released in the 1990s,[168] Cretney remarked with surprise that the Act now on our statute book 'was far more of a compromise than has been appreciated'.[169] But *Law Reform Now* and the 1965 Act cannot be compared without noticing that Gardiner's original model had been compromised.

[164] After much discussion between the two parties, who each wanted to be in sole control. See, eg, KJ Mackenzie (Scottish Office), 'Apportionment of Responsibility for Law Reform Matters between SHHD and LAD with Particular Reference to the Setting Up of the Scottish Law Commission: Summary of Official Consideration', 28 April 1966, NRS HH41/1609; JM Fearn (Scottish Office), 'Responsibility for the Law Reform Commission for Scotland', 14 December 1964, NRS HH41/2048.

[165] *cf* the views of the then Lord President, Lord Clyde, who was at one stage believed to be the anonymous author of 'The Law Commission Bill' 1965 *Scots Law Times (News)* 29: Stott, *Lord Advocate's Diary*, 158; Internal Scottish Office Memorandum, GF Belfourd to RH Law, 23 March 1965, NRS HH41/1609.

[166] HC Deb vol 701 col 884 (10 November 1964) (Norman Wylie).

[167] HC Deb vol 706 col 149 (8 February 1965) (Norman Wylie).

[168] See above n 115.

[169] S Cretney, 'The Law Commission: True Dawns and False Dawns' (1996) 59 *MLR* 631, 634.

A. The Compromise

By February 1964, it seemed likely that something would come of the proposals in *Law Reform Now*. Civil servants suspected that Labour would win the upcoming general election and 'it was known that the Labour Party favoured the proposal in Mr Gardiner's book *Law Reform Now*'.[170] Examining Gardiner's plan, these civil servants found it 'highly undesirable', because it 'would take the consideration of revision of the law out of the hands of the departments responsible for administering it; and it would involve a complete change in our present concept of administrative responsibility'.[171] The Home Office in particular was 'resolutely opposed' to the responsibility for criminal law reform being transferred from it to the LCEW.[172] Such opposition occurred despite Gardiner's argument that the existing bodies responsible for law reform, including government departments, were not able to carry out the huge amount of work needed for the 'steady, planned and co-ordinated' overhaul of English law he felt was necessary.[173]

Gardiner's plan was criticised for six main reasons.[174] First, the civil service felt that it was an exaggeration to say that the law was in such a dire state that it needed a drastic overhaul, and that the present bodies set up to reform the law were completely worthless. The civil service did not, therefore, agree with Gardiner that the entire law needed to be reappraised by the Commissions. Second, Gardiner had not properly defined 'law reform' because 'all Bills … reform the law' and 'no Government, whatever its political complexion' would relinquish that responsibility. What 'law reform' would entail for the Commissions was, therefore, unclear. Third, it was observed that finding parliamentary time for the resultant Bills would be problematic. Fourth, the vague argument that law reform Bills could be 'extremely difficult to prepare' was advanced. Fifth, those who were sceptical of the Commissions worried that finding suitable Commissioners could prove difficult. It was argued that 'there cannot be many barristers and solicitors of sufficient status in their profession who would be prepared to give up their ordinary activities for a period of years to take on this work'.[175] Sixth and finally, it

170 Meeting of C Cunningham (Home Office), G Coldstream (Lord Chancellor's Office), L Helsby (Treasury) and P Allen (Treasury), 'Note for Record, Machinery of Government: Administration of Justice', 25 February 1964, NA T330/18.

171 ibid.

172 C Cunningham (Home Office) to P Allen (Treasury), 13 March 1964, NA T330/18. See also R Crossman, *The Diaries of a Cabinet Minister*, vol 1 (London, Hamish Hamilton and Jonathan Cape, 1975) 56 (*The Diaries of a Cabinet Minister*).

173 Gardiner and Martin, 'The Machinery of Law Reform' 6.

174 Report by P Allen (Treasury), 'Committee on Machinery of Government: Law Reform, Treasury (Prepared after Consultation with the Lord Chancellor's Office, the Home Office, the Treasury Solicitor and the First Parliamentary Counsel)', 16 July 1964, NA T330/18.

175 ibid. See also HL Deb vol 258 cols 1097–98 (11 June 1964) (Lord Chancellor (Manningham-Buller)) and HC Deb vol 706 cols 147–48 (8 February 1965) (Norman Wylie). Decades later, even former Chairman, Sir Michael Kerr, remarked that 'no one who was at the centre of things, on the Bench or at the Bar, wanted to go [to the LCEW], including myself': M Kerr, *As Far as I Remember* (Oxford, Hart Publishing, 2006) 291.

was worried that departmental responsibility for the reform of respective areas of the law would be blurred (or lost).

The government and civil service conceded, however, that a compromise could be reached and that it would be

> possible to work out a reasonably satisfactory scheme—provided that it was accepted that the Law Commission should not operate as an entirely independent body and provided that the programme of legislation with which it was concerned was fitted into the general programme under the ultimate authority of the Cabinet.[176]

Eventually a compromise was indeed reached. Changes were made to Gardiner's plan which essentially eroded (but did not completely remove) the Commissions' independence from government. The Commissions would be advisory bodies, and they would report to the government. The LCEW would function under the Lord Chancellor's authority and the SLC, as noted above, would function under the control of the Lord Advocate and Secretary of State for Scotland.[177] The Commissions would be required to have programmes of law reform (detailing the subjects the Commissions wish to examine) approved by the appropriate Minister and would then report to those Ministers with their proposals for reform. The government could also refer projects to the Commissions directly. In addition, the Commissions would have to report annually on their progress to the Ministers. The Ministers would lay all Commission documents submitted to them before Parliament. There would be no Commission 'Vice-Chancellor' sitting in the House of Commons, guiding Commission Bills through Parliament. Instead, the Chairmen of the Commissions would be members of the judiciary.

Despite criticism of the wide remit Gardiner envisaged for the Commissions and government's preference for a narrower focus, no attempt was made to provide a clearer definition of what the Commissions would actually examine. Gardiner bowed to pressure to alter the Commissions' status to 'planning, research and consultative' bodies, but he would not allow certain areas of the law to be beyond their remit, being adamant that they should be able to examine 'the *whole*' of the law.[178] The meaning of 'law reform' for the Commissions was never fully ascertained by the government, leaving the Commissions' proper scope of activity unclear.

The government suggested at one point that the Commissions could be established without any legislation—the previous British law reform bodies, after all, were not set up on a statutory footing. Gardiner, fearing this would leave the Commissions at the whim of a 'less sympathetic administration' in the future,[179]

[176] P Allen (Treasury) to the Financial Secretary, 'Establishment of a Law Commission: Memorandum by the Lord Chancellor', 12 November 1964, NA T330/18.

[177] Now the Scottish Ministers: 1965 Act, s 6(2).

[178] Lord Chancellor's Office to P Allen (Treasury), 10 November 1964, NA CAB21/6073, emphasis in original.

[179] Record of a Meeting held at the Treasury between G Gardiner et al, 8 January 1965, NA T330/40.

sensibly resisted this proposal.[180] It is possible that Gardiner was again[181] influenced by the New York State Law Revision Commission, which was set up by statute.[182] A further attempt was made to tweak Gardiner's proposal and to try to introduce both Commissions gradually, 'until some experience has been gained of the scale on which and the pace at which the work can proceed'.[183] In the event, only the SLC was given a trial run of this kind because it did not have its full complement of Commissioners from the outset.

Once he was appointed Lord Chancellor, Gardiner wasted no time in implementing his plan. Instructions were sent to Parliamentary Counsel for the drafting of a Bill 'to give effect to the proposals which have now been agreed by Ministers for the setting up of a Law Commission for England and Wales and a separate Law Commission for Scotland' on 16 December 1964.[184]

B. Passage Through Parliament

The Law Commissions Bill was introduced in the House of Commons on 20 January 1965.[185] The White Paper, *Proposals for English and Scottish Law Commissions*, set out the policy that had been agreed.[186] It is clear from background correspondence that the White Paper was considered carefully, so as to attempt not to give 'erroneous ideas of the size of the task and the speed with which it can be carried out', lest the Commissions and the government 'be subjected to misconceived criticism for not moving faster'.[187] Despite the White Paper, concerns about the magnitude of the task facing the Commissions were indeed expressed during the debates on the Bill, with Lord Reid, for example, being 'afraid that the very wide language of this Bill ha[d] already raised many false hopes which [were] unlikely to be fulfilled'.[188]

Scots law was again described in the White Paper as being not in such dire need of repair, although it was conceded that there was 'nevertheless plenty of room in Scotland for systematic review and reform'.[189] The Law Reform Committee for Scotland was (at the request of the Lord Advocate and Secretary of State

[180] Internal Treasury Memorandum, 'Establishment of Law Commissions for England and Wales and for Scotland', 14 December 1964, NA T330/18; 'The Task: To Get Good Judges' (interview with Lord Gardiner), *Sunday Times* (7 February 1965).

[181] See section I.B above.

[182] Laws of New York 1934, ch 597.

[183] P Allen (Treasury) to the Financial Secretary, 'Establishment of a Law Commission: Memorandum by the Lord Chancellor', 12 November 1964, NA T330/18.

[184] 'Law Commission Bill: Instructions to Parliamentary Counsel', 16 December 1964, NA T330/18.

[185] HC Deb vol 705 col 202 (20 January 1965).

[186] Lord Chancellor's Department, *Proposals for English and Scottish Law Commissions* (Cmnd 2573, 1965) (White Paper).

[187] DW Dobson (Lord Chancellor's Office) to JJ Nunn (Cabinet Office), 'Note on Draft White Paper', 8 January 1965, NA CAB21/6073.

[188] HL vol 264 col 1194 (1 April 1965).

[189] White Paper, 4.

for Scotland)[190] to be replaced by the new SLC, whereas the equivalent English bodies[191] were to remain. The justification for the inconsistency was apparently that there would not be enough suitable people or work to sustain two bodies in the smaller jurisdiction.[192] Lord Kilbrandon, the first Chairman of the SLC, was 'puzzled' by the difference—not as to why the Scottish body was being scrapped, but rather as to why the English bodies needed to remain.[193] Others felt that the existing Scottish body should be retained.[194] In the event, the Law Reform Committee for Scotland was not abolished immediately, but received no work after the SLC's establishment and was eventually wound up in 1970.[195] The English equivalents are now defunct, although they did continue to exist and to receive work for some decades after the LCEW came into being.[196] Gardiner and Martin's original plan was that the part-time English bodies would be abolished because there would be 'no need' for them.[197] In the spirit of compromise, however, the bodies were retained with a view to having projects referred to them by the Commissions under section 3(1)(b) of the 1965 Act.[198]

The White Paper also stated that, if the Commissions were to prove worthwhile, then 'means [would] have to be found of facilitating the passage of the necessary Bills through Parliament'.[199] This statement was added to the White Paper at the insistence of the Scots, who were concerned that it was 'tactically unwise' not to mention this potential problem because its resolution would be 'fundamental to the success of the scheme'.[200] Despite this concern, no provisions for finding parliamentary time were contained in the Bill.

The Bill's progress through Parliament was fairly swift and, after the compromises already reached, did not prove too controversial. A comparison of the Bill as introduced and the text of the 1965 Act as enacted reveals few changes, none of real substance. At the House of Commons stage, no one argued against the need for at least a certain amount of law reform, but certain critics felt that the real problem was the lack of parliamentary time (and parliamentary draftsmen), not

190 Gibson to Coldstream, 'Proposed Law Commissions'.

191 See section I.A.i above.

192 HL Deb vol 265 col 541 (27 April 1965) (Lord Hughes).

193 Memorandum by RH Law (Scottish Office) to GF Belfourd (Scottish Office), 'Scottish Law Commission', 17 March 1965, NRS HH41/1609.

194 HC Deb vol 706 col 149 (8 February 1965) (Norman Wylie); HL Deb vol 264 col 1191 (1 April 1965) (Earl of Selkirk); HL Deb vol 264 cols 1199–1200 (1 April 1965) (Lord Reid).

195 HC Deb vol 808 col 384W (16 December 1970).

196 The Law Reform Committee's final report was *Latent Damage* (Cmnd 9390, 1984), which was implemented by the Latent Damage Act 1986.

197 Gardiner and Martin, 'The Machinery of Law Reform' 10.

198 White Paper, 3.

199 ibid 4.

200 Teleprint by JH Gibson (Lord Advocate's Department) to RH Law (Scottish Office), 11 January 1965, NRS HH41/2049; JH Gibson to DW Dobson (Lord Chancellor's Office), 'Law Commission—Draft White Paper', 12 January 1965, NRS HH41/2049.

the lack of a full-time law reform body.[201] Indeed, even strong supporters of the Bill made such comments and worried that having commissions would in fact exacerbate these problems.[202] Gardiner himself admitted that there was 'something' in these criticisms, but felt optimistic that 'if there is a will for law reform, Parliamentary time can be found'.[203]

Certain commentators, however, saw the Commissions as having a more limited role than Gardiner envisaged. References were made to the Commissions being suitable to 'clear away all the cobwebs from the old law', but that a 'hullabaloo' would ensue if they went any further.[204] Politicians from both the main political parties at that time queried what the Commissions' role would be. Certain MPs agreed that a tidying-up exercise was an ideal task for lawyers and was, therefore, well suited to the Commissions, but that actual modernisation and reform of the law was better done by politicians.[205] A narrower remit for the Commissions than that put forward by Gardiner was therefore indicated, but the 1965 Act did not specify any such limitation.

During the House of Commons readings, both ends of the political spectrum expressed some support and some criticism for the Bill. Richard Crossman, in his infamous diaries, even said that the Law Commissions Bill was 'saved' by other parliamentarians who thought the Bill was 'a perfectly sensible idea' despite Gardiner being 'an extraordinarily inept politician'.[206] Gardiner admitted that he had had letters of support from Conservatives.[207] Indeed, one criticism that the Commissions were in fact too small came from the Right,[208] and another Conservative MP remarked that he was 'dismayed by the extent to which [the Commissions'] rôles and … powers have been whittled away from the original conception enunciated by the Minister's noble Friend some years ago'.[209] Yet another Conservative MP described himself as a 'staunch supporter of the Bill'.[210] Others merely doubted whether the Commissions had enough resources to tackle the 'monumental task' of codification,[211] and also (again) queried why the SLC should be so small, wondering '[i]s it to be said that the law of England is in a big mess and that the law of Scotland is in only a little mess?'.[212] In both Houses,

[201] eg, HC Deb vol 706 cols 60, 64–65 (8 February 1965) (Sir John Hobson); col 88 (Sir David Renton).

[202] HC Deb vol 706 col 107 (8 February 1965) (Charles Fletcher-Cooke).

[203] HL Deb vol 264 col 1154 (1 April 1965).

[204] HC Deb vol 706 cols 78–79 (8 February 1965) (Arthur Woodburn).

[205] HC Deb vol 706 cols 96–97 (8 February 1965) (Sir Hugh Lucas-Tooth); HC Deb vol 706 cols 121–29 (8 February 1965) (Leo Abse).

[206] Crossman, *The Diaries of a Cabinet Minister,* 55–56.

[207] HL Deb vol 264 col 1156 (1 April 1965).

[208] HC Deb vol 706 col 132 (8 February 1965) (Daniel Awdry).

[209] HC Deb vol 709 col 267 (22 March 1965) (Geoffrey Howe).

[210] HC Deb vol 709 col 266 (22 March 1965) (Norman St John-Stevas).

[211] HC Deb vol 706 col 146 (8 February 1965) (Norman Wylie).

[212] HC Deb vol 706 col 149 (8 February 1965) (Norman Wylie).

the issue of whether the Secretary of State for Scotland and the Lord Advocate should share the role of overseeing the SLC was discussed.[213]

Gardiner thought that the Conservative peers were 'snooty' towards his Bill during its scrutiny in the House of Lords,[214] but neither political party was completely opposed to the Commissions. One Conservative peer said that Gardiner had 'the whole House with him in trying to make this the best Bill we can make it'.[215] During the House of Lords readings, it was again emphasised that those expressing doubts about the Commissions were not arguing against the need for law reform, although many did not think that the law was in such a terrible state as Gardiner suggested,[216] which is again indicative of a narrower scope of activity for the Commissions. Plenty of support was given for the Bill and there was some hope that the Commissions would work together to bring Scots and English law into harmony.[217] As noted above, such harmonisation was fuelled mainly by plans to make the UK look more attractive to continental Europe, prior to joining what is now the EU. Criticisms of the Bill were as they were in the Commons: the task of reforming the whole law was too ambitious;[218] the Scottish Commission was inadequate, giving Scotland 'the worst of both worlds';[219] and there would be a lack of both parliamentary time[220] and parliamentary draftsmen.[221]

The Bill as originally drafted provided for both Commissions to consist of a Chairman and 'not more than four other Commissioners' apiece.[222] During parliamentary debates, the 'not more than' provision was struck out for England, so that the LCEW would consist of five Commissioners at any given time.[223] A similar amendment was moved for Scotland, but not agreed to, on two bases. First, it was argued on the admittedly shaky ground that it would have taken the Act out of line with what was said in the White Paper.[224] Second, it was reiterated that the need for a commission was not as acute in Scotland.[225] Gardiner did,

[213] The Earl of Selkirk, Lord Reid and Norman Wylie thought that the Lord Advocate should act alone: HL Deb vol 265 col 529 (27 April 1965); HL Deb vol 264 cols 1200–01 (1 April 1965); and HC Deb vol 706 col 150 (8 February 1965), HC Deb vol 709 cols 216–26 (22 March 1965), respectively. Arthur Woodburn thought that the Secretary of State should act alone: HC Deb vol 706 cols 80–81 (8 February 1965).

[214] G Gardiner to H Wilson, 28 November 1966, NA CAB130/214.

[215] HL Deb vol 265 col 434 (14 April 1965) (Earl of Swinton).

[216] See, eg, HL Deb vol 264 cols 1164–65 (1 April 1965) (Viscount Dilhorne).

[217] HL Deb vol 264 col 1178 (1 April 1965) (Lord Silkin).

[218] HL Deb vol 264 cols 1184–85 (1 April 1965) (Viscount Simonds).

[219] HL Deb vol 264 col 1191 (1 April 1965) (Earl of Selkirk).

[220] HL Deb vol 264 col 1201 (1 April 1965) (Lord Reid).

[221] HL Deb vol 264 col 1216 (1 April 1965) (Lord Morris of Borth-y-Gest).

[222] Law Commissions Bill, cls 1(1) and 2(1).

[223] 1965 Act, s 1(1); HL Deb vol 265 cols 830–31 (4 May 1965) (Lord Chancellor (Gardiner), Viscount Dilhorne); HC Deb vol 714 cols 157–59 (14 June 1965) (Sir Eric Fletcher, Sir John Hobson).

[224] HL Deb vol 265 col 840 (4 May 1965) (Lord Hughes). The White Paper provided for a commission of 'five lawyers of high standing' for England and 'a full-time Chairman, and three or four other members' for Scotland: 2 and 4.

[225] HL Deb vol 265 cols 840–41 (4 May 1965) (Lord Hughes).

however, reassure the House that the SLC should not be 'in any sense a subcommittee of the English Law Commission'.[226]

The overall view from both Houses and both main parties was that not everyone was convinced by the idea of the Commissions. Most, however, were not completely opposed and agreed that the Commissions could be launched as 'an experiment',[227] because they could 'do no harm', although it was doubted whether they could do any good either.[228] Even one of the Bill's most vocal critics pleaded that he was not seeking to 'wreck' the Bill, but that he was rather 'endeavouring to be helpful'.[229] The criticisms expressed in Parliament show foresight in predicting issues which have indeed troubled the Commissions and which form the basis of this book. The debates indicate that many issues—such as the proper scope of the Commissions' activities, how parliamentary time would be found for their proposals, how they would be able to codify the law, and the relationship between the two Commissions, including whether or not they should harmonise the law—were still unclear when the Act was passed on 15 June 1965.

C. The Enactment of the Commissions' Six Duties

The 1965 Act sets out the Commissions' framework. Cretney has described it accurately as giving a 'breathtakingly wide' remit to the Commissions.[230] Section 3(1) of the 1965 Act orders the Commissions to 'keep under review all the law' which they are responsible for, without narrowing down what that is—a 'formidable undertaking'.[231] Despite the criticisms of Gardiner's wide notion of 'law reform' and various calls for the Commissions to have a narrower remit, no definition of what the Commissions should or should not examine is to be found in the Act.

The Commissions' work encompasses both proposing that laws should be consolidated or repealed and, more ambitiously, proposing substantive reforms. The former is a fairly uncontroversial tidying function,[232] whereas the latter gives the Commissions such a wide remit that it can prove more divisive. The Commissions' duties can be split into six main areas.

[226] HL Deb vol 265 col 400 (14 April 1965).

[227] HL Deb vol 264 col 1197 (1 April 1965) (Lord Reid).

[228] HC Deb vol 706 col 74 (8 February 1965) (Sir John Hobson).

[229] HL Deb vol 265 col 548 (27 April 1965) (Viscount Dilhorne), whom Gardiner did indeed accuse of trying to 'wreck' the Bill: Box, *Rebel Advocate*, 178.

[230] S Cretney, 'The Politics of Law Reform—A View from the Inside' (1985) 48 *MLR* 493, 493.

[231] Anon, 'The Law Commission Bill' 1965 *Scots Law Times (News)* 29, 29.

[232] *cf* the criticism of the repeal of certain 'harmless' enactments relating to turnpikes: P Samuel, 'Turnpikes under Attack from British Law Reformers' *Toll Roads News* (5 August 2006). The repeals were eventually made by the Statute Law (Repeals) Act 2008, which implemented LCEW and SLC, *Statute Law Repeals: Eighteenth Report* (Law Com No 308 and Scot Law Com No 210 (2008)).

i. *To Propose Areas of Examination and to Suggest How Those Areas Should be Reformed*[233]

Because of their task to review 'all the law', discretion is implied for the Commissions to select which projects they actually wish to examine. One of the Commissions' main tasks is to select areas of law in need of reform, based on a consultation exercise, and to propose to the Ministers that those areas should be examined. The Commissions' ability to suggest areas of law for examination was a departure from how previous law reform bodies in England worked, although the notion was not new in Scotland.[234] Once ministerial approval has been obtained and the Commissions begin undertaking their research for a project, they should survey the law in other jurisdictions.[235]

The Commissions' preliminary thoughts are presented in a Consultation Paper/Discussion Paper[236] which is followed by a 'vital'[237] period of consultation. The careful consideration of consultation responses is invariably evident from a glance at any final report, but is particularly apparent where consultees' responses 'dissuade the Commission from following its instincts'.[238] Miller has argued that '[g]ood law reform must start with effective and appropriate consultation' and has praised the Commissions for having 'pioneered' such consultation.[239] In 1985, North argued that such consultation was designed to afford the Commissions' output with democratic legitimacy, but he cast doubt on the effectiveness of the Commissions' style of consultation to achieve that aim.[240] Modern innovations such as the increased use of social media to reach consultees have partially addressed North's concerns by allowing a more 'direct, effective, economical and … relatively undemanding' way of responding to consultations.[241] But North's argument shows that the Commissions cannot become complacent in their consultation function.[242]

After the consultation stage, a report is published, usually (but not always) accompanied by a draft Bill. The draft Bill procedure initially caused controversy, at least in Scotland, where the SLC was accused by an anonymous

233 1965 Act, ss 3(1)(b), (c) and (f).

234 See section I.A above.

235 1965 Act, s 3(1)(f).

236 The terminology varies between England (the former, previously called 'Working Papers') and Scotland (the latter, previously called 'Memoranda').

237 M McMillan, 'The Role of Law Reform in Constitutionalism, Rule of Law and Democratic Governance: Reflections by the Scottish Law Commission' (Association of Law Reform Agencies of Eastern and Southern Africa Lecture, 2011) 15.

238 P Mitchell, 'Strategies of the Early Law Commission' in Dyson, Lee and Stark, *Fifty Years of the Law Commissions*, 41, discussing LCEW, *Landlord and Tenant: Interim Report on Distress for Rent* (Law Com No 5 (1966)).

239 K Miller, 'Legal Change: The Social Dimension' (1998) 3 *Scottish Law and Practice Quarterly* 117, 118 ('Legal Change').

240 P North, 'Law Reform: Processes and Problems' (1985) 101 *LQR* 338, 340 and 342–44.

241 D Johnston, 'How Law Commissions Work: Some Lessons from the Past' in Dyson, Lee and Stark, *Fifty Years of the Law Commissions*, 235 ('How Law Commissions Work').

242 See ch 7, section III.

critic of usurping the role of the Lord Advocate's Department by drafting its own Bills.[243] The 1965 Act does not require a draft Bill other than in the case of consolidation and repeals.[244] The Act provides for other findings to be presented 'by means of draft Bills or otherwise'.[245] In practice, it is usually helpful for the Commissions to present their work in a draft Bill, because it 'provides Parliament with as much help as possible' if the suggestions are taken forward.[246] Furthermore, if the same draftsman can be recruited to make amendments to the Bill if it is introduced, any 'unnecessary delay and duplication of resources' can be avoided.[247] The production of draft Bills also allows those reading the proposals to see how they translate into 'the crisp language of statute',[248] and ensures that the Commissions do not produce 'theoretical' work.[249] Miller has described the draft Bill procedure as a 'valuable innovation' in allowing 'points of difficulty' to be identified at an early stage.[250] Palmer has described it in even more effusive terms as 'a stroke of genius'.[251] By contrast, the Law Commission of Canada faced criticism for not having draft Bills attached to its reports but for laying out 'a number of recommendations that could be transposed into appropriate legal wording'.[252] Such criticism may have played a part in that Commission being abolished in 2006.

The Commissions are expected to examine many areas of law, including not just technical matters, or so-called 'lawyers' law',[253] but more obviously controversial areas too, such as criminal law and family law. The Commissions, however, tend to avoid certain areas. For example, the press release for the SLC's launch stated that Royal Commissions or Departmental Committees would continue to examine cases 'where important social questions are concerned'.[254] Lord Kilbrandon observed that the Commissions would not be able to recommend 'sweeping social reforms' because bodies which consist solely of lawyers as the Commissions do cannot determine how society lives.[255] It is also widely understood that the

243 Anon, 'The Law Commission Bill' 1965 *Scots Law Times (News)* 29, 30.

244 1965 Act, s 3(1)(d).

245 1965 Act, s 3(1)(c).

246 P Gibson, 'Law Reform Now: The Law Commission 25 Years On' (Denning Lecture, 1991) 11. Unless a method of implementation other than primary legislation is sought: see ch 4, section I.A.

247 H Brooke, 'The Role of the Law Commission in Simplifying Statute Law' (1995) 16 *Statute Law Review* 1, 3.

248 Johnston, 'How Law Commissions Work' 243. See also DM Walker, 'The Second Annual Report of the Scottish Law Commission' 1968 *Scots Law Times (News)* 2, 3 ('The Second Annual Report').

249 M Arden, 'The Work of the Law Commission' (2000) 53 *Current Legal Problems* 559, 565.

250 Miller, 'Legal Change' 119.

251 G Palmer, 'The Law Reform Enterprise: Evaluating the Past and Charting the Future' (2015) 131 *LQR* 402, 414.

252 Y Le Bouthillier, 'The Former Law Commission of Canada: The Road Less Travelled' in Dyson, Lee and Stark, *Fifty Years of the Law Commissions*, 100.

253 See, eg, HL Deb vol 264 col 1160 (1 April 1965) (Viscount Dilhorne).

254 Scottish Office Press Office, 'Scottish Law Commission Appointed', 16 June 1965, NRS HH41/1609.

255 'Aim Will be to Bring Law Up to Date' *The Scotsman* (17 June 1965).

Commissions will not look at anything which is 'political' in nature.[256] The 1965 Act, however, does not mention this understanding. The precise scope of the Commissions' activity is, therefore, unclear from the terms of the 1965 Act. The Commissions have determined their scope of activity independently of (and without much assistance from) the 1965 Act, in particular by reference to project-selection criteria first developed in the 1990s.[257] Despite not examining all the law singlehandedly, the Commissions do have a more general oversight function because they can make proposals as to which agency should carry out the examination of the law, 'whether the Commission or another body'.[258]

ii. To Consolidate, Repeal and Generally 'Tidy Up' Existing Law[259]

As we have seen, Gardiner envisaged a wide scope of activity for the Commissions. For other commentators, however, one of the main problems noted with the law in the years leading up to the Commissions' establishment was not that new laws were needed. It was instead that there were too many laws on the statute book which might no longer be needed because they were 'obsolete, spent or unnecessary or [had] been superseded'.[260] The Commissions are therefore tasked with finding such laws and suggesting that they be repealed. They are also entrusted with consolidation exercises. The amount of work needed in this area is extensive,[261] and such exercises (particularly consolidation exercises) are useful to make the law more user-friendly. They are, however, not very radical—they are merely tidying up exercises which do not alter (or alter only incidentally) the substance of the law. The Commissions' consolidation and repeals function has been described as being, in comparison to their substantive reform function, 'less spectacular and less exciting ... but very important'.[262] How the Commissions were to balance their substantive and tidying functions was not set out in the 1965 Act.

iii. To Strive for the Codification of the Law[263]

Gardiner placed little emphasis on codification in his pre-1965 writings. He saw the value of codification, but thought that it 'must of necessity be preceded

[256] See, eg, HC Deb vol 706 cols 54–55 (8 February 1965) (Sir Eric Fletcher); HL Deb vol 264 cols 1218–19 (1 April 1965) (Lord Chancellor (Gardiner)); L Scarman, *Law Reform: The New Pattern (The Lindsay Memorial Lectures)* (London, Routledge & Kegan Paul, 1968) 25. See further ch 3, section V.A.ii.

[257] See ch 3.

[258] 1965 Act, s 3(1)(b).

[259] 1965 Act, s 3(1)(d).

[260] HC Deb vol 706 col 48 (8 February 1965) (Sir Eric Fletcher).

[261] 'The idea that consolidation of that kind could ever be achieved seems to be becoming more and more fanciful': Hope, 'Do We Still Need a Scottish Law Commission?' 26.

[262] Walker, 'The Second Annual Report' 3. See also DM Walker, 'The Scottish Law Commission under Review' (1987) 8 *Statute Law Review* 115, 118.

[263] 1965 Act, s 3(1).

by reform'.[264] Gardiner's views might again have been influenced by Cardozo, who stated that '[c]odification is, in the main, restatement. What we need … is change'.[265] Yet striving for codification is a distinct task for the Commissions under the 1965 Act, although there appears to have been no discussion at the time as to why such a task was created. It has been argued that harmonisation by codification was intended as a step towards the UK's entry into the Common Market.[266] The Commissions' codification task presents numerous challenges—the formidable job it poses, the uncertainty of its exact meaning and purpose, and the hostility towards codification in common law or mixed legal systems.[267]

iv. To Report to the Ministers[268]

The Commissions have three separate reporting duties in relation to the Ministers: (1) the Commissions must submit programmes of law reform (the areas of law they believe should be examined) to the Ministers for approval; (2) the Commissions must submit annual reports to the Ministers; and (3) the Commissions' reports and draft Bills making recommendations are presented to the Ministers for consideration. The amount of control the Ministers have over the Commissions is the main difference between Gardiner's original view and the 1965 Act. One supporter of the Commissions criticised the degree of control as an 'unnecessary limitation' during the Bill's progress through Parliament.[269] An alternative view is that such control is necessary to ensure the Commissions do not waste their efforts on projects that are later deemed to be unsuitable:

> Nothing should be done, of course, which would stifle the initiation of ideas, but what is of tremendous importance is the sifting and vetting of ideas so that such time and talent as is available may be directed to ideas which will bear fruit.[270]

The Commissions experience a tension between their independence from government on the one hand, and the perceived need for greater cooperation with government in order to improve implementation rates of their proposals on the other. The unresolved need to balance independence and implementation will be examined throughout this book, and particularly in chapter four. It is entirely proper that the Commissions' programme projects are approved by Ministers, and that the Commissions should not be able simply to embark on projects based on the Commissioners' varying interests. It is important, however, that Commissioners and Ministers choose and approve projects on the same basis and by reference

[264] Gardiner and Martin, 'The Machinery of Law Reform' 12.
[265] B Cardozo, 'A Ministry of Justice' (1921–22) 35 *Harvard Law Review* 113, 117.
[266] Gower, 'A Comment' 260.
[267] Those challenges are examined in ch 5.
[268] 1965 Act, ss 3(1)(b) and 3(3). 'Minister', as defined by s 6(2), means the Lord Chancellor for the LCEW and (now) the Scottish Ministers for the SLC.
[269] HC Deb vol 706 col 117 (8 February 1965) (Roderic Bowen).
[270] HC Deb vol 709 col 237 (22 March 1965) (Ian Percival).

to the same criteria. Consistency in choosing and approving projects facilitates good relationships as well as aiding selection of the most deserving projects. A method of achieving such consistency is advanced in chapter three.

v. *To Receive References from Government and Proposals from Other Bodies or Persons*[271]

The 1965 Act provides that the Commissions must 'receive and consider any proposals for the reform of the law which may be made or referred to them'.[272] This provision is widely drafted and has been criticised on the basis that the Commissions must therefore consider references 'from any crackpot who feels like writing to them'.[273] In practice, however, the Commissions need not do more than 'consider' such references—they need not embark on a report, or, in other words, they do not need to give them '*serious* consideration'.[274] This provision was intended to mainly cover bodies such as the Law Societies, the Bar Council and local government.[275] As soon as the SLC had been established, it positively encouraged the legal profession to 'make proposals or suggestions' and to 'continue to do so in the future'.[276] Proposals received from such bodies now form the basis of the Commissions' *Programmes of Law Reform*, although the Commissions formerly embarked on such projects without ministerial approval.[277]

Under sections 3(1)(e) and (ea) of the 1965 Act, the Commissions also receive references from government, and they provide advice to government on a more informal basis. As drafted in the Bill as introduced, the original clause required the Commissions to provide 'assistance' to government departments. After debate in both Houses, the clause was amended to require the provision of 'advice and information'.[278] Although not discussed in Parliament, the amendment was apparently eventually made due to the weight of Lord Scarman's views on the matter. He felt that a judge would not be able to take up a position in either Commission if he was to 'assist' government, because, due to necessary judicial independence, the 'only assistance which a judge can properly offer is *advice*'.[279]

[271] 1965 Act, ss 3(1)(a), (e) and (ea). The SLC must also now advise the Scottish Government under s 3(1)(e). The LCEW must now also advise the Welsh Ministers under s 3(1)(ea).

[272] 1965 Act, s 3(1)(a).

[273] HC Deb vol 709 col 200 (22 March 1965) (Sir John Hobson). See also HL Deb vol 265 cols 547–53 (27 April 1965) (Viscount Dilhorne, Viscount Simonds and Lord Conesford).

[274] HC Deb vol 709 col 237 (22 March 1965) (Sir Eric Fletcher), emphasis added. Projects completed as a result of an individual member of the public's recommendation have, in fact, been exceptionally rare. One example is the SLC's, *Report on Boundary Walls* (Scot Law Com No 163 (1998)), which was inserted into the SLC's *Fifth Programme of Law Reform* (Scot Law Com No 159 (1997)).

[275] HC Deb vol 709 col 244 (22 March 1965) (Sir Eric Fletcher).

[276] Anon, 'Scottish Law Commission' 1965 *Scots Law Times (News)* 148, 148.

[277] See ch 3.

[278] HC Deb vol 709 cols 246–62 (22 March 1965); HL Deb vol 265 cols 567–77 (27 April 1965).

[279] S Cretney, 'The Law Commission: True Dawns and False Dawns' (1996) 59 *MLR* 631, 648, emphasis in original.

Cretney has observed that it was 'strange' that Gardiner continued to be of the opinion that the words 'advice' and 'assistance' were synonymous, when his Chairman-designate was of such a strong opinion.[280]

The Commissions cannot be compelled to embark on projects referred to them by government, although a commission would be unwise to strain relations with government by refusing a reference without good reason, for example the absence of a Commissioner with the necessary expertise or capacity. The relevant section caused confusion, however, when the Bill was introduced. The English tended to think that the Commissions would be bound to examine projects referred to them by government,[281] and the Scots thought that they could refuse to carry out such examinations.[282] The drafting is indeed ambiguous and would benefit from clarification. Whereas section 3(1)(a) outlines the duty to '*receive and consider*' suggestions from other bodies, sections 3(1)(e) and (ea) lay down the duty to actually '*provide* advice and information' to government. A more literal interpretation of these sections, therefore, would suggest that the Commissions *are* obliged to take on work referred to them by government. Any ambiguity was, however, clarified when the *Protocol between the Lord Chancellor (on behalf of the Government) and the Law Commission* was published in 2010.[283] The Protocol made it clear that the LCEW (and, because the same legislation applies, the SLC) can choose whether or not to accept a reference by including a list of factors the LCEW should consider in reaching that decision.[284] The section 3(1)(e) and (ea) duties therefore, like other provisions of the 1965 Act, contain an element of discretion, but that discretion is limited by the need to have regard to the factors listed in the Protocol. In exercising and controlling discretion, it is important that the Commissions and Ministers should make reference to the same criteria to avoid any strained relationships or misunderstandings.

vi. To Act in Consultation with Each Other[285]

The Commissions have an explicit duty to act in consultation with one another under the 1965 Act.[286] The Commissions frequently join forces on projects which require consideration of the law both north and south of the border. When the

[280] ibid.

[281] DW Dobson (Lord Chancellor's Office) to RH Law (Scottish Office), 'Law Commissions Bill', 28 January 1965, NRS HH41/2049.

[282] RH Law (Scottish Office), handwritten file note, 29 January 1965, NRS HH41/2049.

[283] LCEW and Ministry of Justice, *Protocol between the Lord Chancellor (on behalf of the Government) and the Law Commission* (Law Com No 321 (2010)).

[284] ibid para 9. Such factors include whether the LCEW considers the current law in the area to be unsatisfactory enough to warrant examination, and whether it has, or can obtain, the necessary expertise in the area. See too LCEW and Welsh Ministers, *Protocol between the Welsh Ministers and the Law Commission/Protocol Rhwng Gweinidogion Cymru a Comisiwn y Gyfraith* (2015) para 7.

[285] And with the Northern Ireland Law Commission, if it still exists (see ch 6, section III.C): 1965 Act, s 3(4).

[286] ibid.

LCEW and the SLC work together, problems arise due to the difference in size and resources between the two Commissions, as well as the legal differences between the two jurisdictions. Furthermore, the 1965 Act does not make clear the purpose of the Commissions' consultation duty. In 1965, the Secretary of State for Scotland urged the public not to worry about the complete harmonisation of Scottish and English law.[287] As we have seen, however, there was a plan that the Commissions could encourage harmonisation between the two jurisdictions, intended as a precursor to integration into what is now the EU.[288] Far from being harmonised, the UK and its jurisdictions are, since devolution, more fragmented. Since 2008, the Commissions have also had the added duty to consult with the Northern Ireland Law Commission, albeit that its future is currently uncertain.[289] The challenges facing the Commissions in their consultation duty have, therefore, altered since 1965.[290]

D. Composition of the Commissions[291]

Commissioners and Chairmen are appointed to the Commissions by the appropriate Minister for a maximum term of five years, although they may be reappointed.[292] The Chairman of the SLC need not be a judge,[293] although in practice he or she always is. The same used to be true of the LCEW, but since 2007, its Chairman must be someone 'who holds office as a judge of the High Court or Court of Appeal in England and Wales'.[294] By convention, it was previously the case that a High Court judge, when stepping down from his role as LCEW Chairman, would be elevated to the Court of Appeal. For various reasons, including the need for increased transparency, a desire to increase the standing of the LCEW, and the need to secure good Chairmen, incoming LCEW Chairmen are now either existing Court of Appeal judges or are elevated to the Court of Appeal on their appointment to the LCEW.[295] Judicial chairmen are thought to benefit

[287] 'No Complete Assimilation with English Law: Mr Ross Gives Assurance' *The Scotsman* (9 February 1965).

[288] Gower, 'A Comment' 260.

[289] The Justice (Northern Ireland) Act 2002, sch 12, para 9, which came into force in 2007, added this duty to the 1965 Act, s 3(4), but the first Commissioners were not appointed until 2008. For the fate of the Northern Ireland Law Commission, see ch 6, section III.C. The Commissions' duty to consult each other is examined in detail in ch 6 generally.

[290] Such challenges are confronted in ch 6.

[291] A full list of all past Chairmen and Commissioners of both Commissions from 1965 to 2016 can be found in appendix 1.

[292] 1965 Act, ss 1(3) (LCEW) and 2(3) (SLC).

[293] The 1965 Act, s 2 does not distinguish between the Chairman and Commissioners.

[294] 1965 Act, s 1(1A), as added by the Tribunals, Courts and Enforcement Act 2007, s 60(2). A few commentators sought to have this be the case from the beginning: see HL Deb vol 265 cols 425–40 (14 April 1965) (Viscount Simonds, Lord Derwent, Lord Tangley, the Earl of Swinton and Viscount Dilhorne); HL Deb vol 265 cols 831–33 (4 May 1965) (Viscount Dilhorne).

[295] A change that required the increase in the number of Court of Appeal judges from 37 to 38 to deal with the Chairman's absence while at the LCEW. For a full account of the change, see T Etherton, 'Memoir of a Reforming Chairman' in Dyson, Lee and Stark, *Fifty Years of the Law Commissions*, 85–87.

the Commissions in giving the institutions 'more weight'.[296] Particularly in relation to the first Chairmen, Lord Hope has observed that, '[i]t was these men's chairmanships of the two Law Commissions that gave those bodies acceptance in the eyes of a doubting legal profession and set them on the road to the high standing that they both now enjoy'.[297] Hope added that both Lord Kilbrandon and Lord Scarman were 'ideally suited' to be the first Chairmen of these new law reform bodies, because, '[t]hey were both quite different from the ordinary mould of the judges of those days, liberal in character, gentle in manner and unusually ready to mix with people of all kinds'.[298] In addition, judicial chairmen give the Commissions more independence from government than they would have had under Gardiner's plan of ministerial chairmen, while still affording the Commissions with 'prestige' and 'legitimacy'.[299] Experiments with different types of chairmen, such as an academic chair in Canada, have not necessarily been successful.[300]

The appointment of judicial chairmen was not, however, entirely uncontroversial. During the Law Commissions Bill's progress through Parliament, the idea of judicial chairmen was criticised as 'both a derogation from their dignity as judges and a breach of their historic independence'.[301] It was conceded by those supporting the Bill that it would be 'an inconsistency for a High Court judge to act as such while he was a member of the Commission', but that this would not be an issue, because part-time chairmen would never exist.[302] Although LCEW Chairmen technically work full-time in that role,[303] Chairmen of the SLC are now appointed on a part-time basis. The change from full- to part-time SLC Chairmen was recommended in 1996 by Lord Hope who, while Lord President, felt that, due to the 'pace of changes in criminal and civil practice', it was no longer acceptable for a judge to be away from the bench on a full-time basis if he or she intended to return.[304] The current SLC Chairman, Lord Pentland, has argued that it is essential for him to split his time between the Commission and the bench so that 'the Commission stays in touch with what is happening on a day-to-day basis in

[296] RT Oerton, *A Lament for the Law Commission* (Chichester, Countrywise, 1987) 21. See also HL Deb vol 265 cols 425–40 (14 April 1965) (Viscount Simonds, Lord Chancellor (Gardiner), Lord Derwent, Lord Tangley and the Earl of Swinton).

[297] Hope, 'Do We Still Need a Scottish Law Commission?' 18.

[298] ibid 17.

[299] On the pros and cons of judicial chairmen, see W Binchy, 'Law Commissions, Courts and Society: A Sceptical View' in Dyson, Lee and Stark, *Fifty Years of the Law Commissions*, 154.

[300] The Law Commission of Canada is now defunct, although its abolition is not necessarily linked to its academic chair.

[301] HC Deb vol 709 col 207 (22 March 1965) (Percy Grieve).

[302] HC Deb vol 709 col 214 (22 March 1965) (Sir Eric Fletcher).

[303] All LCEW Commissioners and Chairmen are appointed on a full-time basis, although they can, and do, 'undertake other work including judicial training or judicial service': LCEW website, 'Who We Are' www.lawcom.gov.uk/about/who-we-are/.

[304] Hope, 'Do We Still Need a Scottish Law Commission?' 22. SLC Commissioners may also be appointed on a part-time basis.

the courts, both civil and criminal'.[305] It is agreed here that the reasons for such part-time appointments are convincing and they are compatible with the current terms of the 1965 Act.[306]

The Commissioners each head up projects in their respective areas of expertise. Commission reports are, however, read and scrutinised by the Commission as a whole and are therefore documents of the Commission, not of any individual Commissioner. This collective responsibility, or 'homogeny of corporate branding' has been said to insulate the Commissioners against any personalised attacks which, for example, a judge-led review might generate.[307]

Two recent additions have been made to the composition of the Commissions. First, the LCEW now has two non-executive, non-lawyer board members.[308] The first appointment to this role was made in September 2015 in the light of the LCEW's first *Triennial Review* to 'provide a level of support, independent challenge and expertise to the Commission'.[309] The *Review* was concerned that the LCEW did not, given its date of establishment, follow modern 'best practice principles' for public bodies, in particular because it had a judicial Commissioner as Chair rather than a non-executive member.[310] The non-executive board members will not have a role in individual law reform projects, but rather in 'the strategic management of the Commission'.[311] In practice, the two cannot be easily separated. Although the non-executive board members may not have a role in crafting the substantive proposals for reform, it seems inevitable that part of the 'strategic management of the Commission' comprises which new projects to undertake.

Second, at the SLC, a 'landmark' agreement was signed in September 2016 with the Committee of Heads of the Scottish Law Schools to encourage greater cooperation on law reform projects.[312] Essentially, the scheme provides for secondments for academics or postgraduate students to the SLC to work on projects for fixed lengths of time.[313] The scheme is a simple way to harness additional resources, especially important in a small jurisdiction like Scotland. It only

305 B Gillan, 'Ninth Life' (2014) 59(7) *Journal of the Law Society of Scotland* 18, 18. See also Lord Pentland, 'The Scottish Law Commission and the Future of Law Reform in Scotland' in Dyson, Lee and Stark, *Fifty Years of the Law Commissions*, 347.

306 1965 Act, ss 1(4) and 2(4).

307 Lord Carloway, 'To "Mend the Laws, That Neids Mendement": A Scottish Perspective on Lawyers as Law Reformers' (speech at the Commonwealth Association of Law Reform Agencies Conference, Edinburgh, 2015) 19–20.

308 Ministry of Justice and LCEW, *Framework Document* (2015) para 3.5. A second appointment was made after the *Framework Document* was published: LCEW website, 'Bronwen Maddox Appointed Non-Executive Board Member' www.lawcom.gov.uk/bronwen-maddox-appointed-non-executive-board-member/.

309 Ministry of Justice, *Triennial Review: Law Commission, Report of Stage Two* (2014) para 47.

310 ibid para 41.

311 ibid para 47.

312 SLC Press Release, 'Scottish Law Commission and Scottish Law Schools to Work More Closely Together on Law Reform' (15 September 2016).

313 Lord Pentland, 'The Scottish Law Commission and the Future of Law Reform in Scotland' 2016 *Juridical Review* 169, 175–76.

remains to be seen whether any hackles are raised at the additional academic influence on the SLC, and whether similar arrangements can or should be made for practitioners.[314] Its effectiveness beyond academia may be limited by the unpaid nature of such secondments; academics are expected to secure external funding, and/or use their sabbatical terms to work at the SLC. The likelihood of securing such funding is presumably increased by the ability to demonstrate the practical impact of any research project that will hopefully culminate in legislation. It is also a neat way for academics to prove the 'impact' of their research, which is of course much sought after under the current Research Excellence Framework. The LCEW also provides for unpaid 'academic placements', but without any formal agreement with the Committee of Heads of the University Law Schools.[315] The ball is in the court of academics to approach the LCEW if an ongoing project matches their research interests. By contrast, although the SLC is also open to approaches, it will from time to time circulate to the Scottish Law Schools, for onwards transmission to academics and PhD students, a note of current or proposed projects on which research would be particularly welcome.[316] The system is still in its infancy and its success will depend on timing—the right person needs to be available, fully-funded, at the right time. But it is off to a good start with the first secondment currently underway, and it demonstrates that the SLC is willing to take innovative steps to evolve and to improve its output.

The contrasting recent developments in the compositions of the SLC and the LCEW reflect the very different experiences the bodies have with government and with other bodies in their respective jurisdictions. Law reform agencies in smaller jurisdictions may struggle for support and resources, as was the case in Northern Ireland. A different story has emerged in Scotland, however, of a commission reaping the benefits of the close links which can be more easily forged in a smaller jurisdiction.

V. Consequent Issues

It has been important to look back to the Commissions' establishment because the flaws and gaps identified in the 1965 Act have caused problems which persist to this day, and which will remain for as long as the 1965 Act continues in its current form. As McBryde argued, '[t]here is an ambiguity about the valid scope of the Commission's work which, like a defect in a gene, existed at conception, and, miracles of science apart, may never disappear'.[317] By examining the Commissions'

314 Secondments from the private sector were also mooted by Pentland: ibid 176.

315 LCEW website, 'Placements and Internships' www.lawcom.gov.uk/placements-and-internships/.

316 I am grateful to Malcolm McMillan, Chief Executive of the SLC for explaining, in an email discussion in September 2016, how the procedure will work.

317 WW McBryde, 'Law Reform: The Scottish Experience' (1998) 3 *Scottish Law and Practice Quarterly* 86, 89.

establishment, we can understand better, and tackle better, the problems which the Commissions continue to face. In addition, certain provisions of the 1965 Act, such as the codification task, require reappraisal in the light of changes since 1965, such as the UK's probable departure from the EU.

Four main issues for further consideration emerge from the discussion so far: first, what the proper scope of the Commissions' activity should be; second, the difficulty of finding parliamentary time to implement their proposals as legislation; third, how the task of striving for codification was to be interpreted and achieved; and fourth and finally, how the Commissions would interact with each other and, specifically, whether they would harmonise the laws of England and Scotland. Since the Commissions' establishment, those issues have been considered when assessing both the projects the Commissions undertake and the outcome of those projects. For example, the Commissions have been rebuked for examining (or not examining) particular topics,[318] for the implementation rates of their proposals by Parliament declining,[319] for failing to codify the law,[320] and for promoting (or not promoting) the harmonisation of English and Scots law.[321] In the next four chapters, each of those four issues will be examined in turn, and criteria will be developed by which the Commissions should guide their activity and against which their performance should be measured. The four main issues under consideration all stem from the 1965 Act being vague and outmoded. Consequently, the book will propose how the 1965 Act should be clarified and updated in order to put the Commissions and their assessment on a more stable footing.

[318] eg, GJ Borrie, 'Law Reform: A Damp Squib?' (Inaugural Lecture, University of Birmingham, 1970).

[319] Falling implementation is most frequently a concern of the Commissions themselves. See, eg, J Munby, 'Shaping the Law—The Law Commission at the Crossroads' (Denning Lecture, 2011).

[320] eg, F Bennion, 'Additional Comments' in G Zellick (ed), *The Law Commission and Law Reform* (London, Sweet & Maxwell, 1988) 63.

[321] C Davidson, 'Law Reform—Who Cares?' (1992) 37(4) *Journal of the Law Society of Scotland* 130, 131.

3

The Scope of Commission Activity

The Law Commissions Act 1965 (the 1965 Act) tasks the Commissions with taking and keeping under review 'all the law'.[1] Despite the impossibility of that task, the Act is silent as to how the Commissions should prioritise the allocation of their limited resources. Discretion for the Commissions, the Ministers and the rest of government to select, approve or refer certain projects is therefore implied.

Commission projects can originate from three sources: the Commissions themselves; government; or any other party. When a project is selected by the Commissions themselves, it will be set out in a *Programme of Law Reform* and laid before the appropriate Minister for approval.[2] The 1965 Act provides for references to be made to the Commissions by government.[3] Such references can be made to both Commissions by the UK Government, to the Scottish Law Commission (SLC) by the Scottish Government and to the Law Commission for England and Wales (LCEW) by Welsh Ministers.[4] Since the Law Commission Act 2009 (the 2009 Act), the distinction between governmental references and programme work has been increasingly blurred for the LCEW. The 2009 Act has increased the checks required before an LCEW programme project gets the go-ahead, with the result that effectively all projects are, more than ever, a negotiation between the LCEW and government.[5] Projects may also be referred to the Commissions by any other person or body.[6] In practice, such references usually come from professional bodies such as the Law Societies.[7] Projects based on references from individuals are very uncommon.[8] In chapter two, we saw that concern had been expressed that the

[1] 1965 Act, s 3(1).

[2] 1965 Act, s 3(1)(b). 'Minister' means the Lord Chancellor for the LCEW and the Scottish Ministers for the SLC. In practice, proposed projects are already negotiated and agreed with the Commission's Minister before the final programme is laid before him or her.

[3] 1965 Act, ss 3(1)(e) and (ea).

[4] ibid.

[5] The 'virtual necessity' of securing governmental support even pre-2009 is discussed in H Beale, 'The Law Commission and Judicial Law Reform' (2001) 35 *The Law Teacher* 323, 329.

[6] 1965 Act, s 3(1)(a).

[7] See, eg, SLC, *Report on the Married Women's Policies of Assurance (Scotland) Act 1880* (Scot Law Com No 52 (1978)) and LCEW, *Administration Bonds, Personal Representatives' Rights of Retainer and Preference and Related Matters* (Law Com No 31 (1970)), neither of which feature in any programme of law reform.

[8] But see the SLC's *Report on Boundary Walls* (Scot Law Com No 163 (1998)), which was inserted into the SLC's *Fifth Programme of Law Reform* (Scot Law Com No 159 (1997)).

Commissions would find themselves overwhelmed with inappropriate suggestions for projects. The Commissions have not been inundated with such suggestions, or are exercising their discretion to only pursue projects which have genuine merit. Although the Commissions have, in the past, embarked on references from non-governmental sources separate from any programme of law reform, the usual practice now is to interpret the section 3(1)(a) duty as being part of a process of consultation to formulate programmes. The LCEW at least no longer believes it could embark on a section 3(1)(a) reference without governmental approval.[9]

How the wide discretion afforded to the Commissions, Ministers and the rest of the government by the 1965 Act is, and should be, exercised, will be established in this chapter. By doing so, it can be determined what the proper scope of the Commissions' activity should be. The proper scope of the Commissions' activity can be best understood by developing and strengthening three project-selection criteria already used by the Commissions: (i) the availability (and economical use) of resources; (ii) the suitability of the project; and (iii) the importance of the project. Developing these criteria in both their content and their use would both clarify and secure the proper scope of the Commissions' activity by better structuring, and making more transparent, the discretion exercised when selecting, approving and referring projects.

I. The 1965 Act and Discretion

The terms of the 1965 Act necessitate the Commissions, Ministers and the rest of government exercising considerable discretion. The 1965 Act states that: 'It shall be the duty of each of the Commissions to take and keep under review *all the law* with which they are respectively concerned with a view to its systematic development and reform'.[10] Borrie argued that such 'systematic development' requires 'going back to first principles', and he criticised the Commissions for the 'piecemeal reform' which they have in fact achieved.[11] But piecemeal reform can still be systematic. The Commissions, because of their size, can only possibly operate by piecemeal reform. Each Commission is a small body of only five Commissioners and supporting staff. The 1965 Act therefore tasks the Commissions to *take and keep under review* all the law, not to *examine* all the law. Projects deemed worthy of examination can, especially if the proposals in this book are adopted,

[9] House of Commons Justice Committee, 'The Work of the Law Commission', Oral Evidence, HC 858 (2 March 2016) Q6 (Sir David Bean).

[10] 1965 Act, s 3(1), emphasis added.

[11] GJ Borrie, 'Law Reform: A Damp Squib?' (Inaugural Lecture, University of Birmingham, 1970) 2.

be selected systematically. The 1965 Act itself does not set out any such system for prioritisation, or avoidance, of any particular areas of law.

The Commissions exercise discretion when selecting potential projects under section 3(1)(b) of the 1965 Act. The Commissions' Ministers also exercise discretion when deciding which projects to permit the Commissions to examine, and government exercises discretion when deciding which projects to refer directly to the Commissions.[12] The Commissions can choose whether or not to accept a governmental reference.[13] Such a choice is essential because the Commissions might not have the time or expertise to deal with a particular reference, or may doubt its suitability or importance. It may, however, be politically unwise for the Commissions to refuse to consider issues referred to them by their sponsoring bodies without good reason. Good relationships and dialogue between the Commissions and government could be fostered by mutual selection criteria to attempt to ensure that the most deserving references are undertaken, and that the reasons for not undertaking other references are clear.

Discretion has its benefits for the Commissions—it allows freedom to choose projects depending on the circumstances at the time, and it makes it difficult for critics to argue that they are acting ultra vires. Discretion is also essential for Ministers to approve or veto the Commissions' proposed projects, and for government to refer projects to the Commissions. Such discretion is limited—certain areas (such as projects with party political implications) are not, by convention, within the Commissions' remits. Despite the existence of the project-selection criteria, the precise limits of Commission, ministerial and governmental discretion could be clearer. Discretion, although essential, has its dangers if such limits are unclear.[14] The Commissions should not, as publicly funded bodies suggesting reforms solely crafted by lawyers, be allowed unlimited choice. Having wide discretion with indistinct limits could leave the Commissions open to criticism for acting, or failing to act, in certain areas, particularly if outsiders cannot understand how projects have been chosen. The exercise of ministerial and governmental discretion is particularly opaque because it is not made according to the same project-selection criteria. The considerations the government must make before referring a project to the LCEW are set out in the Protocol.[15] On what basis governmental references are made to the SLC, and on what basis programme projects are approved by both Commissions' Ministers is entirely unknown and

[12] 1965 Act, ss 3(1)(c), and 3(1)(e) and (ea) respectively.

[13] Due to the wording of the LCEW and Ministry of Justice, *Protocol between the Lord Chancellor (on behalf of the Government) and the Law Commission* (Law Com No 321 (2010)) (the Protocol) para 9. See also LCEW and Welsh Ministers, *Protocol between the Welsh Ministers and the Law Commission/ Protocol Rhwng Gweinidogion Cymru a Comisiwn y Gyfraith* (2015) (the Wales Protocol) para 7.

[14] KC Davis, *Discretionary Justice: A Preliminary Inquiry* (Urbana, University of Illinois Press, 1971) 25 (*Discretionary Justice*).

[15] Protocol, para 8; Wales Protocol, para 6.

therefore not transparent. If improperly exercised, such discretion could adversely affect the Commissions' independence by not allowing the Commissions to embark on projects that may be demonstrated to be perfectly viable. The project-selection criteria are important to allow the Commissions, the Ministers and government to structure the exercise of their discretion, and to allow such exercise to be assessed by outsiders, such as other lawyers, academics, the public and Parliament. In this chapter, problems with the current use of the criteria are identified, and improvements are proposed. It will ultimately be recommended that the criteria are incorporated into the 1965 Act to address the fact that the Act currently gives a very incomplete picture of how the Commissions actually operate.

II. The Need to Control and Facilitate the Exercise of Discretion

The exercise of the Commissions' discretion was particularly insufficiently structured in their first three decades. The discretion exercised by Ministers and the rest of government in relation to the Commissions (in granting permission for the study of programme projects and in referring projects directly to the Commissions) has always suffered, and continues to suffer, from a lack of transparency. Developing the content and the use of the project-selection criteria would address both problems. Discretion is inevitable and desirable, but its exercise should be controlled and facilitated. If the exercise of the Commissions' discretion is not controlled and facilitated in a transparent manner, it leaves the Commissions vulnerable to criticism for making potentially arbitrary project-selection choices and for wasting public money. The uncontrolled and clandestine exercise of ministerial discretion may limit the Commissions' own discretion if, for example, permission to study a particular project is refused without reference to proper criteria. The uncontrolled exercise of discretion is therefore undesirable for the Commissions, government, legal practitioners and others engaging with the Commissions and the law, and the general public.

The classic account of controlling and facilitating the exercise of discretion is Davis's *Discretionary Justice: A Preliminary Inquiry*.[16] In that work, Davis advanced a thesis endorsing the reduction and control of discretion. His aim was to reduce injustice caused to individuals by the illegitimate exercise of discretionary power. His work did not cover '[b]road policy-making' of the sort carried out by the Commissions,[17] instead concentrating primarily on individual instances of justice (for example, decisions of whether or not to prosecute, or the fixing of sentences).

[16] Davis, *Discretionary Justice*.
[17] ibid 6.

When the Commissions exercise discretion, issues of justice do not arise in the same way. No specific individual is affected in the same way as that person is when she is on trial. Davis's views can, however, be extended to the Commissions—his work was, after all, only *A Preliminary Inquiry*, and he specifically hoped that his work would form a base for 'further study'.[18] Subsequent work has extended the scope of Davis's work beyond the effects on one specific *individual* to specific *groups*. For example, Villiers cites Davis when she considers the effects of insolvency practitioners' 'considerable discretionary freedom' on, for example, employees and other creditors.[19] It is possible to extend Davis's theory further to the work of the Commissions—not in relation to their substantive proposals for law reform, but in relation to their selection of projects. The Commissions make decisions as to which projects to undertake on a case-by-case basis. Like a decision as to whether to prosecute one person but not another, project selection should be carried out according to certain criteria so that one project is not (perhaps unfairly) rejected when another is (perhaps unjustifiably) selected. Those affected by the discretion exercised by the Commissions and Ministers include the Commissions and Ministers themselves, and those of us who have an interest in the Commissions' work. Such interest may be because we are lawyers or otherwise engaged with the Commissions and the law, or simply because we are the taxpayers who fund them—or both. Indeed, the Commissions have already introduced a process of using criteria that bear a striking similarity to the sort of structuring of discretion endorsed by Davis.

Davis was realistic that it is 'both impossible and undesirable' to eliminate all discretionary power.[20] He opined, however, that 'the degree of discretion is often much greater than it should be'.[21] Davis therefore proposed that discretion should first be confined so that any excess 'unnecessary discretionary power' is trimmed, and that the exercise of the discretion which remains should be structured and checked.[22] Those three measures are adopted below and applied to the Commissions. In applying Davis's theory to the Commissions, it can be argued that the Commissions' discretion is already sufficiently confined. It is partially structured and checked, but that structure and checking could be improved. Discretion is essential for the Commissions to function meaningfully. The exercise of that discretion must, however, be structured in a way to ensure that the Commissions use their resources wisely, and to ensure transparency in their operation as publicly funded bodies.

[18] ibid vii.

[19] C Villiers, 'Employees as Creditors: A Challenge for Justice in Insolvency Law' (1999) 20 *Company Lawyer* 222, 228.

[20] Davis, *Discretionary Justice*, 42. See also 216: 'No legal system in world history has been without significant discretionary power. None can be.'

[21] ibid 15.

[22] ibid 26.

A. Confining Discretion

Davis argued that discretion must first be confined.[23] Confining discretion means setting down the broad goalposts, or 'designated boundaries',[24] between which an official or a body may exercise discretion. Dworkin later clarified that without such boundaries, it is unhelpful to talk of discretion existing. Dworkin likened discretion to 'the hole in the doughnut'—it exists 'as an area left open by a surrounding belt of restriction'.[25] Without the doughnut, there is no hole; without certain limits, it is unhelpful to talk about discretion. Davis noted that discretion could be confined by statutory enactment, although it need not be.[26]

Very wide goalposts are already set down for the Commissions. Their broad role is 'confined to the law and law reform', and so clearly non-legal matters are off-limits.[27] So too (most probably) are 'social policy project[s]' with 'minimal legal aspect[s]'.[28] The convention that the Commissions should not examine party political issues further confines the Commissions' discretion. In addition, the 1965 Act makes it clear that the Commissions can make no recommendations for jurisdictions other than their own.[29] Between those very wide sets of goalposts, however, a great deal of discretion remains. That discretion must be structured to ensure the best use of the Commissions' resources.

B. Structuring Discretion

Once the broad boundaries have been set down, Davis said that the exercise of the discretion left between them must then be structured, for example, by way of plans, policy statements or rules.[30] This structure is designed to 'control the manner of the exercise of discretionary power within the boundaries' already set out by the confining of discretion.[31] The Commissions already attempt to structure

[23] ibid ch III.

[24] ibid 97.

[25] R Dworkin, *Taking Rights Seriously* (Cambridge MA, Harvard University Press, 1977) 31.

[26] Davis, *Discretionary Justice*, 97.

[27] E Clive, 'Law Reform and Social Policy' in M Dyson, J Lee and SW Stark (eds), *Fifty Years of the Law Commissions: The Dynamics of Law Reform* (Oxford, Hart Publishing, 2016) 68 (Dyson, Lee and Stark, *Fifty Years of the Law Commissions*).

[28] ibid.

[29] The 1965 Act states that the SLC is to propose reforms to 'the law of Scotland' (s 2(1)). The equivalent LCEW provision tasks the LCEW with proposing reforms to 'the law of England and Wales' (s 1(1), as amended by the Justice (Northern Ireland) Act 2002, sch 12, para 8). The amended version of s 1(1) is much clearer than the section as enacted, which provided that the LCEW should simply examine 'the law'. The original provision was criticised by the Earl of Selkirk as the Bill was progressing: HL Deb vol 265 cols 399–400 (14 April 1965).

[30] Davis, *Discretionary Justice*, 55 and ch IV.

[31] ibid 97.

the exercise of their discretion by using the three project-selection criteria of resources, suitability and importance. Their method of structuring discretion tallies exactly with Davis's example that an agency could state that, in exercising its discretion, it 'will consider three factors'.[32] Thus, it is realistic to use Davis's theory to examine the efficacy of the Commissions' use of project-selection criteria, as well as using other aspects of Davis's work to assess the Commissions', the Ministers' and government's exercise of discretion more generally. The structuring of discretion is central to Davis's theory, and it, together with the actual project-selection criteria adopted by the Commissions, will be expanded on in the rest of this chapter.

C. Checking Discretion

Finally, according to Davis, the exercise of discretion should be subject to supervision or review. Davis goes on to note, however, that 'the principle of check is often at its best when it is limited to correction of arbitrariness or illegality'.[33] This limitation is important because anything beyond that introduces a new discretionary judgement, which 'may itself introduce arbitrariness or illegality for the first time and not be checked'.[34] The Ministers check the Commissions' exercise of discretion when they approve or reject Commission projects. Where a project is referred to a Commission by government or others, the Commission itself must exercise the checking function. The dangers of assuming that all references are viable will be seen later in this chapter. Development of the project-selection criteria could help to ensure that the checking of discretion is exercised in the manner recommended by Davis and endorsed here. In particular, transparent and consistent project-selection criteria are essential to ensure that both the Commissions and the Ministers have the same idea as to the proper selection of Commission projects. Transparency and consistency should not only ensure that the best projects are selected, but should facilitate good dialogue (and hence encourage good relationships) between the Commissions and the Ministers and government more generally.

Outsiders—such as academics, legal practitioners, judges, parliamentarians, the media and members of the public—also check the Commissions' exercise of discretion when they critique the projects they undertake. The checking function by outsiders is important in assessing the Commissions as publicly funded bodies, and also because outsiders can recommend projects for examination by the Commissions. They consequently need to understand why their recommendations may not be taken forward. Use of the criteria in the manner

[32] ibid 103.
[33] ibid 142.
[34] ibid.

developed in this chapter would not only improve the exercise of discretion, but also the assessment of its exercise.

III. Previous Deficiencies in the Control and Facilitation of the Commissions' Exercise of Discretion

The exercise of the Commissions' discretion to choose programme projects was insufficiently structured in their first few decades, leaving the scope of Commission projects unclear. It is important that the Commissions' discretion to choose projects is structured because the Commissions have a duty to keep under review 'all the law',[35] not just the areas of law they feel like reviewing. In addition, the Commissions are publicly funded bodies and should therefore exercise their functions in an accountable and transparent manner. Their finite resources should be targeted towards the most deserving projects, and a way of determining which projects those are is developed in this chapter.

Prior to the development of the project-selection criteria in the mid-1990s, both Commissions selected projects somewhat arbitrarily and without reference to any criteria. Michael Sayers, the Secretary of the LCEW at the time the project-selection criteria were developed, has said that although there were no such criteria beforehand, the criteria 'may have reflected our previous thinking but with greater clarity'.[36] Project-selection criteria, however, were not published, and were not known outside the Commissions, until the mid-1990s. Transparency is particularly important in order that the exercise of discretion can be checked by government or other outsiders such as the public or parliamentarians, or even by the Commissions themselves when the discretion is exercised by government. The lack of published criteria in the Commissions' first three decades was therefore undesirable.

Those appointed to the LCEW prior to the mid-1990s have since spoken of Commissioners at that time being able to 'do anything they wanted'.[37] Lady Hale, for example, has said she could 'tackle more or less what [she] pleased within the area of family law' while Commissioner from 1984–93.[38] A real

[35] 1965 Act, s 3(1).

[36] I am grateful to Michael Sayers for sharing his thoughts with me in a discussion in March 2015. The role of Secretary is now entitled 'Chief Executive'.

[37] I am grateful to various previous Chairmen, Commissioners and staff for discussing their experiences with me in a series of interviews conducted between December 2014 and March 2015. The present statement was made by a previous Commissioner who wished to remain anonymous. The comments in this chapter from Sir Henry Brooke, Andrew Burrows, Michael Sayers, Sir Stephen Silber and certain anonymous Commissioners are taken from the same series of interviews.

[38] B Hale, 'Fifty Years of the Law Commissions: The Dynamics of Law Reform Now, Then and Next' in Dyson, Lee and Stark, *Fifty Years of the Law Commissions*, 21.

sense of independence prevailed during that era. The Commissions should be independent to *propose*, but not necessarily *embark on*, their own projects and certainly to propose the substantive reforms contained therein. Independence cannot, however, be absolute because the Commissions are not academic institutions, but publicly funded law reform agencies. A difference exists between taking a risk on a potentially valuable law reform project which may not be implemented immediately (or ever), and commencing work on a project which concerns an area of law not in need of reform. While discretion should be able to be exercised in order to allow a project of the former type to be embarked on, it should be structured in such a way as to prohibit the latter. Commissioners' own preferences should not be allowed to dictate project selection if those projects do not have merit. The Commissions, being publicly funded bodies with finite resources, must prioritise the areas of law that are most in need of reform.

Sir Stephen Silber, a former Commissioner, describes the LCEW before his appointment as being 'disturbing'. He observes that one particular problem was the number of unfinished projects, a problem largely caused by Commissioners having such wide discretion to choose their own projects that if a project was unfinished by the end of that Commissioner's tenure, his successor may not have the requisite skill or interest or desire to complete it (especially if he was also being promised an ability to choose his own projects). In 1995, the *Sixth Programme of Law Reform* ushered in a new era, and a more organised LCEW.[39] In that programme, various incomplete projects were officially abandoned.[40] Silber felt that once the project selection regime was tightened up, he still had 'total independence' in the substantive reforms he proposed. He notes that such independence was particularly important in order to 'consult widely' with those using, or affected by, the law in question.

Unstructured project selection was also evident at the SLC until the development of the criteria. Outsiders found it difficult to establish how or why a project had been chosen, and criticism ensued. At the turn of the century, McBryde criticised the SLC for, on the one hand, having embarked on projects where Commissioners had little expertise in an area,[41] and, on the other, for having taken on projects based purely (or largely) on Commissioners' interests, but which were not 'of pressing importance'.[42] McBryde cited the SLC's 1970s memoranda on corporeal movables as examples of projects which were not 'of pressing importance', but which were completed due to the interests of then

[39] LCEW, *Sixth Programme of Law Reform* (Law Com No 234 (1995)).

[40] eg, 'civil liability for dangerous things and activities', which had been dormant since 1989 (ibid 12) and private international law, which had been dormant since 1990 (ibid 17).

[41] WW McBryde, 'Law Reform: The Scottish Experience' (1998) 3 *Scottish Law and Practice Quarterly* 86, 95 ('Law Reform: The Scottish Experience') discussing the SLC's *Report on Bankruptcy and Related Aspects of Insolvency and Liquidation* (Scot Law Com No 68 (1981)). See ch 4, section V for McBryde's criticism of that project.

[42] McBryde, ibid.

Commissioner TB Smith.[43] Exemplifying the fact that such projects may falter when their Commissioner is no longer at their helm, only one of the eight memoranda proceeded to report stage.[44] McBryde expressed concern that the impression given, at least in the past, was that SLC projects were selected based 'on the personal interest of the Commissioners'.[45]

In their first few decades, project selection at both Commissions was unstructured and, to their detriment, was perceived by outsiders, such as McBryde, to be deficient. Public resources were being wasted and, to survive, the Commissions needed to rectify that deficiency.

IV. The Project-Selection Criteria

The project-selection criteria already used by the Commissions are central to this book. The criteria provide a basis for the proper structuring of the Commissions', the Ministers' and the rest of government's exercise of discretion. They require development, however, both in their content and their use. By developing the criteria already used by the Commissions, realistic proposals for the reform of the Commissions' project selection can be made. First, we must establish why and how the criteria were introduced, how they have been used since 1997 and why they are in need of development in this book.

A. The Introduction of the Criteria

The project-selection criteria were first explicitly mentioned (then called 'relevant considerations') in 1997, in the LCEW's annual report published that year.[46] No reasons have ever been published as to why a need for such criteria was felt, why these particular criteria were chosen, or who chose them. I am grateful to previous and current Chairmen, Commissioners and staff, certain of whom wish to remain anonymous, for their recollections of the genesis and evolution of the criteria.

The development of the criteria began under Sir Henry Brooke's chairmanship from 1993 until 1995. Brooke and former Commissioner Andrew Burrows both recall that the criteria began to be formulated in the mid-1990s by civil servants in consultation with Brooke and the then Secretary of the LCEW, Michael Sayers. Brooke recalls pressure from the civil service to demonstrate 'value for money'.

[43] SLC Memoranda Nos 24–31 inclusive, all 1976.

[44] SLC, *Corporeal Moveables—Lost and Abandoned Property* (Scot Law Com Memorandum No 29 (1976)) which resulted in *Report on Lost and Abandoned Property* (Scot Law Com No 57 (1980)).

[45] McBryde, 'Law Reform: The Scottish Experience' 97.

[46] LCEW, *Thirty-First Annual Report: 1996* (Law Com No 244 (1997)) app A.

Brooke was himself concerned about the LCEW's falling implementation rate. He therefore endeavoured to devise a set of criteria, the proper consideration of which would ensure that projects were chosen which had genuine merit, and which might consequently have a better chance of implementation. The criteria were therefore at least partially created in response to a lack of enactment of LCEW proposals and were designed to improve implementation rates. If they are properly developed, as recommended in this book, further implementation measures such as the Law Commission Act 2009 would become less necessary.[47]

The evolution of the project-selection criteria took a number of years. In December 1994, a two-day residential meeting was held between the LCEW and the Lord Chancellor's Department. At this meeting, the LCEW (including Brooke, Sayers and the Commissioners) and civil servants discussed and devised the project-selection criteria together. The meeting successfully allowed both the LCEW and the government to have 'a clearer understanding of their respective roles and of the ways in which [they] can work together most effectively without imperilling [the LCEW's] independence'.[48] The first results of that meeting can be seen in the *Sixth Programme of Law Reform*, published in 1995.[49] The *Sixth Programme* does not mention the criteria, instead describing how the LCEW would choose to examine areas of law which were unfair, out of date, uncertain or expensive to use. This programme can be seen as Brooke's first attempt to add structure to how the LCEW chose its projects, and it paved the way for the greater transparency which followed.

As noted above, the criteria were first published in 1997. By that time, Dame Mary Arden had succeeded Brooke as LCEW Chairman. Carrying on the work started by Brooke, she continued striving for greater transparency of project selection by developing the project-selection criteria. She was responsible for the first public mention of the criteria which has continued to this day: availability of resources, suitability of subject matter and importance of subject matter.

Because the LCEW is publicly funded, the public should be able to see how projects are selected. Moreover, projects should be selected on the basis that they will do public good, not that they are simply academically interesting. Use of the criteria should allow outsiders, such as government and the public, to see how projects are selected. Such transparency allows for better understanding of the Commissions as well as attempting to ensure that decision-making inside the Commissions is better than it might otherwise be if such decisions were allowed to remain secret. One previous Commissioner who wished to remain anonymous went so far as to say that had the project-selection criteria not been introduced, the LCEW would 'probably not' have survived. Burrows has described the introduction of the criteria as being a 'bridge' between the total independence of the

[47] For a full discussion of the 2009 Act, see ch 4, section IV.B.iv.

[48] LCEW, *Twenty-Ninth Annual Report: 1994* (Law Com No 232 (1995)) para 3.7.

[49] LCEW, *Sixth Programme of Law Reform* (Law Com No 234 (1995)).

previous Commissioners and a certain loss of independence under the Protocol between the LCEW and the Lord Chancellor made in 2010.[50]

B. The LCEW's Use and Development of the Criteria

Since they were first published in 1997, the project-selection criteria have been referred to routinely by the LCEW. They are noted in programmes,[51] annual reports[52] and on the LCEW website.[53] The criteria should, therefore, be widely known. The LCEW does not, however, demonstrate how each new project measures up to the criteria. It cannot therefore be known how, and even whether, each new project chosen (or rejected) has been considered against the criteria. Although no evidence exists to suggest that the LCEW does not consider the criteria properly, it is problematic that such consideration cannot be known or tested. Proposals are made later in this chapter as to how the Commissions (and Ministers and the rest of government) could demonstrate consideration of the criteria. Doing so would allow for easier checking to ensure that the criteria have been considered, and to understand to what extent the project meets (or does not meet) each criterion. Requiring publication of the consideration of the project-selection criteria would not be unduly onerous because it would simply require recording briefly what should already be taking place. Furthermore, arguments are advanced below as to why such a duty would not leave the Commissions, the Ministers or government vulnerable to challenges of their exercise of discretion. Although the choice of projects may not be arbitrary, and the criteria may be applied consistently, it is problematic that it cannot be *known* whether they are being so applied. Greater transparency in the use of the criteria is needed.

Despite routine mention of the criteria since 1997, the 2010 Protocol listed nine considerations which the LCEW should take account of in selecting projects.[54] The nine considerations mentioned in the Protocol are a potential source of confusion and inconsistency because they have not been referred to as a whole, before or since the Protocol, in programmes, annual reports or on the LCEW website. On occasion, certain of the nine considerations are referred to together with the criteria.[55] The nine considerations show the LCEW's development of the criteria, and are best viewed as sub-criteria of the original three criteria as illustrated in Figure 1.

[50] Protocol, discussed at length in ch 4, section IV.B.iv.
[51] See, most recently, LCEW, *Twelfth Programme of Law Reform* (Law Com No 354 (2014)) para 1.15.
[52] See, most recently, LCEW, *Annual Report 2015–16* (Law Com No 367 (2016)) 57.
[53] LCEW website, 'How We Work' www.lawcom.gov.uk/about/how-we-work/.
[54] Protocol, para 5.
[55] See, eg, LCEW, *Twelfth Programme of Law Reform* (Law Com No 354 (2014)) para 1.16.

1. Considerations relevant to the availability and economical use of resources

(i) Whether the Commissioners and staff have or have access to the relevant experience.
(ii) Whether project-specific funding is available (if relevant).
(iii) The degree of departmental support, and the information provided by the department in accordance with paragraph 7 below.[56]
(iv) The priority that should attach to the project when compared with other ongoing or potential projects.
(v) Whether there is a Scottish or Northern Irish dimension to the project that would need the involvement of the Scottish and/or Northern Ireland Law Commission(s).
(vi) Whether there is a Welsh dimension that would need the involvement of the Welsh Assembly Government.

2. Considerations relevant to the suitability of the project

(vii) Whether the independent non-political Commission is the most suitable body to conduct a review in that area of the law.

3. Considerations relevant to the importance of the project

(viii) The extent to which the law in that area is unsatisfactory.
(ix) The potential benefits that would flow from reform.

Figure 1: The nine considerations of the 2010 Protocol as sub-criteria of the three project-selection criteria[57]

It is preferable, in the interests of clarity and consistency, to refer regularly to the three broad criteria, rather than making occasional reference to the existence of nine considerations, or certain of those considerations. The nine considerations do, however, have a valuable role to play in aiding the understanding of the three criteria. They are important considerations which should be taken into account before a Commission embarks on a project and which can guide and inform the Commissions' proper consideration of the three criteria. As such, they can be improved on, and a revised set of sub-criteria is presented in Figure 2 on page 84.

Similarly in the LCEW's annual reports, a new fourth criterion has started to creep in: 'the strength of the need for law reform'.[58] While undoubtedly a crucial consideration, this new criterion does not really add anything to the other criteria.

[56] Para 7 of the Protocol covers governmental input into the most appropriate method of the LCEW presenting its findings (eg, draft Bill) and the prospects for implementation specific to that method.

[57] The nine considerations could plausibly fit into more than one of the three project-selection criteria—I present here the most logical fit in my view.

[58] The first mention of this criterion appears to be in LCEW, *Annual Report 2012–13* (Law Com No 338 (2013)) para 4.2.

A project will be *important* if there is a strong need for reform. It will be a good use of *resources* if it is likely to result in a change to the law. A set of three, unchanging criteria would be preferable in the interests of those criteria being well established, well known and therefore consistently applied. It is undesirable to have a different set of criteria in annual reports and on the LCEW website, for example (where the 'strength' criterion does not appear).

C. The SLC's Use and Development of the Criteria

The SLC has adopted project-selection criteria similar to the LCEW's criteria, with the first public mention of the criteria being in its *Seventh Programme of Law Reform* published in 2005.[59] Since then, the SLC has usually cited the project-selection criteria in programmes and annual reports.[60] Recent annual reports make no mention of the criteria,[61] but no alternative criteria are proposed and so it is assumed that the same criteria still apply. It is more important that project-selection criteria are cited in programmes of law reform to show how those projects have been selected, although their absence from annual reports is still an unfortunate backward step in terms of transparency. This is particularly so since without widespread and consistent use, the criteria cannot be well known.[62]

The SLC apply the criteria to each project as it is being considered for inclusion in a programme.[63] Like the LCEW, however, the SLC does not demonstrate whether and how each new project has actually been considered against the project-selection criteria. Although, therefore, the criteria themselves are (somewhat) transparent, their proper and consistent use cannot be ascertained. Although it may well be that the criteria are being consistently applied, it is highly undesirable that any doubt should exist as to that fact. Such doubt could easily be removed by use of the method of transparent criteria-consideration endorsed below. Like the UK Government and Ministers, the Scottish Ministers and government do not (or at least do not openly) consider the criteria when making a reference or approving a programme project. Reasons why they should are advanced below.

In its *Ninth Programme of Law Reform*, the SLC showed its first real development of the criteria. The 'suitability of the project' criterion was split into two parts:

(a) whether the issues concerned are predominantly legal rather than political; and whether there is any other body better placed to examine the topic in question; and

[59] SLC, *Seventh Programme of Law Reform* (Scot Law Com No 198 (2005)) para 1.2.

[60] See, most recently, SLC, *Ninth Programme of Law Reform* (Scot Law Com No 242 (2015)) para 1.4 and SLC *Annual Report 2014* (Scot Law Com No 241 (2015)) 13.

[61] See, eg, SLC, *Annual Report 2015* (Scot Law Com No 244 (2016)).

[62] On giving a paper on law reform to an audience at the University of Glasgow in September 2015, I asked how many people knew of the criteria. The audience included former SLC legal assistants and other legal academics interested in the field of law reform. Most were unaware of the existence of the criteria.

[63] I am grateful to Malcolm McMillan for sharing his views with me in December 2014.

(b) whether a Bill on the topic may be suitable for the special Parliamentary law reform processes, in particular the new procedure in the Scottish Parliament.[64]

Part (a) summarises the usual understanding of the 'suitability of the project' criterion. Part (b) introduces a new consideration in relation to this criterion. It makes reference to special parliamentary procedures in the House of Lords and the Scottish Parliament to aid implementation of the most technical and least controversial Commission proposals.[65] The new Scottish Parliament procedure specifically excludes proposals which 'relate directly to criminal law reform'.[66] Because of concerns that technical law reform proposals struggle most to find legislative time due to their lack of political appeal, the new procedures were designed to level the playing field for such proposals. Giving priority to the selection of those projects over other, potentially more deserving, projects could tip the balance too far in the other direction. The new SLC interpretation of the 'suitability of the project' criterion prioritises technical law reform and could mean that criminal law reform will be less likely to be seen as 'suitable' for the SLC because criminal law reform Bills cannot pass under the new Holyrood procedure. The prospect of implementation is only one consideration that should be taken into account in allocating resources. The SLC must be careful not to neglect its duty to take and keep under review all the law, including the criminal law.

The project-selection criteria have shown a considered move away from the arbitrary and undisclosed selection of projects in the Commissions' first three decades. The criteria have been a positive step towards ensuring transparency and proper allocation of resources. They are, however, in need of development, both in their content and their use.

V. Developing and Strengthening the Criteria

The project-selection criteria already used by the Commissions provide a basis for the development of the proper structuring of the Commissions' exercise of discretion. The criteria reflect the main considerations which are, and should be, taken into account in deciding whether a project is viable. The further development proposed in this book is more practicable and therefore preferable to suggesting a complete departure from current practice. The developments proposed to the criteria can be split into two categories: developing the content of the criteria; and developing the use and transparency of the criteria.

[64] SLC, *Ninth Programme of Law Reform* (Scot Law Com No 242 (2015)) para 1.4.

[65] Discussed in ch 4, sections IV.A.iv and IV.C.ii respectively.

[66] Scottish Parliament Official Report, 28 May 2013, col 20377 (Nigel Don); Scottish Parliament Business Bulletin (93/2013) 1. The House of Lords procedure makes no such exclusion.

A. The Content of the Criteria

The criteria first require development as to their content. The three broad criteria work well in covering the most important issues to be considered before embarking on a project. The criteria do, however, require refocusing and fuller explanation. As already explained, any attempts to develop other criteria should be resisted in the interests of having three criteria that become well known and consistently applied.

i. Availability and Economical Use of Resources

In choosing whether or not to undertake a project, the Commissions currently consider the availability of their resources, in both a human and financial sense. As we have seen, the Commissions are small bodies and they have increasingly limited resources. Realistically, they cannot possibly examine 'all the law' that the 1965 Act requires them to take and keep under review. Commission, ministerial and governmental discretion to pick and choose projects is therefore implied. While he was Chairman of the LCEW, Sir Michael Kerr remarked that the Commissions do not deal with certain topics, such as tax, not only because of the 'specialised character' of such areas which makes them more suitable for reform by government departments, but also because of the limitations of the Commissions (and Commissioners) themselves.[67] Kerr argued that the scope of the Commissions' activity should not be defined on the basis of whether issues were political or technical, but 'by the logistics of what is possible within a relatively small organisation'.[68]

The 1965 Act does not prescribe which areas of law the Commissions should or should not examine, and it should not seek to do so. The Commissions will find that certain projects fit well at certain times depending on, in particular, the expertise and capacity of Commissioners. Being too prescriptive in what they can and cannot examine is unwise when individual Commissioners change every five years or so. Commissioners are chosen to work in their own broad area of expertise (although they scrutinise all Commission publications). The Commissions must therefore have a range of projects in terms of subject matter so that each Commissioner has a roughly equal load. The Commissions therefore have a varied workload and no single area of law dominates their output. A Commission's output at any given time is largely driven by the expertise of its current Commissioners, which might reflect the perceived needs of the time. For example, the government sought a lot of guidance from the Commissions on private international law matters during the UK's entry into what is now the

[67] M Kerr, 'Law Reform in Changing Times' (1980) 96 *LQR* 515, 526.
[68] ibid.

European Union (EU), and during the adoption of various international instruments.[69] A high family law output partially corresponds with Stephen Cretney and Lady Hale's terms as family law Commissioners (1978–83 and 1984–93 respectively). The LCEW no longer has a dedicated family law Commissioner,[70] and the number of family law projects undertaken has declined markedly.

The SLC also looks at a wide variety of projects. As with the LCEW, the appointment of individual Commissioners corresponds with certain productivity rates. For example, the appointment of Kenneth Reid as property law Commissioner in 1995 tallies with a sharp increase in property law projects. In contrast, there has been no Commissioner responsible for criminal law since the retirement of Patrick Layden in 2014. Consequently, there are no criminal law projects in the SLC's *Ninth Programme*,[71] and a project on homicide from the *Eighth Programme* has been suspended.[72] In June 2013, the then Justice Secretary, Kenny MacAskill, indicated his intention to refer a project to the SLC on the not proven verdict.[73] No project was ever commenced, perhaps partly because of a lack of suitable expertise.[74]

The availability of resources is an essential criterion to consider—a project, no matter how valuable, cannot be embarked on if the resources (either human or financial) do not exist, or if they cannot be found. In the LCEW's case, funding is provided by way of a combination of core funding from Parliament received via the Ministry of Justice, and contributions from the relevant governmental department on a project-by-project basis.[75] Although a practical solution to decreased core funding, the LCEW is aware of the risks of project-by-project funding.[76] Funding projects on an individual basis is problematic because a project may simply be vetoed by governmental refusal of funds, unless the funding can be taken from the core supply. Although it may not currently be practically possible, it would be preferable for the LCEW's funding to be given as a lump sum—as it

[69] Such as LCEW and SLC, *Hague Convention on Recognition of Divorces and Legal Separations* (Law Com No 34 and Scot Law Com No 16 (1970)); and LCEW and SLC, *Report on the Council of Europe Conventions on Foreign Money Liabilities (1967) and on the Place of Payment of Money Liabilities (1972)* (Law Com No 109 and Scot Law Com No 66 (1981)).

[70] Professor Nick Hopkins currently heads the 'property, family and trust law' team: LCEW website, 'Who We Are' www.lawcom.gov.uk/about/who-we-are/.

[71] SLC, *Ninth Programme of Law Reform* (Scot Law Com No 242 (2015)).

[72] SLC, *Eighth Programme of Law Reform* (Scot Law Com No 220 (2010)) paras 2.13–2.14; *Ninth Programme*, ibid para 1.5 and app A.

[73] SLC, *Annual Report 2014* (Scot Law Com No 241 (2015)) 20.

[74] Although there are other possible reasons such as the Scottish Government's desire for further research into jury behaviour, which stymied a Member's Bill on the topic. For further discussion, see J Chalmers, F Leverick and SW Stark, 'The Process of Criminal Evidence Law Reform in Scotland: What Can We Learn?' in P Duff and P Ferguson (eds), *Current Developments in Scottish Criminal Evidence Law* (Edinburgh, EUP, forthcoming 2017).

[75] LCEW, *Annual Report 2015–16* (Law Com No 367 (2016)) app B.

[76] E Lorimer, 'Commissioning the Future—A Chief Executive's Perspective' in Dyson, Lee and Stark, *Fifty Years of the Law Commissions*, 365–66.

is at the SLC—in order for the Commissions to decide how best to allocate it, using the project-selection criteria as a guide and with ministerial approval. The Commissions must also consider whether the project requires any collaboration from another Commission or Commissions.[77] If so, the available or obtainable resources at both or all Commissions must be considered.

The resources criterion requires further development. If the resources are available (or obtainable), the Commissions should then consider whether a project would be an *economical use* of those resources. It appears, from the sub-criteria listed in Figure 1, that the Commissions do (or at least the LCEW does) already interpret the criterion in such a way. This interpretation should, however, be more explicit, and the criterion should be more developed.

Only once it has been ascertained that the necessary resources are available or obtainable can it be decided whether a project is also an economical use of those resources. That decision will involve, for example, considering a project's likelihood of implementation. A project which is uncertain of implementation might ostensibly seem like a poor use of resources, but it may be sufficiently important to justify its examination.[78] It will also involve estimating the size of the proposed project. A particularly large project may seem like a poor use of resources because it may reduce the number of other smaller projects which can be carried out simultaneously. In his *Quinquennial Review of the Law Commission*, Halliday expressed the view that the LCEW should concentrate on 'more tightly focused' projects, rather than the longer, more elaborate ones, which were increasingly being favoured.[79] Any '[l]ong term, multi-faceted pieces of work', he recommended, 'should be broken down into discrete projects'.[80] Similar recommendations have been made in relation to other law reform bodies. Writing about the New York State Law Revision Commission, MacDonald said '[i]t would not be wise' for it to be engaged in long projects which take many years to complete, because they prevent it from simultaneously carrying out other projects.[81] A large project will potentially require substantial resources and could impact negatively on the progress of other existing or proposed projects. Large projects, which take a long time to complete, may also be undesirable because of a risk of the project not being completed before the tenure of the lead Commissioner is over, or the risk of the government losing interest in the project. In addition, projects that take a long time to complete are at greater risk of being superseded by ongoing developments,[82] albeit that such a risk exists in any project. Certain large projects have,

[77] One of the nine considerations under the Protocol, para 5. See also the Wales Protocol, para 7 and ch 6.

[78] The possible benefits of projects which are not immediately (or ever) implemented are advanced in ch 4.

[79] J Halliday, *Quinquennial Review of the Law Commission* (2003) para 3.11.

[80] ibid.

[81] JW MacDonald, 'The New York Law Revision Commission' (1965) 28 *MLR* 1, 16.

[82] R Carnwath, 'Introduction' in Dyson, Lee and Stark, *Fifty Years of the Law Commissions*, 125.

however, been important and successful. For example, in 2001, the LCEW completed an extremely large and long-term project on Land Registration. The Draft Land Registration Bill annexed to *Land Registration for the Twenty-First Century*[83] was 133 clauses and 13 schedules long. The project took over six years to complete and was conducted jointly with HM Land Registry.[84] The report itself describes the reforms as a 'conveyancing revolution'.[85] The Land Registration Act 2002 implemented the LCEW's reforms in full, and the Act received Royal Assent a mere seven months after the publication of the report. Many successfully implemented SLC projects have been huge endeavours, such as the quasi-codification of bankruptcy law;[86] the abolition of feudal tenure;[87] and a complete overhaul of the law on sexual offences.[88] Such projects indicate that, although large projects may prevent the Commissions from examining many other smaller projects simultaneously, they need not be out of bounds if they meet the following two criteria: if they are sufficiently suitable for a Commission to examine; and if they are sufficiently important to warrant examination.

ii. Suitability of Subject Matter

The second criterion the Commissions consider when selecting projects is the suitability of the subject matter. Essentially the question they ask currently is whether an 'independent non-political Commission' is the appropriate body to carry out the project.[89] As we have seen, the Commissions do not, by convention, look at things which are 'political' in nature.[90] This convention is not mentioned in the 1965 Act and it is unclear what political means. The lack of statutory definition is unsurprising because it is difficult to define what political means in this (and other) contexts. It is easier first to state what it does *not* mean. 'Political', in this instance, cannot be defined merely by how controversial a subject is. The Commissions do look at obviously controversial areas, such as criminal law and family law. In family law, for example, the LCEW has examined projects on the

[83] LCEW, *Land Registration for the Twenty-First Century: A Conveyancing Revolution* (Law Com No 271 (2001)).

[84] The project originated in the LCEW's *Sixth Programme of Law Reform* (Law Com No 234 (1995)), which resulted in a first report the same year (LCEW, *Land Registration: First Joint Report with HM Land Registry* (Law Com No 235 (1995))) and the Land Registration Act 1997.

[85] Law Com No 271, para 1.1 and in the subtitle of the report.

[86] SLC, *Report on Bankruptcy and Related Aspects of Insolvency and Liquidation* (Scot Law Com No 68 (1981)). See also *Report on the Consolidation of Bankruptcy Legislation in Scotland* (Scot Law Com No 232 (2013)).

[87] SLC, *Abolition of the Feudal System* (Scot Law Com No 168 (1999)).

[88] SLC, *Report on Rape and Other Sexual Offences* (Scot Law Com No 209 (2007)).

[89] LCEW website, 'How We Work' www.lawcom.gov.uk/about/how-we-work/. But see the SLC's recent development of this criterion, discussed above.

[90] See, eg, HC Deb vol 706 cols 54–55 (8 February 1965) (Sir Eric Fletcher); HL Deb vol 264 cols 1218–19 (1 April 1965) (Lord Chancellor (Gardiner)); L Scarman, *Law Reform: The New Pattern (The Lindsay Memorial Lectures)* (London, Routledge & Kegan Paul, 1968) 25 (*The New Pattern*).

grounds for divorce,[91] proof of paternity,[92] polygamous marriage,[93] and the rights of illegitimate children,[94] which have all been successfully implemented. It is currently proposing to examine a project on surrogacy in its forthcoming *Thirteenth Programme of Law Reform*.[95] Surprise at a high implementation rate in family law has been expressed by family law Commissioners themselves, such as Cretney.[96] In chapter four, however, we will see that implementation is often a particular problem for more technical areas. We should not be surprised that more attention grabbing reforms sometimes find their way more easily into the parliamentary schedule. Another former family law Commissioner, Lady Hale, has remarked that the previous productivity and success rates in family law were partly to do with it being within the remit of the Lord Chancellor's Department and partly to do with the LCEW's concentration on remedies rather than rules which are deemed to be 'less controversial'.[97]

In addition, it is not always obvious what a 'controversial' project might be.[98] Steering away from political issues does not, therefore, necessarily lead to everything the Commissions do being anodyne. Items on Commission agendas may be 'highly topical and socially controversial', despite being apolitical.[99] The Commissions typically, however, do not look at subjects which are *party* political. In such cases, the Commissions are inevitably drawn into politics by siding with one party, when the Commissions should remain neutral on that front. As well as being contrary to the ethos of the independent and politically-neutral nature of the Commissions, questions of policy are best left to elected representatives, not the lawyers of the Commissions. Because the Commissions cannot possibly examine 'all the law', their efforts should be concentrated on areas where their examination can be most beneficial because of their expertise. The Commissions should steer away from issues which are clearly divided on party lines and better decided by politicians—or indeed by the public via a referendum—than lawyers. Such issues are frequently matters of constitutional importance. For example, the Commissions would not have been appropriate bodies to answer questions such as whether the UK should leave the EU or whether Scotland should become an

91 LCEW, *Reform of the Grounds of Divorce: The Field of Choice* (Law Com No 6 (1966)) and LCEW, *The Ground for Divorce* (Law Com No 192 (1990)) (the latter was enacted in the Family Law Act 1996, but never brought into force).

92 LCEW, *Blood Tests and the Proof of Paternity in Civil Proceedings* (Law Com No 16 (1968)).

93 LCEW, *Family Law: Report on Polygamous Marriages* (Law Com No 42 (1971)).

94 LCEW, *Family Law: Illegitimacy* (Law Com No 118 (1982) and Law Com No 157 (1986)).

95 LCEW website, 'Should we Include These Projects in the 13th Programme?' www.lawcom.gov.uk/13th-programme-potential-projects/.

96 S Cretney, 'The Politics of Law Reform—A View from the Inside' (1985) 48 *MLR* 493, 499. Cretney served as an LCEW Commissioner from 1978 until 1983.

97 B Hale, 'Fifty Years of the Law Commissions: The Dynamics of Law Reform, Now, Then and Next' in Dyson, Lee and Stark, *Fifty Years of the Law Commissions*, 21.

98 See, eg, below n 138.

99 N Brotchie, 'The Scottish Law Commission: Promoting Law Reform in Scotland' (2009) 9 *Legal Information Management* 30, 32.

independent country. Within those areas, however, there may still be a role for the Commissions.

In the 1970s, the SLC was asked to give its opinion on the impact of Scottish and Welsh devolution,[100] showing that it is never easy to say that a subject is off-limits for the Commissions. The more politically charged content can be explained partially by the fact that this project was referred to the SLC by government. Such projects are frequently, but not always, concerned with more contentious issues. Furthermore, a project may appear to be highly political, but the Commissions' remit may be limited to more technical aspects. For example, when examining devolution, the SLC's role was restricted to giving advice on the consequences of devolution. The SLC was patently aware that policy matters (including whether or not devolution should be pursued) were to be left for government.[101] More recently, the Commissions, together with the Northern Ireland Law Commission (the NILC), have embarked on a project to reform electoral law.[102] The project appears to be highly political, but its scope is restricted to cover more technical issues. For example, the Commissions will not be changing voting systems or electoral boundaries,[103] but will examine, for example, pre-election deadlines for registering to vote, and the meaning of 'residence' for electoral registration purposes. A particularly stark example of a project which appears to be political, but which is actually highly technical, might in the future be a project to consolidate the sources of the British constitution. In 2014, a parliamentary consultation considering whether the UK should have a codified constitution suggested that the three Commissions were 'well situated' to carry out the task, provided that it was merely a 'technical exercise' of consolidating various constitutional sources into one statute.[104] It was acknowledged that any 'political contentiousness' would have to be resolved before the Commissions became involved.[105] In addition, areas of law that at one point have been highly politicised sometimes become suitably uncontroversial for the Commissions to deal with. For example, the LCEW carried out various projects on renting homes only after the area had become more stable after swinging wildly between the different policies of recent governments.[106] Therefore, the Commissions need not be prohibited from examining any particular broad

[100] SLC, *Comments on White Paper: 'Our Changing Democracy: Devolution to Scotland and Wales'* (Scot Law Com Memorandum No 32 (1976)).

[101] ibid para 1.

[102] The future of that project is uncertain given the fate of the NILC: see SW Stark and N Faris, 'Law Reform in Northern Ireland: Cheshire Cat or Potemkin Commission?' [2016] *PL* 651.

[103] LCEW, SLC and NILC, *Electoral Law: An Interim Report* (2016) para 1.5.

[104] House of Commons Political and Constitutional Reform Committee, *A New Magna Carta?* (2014, HC 463) 376. The consultation considers three types of constitution, of which a consolidating statute is only one option.

[105] ibid 377.

[106] eg, LCEW, *Renting Homes: The Final Report* (Law Com No 297 (2006)) and LCEW, *Housing: Encouraging Responsible Letting* (Law Com No 312 (2008)).

topic, as long as they are not deciding issues that are more political than legal—which should be reserved for government.

The phrase 'lawyers' law' has been used to describe technical, uncontroversial areas of the law which are sometimes regarded as particularly suited for the Commissions' examination.[107] The expression has, however, been subject to criticism, because it has been questioned whether any area of the law is totally uncontroversial.[108] The press release for the SLC's launch stated that Royal Commissions or Departmental Committees would continue to examine areas of law 'where important social questions are concerned'.[109] Lord Kilbrandon, the first SLC Chairman, observed that the SLC would not be able to recommend 'sweeping social reforms' because bodies which consist solely of lawyers, as the Commissions do, cannot determine how society lives.[110] Once the Commissions had been in existence for a decade, he confirmed his view in a judicial ruling: 'If there is one lesson which has been learned since the setting up of the Law Commissions it is this, that law reform by lawyers for lawyers (unless in exceptionally technical matters) is not socially acceptable'.[111] Even Gardiner eventually accepted that there were certain areas which the Commissions should not examine. He stated that 'lawyers' law reform' was certainly within their remit and 'political law reform' was not, but that areas of a 'mixed character' between these extremes could also be suitable for the Commissions to examine.[112]

It is not entirely clear, however, where a line can be drawn beyond which the Commissions should not act. For example, during parliamentary debates on the Law Commissions Bill, the Secretary of State for Scotland gave the subject of divorce as an example of something which was too much of a 'personal matter' for the Commissions to deal with.[113] Both Commissions received references from government to examine divorce law just over a year later.[114] From the very outset a fundamental confusion existed as to the Commissions' remits.

Lord Scarman, the first LCEW Chairman, doubted whether any such thing as lawyers' law really existed: 'There is no cosy little world of lawyers' law in which

[107] See, eg, HL Deb vol 264 col 1160 (1 April 1965) (Viscount Dilhorne).

[108] Scarman, *The New Pattern*, 27–28; M Kerr, 'Law Reform in Changing Times' (1980) 96 *LQR* 515, 515.

[109] Scottish Office Press Office, 'Scottish Law Commission appointed', 16 June 1965, National Records of Scotland (NRS) HH41/1609.

[110] 'Aim Will be to Bring Law Up to Date' *The Scotsman* (17 June 1965).

[111] *DPP for Northern Ireland v Lynch* [1975] AC 653, 700. The case was concerned with whether the defence of duress was available for murder. The LCEW had recently published a Working Paper which included a discussion of that issue: LCEW, *Codification of the Criminal Law, General Principles: Defences of General Application* (Law Com CP No 55 (1974)), which was followed by LCEW, *Criminal Law: Report on Defences of General Application* (Law Com No 83 (1977)). The LCEW's recommendations were rejected by government.

[112] HL Deb vol 264 col 1218 (1 April 1965) (Lord Chancellor (Gardiner)).

[113] HC Deb vol 706 col 158 (8 February 1965) (William Ross).

[114] SLC, *Divorce: The Grounds Considered* (Scot Law Com No 6 (1967)); LCEW, *Reform of the Grounds of Divorce: The Field of Choice* (Law Com No 6 (1966)).

learned men may frolic without raising socially controversial issues'.[115] Decades later, former SLC Commissioner, George Gretton, agreed:

> But what law is just for lawyers? ... It is sometimes suggested that 'technical law reform' is for the benefit of lawyers. That is evidently untrue. 'Technical law' exists for the benefit of citizens, including citizens who have to pay their lawyers fees for research and for litigation that better 'technical law' would have rendered unnecessary ... People know vaguely that under city streets are various pipes and cables but they are unlikely to have views about their construction, so long as the power supply, the water supply, the drainage and so on work ... Nobody speaks of plumbers' plumbing; lawyers' law is as absurd.[116]

The SLC has said from the outset that '[a]ll law has social implications, and it is impossible to draw any dividing line between "social law" and "lawyers' law"'.[117] With that impossibility in mind, the SLC has been keen to stress that it considers its remit to cover '*all* the law' and it does not think it is 'in any way confined to what is loosely referred to as "lawyers' law"'.[118]

The SLC is, however, sometimes 'seen as a suitable body for examining areas of private law and, to a much lesser extent, criminal law' (or public law or court procedure).[119] The reasons advanced for this view are equally applicable to the LCEW. Walker has said that public law is more likely to be dealt with by the government, so there is less need for the Commissions to step in.[120] Private law, by contrast, may be much neglected and provides a valuable focus for the Commissions. This focus is not exclusive to Britain—the New York State Law Revision Commission has also historically thrived in the area of private law.[121] It is true that the Commissions frequently examine private law issues, and they have had many proposals successfully implemented in that broad area. They therefore provide a valuable service in reforming that area of law. Indeed, the lack of another body able or willing to reform the law is one consideration that indicates a potential Commission project's suitability. But the Commissions also examine (successfully) many non-private law and/or more obviously contentious projects, as we saw earlier in relation to family law. Not all those projects would have necessarily found places in government agendas. Furthermore, Walker also argued that areas relating to public law are more likely to be shared throughout Britain, making it less suitable

[115] Scarman, *The New Pattern*, 27.

[116] G Gretton, 'Of Law Commissioning' (2013) 17 *Edinburgh Law Review* 119, 127 ('Of Law Commissioning'). See also A Diamond, 'The Law Commission and Government Departments' in G Zellick (ed), *The Law Commission and Law Reform* (London, Sweet & Maxwell, 1988) 23, where it is noted that 'law reform is hardly worth doing if the changes that are made have no impact on people's lives'.

[117] SLC, *First Annual Report* (Scot Law Com No 3 (1966)) para 9.

[118] ibid, emphasis in original.

[119] HRM Macdonald, JC Mullin, TB Smith and JF Wallace, *The Laws of Scotland: Stair Memorial Encyclopaedia*, vol 22 (Edinburgh, Law Society of Scotland, 1987) para 666. A similar view has been expressed more recently: D Cusine, 'Civil Law Reform: Where are We and Where are We Going?' 2015 *Scots Law Times (News)* 27, 28.

[120] DM Walker, 'The Scottish Law Commission under Review' (1987) 8 *Statute Law Review* 115, 118 ('The Scottish Law Commission under Review').

[121] JW MacDonald, 'The New York Law Revision Commission' (1965) 28 *MLR* 1, 2.

for only one Commission to examine.[122] This argument ignores the fact that the Commissions can (and frequently do) work in conjunction with each other. It also ignores the fact that certain areas of law, such as criminal law, are neither private-law based nor the same on both sides of the border.

The perception that the Commissions concentrate on technical law is in contrast to certain other law commissions, which have broader acceptable remits. The Australian Law Reform Commission (ALRC) is one body which notably deals with topics that are 'rather spicier' than the ones the GB Commissions deal with.[123] For example, the ALRC has published projects examining human tissue transplants,[124] complaints against the police[125] and multiculturalism.[126] These topics lend themselves to a lot of public interest. The ALRC therefore makes use of public hearings, which are even advertised in the popular press and on radio and television, and it is not unusual for Commissioners to be interviewed or take part in televised debates.[127] The ALRC's neighbour, the New Zealand Law Commission (NZLC), has also looked at some controversial topics, including compulsory treatment for drug and alcohol dependence,[128] safeguarding rights in national emergencies (for example, controlling executive power)[129] and the treatment of Maori women by the New Zealand legal system.[130] Geoffrey Palmer, President of the NZLC from 2005–10, has remarked that the GB Commissions should also take on even projects with 'heavy social policy'.[131] Such a view has proved controversial with law reformers in Great Britain,[132] and reflects the sometimes very different approaches of different law reform bodies.[133]

The GB Commissions are not, however, completely technical bodies. As we have already seen, the Commissions have examined many potentially controversial issues. Furthermore, as noted earlier, projects which the Commissions

[122] Walker, 'The Scottish Law Commission under Review' 118.

[123] M Zander, *The Law-Making Process*, 6th edn (Cambridge, CUP, 2004) 475 (the statement does not appear in the 7th edn) (*The Law-Making Process*).

[124] ALRC, *Human Tissue Transplants* (ALRC 7 (1977)).

[125] ALRC, *Integrity: But Not By Trust Alone* (ALRC 82 (1996)).

[126] ALRC, *Multiculturalism and the Law* (ALRC 57 (1992)).

[127] Zander, *The Law-Making Process*, 509–10 (the statement does not appear in the 7th edn).

[128] NZLC, *Compulsory Treatment for Substance Dependence: A Review of the Alcoholism and Drug Addiction Act 1966* (NZLC R118 (2010)).

[129] NZLC, *Final Report on Emergencies* (NZLC R22 (1991)).

[130] NZLC, *Justice: The Experiences of Maori Women* (NZLC R53 (1999)).

[131] G Palmer, 'The Law Reform Enterprise: Evaluating the Past and Charting the Future' (2015) 131 *LQR* 402, 414.

[132] E Clive, 'Law Reform and Social Policy' in Dyson, Lee and Stark, *Fifty Years of the Law Commissions*, 64, 71–72; and D Lloyd Jones, 'Looking to the Future' in Dyson, Lee and Stark, ibid 358.

[133] See also the South African Law Reform Commission (SALRC), which has reported on, eg, *Euthanasia and the Artificial Preservation of Life* (Project 86 (1998)). A former LCEW Chairman has doubted whether such a topic would be appropriate for the LCEW to examine: Lloyd Jones, 'Looking to the Future', ibid 359. *cf* some coverage of euthanasia despite the 'fundamental issues' of the topic being excluded from the terms of reference of LCEW, *Murder, Manslaughter and Infanticide* (Law Com No 304 (2006)) para 1.1.

have referred to them by government are also frequently (but not always) more provocative than the ones chosen by the Commissions themselves. An increase in such references has resulted in 'spicier' projects.[134] The ALRC does not have the power to choose its own projects—it only receives references from the Attorney-General, although it can suggest projects to the Attorney-General it wishes to have referred to it.[135] The GB Commissions' ability to choose their own projects, as part of their independence, is a strength which should be protected, so that certain areas of law are not neglected. Therefore, the bare fact that the ALRC examines 'spicier' projects is not necessarily anything to be envious of. The ALRC's remit is also partly due to the fact that it is a federal law reform body and more 'technical law reform' tends to be carried out at state level.[136] Comparisons with the GB Commissions may not therefore be wholly appropriate. In any event, the claims that the GB Commissions are tools of private law reform are no longer valid (if they ever were); we need to revisit our expectations of the Commissions based on their actual performance to date.

The Commissions' work does generate some public interest, even in ostensibly technical areas. Gretton, a former SLC Commissioner, has mooted that the Commissions should shy away from more controversial areas because 'the more often commission projects appear on the front pages, the greater the risk that commissions will incur opposition, and run the risk of abolition'.[137] It may not always be easy to predict, however, which projects will prove to be headline worthy. For example, a seemingly innocuous LCEW project examining landowners' right to light generated much (negative) media interest.[138] This example is not the first time the LCEW has been lampooned in the press, particularly in relation to its family law projects. The *Daily Mail* was notoriously critical of the LCEW's *Report on Domestic Violence and Occupation of the Family Home*,[139] expressing its

[134] J Halliday, *Quinquennial Review of the Law Commission* (2003) annex 5 para 7.

[135] Australian Law Reform Commission Act 1996 (Cth), s 20(1). The NZLC operates similarly to the GB Commissions in both selecting its own projects and receiving references: Law Commission Act 1985 (New Zealand), s 6. The SALRC's founding legislation does not give any specific power to government to make references to the SALRC, it simply receives project suggestions from 'any person or body' (including government) and submits programmes to the Minister for approval or amendment: South African Law Reform Commission Act 1973, s 5.

[136] K Tranter, 'Citation Practices of the Australian Law Reform Commission in Final Reports 1992–2012' (2015) 38 *University of New South Wales Law Journal* 323, 337. *cf* the position in Canada, where the (now defunct) Law Commission of Canada dealt with both federal and provincial matters: Y Le Bouthillier, 'The Former Law Commission of Canada: The Road Less Travelled' in Dyson, Lee and Stark, *Fifty Years of the Law Commissions*, 99.

[137] Gretton, 'Of Law Commissioning' 127.

[138] LCEW, *Rights to Light* (Law Com No 356 (2014)). See, eg: '"Right to Light" Important to Protect the "Little Man" says Businessman who won Landmark Case' *The Telegraph* (19 February 2013); 'Will our Right to Light Soon be Blotted Out? Laws that Allow Homeowners to Stop Development that will Block out Sunlight could be Reined in' *Daily Mail* (18 February 2013); 'Millions of Householders Could Lose Right to Challenge Developers' *The Times* (19 February 2013).

[139] LCEW, *Report on Domestic Violence and Occupation of the Family Home* (Law Com No 207 (1992)).

vehement concern that the reforms eroded family values and comprised a 'charter for live-in lovers'.[140] Such debate demonstrates that the Commissions are certainly not solely concerned with technical reform and, even where such reform appears to be technical, it is not necessarily uncontroversial. Kerr was correct, therefore, when he remarked that there is no such thing as 'lawyers' law' because no reform 'can ever be immune from controversy'.[141]

Kerr also suggested that the Commissions could recommend the reform of 'any part of the law which can appropriately be put forward by a body of lawyers on the basis of legal principle and pragmatic common sense, after due public consultation'.[142] The Commissions should avoid party political issues on the basis that they are not the best bodies to examine such matters; these issues will be adequately and more appropriately considered in the political sphere. The government can, however, refer more topical issues to the Commissions for advice as it sees fit. Furthermore, the Commissions need not shy away from any particular area of the law, especially if there is no other body able or willing to examine it. Even in ostensibly controversial areas, the Commissions may have a technical contribution to make, befitting their legal expertise. For example, the Commissions would not have been the best bodies to decide whether there should be an equal right to marriage for same-sex couples in the British jurisdictions. As Lord Kilbrandon said, a group of lawyers should not decide how society should live.[143] No area of law, however, need be off-limits for the Commissions. The 'suitability' criterion should not be equated with 'lawyers' law'. As we have seen, controversial sounding projects can be technical, and technical sounding projects can be controversial. So, the Commissions should not tell us whether we should *have* an equal right to marriage for same-sex couples, but once the policy has been agreed, the Commissions *are* good bodies to advise on the *technical and practical consequences* of that policy. For example, in the case of equal marriage, the Commissions could examine consequences in relation to succession law, or the grounds for divorce (again) because adultery cannot currently be committed with a person of the same sex.[144] The broad area of law does not reveal very much about its potential content and so it is not a good way to define the Commissions' scope of activity. In addition, Beale has argued that the Commissions can perform a 'useful role' in contentious areas by providing a 'cool and independent' perspective.[145]

[140] Zander, *The Law-Making Process*, 470 (the statement does not appear in the 7th edn). See also Sir Henry Brooke, 'The Law Commission's Family Homes and Domestic Violence Bill in 1995', *Musings, Memories and Miscellanea* (4 December 2015) sirhenrybrooke.me/2015/12/04/the-law-commissions-family-homes-and-domestic-violence-bill-in-1995/.

[141] M Kerr, 'Law Reform in Changing Times' (1980) 96 *LQR* 515, 515. See also above nn 115 and 116.

[142] Kerr, ibid 516. The importance of consultation is examined in ch 2, section IV.C.i and ch 7, section III.

[143] 'Aim Will be to Bring Law Up to Date' *The Scotsman* (17 June 1965).

[144] See, eg, *Dennis v Dennis* [1955] 2 WLR 817.

[145] H Beale, 'The Law Commission and Judicial Law Reform' (2001) 35 *The Law Teacher* 323, 331.

Exclusively political decision-making is off-limits for the Commissions, in contrast to technical projects, which are acceptable. Many projects, however, are somewhere in the middle. The Commissions' discretion again comes into play here, in allowing the Commissions to tailor each project in a specific way. Lay involvement in advisory groups or in running the project can help validate more social reforms, but can also benefit technical reforms. For example, on a project to overhaul the Scottish land registration system, Registers of Scotland seconded members of their staff to work at the SLC.[146] The NILC was obliged by statute to have one lay Commissioner.[147] Better than a lay Commissioner is the LCEW and the SLC's power to bring in ad hoc members on specific Commission projects.[148] In addition, we should not underestimate the contribution that can be made at the consultation stage, once again highlighting the importance of proper consultation. Consultation with appropriate non-legal experts is often required for 'casting light on technical details'.[149] Sometimes, as with an LCEW project examining hate crime, 'easy read' documents are helpful when responses from the general public are encouraged.[150] Increased public interaction can give the Commissions more credibility when suggesting more social reforms. Each project must be chosen and structured on its own terms. The resources criterion is also relevant here—there have to be enough resources to allow the Commissions to bring in ad hoc members or pay for specific styles of written materials if they are needed, and this should be taken into account before starting a project.

As we have already seen, the Commissions do not typically examine certain areas if they are covered adequately by government departments. One notable example is tax law. It has already been demonstrated that certain government departments were particularly perturbed about the arrival of the Commissions, and felt that they could adequately oversee the reform of the law in their own areas.[151] In this instance, there is no point in the Commissions pressing the issue. In assessing suitability, therefore, more account should be taken of whether there is any other body equally (or better) placed to carry out that reform.[152] If such a

[146] SLC, *Land Registration* (Scot Law Com No 222 (2010)) para 1.30.

[147] Justice (Northern Ireland) Act 2002, s 50(4)(d). At the time of writing, the position is vacant—for the fate of the NILC, see ch 6, section III.C. The first (and so far only) lay Commissioner was Robert Hunniford, a former police officer. See too the Law Commission of Canada Act 1996, s 7(2).

[148] The 1965 Act provides that the Ministers may 'appoint such officers and servants' to the Commissions as they determine (ss 5(1) and (2)) in addition to the provision for a Chairman and four other Commissioners (ss 1(1) and 2(1)).

[149] P Mitchell, 'Strategies of the Early Law Commission' in Dyson, Lee and Stark, *Fifty Years of the Law Commissions*, 42–43, discussing LCEW, *Blood Tests and the Proof of Paternity in Civil Proceedings* (Law Com No 16 (1968)).

[150] LCEW, *Hate Crime: Should the Law Cover Other Victim Groups?* (Easy Read Version of Law Com CP No 213 (2013)).

[151] See, eg, ch 2, section IV.A.

[152] SLC, *Ninth Programme of Law Reform* (Scot Law Com No 242 (2015)) para 1.4.

body exists, then the Commissions do not need to examine that area. But even if a body is willing to examine an area of law, the Commissions may still suggest that they intervene if they feel that they are better placed to carry out the examination. Gane, for example, has criticised the SLC's lack of involvement in criminal law reform, even when reform has taken place through the courts.[153] As Lord Rodger pointed out,[154] law reform should be assessed holistically—the question is not whether the Commissions are keeping the law up to date, but whether the law as a whole is being kept up to date by whatever means necessary. The Commissions may tend to be involved in certain subject areas more frequently than others, but no particular subject need be out of bounds if it can be shown that (a) it is suitable for examination by a body of lawyers with other input as required and (b) there is no other body able or willing to carry out that examination to a sufficient standard.

If the Commissions decide that they are not the best bodies to examine an area of the law, or if they are denied permission to do so, they have the power to recommend that some other body takes on the project.[155] This power has been invoked much less frequently than appears to have been intended at the Commissions' outset,[156] but it has been used. For example, in its early years, the SLC suggested that the law of criminal procedure be examined by a departmental committee.[157] In its *Ninth Programme of Law Reform* in 2005, the LCEW recommended that the government (or some other body) should carry out research into the law relating to contagious and infectious diseases, having been denied permission to look at the area itself.[158] The benefit of the independence and continuing existence of the Commissions is that they have the power to hold government to account for areas of the law in need of reform (and for its failure to act on Commission proposals). Civil servants worried about this power when the Commissions were being proposed—unlike Royal Commissions, these new bodies would stick around reminding government of its failure to take action which could, they feared, prove

[153] CHW Gane, 'Criminal Law Reform in Scotland' (1998) 3 *Scottish Law and Practice Quarterly* 101, 101.

[154] A Rodger, 'The Bell of Law Reform' 1993 *Scots Law Times (News)* 339, 340.

[155] 1965 Act, s 3(1)(b) states that in recommending areas of the law for reform, the Commissions should make 'recommendations as to the agency (whether the Commission or another body) by which any such examination should be carried out'.

[156] The White Paper accompanying the Law Commissions Bill envisaged that the Commissions would recommend projects for examination by the Law Reform Committees, the Criminal Law Revision Committee, government departments or Royal Commissions: *Proposals for English and Scottish Law Commissions* (Cmnd 2573, 1965) 3.

[157] SLC, *Second Programme of Law Reform* (Scot Law Com No 8 (1968)) item no 13. This suggestion led to the extensive review of Scots criminal procedure carried out by the Thomson Committee in the 1970s: see J Chalmers, F Leverick and SW Stark, 'The Process of Criminal Evidence Law Reform in Scotland: What Can We Learn?' in P Duff and P Ferguson (eds), *Current Developments in Scottish Criminal Evidence Law* (Edinburgh, EUP, forthcoming 2017).

[158] LCEW, *Ninth Programme of Law Reform* (Law Com No 293 (2005)) paras 4.2–4.11.

to be 'embarrassing'.[159] The 1965 Act gives the Commissions an oft-overlooked role of 'overview and co-ordination of reform across the legal system'.[160] The power of the Commissions in this regard is valuable, and more use could be made of it to bring attention to problems which the Commissions themselves cannot solve. The suitability criterion targets the Commissions' limited resources to the areas where their expertise is best suited and which might otherwise be neglected. But it does not prevent them from highlighting problems in areas beyond that remit.

iii. Importance of Subject Matter

The third and final criterion which the Commissions take into account before beginning a project is importance. The Commissions currently consider how unsatisfactory the law is (for example, it could be 'unfair, unclear, inefficient, unduly complex or outdated')[161] and how much it would benefit from reform. Such consideration should also take into account whether, and how frequently, the existing law actually causes problems in practice. In chapter six, we will see that the importance criterion can include consideration of whether harmonisation of the law of the British jurisdictions would alleviate any problems in the existing law. In its latest annual report, the LCEW stressed that it intends to focus its energies on projects where reform is not only most necessary, but also where implementation is most likely.[162] The Commissions should, however, think carefully about the importance criterion. The Commissions should not consider how important it is that changes to an area of law are *implemented*, but should instead consider how important it is that that area of law is *examined*. The likelihood of a project's implementation is, as outlined above, better taken into account when considering whether a project is an economical use of resources. The Commissions, as independent bodies, should be able to challenge the current law without undue emphasis being placed on implementation, otherwise the advantages of being separate from government are lost. In addition, the importance criterion puts emphasis on the substantive quality of the project—but only if it is not equated with implementation since the mere fact that a proposal is implemented does not mean that it was important.

As we saw in chapter two, the Commissions propose substantive reforms to the law, as well as attempting to declutter the statute book by way of both consolidation

[159] 'Law Reform Commission: Functions of Commission as Presented to Home Affairs Committee', 13 November 1964, NRS HH41/2048. In fact, the view was expressed that the Commissions should not produce annual reports because of the risk of using the opportunity to criticise the government. It was eventually conceded that with or without annual reports, it would be impossible to prevent a Commission from 'voicing its displeasure with Government action or inaction if it felt moved to do so'.

[160] Lord Carloway, 'To "Mend the Laws, That Neids Mendement": A Scottish Perspective on Lawyers as Law Reformers' (speech at the Commonwealth Association of Law Reform Agencies Conference, Edinburgh, 2015) 9.

[161] SLC, *Ninth Programme of Law Reform* (Scot Law Com No 242 (2015)) para 1.4.

[162] LCEW, *Annual Report 2015–16* (Law Com No 367 (2016)) 57.

and repeals. Consolidation and repeals projects are both unlikely to be as important as substantive reform. Although both consolidation and repeals are valuable to make the law more accessible to lawyers and laypersons, spring cleaning should not take priority over areas of the law where there is injustice, unfairness, or where the law is outdated. Consolidation and repeals projects do not take up the same amount of resources as more substantive law reform because they are carried out by teams within the Commissions with little or no Commissioner input. Technically, therefore, they should not impact on the Commissions' substantive work. Those teams, however, especially the parliamentary draftsmen, may be better employed on projects which propose substantive reform.

Although they are often considered together, it is important to distinguish between consolidation projects and repeal projects. Consolidation may provide a useful function in making the law more accessible and clearer, whereas repeals tend to concern legislation that is in desuetude and not causing a problem anyway.[163] Statute law repeals projects are conducted jointly by the Commissions, and the LCEW now states that it will 'narrow its focus' to the repeal of statutes which are likely to cause confusion.[164] Even consolidation, however, is arguably less important now that statutes are available electronically in an amended and updated form.[165] Certain critics have queried the need for the Commissions' consolidation and repeals role on the basis that there is rarely any 'urgency' or 'pressing need' for such work, particularly the repeal of old statutes which are not causing any problems in practice.[166] Mostly, however, the Commissions have been praised for their consolidation and repeals work. It is a role which the Commissions perform very successfully,[167] and in which they have been historically very active, although it has declined in recent years. In the 1980s, Walker suggested that the SLC's most valuable function was its aim to consolidate and repeal the law, and praised the 'wholly beneficial' work it had achieved in pursuit of that aim.[168] He recommended that such work should be encouraged and 'should be pursued with unrelenting energy'—although the work is 'unspectacular' it is 'quite the most valuable'.[169] The government, however, does not prioritise consolidation and repeals work and the LCEW has complained that it has had to abandon

[163] GL Gretton, 'The Duty to Make the Law More Accessible?: The Two C-Words' in Dyson, Lee and Stark, *Fifty Years of the Law Commissions*, 93 ('The Two C-Words'). *cf Annual Report 2015–16*, ibid 59, which discusses the increasing problem of unrepresented litigants seeking to rely on out of date legislation.

[164] *Annual Report 2015–16*, ibid.

[165] But see the converse argument that increasing public availability actually increases the need for reliable legislation: *Annual Report 2015–16*, ibid.

[166] GJ Borrie, 'Law Reform: A Damp Squib?' (Inaugural Lecture, University of Birmingham, 1970) 2.

[167] 100% of LCEW and SLC proposals relating to consolidation and repeals have been implemented successfully in their entirety. This success is at least partly due to a more streamlined parliamentary procedure for consolidation and repeals Bills, which is discussed in ch 4, section I.B.

[168] Walker, 'The Scottish Law Commission under Review' 118.

[169] ibid.

such work (sometimes at a very late stage) when governmental support has been withdrawn.[170] A cut in the number of Parliamentary Counsel seconded to the LCEW has necessitated a decline in the amount of consolidation work that can be carried out.[171] The LCEW now accepts that consolidation 'can no longer be considered a priority'.[172] Despite the Commissions fulfilling their consolidation and repeals function very successfully, their current approach indicates that they consider other areas of their output to be more important, in large part because of the lack of importance attached to consolidation and repeals by government.

iv. Summary: Improved Sub-Criteria

The above discussion allows sub-criteria to be developed. These sub-criteria are set out below in Figure 2. They may be compared with the nine considerations stated in the 2010 Protocol and set out as sub-criteria above in Figure 1. Both sets of sub-criteria are similar, but the version advanced here draws together the improvements recommended above. In particular, it ensures that the Commissions and Ministers consider issues such as size and substantive reform to ensure they are guided towards only the most deserving projects.

B. The Use of the Criteria and Transparency

The criteria also require development as to their use and the transparency of that use. They should be used not only by the Commissions, but also by the Ministers and the rest of government. They should be used more transparently, with each project being openly considered against the criteria. Enshrining them in statute would help with both those developments.

i. When and by Whom the Criteria Should be Used

The criteria should of course continue to be used by the Commissions when selecting programme projects. They should also be used by the Ministers when deciding whether to permit a Commission to embark on a programme project. Ministers should limit their power of veto to only those projects which, in their view and using Figure 3 below as guidance, do not satisfy all three criteria. The criteria should also be used by government before referring a project to the Commissions, and indeed by any other body or person when suggesting a project

[170] LCEW, *Annual Report 2010–11* (Law Com No 328 (2011)) reveals that projects consolidating pension law (para 2.83) and Representation of the People legislation (para 2.84) both had to be abandoned due to lack of governmental support.

[171] N Paines, 'Reflections on Statutory Implementation in the Law Commission' in Dyson, Lee and Stark, *Fifty Years of the Law Commissions*, 199. The SLC only has one part-time Parliamentary Counsel. On the decline of consolidation at the SLC, see Gretton, 'The Two C-Words' 92.

[172] LCEW, *Annual Report 2015–16* (Law Com No 367 (2016)) 59.

1. Considerations relevant to the availability and economical use of resources

Availability

(i) Whether sufficient expertise (eg, a suitably qualified Commissioner, Parliamentary Counsel and possible expert/non-legal input) is available or obtainable.

(ii) Whether financial resources are available or obtainable including, if necessary, to arrange special consultation materials or measures (eg, easy read documents or public meetings).

(iii) Whether involvement of the LCEW/SLC/NILC is required and, if so, their availability of resources.[173]

Economical use

(iv) The size of the project, including the length of time the project may take to complete and the possible impact on other projects.

(v) The likelihood of implementation (including whether implementation would be by Westminster, the Scottish Parliament and/or the Welsh Assembly, or another method).

2. Considerations relevant to the suitability of the project

(i) Whether the issue is suitable for examination by a body of lawyers (with other input as required) (ie, whether the issue is more legal than political).

(ii) Whether any other body is able or willing to carry out that examination.

3. Considerations relevant to the importance of the project

(i) Whether the law is unfair, unclear, inefficient, unduly complex or outdated.

(ii) Whether there is evidence of the law causing difficulty in practice (including the potential benefits to be derived from harmonisation of the law of the instant and neighbouring jurisdictions).[174]

(iii) Whether the project is one of substantive reform, consolidation, or repeal.

Figure 2: Proposed new sub-criteria of the three project-selection criteria

under section 3(1)(a) of the 1965 Act. Where a reference is made to the Commissions, the Commissions themselves must exercise the checking function[175] to ensure that the three criteria are considered before embarking on the project.[176] Disagreements over the fulfilment of the criteria (and particularly of the 'importance' criterion) would still ensue, but at least the exercise of discretion would be structured and consistent. Shared criteria should facilitate a healthy dialogue between the Commissions, the Ministers and the rest of government, as well as other parties

[173] See ch 6.

[174] See ch 6.

[175] Described at section II.C above.

[176] The LCEW already has a broad duty along such lines under the Protocol, para 9, and the Wales Protocol, para 7.

proposing projects. One party could more clearly demonstrate to the other the value of a project (or reasons for its rejection).

A Commission cannot be forced to accept a reference from government if it feels it does not have the resources to do so. If government wishes to pursue that reference, it will have to provide the Commission with the necessary resources, whether financial or by way of extra staff or both, in order to make its completion possible. Even then, a Commission should be able to reject a reference on the basis that it is not important enough, or that it would more suitably be carried out elsewhere. Use of the criteria could protect the Commissions from embarking on undeserving references which divert the Commissions away from their programme projects. The Commissions should not assume that a governmental reference is automatically an appropriate use of their time. For example, in 1982, the Lord Chancellor asked the LCEW to report on whether reforms to the law of implied terms in contracts for the supply of services were necessary. Four years later, the LCEW reported that a comprehensive review of the area would be 'premature'.[177] It is unlikely that such a project was the best use of the LCEW's resources because no reform to the law was proposed. Although that advice may well have been useful for government, areas of law which are unfair, unclear, inefficient, unduly complex or outdated, and which are actually causing difficulties in practice, are more likely to fulfil the 'importance' criterion.

It might be thought that if the government refers a project to the LCEW, it should have a better chance of being implemented. The statistics show that this is true, but only marginally so; a reference to examine a topic is by no means a guarantee of the eventual project's implementation. Between 1965 and 2014, 70 per cent of LCEW programme projects were implemented, compared with 75 per cent of governmental references. For the SLC during the same period, 75 per cent of programme projects were implemented, compared with 77 per cent of governmental references.[178]

No evidence has been found of the Commissions ever refusing a governmental reference. Malcolm McMillan, the current SLC Chief Executive, has said that, in practice, potential references which the government has in mind are negotiated with the SLC, in particular to determine whether the resources or expertise exist for a particular reference to proceed.[179] The LCEW agrees, and adds that

[177] LCEW, *Implied Terms in Contracts for the Supply of Services* (Law Com No 156 (1986)) para 1.7.

[178] My calculations, using the method of calculation endorsed in ch 4. The figures above are lower than the implementation figures given in ch 4, section I.A because the figures in ch 4 include consolidation and repeals work whereas the figures above include only projects proposing substantive reform. The figures also exclude certain projects that come neither from a reference nor a programme, eg, when the SLC joins an LCEW project such as LCEW and SLC, *Level Crossings* (Law Com No 339 and Scot Law Com No 234 (2013)). Certain projects have started off as programme projects, but references are received to focus on a particular issue, eg, SLC, *Report on Prescription and Limitation of Actions (Latent Damage and other Related Issues)* (Scot Law Com No 122 (1989)). Such projects are counted as references.

[179] I am grateful to Malcolm McMillan for his views on this matter, which he discussed with me in December 2014.

'practical considerations' such as 'lack of funding [or] lack of capacity' might make it 'impractical' to take on a project 'in the short term'.[180] We have already encountered in this chapter a project which was intended to be referred to the SLC, but which never transpired—a reference to examine the not proven verdict. Part of the reason for that project not going ahead was perhaps the lack of suitable expertise.[181] Current practice does not, however, allow adequately for the situation where a reference should simply not be embarked on, even if the necessary resources are available. No Commission would want to make such refusals without good reason for fear of straining relationships with government. If the project-selection criteria were, however, used more transparently and by the Ministers and the rest of government as well as the Commissions, it would facilitate the dialogue between the parties. An alternative would be to move to the South African model, where the government has no distinct power to make references to the Commission. The South African Law Reform Commission (SALRC)'s founding legislation simply directs it to compile programmes for submission to the Minister for approval. Such programmes should incorporate suggestions 'from any person or body', which implicitly includes the Minister and other governmental actors.[182] A shift to the South African model is not proposed here for two main reasons. First, such a change is unlikely to have much effect in practice. Under the South African model, the government can still make suggestions to the SALRC just as any other person or body can. Although the public plays an important role in project selection, ministerial proposals make up a large part of the SALRC's programme.[183] The government's power may not be a distinct power under the legislation, but the weight of a request from a governmental actor may be great given the relationship between any commission and government. In addition, the Minister still has to approve a programme and can 'amend' it.[184] This method of working does, however, have the distinct advantage that a law reform body can better plan its activities rather than receiving ad hoc references, which disrupt its programmes. Despite that advantage, the second reason for not proposing such an amendment is a practical one. It would be difficult to achieve such a change for the GB Commissions because it would rely on government ceding its existing, explicit power—an unlikely prospect.

ii. How the Criteria Should be Used and their Weighting

Because the Commissions do not currently provide information as to how the criteria have been used and how each project has measured up against the criteria,

[180] I am grateful to Catherine Vine for discussing the views of the LCEW on this matter with me in March 2015.

[181] In addition to other possible reasons: see above n 74.

[182] South African Law Reform Commission Act 1973, s 5(2).

[183] I am grateful to Dellene Clark of the SALRC for this information.

[184] South African Law Reform Commission Act 1973, s 5(3).

it cannot be known whether the criteria have been used appropriately, if at all. The Commissions, the Ministers and the rest of government should explicitly note in writing how each proposed project has been judged against the criteria. Doing so would not be laborious because the Commissions (and, according to the proposals in this chapter, the Ministers and government) should be making the considerations anyway. Transparency in how the Commissions and Ministers have decided that a project is, or is not, viable would allow others to check that the criteria have been used consistently and that the decisions have been proper. Each project could be marked as satisfying each criterion (taking the sub-criteria into account) to a greater or lesser extent as depicted in Figure 3 below.

Marking a potential project against each criterion on a scale of 0–3:

(i) Availability and economical use of resources

Where 0 = necessary resources (financial and human, and at the other Commission(s) if necessary) **not** available **and cannot** be obtained;

and 3 = necessary resources (financial and human, and at the other Commission(s) if necessary) **are** available **and no** negative impact on other projects foreseen **and** prospects of implementation are good.

(ii) Suitability of project

Where 0 = a **political** issue, **and** another body able/willing to examine the area;

and 3 = a **legal** issue, **and** no other body able/willing to examine the area.

(iii) Importance of project

Where 0 = current law **not** unfair, unclear, inefficient, unduly complex or outdated, **or** causing difficulty in practice, **and** project would **not** substantively reform the law;

and 3 = current law unfair, unclear, inefficient, unduly complex or outdated, **and** clear and recent evidence of it causing difficulty in practice, **and** project would substantively reform the law.

If a potential project scores 0 in any category, it cannot be embarked on.

If a potential project scores 5 or above in total*, it is a potentially viable project.

* 5 has been chosen as the minimum score so that any project scoring poorly in two categories must score highly in the third category to be potentially viable (eg, 1+1+3).

Figure 3: Assessing the viability of a Commission project

According to the method advanced in Figure 3, a project satisfying all three criteria would only be a potentially viable project. Crossing the threshold recommended in Figure 3 would not automatically guarantee that a project will be embarked on, because many more projects may be potentially viable than the Commissions have the resources actually to undertake. The Commissions and Ministers would retain the discretion to choose which projects should be embarked on from the pool of potentially viable projects. In so doing, a Commissioner or Minister may wish to give more weight to one or more of the criteria.

The criteria are the three main considerations that should be taken into account before embarking on a project. All three criteria should be taken into account and all should be satisfied to at least a certain extent. There should be a rebuttable presumption that all three criteria have equal weight. No one criterion should automatically outweigh the others because the criteria can only allow for the selection of the most deserving projects when used in combination. For example, if the 'resources' criterion was always the most important, many 'important' or 'suitable' projects (such as the LCEW's Land Registration project described above)[185] would not be embarked on simply because they were a gamble in the implementation stakes, and/or because they would require the use of a large amount of resources. Obviously, however, if the resources simply cannot be obtained, the project is not viable. Allowing 'suitability' or 'importance' to take priority would be impractical and unworkable—no matter how suitable or important, a project needs resources to be commenced. If, however, a project is clearly not suitable, or it is not important, it should not be embarked on even if there are the resources (for example, a very keen Commissioner). The criteria are, therefore, all initially presumed to be equally important although a project will not necessarily score equally across all three criteria. It is recommended that a Commissioner, or Minister, should be able to rebut the presumption of the equal weighting of the criteria by demonstrating that a project should be embarked on because of an overwhelmingly high score in one particular criterion—provided that the other criteria are satisfied to at least a certain extent. The criterion which is most likely to cause controversy is the importance criterion. The use of resources and a project's suitability for examination by a law commission, although not entirely binary choices, are less open to interpretation than a project's importance. The marking system in Figure 3 has been adopted for its simplicity, but it is possible that scoring a '3' will not always do justice to the overwhelming importance of a project, particularly if it is considered to be urgent. It is possible that there are other unforeseen circumstances where a Commissioner or Minister may wish to argue for the overwhelming need to examine a certain project, thus it is important to retain the discretion for him or her to be able to do so. There is, therefore, an additional exercise of discretion in choosing the eventual projects to be undertaken from the pool of potentially viable projects. A practice could be developed whereby projects are listed in order of preference. The SALRC's founding legislation mentions listing programme projects 'in order of preference', but priority was determined by the Minister and the practice has fallen away in recent years.[186]

[185] Section V.A.i.

[186] South African Law Reform Commission Act 1973, s 5(1). I am grateful to Dellene Clark of the SALRC for this information.

iii. The Legislative Enactment of the Criteria

Davis argued that all measures used to structure the exercise of discretion should be open because '[o]penness is the natural enemy of arbitrariness'.[187] Davis's endorsement of publicising such measures echoes Brandeis's oft-quoted remark that '[s]unlight is said to be the best of disinfectants'.[188] Where measures used to structure the exercise of discretion (such as project-selection criteria) are secret, they cannot be used by outsiders to test decisions against. The reasons behind a decision cannot be known. The criteria themselves are not a secret. They are cited with a degree of regularity in annual reports and programmes, and can be found on the LCEW's website. Anyone can, therefore, see how the Commissions purport to select projects and can scrutinise project selection against the project-selection criteria. As we have seen, however, there has been a tendency to cite different criteria in different places, leaving outsiders uncertain as to which criteria actually apply. In addition, the criteria's proper and consistent use cannot be known because the Commissions do not demonstrate that they actually have considered the criteria in relation to every potential project, and they do not state what the result of such consideration is.

Davis noted that '[l]egislative clarification of objectives may sometimes be undesirable, even though it is always desirable when the legislative body knows what it wants'.[189] Structuring discretion may therefore be done by legislative enactment or otherwise.[190] The statutory embodiment of the project-selection criteria would solidify their existence to put an end to the trend of the Commissions citing different criteria in different places. It would also clarify their status, which is unclear at present. It cannot be ascertained whether the Commissions do in fact use the criteria, and indeed whether the Commissions are *obliged* to consider them. In addition, the project-selection criteria do not currently apply to decision-making by the Ministers or government, but the application of the criteria could easily be extended by legislation. Former LCEW Commissioner Elizabeth Cooke has argued that the project-selection criteria can be used to persuade a Minister that a potential project is viable, and has said that such an approach was taken on the *Rights to Light* project.[191] The Commissions' position could be further strengthened by requiring the Ministers to consider the same criteria as a matter of course. By making it mandatory for the Commissions, the Ministers and government to consider the criteria, it would secure the Commissions' discretion,

[187] Davis, *Discretionary Justice*, 98.

[188] LD Brandeis, *Other People's Money and How the Bankers Use it* (Mansfield Centre, Martino Publishing, 2009) 92.

[189] Davis, *Discretionary Justice*, 49.

[190] ibid 97.

[191] LCEW, *Rights to Light* (Law Com No 356 (2014)). I am grateful to Elizabeth Cooke for sharing her views with me in an interview conducted in March 2015.

and reduce the unstructured and non-transparent ministerial and governmental exercise of discretion.

Giving the project-selection criteria legislative status might not do much to increase their profile—they could become well known simply through publication in Commission publications and on their websites. It would, however, increase accountability and consistency. The current system is not ideal because Ministers and government have no obligation to use the criteria. It cannot be known whether the Commissions themselves do, or must, consider the criteria. A legislative duty to use the criteria would remove any ambiguity as to the legal status of the criteria by imposing a legal duty on all parties to consider the criteria. It would also encourage the Commissions, Ministers and government to make public their decision-making by noting how they have considered the criteria and how each project has measured up. Although a legislative duty may not absolutely guarantee that the criteria were used by all relevant parties, it should at least improve the chance that they are.[192] Furthermore, it is desirable to consolidate the Commissions' effective constitution because they are bodies which aim to consolidate and simplify themselves. Their own founding legislation, the 1965 Act, should be a more comprehensive source of their duties and powers. Those duties and powers should not be found scattered in various sources. At the moment, the 1965 Act alone gives a very incomplete picture of how the Commissions actually operate. Indeed, the Ministry of Justice's first triennial review of the LCEW was critical of the LCEW's terms of reference being 'spread across several documents'.[193] Instead of legislating, the criteria could be added to the Protocol,[194] but the Protocol does not apply to Scotland and a Protocol on other matters in Scotland would be unnecessary (and perhaps even harmful) because of the good relations between the SLC and the Scottish Government.[195]

The criteria have, so far as we can tell, been used since 1997 and have been demonstrated to be the proper considerations for selecting the worthiest projects. It is now time for them to be enshrined in statute so that their permanence is guaranteed. As we saw in chapter two, Gardiner fought to have the Commissions founded by statute to ensure their permanence, and the same principles can apply to the project-selection criteria. In chapter five we will see that rules should be tried and tested before being codified—the project-selection criteria have been so tested. Considering the proposed amendments to the 1965 Act in appendix two, it is logical and clear to include the criteria because they link up with other proposed changes. For example, it is proposed that the 1965 Act should be amended to clarify that the Commissions are not obliged to take a reference from

[192] As will be seen in ch 4, the Lord Chancellor's statutory duty to report on the disposal of LCEW proposals has not always been adequately discharged.

[193] Ministry of Justice, *Triennial Review: Law Commission, Report of Stage Two* (2014) para 22.

[194] The 1965 Act, s 3B provides that the Protocol must be reviewed and revised from time to time.

[195] A matter which will be discussed in ch 4, section IV.C.i.

government.[196] Because decisions on whether to take a reference will be based on the project-selection criteria, it is more user-friendly to include the criteria in the same legislation. There would be little point in legislating if the content and meaning of the criteria were not being changed. As we have seen, however, the content of the criteria does require clarification. In particular, the development of the criteria by the Commissions has not always been desirable.[197] Statutory embodiment could reverse such development and prevent future unwanted development.

In appendix two, proposals have been made as to how the 1965 Act could be amended to incorporate the project-selection criteria. Section 3(1A) would establish that the Commissions, their Ministers and government 'shall take into account' the project-selection criteria. The wording has been chosen carefully to ensure that, although the Commissions, the Ministers and government must consider the criteria before the outset of a project, it would be difficult to challenge proper exercises of discretion. The wording has been adapted from section 2(1) of the Human Rights Act 1998, where it is established that domestic courts 'must take into account' judgments of the Strasbourg Court (among other things). Although that section has certainly not been uncontroversial,[198] the wording would ensure that as long as the criteria are considered, the Commissions' actual project selection would not be susceptible to challenge.[199] Importantly, however, it is not recommended that the sub-criteria developed at Figure 2 above should be enshrined in legislation. Those sub-criteria are, unlike the three main criteria, too susceptible to change to be included in the statutory wording. For example, one of the sub-criteria mentions the NILC—given its uncertain status, it would be unwise to mention it in a statute. A memorandum of understanding or other similar document recording the content of the sub-criteria from time to time should be prepared between the Commissions and the Ministers.

Seeing how the criteria have been taken into account aids transparent project selection and attempts to ensure consistent application of the criteria (which cannot at present be known). The Commissions may be equally susceptible to criticism, and even legal challenge, at present. Because it cannot be known that the criteria have been properly applied, suspicions may arise as to whether the Commissions' exercise of discretion in relation to a particular project has been proper. Enshrining the criteria in legislation would not pose a greater risk to the Commissions' exercise of discretion, and could in fact better protect it.

[196] Appendix 2, ss 3(1)(e) and (ea), and see ch 2, section IV.C.v.

[197] eg, the SLC's development of the 'suitability' criterion (section IV.C).

[198] See, eg, Conservative Party, *Protecting Human Rights in the UK: The Conservatives' Proposals for Changing Britain's Human Rights Laws* (2014) 4.

[199] On his 'surprise' at the controversy surrounding s 2(1), see D Irvine, 'A British Interpretation of Convention Rights' [2012] *PL* 237, 238.

VI. Conclusion: Clarifying and Securing the Scope of Commission Activity

The 1965 Act leaves the Commissions' scope of activity unclear by mandating that they should keep under review 'all the law'. The Commissions cannot actually propose reforms to 'all the law' at any one time because of their limited resources. Discretion exists, therefore, for the Commissions, the Ministers and government to select, approve or refer certain projects. Project-selection criteria have developed, independently of the 1965 Act, to attempt to ensure that the Commissions only embark on the most appropriate and deserving projects. Those criteria have been used as a basis in this chapter for further development. In particular, the Commissions, Ministers and government should be more transparent about how each project measures up against the criteria. In so doing, each party could better demonstrate why certain projects have been chosen, and why certain others have been rejected. The Commissions would also be protected from potentially arbitrary ministerial control because the Ministers do not currently make transparent decisions in relation to the approval of potential programme projects.

Appropriate development of both the content and the use of the criteria would help to ensure that the Commissions only embark on projects that have genuine potential merit. By ensuring that the importance criterion reflects the importance of *examination* rather than the importance of *implementation*, more emphasis can be placed on the substantive potential benefits of the project, rather than by predicting its end result. Certain projects are sufficiently important to justify their examination, even if implementation is uncertain. Repeals projects, and even consolidation projects, on the other hand, despite their guaranteed implementation, are less likely to be important. Development and statutory embodiment of the project-selection criteria would clarify and secure the scope of Commission activity and would ensure that their resources are allocated to only the most deserving projects.

The criteria were at least partly introduced as a sword to ensure that the Commissioners did not make capricious project choices based purely on their own interests. That in itself is a valuable aim. The project-selection criteria can, however, also be used as the Commissions' shield, to allow them to (a) defend their project choices, and (b) reject unsuitable governmental references. In all instances, the goal is the same—to ensure the proper allocation of the Commissions' resources to the most deserving projects.

4

The Extent of Implementation

The Commissions rely on the Westminster Parliament, the Scottish Parliament and the National Assembly for Wales to implement their proposals as legislation. After a successful start, implementation rates for both Commissions have dropped almost every decade since 1965.[1] The Law Commission for England and Wales (LCEW)'s own research suggests a recent implementation rate of 66 per cent.[2] It is more difficult to give a figure for the Scottish Law Commission (SLC) due to the fact that it does not release official implementation rates. Implementation for the SLC in devolved matters in the ten years following devolution was under 50 per cent,[3] but that figure has been 'rising' in recent years,[4] and recent figures put it on a par with the LCEW.[5]

The current understanding of what it means for a Commission proposal to be implemented is inadequate, leading to the failure of many implementation figures, including the official figure released by the LCEW, to reflect adequately the Commissions' true contribution to law reform. The LCEW and the SLC have faced different challenges in respect of implementation since 1965, leading to different attempts to curb falling implementation rates. Certain of those attempts, notably the Law Commission Act 2009, erode independence from government by concentrating too much on immediate implementation, and too little on the

[1] Implementation rates by decade for the LCEW, including consolidation and repeals and partially implemented projects, are: 96% (1965–74); 85% (1975–84); 83% (1985–94); 72% (1995–2004) and 50% (2005–14). The corresponding figures for the SLC are: 96% (1965–74); 97% (1975–84); 87% (1985–94); 76% (1995–2004); and 61% (2005–14). Percentages have been calculated using the method advanced in this chapter. The figures relate to reports published during the relevant time periods, although their implementation may have occurred later, eg, a report published in 2004 may not have been implemented until 2006, but is classed as an implemented report in the 1995–2004 time period; a report published in 2014 may yet be implemented. The 2005–14 figures in particular may therefore rise.

[2] LCEW, *Annual Report 2015–16* (Law Com No 367 (2016)) 37.

[3] M McMillan, 'The Role of Law Reform in Constitutionalism, Rule of Law and Democratic Governance: Reflections by the Scottish Law Commission' (Association of Law Reform Agencies of Eastern and Southern Africa Lecture, 2011) 4.

[4] ibid 5.

[5] Implementation rates of 66.8% for the LCEW and 66.7% for the SLC were calculated by G Hammond, 'The Legislative Implementation of Law Reform Proposals' in M Dyson, J Lee and SW Stark (eds), *Fifty Years of the Law Commissions: The Dynamics of Law Reform* (Oxford, Hart Publishing, 2016) 177 ('The Legislative Implementation of Law Reform Proposals'; and Dyson, Lee and Stark, *Fifty Years of the Law Commissions*).

Commissions' other ways of promoting law reform. Implementation is not the only criterion by which to measure the success of a Commission proposal. A project which is deemed viable when judged against the project-selection criteria developed in the previous chapter should not automatically be vetoed simply because implementation is uncertain. As we saw in chapter three, the likelihood of implementation is just one consideration to be taken into account when considering whether a project is an economical use of resources. That being said, however, implementation cannot be ignored. If a trend for declining implementation rates were to be left unchecked, the Commissions could be in real danger of abolition by an unsympathetic government.[6] We can better protect the Commissions' independence by correcting the way we view and measure implementation.

I. Preliminary Issues

Before beginning a detailed examination of the matter of implementation, certain preliminary issues must be considered. First, the extent of implementation achieved by the Commissions depends on what is meant by 'implementation'. The definition, therefore, of when a proposal is classed as 'implemented' must be ascertained. Second, the difference between consolidation and repeals projects and substantive law reform projects bears noting, because implementation only poses a problem for the latter. Third, the different manners in which non-implementation can occur must be understood in order to address them.

A. The Meaning of 'Implementation'

Frequently, only part of what the Commissions propose becomes law. In such cases, the LCEW defines widely when a project has been at least partially implemented.[7]

[6] Abolition of law commissions is not unheard of. For example, in 1993, the Law Reform Commission of Canada (established in 1971) was abolished. Its successor, the Law Commission of Canada, was established in 1997. In 2006, the Canadian Government withdrew funding, forcing the Law Commission of Canada to close: see Y Le Bouthillier, 'The Former Law Commission of Canada: The Road Less Travelled' in Dyson, Lee and Stark, *Fifty Years of the Law Commissions*, ch 11.

[7] eg, LCEW, *Legislating the Criminal Code: Involuntary Manslaughter* (Law Com No 237 (1996)) is classed as 'implemented in part' (LCEW, *Annual Report 2015–16* (Law Com No 367 (2016)) app A) even though the Corporate Manslaughter and Corporate Homicide Act 2007 enacted just a small part of the proposed reforms. LCEW, *Legislating the Criminal Code: Offences against the Person and General Principles* (Law Com No 218 (1993)) is also classed as 'implemented in part' (*Annual Report 2015–16*, ibid), despite only one of its recommendations being implemented by the Domestic Violence, Crime and Victims Act 2004.

The SLC takes a narrower approach, counting as implemented only those projects which result in legislation based significantly on its recommendations.[8] No consensus exists, therefore, between the Commissions as to what proportion of their proposals must be taken forward before a project is classed as being at least partially implemented. The Commissions have not, so far as any current or recent Commission personnel are aware, had any formal exchanges about the calculation of implementation rates, or endeavoured to develop a uniform method of calculation. No public record exists as to how the SLC calculates implementation figures because the SLC takes the view that the calculations it makes are made primarily for internal purposes and, unlike the LCEW, it does not calculate and publish implementation rates.[9] The LCEW believes that both Commissions calculate implementation figures in the same manner,[10] although that does not appear to be the case with respect to consolidation and repeals,[11] or partially implemented projects. This lack of consensus leads to inaccurate comparisons being made between Commission implementation rates. It can also lead to anomalies where reports have been conducted jointly between the two Commissions.[12] Furthermore, it is unclear whether the recording of implementation rates is consistent over time within each Commission, because the precise criteria according to which a project is classed as implemented, partially implemented, or not implemented have never been published. The current methods of recording implementation rates are therefore inadequate. Even if implementation calculations are only used for internal purposes, the Commissions cannot escape the fact that outsiders will attempt their own implementation calculations. The Commissions can better protect themselves from attack by being more open and transparent with their calculations. By employing too narrow an interpretation of when a project has been implemented, the SLC does not take credit for the contribution it has made to small pieces of enacted law. Consequently, the SLC is left open to unfair criticism for having a lower implementation rate than may really reflect reality—although the fiercest critics of implementation rates are often the Commissions

[8] eg, only 2 of the 68 recommendations contained in SLC, *Report on Succession* (Scot Law Com No 124 (1990)) were implemented (by the Family Law (Scotland) Act 2006, s 19 and sch 3) and the report is described as 'almost entirely unimplemented': SLC, *Discussion Paper on Succession* (Scot Law Com DP No 136 (2007)) para 1.2.

[9] Although it does, like the LCEW, publish a note of implementing legislation, it does not give an implementation rate as such. I am grateful to SLC Chief Executive, Malcolm McMillan, for his insights into these matters in December 2014.

[10] I am grateful to Catherine Vine at the LCEW for providing me with information as to how the LCEW calculates implementation rates in a discussion in March 2015.

[11] See text accompanying below n 40.

[12] eg, the Legislative Reform (Limited Partnerships) Order 2009 implemented a small part of LCEW and SLC, *Partnership Law* (Law Com No 283 and Scot Law Com No 192 (2003)). The LCEW classes the report as 'implemented in part' (*Annual Report 2015–16*, app A) and the SLC as unimplemented (SLC website, 'Table of Implementing Legislation' www.scotlawcom.gov.uk/publications/implementing-legislation/).

themselves.[13] An alternative method of recording implementation rates which reflects more accurately the Commissions' contribution to law reform, and which is more open and consistently applied, is proposed in this chapter.

Commission projects may not be implemented immediately. An examination of all LCEW reports completed between 1965 and 2009 and implemented by legislation reveals an average time between publication of the report and Royal Assent of approximately two years and eight months.[14] In recording implementation rates, therefore, it is sensible to adopt Cretney's approach whereby Commission projects completed within the previous two years are disregarded on the basis that implementation cannot necessarily be expected to occur within that time.[15] The Commissions currently count reports in implementation figures as soon as they are published due to the 'uncertain science' of when to otherwise begin including a report.[16] But every recent report will add to the 'not implemented' figure. It is illogical to count a freshly published report as 'not implemented' when there has been no opportunity for such implementation to have taken place. The two-year period chosen here, although still something of an 'uncertain science', has been justified by the evidence of average time from publication to implementation. Given that reports may be implemented after two years have passed, implementation rates should be recalculated periodically, and not only in relation to more recent reports.

The extent to which the Commissions' proposals can be altered by government or Parliament must also be considered. Commission recommendations may be 'implemented' in the sense that the draft Bill annexed to the Commission report (if there was one) forms the basis of legislation, but that legislation is unlikely to be verbatim what the Commission proposed,[17] and in certain cases may bear little resemblance to it.[18] It is important that such changes can be made. Even previous Commissioners, who have spoken of eventual legislation being 'mangled' by Parliament, concede that it is the prerogative of our democratically elected

[13] See, eg, Sir James Munby's assertions that implementation has been a 'grave concern' to successive LCEW Chairmen, and that although the LCEW has a 'good [implementation] record ... we believe it could—and should—be considerably better': J Munby, 'Shaping the Law—The Law Commission at the Crossroads' (Denning Lecture, 2011) 3–4. See also SLC, *Annual Report 2008* (Scot Law Com No 214 (2009)) Chairman's foreword.

[14] My own calculation. The shortest length of time before implementation occurred was one month and the longest was 22 years 11 months. The figure includes both consolidation and repeals projects and projects proposing substantive reform, and projects implemented either fully or substantially, or partially.

[15] S Cretney, 'The Politics of Law Reform—A View from the Inside' (1985) 48 *MLR* 493, 498, fn 23.

[16] I am grateful to Malcolm McMillan and to Catherine Vine for this information.

[17] Even where the resultant legislation is very similar, small changes are likely to have been made. Compare, eg, the Theft (Amendment) Act 1996 with the draft Theft (Amendment) Bill annexed to LCEW, *Offences of Dishonesty: Money Transfers* (Law Com No 243 (1996)).

[18] Compare, eg, the draft Partnerships Bill annexed to LCEW and SLC, *Partnership Law* (Law Com No 283 and Scot Law Com No 192 (2003)) with the small part of that report implemented by the Legislative Reform (Limited Partnerships) Order 2009.

representatives to be able to make such amendments.[19] The Commissions' role is, after all, only advisory. Indeed, one commentator worried that Parliament was not having *enough* input into moulding Commission proposals, saying:

> However much we may admire the Scottish Law Commission, [it] is not a substitute for parliamentary scrutiny and for independent judgment ... Therefore, we must not just look at those decisions and say that because the Scottish Law Commission did it, it is good.[20]

We will see later that attempts to allow Commission proposals to be implemented by statutory instrument had to be drastically curtailed due to concerns about a lack of democratic scrutiny. Governmental and parliamentary changes are usually a necessary stage between Commission proposals and enacted law.

In this book, all reports which have become law (whether by legislation or other means) are classed as implemented, even if the report was not implemented in its entirety. Overall implementation figures include projects that have been 'fully or substantially implemented' and those which have been 'partially implemented'. In the interests of transparency, it is important to acknowledge that overall implementation figures cover projects where a very small, as well as a very significant, part of what a Commission proposed was enacted. A Commission report should be classed as 'fully or substantially implemented' if the majority (half or more) of the Commission's recommendations (or the majority of the clauses of the draft Bill, if there was one) became law, even if alterations were made to those recommendations. The term 'fully or substantially' is used because, as noted above, even Bills taken forward in their entirety are likely to have at least cosmetic changes made to them.

Commission reports where a minority (fewer than half) of the proposals (or draft clauses) were taken forward should be counted as 'partially implemented'. Partial implementation should be included in the overall figures because there is often little difference between 'substantial implementation' and 'partial implementation'.[21] Although partial implementation can be achieved even if only a very small part of the project was implemented, such projects are relatively rare (some examples were mentioned above). The exclusion of partially implemented projects in overall implementation figures cannot be justified when the difference may simply be that four, rather than five, out of ten proposals were implemented.[22] It is essential in the interests of transparency, however, to state explicitly that overall figures do include partially, as well as fully or substantially, implemented projects.

[19] B Hale, 'A Justice of the Supreme Court in Conversation' (JUSTICE Student Human Rights Network Lecture, 16 November 2011) (unpublished attendance notes).

[20] HL Deb vol 457 col 1268 (4 December 1984) (Lord McCluskey).

[21] The Commissions already include projects defined (by their own standards) as 'partially implemented' in overall implementation figures: I am grateful to Malcolm McMillan and to Catherine Vine for this information.

[22] See too Hammond, 'The Legislative Implementation of Law Reform Proposals' 178.

In addition, Commission reports that have been implemented by non-traditional means (such as secondary legislation or the common law—both discussed later) should also be included in implementation figures.[23] The Commissions increasingly consider alternative outputs to primary legislation for their proposals. Such an approach is allowed for under the terms of the Law Commissions Act 1965 (the 1965 Act). While consolidation and repeals work must be presented to government by way of a draft Bill, substantive law reform proposals may be submitted 'by means of draft Bills or otherwise'.[24] Although the draftsman's intention may have simply been that someone else would draft the Bill, the wording allows the Commissions to choose non-statutory outputs.[25] Non-statutory outputs may be attractive for various reasons. They may be more appropriate if the law in need of reform is itself non-statutory. The Commissions, after all, must take and keep under review *all* the law, and that law will comprise common law and secondary legislation, for example, as well as primary legislation.[26] In addition, it may be prudent to consider alternative routes to implementation to avoid the parliamentary bottleneck. The Protocol agreed between the LCEW and the Lord Chancellor expressly states that the parties will consider whether the best output for a Commission proposal might be 'policy recommendations, a draft bill, [or] draft guidance'.[27] Both the SLC and the LCEW have, for example, had recommendations partially implemented by Court Rules.[28]

Only Commission reports that have resulted in no enacted provisions whatsoever, and have not been implemented (fully or substantially, or partially) by any other means, should be classed as 'not implemented'. This method of calculating and recording implementation rates would be more transparent and would allow the Commissions to calculate and record consistent implementation figures, both between the two bodies and within each body over time.[29] It would also mean that

[23] As they currently are by the Commissions: I am grateful to Malcolm McMillan and to Catherine Vine for this information.

[24] 1965 Act, ss 3(1)(d) and 3(1)(c) respectively.

[25] See SW Stark, 'Promoting Law Reform: By Means of Draft Bills or Otherwise' in Dyson, Lee and Stark, *Fifty Years of the Law Commissions*, 140–41 ('Promoting Law Reform') and HL MacQueen, 'Implementation by Statute: What the Future Holds' in Dyson, Lee and Stark, ibid 201.

[26] Stark, ibid 140.

[27] LCEW and Ministry of Justice, *Protocol between the Lord Chancellor (on behalf of the Government) and the Law Commission* (Law Com No 321 (2010)) para 7. See also LCEW and Welsh Ministers, *Protocol between the Welsh Ministers and the Law Commission/Protocol Rhwng Gweinidogion Cymru a Comisiwn y Gyfraith* (2015) para 6.

[28] SLC, *Recovery of Possession of Heritable Property* (Scot Law Com No 118 (1989)) and LCEW, *Expert Evidence in Criminal Proceedings in England and Wales* (Law Com No 325 (2011)) discussed in Stark, 'Promoting Law Reform' 144. See too D Ormerod, 'Reflections on the Courts and the Commission' in Dyson, Lee and Stark, *Fifty Years of the Law Commissions*, 333–34 and, on the other ways in which *Expert Evidence* was implemented, see LCEW, *Annual Report 2015–16* (Law Com No 367 (2016)) 51. On *Recovery of Possession of Heritable Property*, see *Oliver and Son Ltd, Petitioners* 1999 SC 656, 658.

[29] The Commissions accept that their implementation rates may not have been calculated in a consistent manner over time: I am grateful to Malcolm McMillan and to Catherine Vine for this information.

outsiders could check those implementation figures more easily. Furthermore, the meaning of implementation proposed here reflects more realistically the effect the Commissions have had on the law, and their duties under the 1965 Act, which are not limited to suggesting statutory reforms. Consequently, using the method of calculation proposed here, the Commission's implementation rates are actually higher than their official figures quoted above: 78 per cent for the LCEW and 84 per cent for the SLC.[30]

These figures can be put into context by considering the implementation rates of other law commissions around the world.[31] For example, the current implementation figure for the Australian Law Reform Commission (ALRC) is 'over 85 per cent'.[32] The Law Reform Commission of Ireland has an implementation figure of 76.7 per cent.[33] The New Zealand Law Commission (NZLC) has a much lower implementation rate, despite being one of the bodies the SLC has envied.[34] The implementation rate of NZLC proposals from its establishment in 1986 until 2006 was 66 per cent.[35] A 100 per cent implementation rate is neither necessary nor desirable. Such an implementation rate could indicate that a commission was merely undertaking the projects and proposing the reforms the government wanted to hear, thus removing the benefits of independent law reform (such as being able to propose reform after consulting widely and objectively). Commission implementation rates should not, however, be allowed to drop below 50 per cent. Being publicly funded bodies, the majority of Commission work should become law. Any other role the Commissions play, (such as informing scholarly or parliamentary debate) although important, must be ancillary because they are not part of the Commissions' role under the 1965 Act. The ideal Commission implementation rate must therefore lie somewhere between 50 and 100 per cent. It is submitted here that an implementation rate of around 75–85 per cent is desirable.[36] Such a rate strikes a balance between a clear majority of Commission proposals being implemented, and allowing a minority of projects to fulfil those other, ancillary functions. It is evident that both the LCEW and the SLC have healthy implementation rates, at least when the method of calculation proposed here is used.

[30] Reports published between 1965 and 2014 and implemented as at December 2016, my own calculations. The figures include consolidation and repeals projects. Excluding those projects, the figures are 72% for the LCEW and 77% for the SLC.

[31] Although methods of calculation may vary. See too Hammond, 'The Legislative Implementation of Law Reform Proposals' 177–78.

[32] ALRC website, 'About' www.alrc.gov.au/about.

[33] Hammond, 'The Legislative Implementation of Law Reform Proposals' 177.

[34] 'Holyrood Too Slow in Laying Down the Law' *The Herald Scotland* (19 May 2012).

[35] M Thompson (Special Projects Adviser, NZLC) to M McMillan (Chief Executive, SLC), 'Implementation of Law Reform Recommendations', 19 February 2009, SLC file. See too Hammond, 'The Legislative Implementation of Law Reform Proposals' 179.

[36] The average implementation rate in Hammond's analysis was 68.3%, but it seems undesirable to strive for a figure which includes, eg, the Law Commission of India's 47.9% implementation rate: 'The Legislative Implementation of Law Reform Proposals' 178.

B. Focus on Substantive Reform

In discussing the extent of implementation of Commission proposals, this chapter focuses mainly on the Commissions' substantive law reform proposals. Implementation is not a problem for the Commissions' Statute Law (Repeals) Bills and consolidation Bills, because they enjoy a 'relatively speedy [parliamentary] procedure … and do not have to compete for a place with ordinary legislation'.[37] Statute Law (Repeals) Bills and consolidation Bills are normally introduced in the House of Lords and, after their second reading, are referred to the Joint Committee on Consolidation Bills. Thereafter, the Bills are not debated. This procedure was adopted early in the Commissions' existence and is made possible by the relatively uncontroversial nature of consolidation and repeals Bills because they do not propose any (or propose only incidentally) substantive reform to the law. The parliamentary procedure has resulted in a 100 per cent implementation rate for such proposals.[38] Concern about implementation, therefore, does not extend to consolidation and repeals projects, and they are not affected by much of the discussion which follows. Consolidation and repeals projects are, however, included in the implementation figures quoted above.[39] Because of their implementation record, consolidation and repeals projects should be taken into account to provide an accurate picture of how the Commissions have actually contributed to reforming the law, or at least making law more accessible. Although less important and now less prevalent, consolidation and repeals work undertaken by the Commissions contributes to their statutory duty under section 3(1) of the 1965 Act to strive for the 'elimination of anomalies, the repeal of obsolete and unnecessary enactments, the reduction of the number of separate enactments and generally the simplification and modernisation of the law'. To not take account of the Commissions' consolidation and repeals work would not reflect the efforts made by the Commissions pursuant to that duty. The SLC does currently include consolidation and repeals projects in its implementation figures, but the LCEW does not.[40]

C. The Manner of Non-Implementation

Non-implementation of Commission proposals can occur in three different ways. First, the proposal might not be examined at all—it might simply gather dust after its publication. Second, the proposal might be examined but, after consideration, be deemed unsuitable for implementation. The government might

[37] N Marsh, 'Law Reform in the United Kingdom: A New Institutional Approach' (1971) 13 *William & Mary Law Review* 263, 282.

[38] By my own calculations.

[39] See above n 30.

[40] I am grateful to Malcolm McMillan and to LCEW Chief Executive, Phil Golding, for this information.

disagree with the Commission's conclusions or think the area of law is not ripe for reform. Sir Peter Gibson, a previous LCEW Chairman, and Sir Peter North, a previous Commissioner, have both suggested that non-examination of a proposal is a worse result for the Commissions than disagreement.[41] Sir Michael Kerr, another previous LCEW Chairman, expressed a similar view when he remarked that 'the least that the relevant government departments could do was to tell us why they were doing nothing'.[42] Both Commissions have also argued that it is better if government can reach a decision about implementation of their reports (whether positive or negative) timeously, because it can impact on other ongoing projects.[43] Timely decisions are indeed important. Equally important, however, would be a requirement (which does not currently exist) for rejected recommendations (either entire projects or the rejected parts) to be revisited periodically in case the situation changes sufficiently to make them more appealing. The advantages of the Commissions' independence are that they can propose their own projects, and propose reforms based on independent consultation and thorough research. Such reforms may not be palatable for implementation immediately,[44] but they may contribute to a discussion—particularly in academia, the courts, the legal profession and Parliament—which can lead to implementation in the future. The rejection of a Commission proposal, therefore, should be viewed as a rejection *for now*. The third manner of non-implementation was observed by Lord Davidson, a previous SLC Chairman—the proposal might be examined and approved, but parliamentary time might not be found for its implementation.[45] Attempts to remedy all these obstacles to implementation have been made and are discussed below.

II. Reasons for Non-Implementation

Various reasons have been advanced to explain why the Commissions' proposals are not always implemented. The reasons for non-implementation explain

[41] P Gibson, 'Law Reform Now: The Law Commission 25 Years On' (Denning Lecture, 1991) 27; P North, 'Law Reform: Processes and Problems' (1985) 101 *LQR* 338, 354–55 ('Law Reform: Processes and Problems').

[42] M Kerr, *As Far as I Remember* (Oxford, Hart Publishing, 2006) 295.

[43] 'It becomes very difficult for us to plan our work if the Government does not express a view … within a reasonable time': LCEW, *Fifteenth Annual Report: 1979–80* (Law Com No 107 (1981)) para 1.6. The SLC halted their family law projects until the outcome of their 1967 report *Divorce: The Grounds Considered* (Scot Law Com No 6 (1967)) was known: SLC, *Seventh Annual Report: 1971–72* (Scot Law Com No 28 (1973)) para 27.

[44] See, eg, the abolition of the crime of blasphemy which implemented a 23-year-old LCEW report, referred to below at n 261.

[45] C Davidson, 'Law Reform—Who Cares?' (1992) 37(4) *Journal of the Law Society of Scotland* 130, 132.

why the three broad manners of non-implementation discussed above occur: why the proposals are not examined; why the proposals are disagreed with; or why the proposals are agreed with, but time is not found to implement them. Certain reasons have existed since the Commissions' creation and others have emerged over time, creating new challenges for the Commissions—sometimes together and sometimes individually. As these new challenges emerged, implementation rates for both Commissions dropped, leading to the introduction of various measures to improve implementation rates. Examination of the reasons for non-implementation, therefore, provides the backdrop to understanding why such measures have been thought necessary.

A. Disagreement

The first and most straightforward reason for non-implementation is that the Commissions' proposals are given due consideration, but the government simply rejects them.[46] In this case, the best the Commissions can hope for is detailed and timeous reasoning for the rejection, so that they understand why their proposals are not being taken forward. Measures have been introduced, as we will see below, to attempt to ensure that Commission proposals are at least considered. And, as mentioned above, rejected proposals should also be reconsidered periodically in case they become more suitable for implementation over time—the government is not currently obliged to re-examine previously rejected Commission proposals.

Provided it is at least considered, it is not a disaster that a Commission proposal is simply disagreed with. We should value the Commissions' independence and, as we saw earlier, we should not expect 100 per cent implementation. The Commissions should recommend what is, in their opinion after extensive consultation and research, the best reform and not what they think government wants to see. Measures, therefore, which attempt to ensure that the Commissions make recommendations designed to please the government should be resisted. Compromises may, however, have to be made based on the scope of the project. For example, the government's terms of reference to the LCEW to review the law of homicide explicitly directed that the mandatory life sentence for murder was not for review. The criminal Commissioner at the time would perhaps have proposed different reforms had that not been the case.[47] In addition, Commissioners often have to be pragmatic and not base their reports on their own personal views if they suspect or know those to be particularly controversial with stakeholders.[48] But toning down one's own views in the light of extensive consultation is entirely different from toning them down to pander to government. The former is a great strength

[46] And the proposals are not implemented by another means, eg, by the courts or by a Private Member's Bill (see below).

[47] J Horder, *Homicide and the Politics of Law Reform* (Oxford, OUP, 2012) ch 8, especially 235.

[48] See ch 7, section III.

of the sort of consultation the Commissions undertake; the latter is an undesirable erosion of independence.

North, a previous LCEW Commissioner, opined that it is dangerous to equate implementation with success for two reasons.[49] First, doing so is likely to influence the projects undertaken by the Commissions because they may be tempted to select projects based on their likelihood of implementation, rather than on any other quality. It is agreed here that this is a real danger which risks usurping the chapter three project-selection criteria and leaving areas of law neglected because they are unlikely to be reformed by government without prompting. Second, the conclusions reached by the Commissions in projects undertaken could be tailored to 'satisfy the particular partisan interests of the Government of the day'.[50] North argued, however, that it is even worse to propose solutions which it is known will never be implemented, because that 'condone[s] the continuation of the law in the present unsatisfactory state'.[51] The correct answer is, North believes, to give another possible option for reform where the preferred option is known to be controversial.[52] In advocating this compromise, North highlights how difficult it is for the Commissions to strike a balance between their independence and achieving implementation.

The Commissions have occasionally presented more than one option for reform. For example, in the SLC's *Report on Succession*,[53] two different options to deal with the situation where parents attempt to wholly disinherit their children were set out,[54] together with two alternative parts of the draft Bill.[55] Two options were offered because the SLC's original recommendation presented in the preceding discussion paper was 'radical' and proved to be 'very controversial' with consultees 'almost evenly divided for and against it'.[56] The SLC therefore felt unable to present one clear option for reform in the subsequent report because the choice was 'a political question for the Scottish Parliament'.[57] The report was partially implemented by the Succession (Scotland) Act 2016, which did not deal with the issue. In the SLC's, *Double Jeopardy* report,[58] 'no recommendation' was made as to whether there should be a new evidence exception to the new double jeopardy rules, because there were 'strong arguments on both sides, and a division of opinion within the Commission'.[59] The implementing legislation does contain a new evidence exception.[60]

[49] North, 'Law Reform: Processes and Problems' 347.
[50] ibid.
[51] ibid 347–48.
[52] ibid 348.
[53] SLC, *Report on Succession* (Scot Law Com No 215 (2009)).
[54] ibid paras 3.14–3.99.
[55] ibid draft Bill, parts 2 and 3.
[56] ibid para 3.17.
[57] ibid para 3.35.
[58] SLC, *Report on Double Jeopardy* (Scot Law Com No 218 (2009)).
[59] ibid para 4.43. There was no majority because the SLC was functioning with only four Commissioners (as opposed to the usual five) at that time.
[60] Double Jeopardy (Scotland) Act 2011, s 4.

A better solution when Commissioners cannot agree, rather than failing to reach a firm conclusion, is to employ the technique used by the LCEW in *Criminal Law: Offences against Religion and Public Worship*.[61] In that report, the proposals reflected the view of the majority of Commissioners and a note of dissent of two Commissioners was appended.[62] Better still, Commissioners should strive to reach a firm and unanimous conclusion, because the Commissions act in an advisory capacity and should therefore give clear advice.[63] Where the question is a policy one not best resolved by a body consisting solely of lawyers, or where the issue is particularly controversial, the presentation of options can be resorted to. Compromises may be needed, but that does not mean the Commissions should always say exactly what they think government wants to hear.

B. Governmental and Parliamentary Lack of Interest in Law Reform

At one stage, Commission proposals were 'increasingly left unjustifiably to gather dust in Whitehall pigeon-holes'.[64] In 2007, almost half of all LCEW proposals made between 1996 and 2005 had not even been acknowledged by the government.[65] Certain projects were only implemented after 'truly shocking' delays of up to 16 years.[66] It has been acknowledged that although such delays are not ideal from the LCEW's point of view, '[i]t is for the democratically elected government to decide precisely when reports should be enacted, and in some cases this happens a decade or more after the reports are published'.[67] Implementation may become more difficult if it does not happen reasonably quickly because proposals may become outdated and/or the same Commission personnel may no longer be available to aid the implementation process. That being said, we should value the Commissions' ability to push legal boundaries and we should not expect all projects to be implemented immediately. Commission proposals should, however, at least be given due consideration, and the lack of governmental time traditionally afforded to Commission proposals has caused certain proposed reforms

[61] LCEW, *Criminal Law: Offences against Religion and Public Worship* (Law Com No 145 (1985)).

[62] ibid 41–45.

[63] See, eg, Maher's account as Commissioner responsible for the SLC's *Report on Rape and Other Sexual Offences* (Scot Law Com No 209 (2007)). One Commissioner was 'not personally convinced' on one issue, but did not dissent because he felt that 'the need for unanimous recommendations on a key part of the whole project outweighed any point in insisting on his position': G Maher, 'Principles and Politics in Law Reform: Sexual Offences in Scots Law' 2013 *Juridical Review* 563, 581. *cf* Gretton, who notes that he did not dissent in a different discussion paper but 'now wish[es] [he] had': G Gretton, 'Of Law Commissioning' (2013) 17 *Edinburgh Law Review* 119, 138.

[64] S Cretney, 'The Politics of Law Reform—A View from the Inside' (1985) 48 *MLR* 493, 498.

[65] T Etherton, 'Law Reform in England and Wales: A Shattered Dream or Triumph of Political Vision?' (Bar Law Reform Committee Lecture, 2007) 13 ('A Shattered Dream?').

[66] See ibid 13–14 and the examples contained therein.

[67] ibid 24.

to stall.[68] Lady Hale has, however, warned of 'press[ing] government too hard for an answer'.[69] Sometimes projects simply do not arrive at the most opportune moment, but they might be implemented eventually, albeit that work may be needed to 'refresh' them before implementation.[70]

As we saw in chapter two, concerns were expressed over a lack of parliamentary time during the Commissions' creation, but Gardiner was optimistic that sufficient time would be found. Less than a year after the Commissions were established, however, Gardiner admitted that a lack of parliamentary time could thwart the progress of their proposed reforms.[71] In fact, parliamentary time is even more of a problem than originally envisaged, because the Commissions are more industrious than certain parties had anticipated, and more Bills than ever jostle for parliamentary time. In Scotland, concerns were expressed privately shortly after the Commissions' establishment that they were both 'trying to do too much for Parliament to swallow' and 'the right answer' was thought to be 'that they slow down and take longer over it'.[72] Hardly an appropriate response for Commissions keen to demonstrate their value—both then and now.

In 1993, Lord Bingham complained about 'the 38 reports of the Law Commission which currently await implementation':

> These reports, produced at quite considerable public expense, represent clear, well-argued and compelling proposals for improving the law; only two of the 38 have been specifically rejected by the government of the day; they gather dust not because their value is doubted but because there is inadequate parliamentary time to enact them.[73]

But the real problem for the Commissions is not only the lack of parliamentary time, but also the lack of governmental, parliamentary and public interest in law reform. Indeed, a study commissioned by the LCEW in 1994 observed that many Commission Bills do not actually take up a lot of time on the floor of either House. Small Bills, based completely on Commission proposals, pass far more quickly through both Houses than much other legislation. The study calculated that the average time spent debating '[m]ajor Government Bills based partly on Law Commission Reports'[74] was 34 hours and 39 minutes in the Lords, and 14 hours

[68] eg, in the LCEW's *Annual Report 2006–07* (Law Com No 306 (2007)), it was noted that governmental responses were still mostly awaited on several damages for personal injury reports published in 1998 and 1999 (paras 3.50–3.52). The recommendations remain largely unimplemented.

[69] B Hale, 'Fifty Years of the Law Commissions: The Dynamics of Law Reform Now, Then and Next' in Dyson, Lee and Stark, *Fifty Years of the Law Commissions*, 22.

[70] J Munby, 'Shaping the Law—The Law Commission at the Crossroads' (Denning Lecture, 2011) 7 ('Shaping the Law').

[71] G Gardiner (Lord Chancellor) to H Wilson (Prime Minister), 'New Statement of Policy', 7 February 1966, National Archives (NA) CAB130/214.

[72] Handwritten file note by RH Law to JM Fearn, Scottish Office, undated (c 1966), National Records of Scotland (NRS) HH83/702.

[73] TH Bingham, 'The European Convention on Human Rights: Time to Incorporate' (1993) 109 *LQR* 390, 392.

[74] Where the 'relevant Law Commission reports formed only a part, sometimes a very small part, of the Bills introduced into Parliament': P Hopkins, *Parliamentary Procedures and the Law Commission: A Research Study* (1994) app 3.

and 56 minutes in the Commons.[75] The contrasting average times for '[m]inor Bills implementing Law Commission law reform proposals'[76] was only one hour 49 minutes in the Lords and one hour 11 minutes in the Commons.[77] Smaller projects with smaller Bills can be more easily accommodated in the busy parliamentary schedule and are sometimes more easily implemented. The problem, however, is not simply a lack of parliamentary time, but the lack of weight given to Commission proposals in taking up such valuable time.

Sir James Munby, a former LCEW Chairman, complained of a lack of will for 'systematic law reform' in government and Parliament.[78] Despite Gardiner's claim that in the 1960s, law reform was popular among lawyers, it has been observed that '[m]any lawyers are cool, or even hostile, to large-scale law reform' simply because 'they regard it as an intolerable extra burden to have to learn a whole new scheme of law'.[79] This hostility has been advanced by the government as one reason to reject LCEW proposals.[80] Lord Carloway has added that the legal profession can be '[r]eactionary or excessively defensive' in a way which is 'obstructive' to law reform, especially because of financial motivations.[81] The SLC increasingly publishes commentaries on and explanations of its recent proposals in professional law journals.[82] Such publications are an admirable and simple step to smoothing the law reform process, and the relationships within it. Public, or at least professional, interest in law reform could lead to greater governmental or parliamentary interest.

From the outset, it was doubted whether the Commissions would in fact make great inroads into law reform. The reason the law was in need of reform, it was argued, was not because of a lack of a full-time law reform body, but because government and Parliament were uninterested in reform which was of 'little significance to the public'.[83] There continues to be little appetite for law reform in Parliament, and it has been observed that '[w]hen law-reform matters are under discussion the House of Commons is normally virtually empty'.[84] It has been said

[75] Calculated from figures in ibid.

[76] '"[P]ure" Law Commission Bills, based only a Law Commission Report (or Reports) and implementing those proposals directly': ibid.

[77] ibid.

[78] Munby, 'Shaping the Law' 12.

[79] C Davidson, 'Law Reform—Who Cares?' (1992) 37(4) *Journal of the Law Society of Scotland* 130, 132.

[80] Ministry of Justice, *Report on the Implementation of Law Commission Proposals* (2012, HC 1900) para 50, where the government rejected LCEW, *Intoxication and Criminal Liability* (Law Com No 314 (2009)) on the basis that (inter alia) it would replace 'a complex but well understood process with a complicated new test which practitioners would need to master'.

[81] Lord Carloway, 'To "Mend the Laws, That Neids Mendement": A Scottish Perspective on Lawyers as Law Reformers' (speech at the Commonwealth Association of Law Reform Agencies Conference, Edinburgh, 2015) 10.

[82] See the examples given in HL MacQueen, 'Implementation by Statute: What the Future Holds' in Dyson, Lee, and Stark, *Fifty Years of the Law Commissions*, 213.

[83] 'Law Reform' *The Scotsman* (8 February 1965).

[84] M Zander, *The Law-Making Process*, 6th edn (Cambridge, CUP, 2004) 511 (the statement does not appear in the 7th edn).

that the excuse of a lack of parliamentary time for Commission proposals did 'not always ring completely true' and instead was used to mask 'a number of problems' facing the Commissions,[85] including the lack of governmental and parliamentary interest in law reform. Three main reasons can be advanced for that lack of interest.

First, Commission Bills are often (although not always) technical and do not inspire debate, because few MPs or peers 'have the detailed knowledge and also the interest to make much of a contribution to debates on these highly technical matters'.[86] Such Bills struggle to be attention-grabbing enough to be selected for inclusion in the parliamentary timetable in the first place. Measures have been employed to even the playing field for the more uncontroversial Commission reforms, as we will see later.

Second, law reform Bills may often be ignored by government (including civil servants) in favour of legislation that 'has to be introduced quickly because of public pressure'.[87] In chapter three we saw that, although not all Commission projects are technical, they typically do not deal with issues which are highly topical because these are adequately (and more appropriately) dealt with by the government. Commission Bills are, therefore, less likely to require to be dealt with urgently. The Commissions may have an especially difficult struggle to win legislative time for their more technical proposals, even when the government has approved them in principle.[88] When the government approves the Commission's recommendations, the fact that those recommendations are not implemented immediately demonstrates their low priority in the government's eyes.

Third, an increase in legislating on promises made in election manifestos has led to even less interest in 'non-political, non-party Law Commission reports' which will not sway voters.[89] In 1965, law reform *was* part of Labour's election manifesto.[90] It was even remarked in the public press that 'Law reform is a high-sounding topic always safe for insertion into party manifestos'.[91] Successful reforms were easy to achieve because they were carried along on the 'tide of public opinion'.[92] It will be remembered from chapter two, however, that the general public was not clamouring for law reform of the type typically carried out by the Commissions. Oerton noted in the 1980s that certain government departments were 'not prepared to make the necessary sacrifice of time and energy for Bills designed, not to win votes for the Government of the day nor to further Government policies, but merely to

[85] DJ Cusine, 'Law Reform—Who Cares?' (1993) 38(3) *Journal of the Law Society of Scotland* 101, 102–03 ('Law Reform—Who Cares?').

[86] ibid 103.

[87] ibid, which cites the example of the Dangerous Dogs Act 1991, rushed through Parliament as a response to tabloid outrage at a spate of attacks on children by certain dog breeds.

[88] See section IV.A.iv below.

[89] Etherton, 'A Shattered Dream?' 18.

[90] Labour Party, *The New Britain* (1964 manifesto).

[91] 'Law Reform' *Glasgow Herald* (6 January 1965).

[92] D Hope, 'Do We Still Need a Scottish Law Commission?' (2006) 10 *Edinburgh Law Review* 10, 24.

improve the law'.[93] Sir Roger Toulson, a former LCEW Chairman, has added that, '[t]he difficulty for the reformer is that these issues are not the ones on which MPs are bombarded by their constituents or on which tabloid editorials are written'.[94] It has similarly been noted in Scotland that '[n]either politicians nor administrators are greatly interested in proposals for law reform unless they have obvious popular appeal, and, unless they are urgent, [they] may not be regarded as politically important'.[95] Government and Parliament, therefore, have little interest in law reform that is, in turn, of little interest to the public.

Certain other commentators have, however, rejected the suggestion that the government is not supportive of law reform. Lord Rodger felt it was axiomatic that the government thought the SLC produced 'extremely important' work and that the record of implementation to date was 'eminently respectable'.[96] It has also been observed that the Commissions' projects may find favour immediately before and after general elections or when a minority government is in place.[97] Commission proposals tend to be politically uncontroversial and therefore, it is argued, provide an 'anodyne stop-gap' in the legislative timetable when controversial reforms are unappealing.[98] A trend for apparently non-contentious legislation was noted when Scotland had a minority government,[99] although, as we will see later, this trend did not benefit the SLC. Nor can it be said that the Coalition UK Government of 2010–15 had a positive impact on implementation rates.[100]

Additional reasons have affected the implementation of the SLC's proposals. Scottish commentators have chastised the UK Government and Parliament for having little time for Scottish legislation in general, and SLC proposals in particular.[101] One previous SLC Chairman lamented that the problem of finding parliamentary time, particularly in the House of Commons and particularly for Scottish Bills, pre-devolution, was 'notorious'.[102] It had been expressed with vitriol

[93] RT Oerton, *A Lament for the Law Commission* (Chichester, Countrywise Press, 1987) 92.

[94] R Toulson, 'Forty Years On: What Progress in Delivering Accessible and Principled Criminal Law?' (2006) 27 *Statute Law Review* 61, 71.

[95] HRM Macdonald, JC Mullin, TB Smith and JF Wallace, *The Laws of Scotland: Stair Memorial Encyclopaedia*, vol 22 (Edinburgh, Law Society of Scotland, 1987) para 625 (*Stair Memorial Encyclopaedia*).

[96] A Rodger, 'The Bell of Law Reform' 1993 *Scots Law Times (News)* 339, 339.

[97] See, eg, on the 'flurry of activity' just before Labour came to power in 1997, A Burrows, 'Some Reflections on Law Reform in England and Canada' (2003–04) 39 *Canadian Business Law Journal* 320, 326.

[98] M Kerr, 'Law Reform in Changing Times' (1980) 96 *LQR* 515, 533. See also J Beatson, 'Challenges for Independent Law Reformers from Changing External Priorities and Shorter Timescales' in Dyson, Lee and Stark, *Fifty Years of the Law Commissions*, 253.

[99] A Ross, H Nash and CT Reid, 'The Implementation of EU Environmental Law in Scotland' (2009) 13 *Edinburgh Law Review* 224, 238.

[100] See above n 1. Although recent implementation rates may yet rise, that rise cannot then be attributed to the Coalition Government.

[101] See, eg, EE Sutherland, 'Child and Family Law: Progress and Pusillanimity' in EE Sutherland, KE Goodall, GFM Little and FP Davidson (eds), *Law Making and the Scottish Parliament: The Early Years* (Edinburgh, EUP, 2011) 58–59.

[102] C Davidson, 'Law Reform—Who Cares?' (1992) 37(4) *Journal of the Law Society of Scotland* 130, 132.

that parliamentary procedures for Scottish law reform measures were 'grossly inadequate'.[103] At one stage, the government mooted making increased use of the Scottish Grand Committee to debate SLC Bills off the floor of the House of Commons.[104] Some use was made of this procedure,[105] yet many SLC reports still languished in Whitehall. Scots lawyers argued that the SLC faced 'additional obstacles' to the LCEW because of the subordination of Scots law by Whitehall government departments.[106]

It has been said, however, that the correlation between anti-Scottish bias in Whitehall and poor implementation rates did not quite ring true, because implementation was (and still is) also a concern for the LCEW.[107] The 'Scottishness' of the proposals, however, was not the only reason for their foundering, but it was often an extra obstacle in their way. Whitehall and Westminster would not devote as much time to purely Scottish legislation as they would to legislation for England and Wales.[108] A practice had developed of 'tucking legislative amendments of Scots law into corners, or even schedules, of English legislation' which was regarded as 'most objectionable' by Scottish commentators.[109] The SLC still relies on Westminster to implement reports on reserved matters,[110] which makes up a minority of its work—a full discussion of the post-devolution situation is returned to later.

In summary, it has always been a struggle for the Commissions to have their proposals timeously examined by government and, if that examination is favourable, for them to find a slot in the parliamentary timetable. Various mechanisms to improve the Commissions' chances at both stages have been introduced, and are evaluated later in this chapter.

C. Lack of Leadership in Parliament

Lord Scarman argued that a lack of parliamentary driving force limited the implementation of Commission proposals.[111] The problem, he suggested, was not only the lack of parliamentary interest in law reform, but that a draft Commission Bill lacked a 'pilot to steer it on its way'.[112] This deficiency was, historically, particularly

[103] Cusine, 'Law Reform—Who Cares?' 101.

[104] Scottish Office, *Scotland in the Union: A Partnership for Good* (White Paper, Cm 2225, 1993) para 6.13.

[105] eg, the procedure was used for the Children (Scotland) Act 1995, which implemented part of SLC, *Report on Family Law* (Scot Law Com No 135 (1992)).

[106] *Stair Memorial Encyclopaedia*, para 625.

[107] N Brotchie, 'The Scottish Law Commission: Promoting Law Reform in Scotland' (2009) 9 *Legal Information Management* 30, 31.

[108] Or Great Britain or the UK as a whole.

[109] DM Walker, 'The Scottish Law Commission under Review' (1987) 8 *Statute Law Review* 115, 122.

[110] As defined by the Scotland Act 1998, sch 5. Anything not specified therein is a devolved matter.

[111] L Scarman, *Law Reform: The New Pattern (The Lindsay Memorial Lectures)* (London, Routledge & Kegan Paul, 1968) 39–42.

[112] ibid 39.

true for SLC proposals. Smith noted that the problem of finding parliamentary time for Scottish law reform was partly due to a shortage of Scottish representatives in Parliament pushing for their enactment.[113]

We saw in chapter two that Gardiner originally proposed that his law reform body would be headed by a Cabinet Minister. This proposal was unpopular, however, because the government observed that it would then be difficult for it 'to do other than accept the Commission's recommendations'.[114] The Commissions are headed by judicial Chairmen and consequently lack the parliamentary driving force or 'direct line to implementation' they would have had under Gardiner's plan.[115] Despite this deficiency, judicial Chairmen are the better option—the Commissions could not have enjoyed the independence which they now have if they were headed by members of the executive.

In the 1990s, Cusine said that once a Commission submits a report to the Minister 'its task is complete',[116] but that statement is no longer accurate. The Commissions now have work to do even after their proposals are published. Increasingly, both Commissions offer an 'after-sales service' to government and Parliament, being contactable to explain further their drafting; to assist with governmental amendments to draft Bills; to give evidence once Bills are introduced; and to help generally with their draft Bill's onward journey.[117] This service results in 'additional potentially time-consuming work' for Commissioners and staff, but the SLC has stated that priority should be given to governmental or parliamentary requests over ongoing projects, 'on the basis that the Commission must do what [it] can to facilitate the implementation of outstanding reports'.[118] The after-sales service assists government, Parliament and the Commissions themselves: government and Parliament hope for a better explanation of the Commissions' thinking, and the Commissions hope for an increased chance of implementation. Although the work is 'time-consuming' the SLC recognises that post-project work is useful to encourage implementation and must be accommodated alongside work on fresh projects. The Commissions certainly seem to be managing a successful balancing act in that regard. The problem of a lack of Commission 'pilot' in Parliament has therefore been partially alleviated. The SLC, despite its enthusiasm for the after-sales service has admitted that there are 'challenges' of working with government

[113] TB Smith, 'Little Sympathy for its Ideas' *The Scotsman* (16 January 1965).

[114] Note of a Meeting held between the Secretary of State for Scotland et al, 30 October 1964, NRS HH41/2048.

[115] B Hale, 'Fifty Years of the Law Commissions: The Dynamics of Law Reform Now, Then and Next' in Dyson, Lee and Stark, *Fifty Years of the Law Commissions*, 18 ('The Dynamics of Law Reform').

[116] Cusine, 'Law Reform—Who Cares?' 101.

[117] The after-sales service was put on a semi-formal footing by the LCEW in 2004: LCEW, *The Law Commission and Government—Working Together to Deliver the Benefits of Clear, Simple, Modern Law* (2004) paras 1.12, 2.7.7–2.7.11.

[118] SLC internal memo, 'Implementation of Scottish Law Commission Recommendations: Update' (February 2012), SLC file, para 13.

and Parliament 'to encourage and ensure the implementation' of its proposals.[119] Such involvement is particularly required when use is made of the new parliamentary procedures for non-controversial Commission Bills.[120]

A good relationship between the Commissions and government is critical because the Commissions rely on government to introduce their proposals as Bills into Parliament. Parliamentary support is, however, also essential to aid implementation. Parliamentary opinions about the Commissions are mixed. On the one hand, the LCEW has been described in Parliament as an 'unrepresentative quango'.[121] On the other hand, and more recently, the LCEW has been able to publish a selection of comments gathered from Hansard supporting its work.[122] Sections 3(2) and 3(3) of the 1965 Act oblige the Commissions' Ministers to lay the Commissions' programmes of law reform, annual reports and reports proposing law reform before Holyrood and Westminster. The laying obligation is important to the Commissions' independence—their proposals cannot be 'suppressed' by a Minister.[123] Recent developments to increase implementation rates have sometimes focused on increasing parliamentary oversight of governmental disposal of Commission proposals, such as by requiring the Lord Chancellor to lay her responses to LCEW proposals before Parliament.[124] Because of such obligations, the Commissions have reasonably high profiles in Parliament. Their reforms are brought to the attention of parliamentarians who may choose to take forward Commission draft Bills as Private Members' Bills. A high number of Private Members' Bills have made an extremely valuable contribution to implementation rates.[125] Indeed, the Law Commission Act 2009 was itself a private peer's Bill introduced by Lord Lloyd of Berwick.[126] Cusine has even suggested that there should be a convention that reports from the SLC are 'at least debated' in the Scottish Parliament.[127] Though this, at first sight, seems like a radical suggestion, it would, in theory, be workable in practice given the small number of SLC reports

[119] M McMillan, 'The Role of Law Reform in Constitutionalism, Rule of Law and Democratic Governance: Reflections by the Scottish Law Commission' (Association of Law Reform Agencies of Eastern and Southern Africa Lecture, 2011) 3.

[120] Discussed at sections IV.A.iv and IV.C.ii below.

[121] HL Deb vol 568 col 290 (11 January 1996) (Lord Rawlinson of Ewell). For other references to criticisms of the LCEW, see S Cretney, 'The Law Commission: True Dawns and False Dawns' (1996) 59 *MLR* 631, 634, fn 29.

[122] eg, LCEW, *Annual Report 2013–14* (Law Com No 352 (2014)) 8 and 12.

[123] SW Stark and N Faris, 'Law Reform in Northern Ireland: Cheshire Cat or Potemkin Commission?' [2016] *PL* 651, 665.

[124] See T Etherton, 'Memoir of a Reforming Chairman' in Dyson, Lee and Stark, *Fifty Years of the Law Commissions*, 80–81 ('Memoir of a Reforming Chairman') and sections IV.B.iii, IV.B.iv and IV.C.i below.

[125] Between 1965 and 2010, 32 LCEW reports were implemented by 29 Private Members' Bills: figures calculated from House of Commons Information Office, *The Success of Private Members' Bills* (2010).

[126] Etherton, 'Memoir of a Reforming Chairman' 80.

[127] D Cusine, 'Civil Law Reform: Where are We and Where are We Going?' 2015 *Scots Law Times (News)* 27, 28.

produced each year.[128] There should be an exception to the convention, however, for reports dealing with reserved matters. Given the closeness of the institutions in Scotland, such a proposal at least has more merit than it would have in relation to the debate of LCEW proposals in Westminster.

The relationship with Parliament is also important when it comes to Commission Bills being scrutinised. Rarely, a Commission Bill may falter in Parliament and be withdrawn, particularly if one of the special measures to aid implementation has been attempted and the Bill proves to be too contentious.[129] Making changes to, or even rejecting, Commission proposals is Parliament's democratic prerogative. Parliament cannot be said to be a real obstacle to the implementation of Commission proposals if the liberal interpretation of implementation endorsed above is employed so as to include projects where many amendments were made to the proposals (and the draft Bill, if there was one). Such an approach should be employed because the Commissions have still had an impact in law reform, notwithstanding parliamentary changes being made. It would be more dangerous to suggest that Parliament, with its democratic mandate, could *not* make such changes. As we will see later, such a proposal proved highly controversial in the Legislative and Regulatory Reform Bill.[130]

Despite not having the clear leadership in Parliament that Gardiner proposed, measures such as the after-sales service and Private Members' Bills have ensured that the Commissions have a parliamentary voice.

D. LCEW: Institutional Bias

Based on his time working at the LCEW, Oerton alleged that there was an institutional bias in government against the LCEW.[131] Despite the particular problems faced by the SLC at Whitehall and Westminster, its political relations are not as fraught as the LCEW's. Reasons for, and consequences of, such better relationships are discussed below.

i. Government Departments

As we saw in chapter two, during the Commissions' creation, certain government departments expressed concern that their law reform duties were being usurped by the LCEW. Such concern occurred despite the fact that those departments were struggling to keep the law up to date due to the pressures of other work. The Home Office, responsible for criminal law reform, was particularly outspoken. It has been argued that the department responsible for an area of law reform has a bearing on

[128] See section V below.
[129] See, eg, below nn 278 and 407–08.
[130] See section IV.A.iii below.
[131] RT Oerton, *A Lament for the Law Commission* (Chichester, Countrywise Press, 1987) generally and 92, 96 and 99 specifically (*A Lament*).

the likelihood of LCEW proposals in that area being implemented. At one point, a correlation was noted between projects within the remit of the Home Office or the former Department of the Environment and projects with low implementation rates.[132] Conversely, projects within the Lord Chancellor's remit have historically had a better chance of being implemented.[133] Other commentators have expressed their disdain for the 'negative attitude' which certain departments have shown towards Commission proposals.[134] Oerton wrote in particularly candid terms: 'I was shocked—not just because of what they said about the project but because their attitude showed so clearly that, in their eyes, the Law Commission really did not exist'.[135] Relationships between the LCEW and government departments may not, however, be as fraught as they once were. For example, the implementation rate of criminal law projects is much improved.[136]

Dame Mary Arden, a previous LCEW Chairman, has argued that, despite certain government departments' historic dislike of the LCEW, certain areas of law would be neglected without the Commissions, because government departments prioritise more urgent matters.[137] Such urgent matters include manifesto promises or highly topical areas, which the Commissions do not get involved in because they are more adequately and appropriately dealt with by government. In chapter three we saw that the suitability of a Commission project is based partly on it being unlikely that any other party (including government) will consider undertaking (or be capable of undertaking) reform in that area of law. It follows logically, therefore, that the law in certain areas would be neglected without the Commissions.

ii. Lord Chancellor

Oerton has accused the Lord Chancellors following Gardiner of not cooperating with the LCEW in the 1970s and 1980s, saying provocatively, 'with the Lord Chancellor's Department for a friend the Law Commission has no need of enemies'.[138] This accusation, however, has not been consistently true.[139] The Lord Chancellors following Gardiner were not strangers to law reform. For example, the Lord Chancellor from 1974 until 1979, Lord Elwyn-Jones, had co-authored (with

[132] S Cretney, 'The Politics of Law Reform—A View from the Inside' (1985) 48 *MLR* 493, 509. Cretney's finding tallies with Oerton's statement that the LCEW were to 'suffer much' at the ends of the Department of the Environment (now the Department for Environment, Food and Rural Affairs): Oerton, ibid 82. North added that the main problem with these departments was 'non-implementation by inaction': P North, 'Law Reform: Processes and Problems' (1985) 101 *LQR* 338, 355.

[133] Cretney, ibid 510; Hale, 'The Dynamics of Law Reform' 21.

[134] M Kerr, 'Law Reform in Changing Times' (1980) 96 *LQR* 515, 531.

[135] Oerton, *A Lament*, 96, on the Department of the Environment's reaction to the LCEW's *Report on the Law of Positive and Restrictive Covenants* (Law Com No 127 (1984)), which was not implemented.

[136] eg, of seven criminal law projects carried out between 1975 and 1984, four (57%) were implemented. Between 1995 and 2004, 13 criminal projects were carried out and 11 (85%) were implemented.

[137] M Arden, 'The Work of the Law Commission' (2000) 53 *Current Legal Problems* 559, 593.

[138] Oerton, *A Lament*, 99.

[139] See above n 133.

Gardiner) a chapter in *Law Reform Now*.[140] Former LCEW Chairman, Sir Michael Kerr, described Elwyn-Jones as having a 'strong commitment to the work of the Commission'.[141] Lord Mackay, Lord Chancellor from 1987–97, was a Commissioner at the SLC between 1976 and 1979 and Lord Advocate from 1979 to 1984. Indeed, on the occasion of the Commissions' thirtieth anniversary, Lord Mackay had much praise for their work, saying that their reports were always based on 'careful research and wide consultation' and that, as such, he always assumed that they should be implemented.[142] Contrary to Oerton's statement, Sir Terence Etherton has observed that although varying in their 'enthusiasm and success', successive Lord Chancellors tried to solve the problems the LCEW was facing.[143] Measures taken include investigating the concern over parliamentary time not being found for Commission proposals, and attempting to strengthen the relationship between the LCEW and government departments.[144]

E. LCEW: Changes to the Role of Lord Chancellor

As opposed to the changing *personalities* of Lord Chancellors causing a strained relationship with the LCEW on occasion, changes to the *role* of Lord Chancellor pose a greater problem. The importance of the Lord Chancellor's relationship with the LCEW was noted during the 1965 Act's passage through Parliament.[145] Alterations to the role of Lord Chancellor, most notably by the Constitutional Reform Act 2005 (the 2005 Act), adversely affected the LCEW by removing the Lord Chancellor's independence from party politics and making the role that of 'a fully fledged party politician, shorn of any independent judicial or legislative role'.[146]

Due to a perceived lack of separation of powers between the legislature, the executive and the judiciary, the Lord Chancellor's role was radically reformed.[147] A 'process of politicisation',[148] culminated in the creation of the Ministry of Justice in 2007, with the Lord Chancellor, now also with a role as Secretary of State for Justice, at its helm. The changes resulted in 'a new party political edge to [her]

[140] G Gardiner and F Elwyn Jones, 'The Administration of Justice' in G Gardiner and A Martin (eds), *Law Reform Now* (London, Victor Gollancz, 1963) ch 2.

[141] M Kerr, *As Far as I Remember* (Oxford, Hart Publishing, 2006) 293.

[142] LCEW, *Thirtieth Annual Report: 1995* (Law Com No 239 (1996)) para 1.2.

[143] T Etherton, 'Law Reform in England and Wales: A Shattered Dream or Triumph of Political Vision?' (Bar Law Reform Committee Lecture, 2007) 20 ('A Shattered Dream?').

[144] The former attempted by Lord Mackay (discussed at section IV.A.ii below) and the latter attempted by Lord Irvine (discussed at section IV.B.i below).

[145] HC Deb vol 709 col 200 (22 March 1965) (Sir John Hobson).

[146] Etherton, 'A Shattered Dream?' 15.

[147] See, eg, Lord Windlesham, 'The Constitutional Reform Act 2005: Ministers, Judges and Constitutional Change' [2005] *PL* 806 and 'The Constitutional Reform Act 2005: The Politics of Constitutional Reform' [2006] *PL* 35.

[148] Etherton, 'A Shattered Dream?' 16.

position'.[149] The Lord Chancellor remains, however, the person to whom the LCEW must address its publications and so the changes have necessarily impacted on the LCEW.

Sir Terence Etherton, a previous LCEW Chairman, has noted that the new Ministry of Justice and politicised Lord Chancellor did not know quite what to do with the LCEW. The LCEW was, at one stage, pigeon-holed within the 'Her Majesty's Courts Service' section of the Ministry of Justice (now Her Majesty's Courts and Tribunals Service). In Etherton's view, this pigeon-holing reflected 'an awkward confusion or embarrassment as to how to deal with the Commission and, more particularly, a reflection of its low priority within a Department dealing with a wide range of highly politically charged and resource intensive functions'.[150] The LCEW now sits slightly more comfortably in the Ministry of Justice's Justice and Courts Policy group.

Etherton has argued that it would be 'logical and more appropriate' for the LCEW to report to the Prime Minister, rather than the Lord Chancellor, as this would 'send the clearest message throughout the executive as to the importance of the work of the Commission'.[151] This proposal is, however, flawed for two main reasons. First, the Lord Chancellor is already an extremely important figure and is better suited, despite changes to her role (including no longer necessarily being legally qualified), to deal with matters pertaining to law and law reform. The Lord Chancellor has, after all, a duty to uphold the rule of law,[152] and the LCEW is 'an exemplar of the promotion of the rule of law' because it plays 'a vital role as a champion of accessibility and modernisation of the law'.[153] Second, if the Lord Chancellor has no time for law reform because of dealing with more 'highly politically charged' matters, that problem is hardly alleviated by passing the responsibility to the Prime Minister. Criticisms of Etherton's argument notwithstanding, it is true that the LCEW's relationship with the Lord Chancellor has been altered by virtue of her new role—and it has had to fight harder than ever for its share of her time.

F. SLC: After Devolution

The creation of a new Scottish Parliament in 1999 marked 'a momentous political, constitutional and social happening in Scotland'.[154] It has been noted, however,

[149] ibid 17.
[150] ibid 18.
[151] ibid 33–34.
[152] Constitutional Reform Act 2005, ss 1 and 17; Promissory Oaths Act 1868, s 6A.
[153] R Toulson, 'Democracy, Law Reform and the Rule of Law' in Dyson, Lee and Stark, *Fifty Years of the Law Commissions*, 138.
[154] EE Sutherland, KE Goodall, GFM Little and FP Davidson, 'Law Making and the Scottish Parliament: The Early Years in Context' in EE Sutherland, KE Goodall, GFM Little and FP Davidson (eds), *Law Making and the Scottish Parliament: The Early Years* (Edinburgh, EUP, 2011) 3.

that the campaigns leading up to this major development did not promise 'sweeping legal reform in Scotland',[155] because such 'radical reform' was not felt to be needed.[156] Nevertheless, hopes were high that bringing Parliament closer to the SLC would be beneficial, particularly in the light of the arguments we have seen about Scottish law reform being neglected by the UK Government and Parliament. Despite the establishment of a Scottish Parliament in 1999, however, finding parliamentary time for SLC proposals was still a problem. It has been noted with surprise that devolution did not initially have positive consequences for the SLC.[157] Since devolution, the SLC has increasingly been used by the Scottish Ministers to examine points of law referred to them, as well as still receiving references from the UK Government. References from government therefore, although having 'always formed a key part' of the SLC's work, took on a 'greater significance and occupied more … resources' post devolution.[158] Many proposals resulting from those references remain unimplemented. The SLC's implementation rate for devolved matters in the ten years following devolution was around 50 per cent.[159] Although it can be demonstrated that this figure is actually higher if a more realistic definition of implementation is employed, and that rates have since started to rise,[160] reasons for that disappointing implementation rate should be examined.

The devolution settlement for Scotland in 1999 'changed the constitutional landscape within which law reform in Scotland operates'.[161] Certain commentators thought that devolution would be a positive development for the SLC. Brotchie, for example, hoped that it would lead to 'improved attention to Commission proposals' due to an increase in parliamentary time for purely Scottish legislation.[162] The SLC realised, however, that devolution was a mixed blessing for law reform. On the one hand, there were 'new legislative opportunities', but on the other, 'additional burdens imposed on the Scottish Parliamentary counsel … impeded progress' on SLC projects and left it 'frustrated'.[163] The Commissions are reliant on Parliamentary Counsel to write the draft Bills that usually accompany their reports, as well as to continue the drafting process should the Bill be introduced into Parliament. Scottish Parliamentary Counsel's increased engagement, therefore, in drafting other Bills (including the Scotland Bill, which established the Scottish Parliament) took them away from SLC work and stalled both the

[155] ibid 4.

[156] ibid 6.

[157] M McMillan, 'The Role of Law Reform in Constitutionalism, Rule of Law and Democratic Governance: Reflections by the Scottish Law Commission', Association of Law Reform Agencies of Eastern and Southern Africa Lecture, 2011) 4 ('The Role of Law Reform').

[158] SLC, *Annual Report 2006* (Scot Law Com No 205 (2007)) 8.

[159] McMillan, 'The Role of Law Reform' 4.

[160] ibid 5.

[161] ibid 2.

[162] N Brotchie, 'The Scottish Law Commission: Promoting Law Reform in Scotland' (2009) 9 *Legal Information Management* 30, 31 ('The Scottish Law Commission').

[163] SLC, *Thirty-Fourth Annual Report: 1998–99* (Scot Law Com No 179 (2000)) Chairman's foreword.

production and implementation of SLC reports. The impediment to the SLC's progress is evidenced by a decline in the SLC's productivity over the relevant time period,[164] and a reduced implementation rate. Nevertheless, in the first few years following devolution, several significant SLC proposals were implemented, including a large project which abolished feudal tenure.[165] Certain successes notwithstanding, the implementation rate for devolved projects was considerably lower than that of reserved ones.[166] In 2011, the first majority government was formed in Scotland.[167] Because the Commissions are politically neutral and their proposals 'less liable to fall foul of parliamentary voting patterns', the previous lack of majority government should not have adversely affected the SLC.[168] In fact, as noted above, non-controversial reforms should be popular at such times.[169] Certain reasons, however, resulted in devolution not initially having a positive impact on the SLC.

First, the constitutional structure within which the SLC now finds itself is 'more complicated'.[170] Certain areas of law are reserved to Westminster and the remainder is devolved to Holyrood. The SLC must now, therefore, deal with two governments and two parliaments. At the outset of devolution, it was queried what the SLC's role would be—it was uncertain whether it would deal with both reserved and devolved matters, or only with devolved matters.[171] In the event, the former was decided upon and rightly so—the alternative would have left a 'gaping hole' in the maintenance of Scots law.[172] In practice, SLC proposals now relate mainly to devolved matters (because that comprises the majority of Scots law), but it does still interact with Whitehall and Westminster on certain occasions. As well as presenting reports on reserved matters to Scottish Ministers for laying before Holyrood, the SLC usually also presents such reports to the Secretary of State for Scotland for laying before the UK Parliament, although the 1965 Act does not technically give the Secretary of State such a role.[173] In summary, the 'challenges'

[164] eg, the SLC completed 47 projects in the period from 1985 to 1994 and just 38 projects the following decade. Such counting exercises are, however, somewhat crude because the number of projects completed depends on many other factors, such as the size and complexity of the projects.

[165] The Abolition of Feudal Tenure etc (Scotland) Act 2000 implemented SLC, *Abolition of the Feudal System* (Scot Law Com No 168 (1999)).

[166] The implementation rate of devolved projects published between 1999 and 2014 (according to my definition of implementation) was 58%; the implementation rate of reserved projects published over the same period was 93%, although it must be remembered that many more projects are devolved rather than reserved. Projects of a mixed devolved and reserved nature have been disregarded.

[167] Following a Labour/Liberal Democrat coalition between 1999 and 2007, and a minority SNP government from 2007 to 2011. Because elections to the Scottish Parliament are made using the Additional Member System, minority governments and coalitions were not unexpected.

[168] Brotchie, 'The Scottish Law Commission' 32.

[169] See above n 99.

[170] McMillan, 'The Role of Law Reform' 2.

[171] ibid 3.

[172] Lord Pentland, 'The Scottish Law Commission and the Future of Law Reform in Scotland' in Dyson, Lee and Stark, *Fifty Years of the Law Commissions*, 348.

[173] The 1965 Act, s 6(2) defines 'the Minister' in relation to the SLC as the Scottish Ministers. Gretton has noted that reports on reserved matters, such as *Unincorporated Associations* (Scot Law Com No 217 (2009)), should be presented to either the Advocate General for Scotland or the Secretary

of working with government and Parliament referred to above are now greater for the SLC.[174]

Second, as already mentioned, eagerness at the new legislative opportunity has placed huge demands on parliamentary draftsmen and the Scottish Parliament itself. Upon its creation, Holyrood was soon overburdened, full of a 'busy legislative programme put forward by the new Scottish administrations, newly elected and keen to make progress with the political and other priorities set out in their manifestoes'.[175] As even the current Chief Executive of the SLC admits, the prioritisation of manifesto promises is 'understandable'.[176] Such prioritisation led to the familiar story of Commission proposals being seen as less urgent and being pushed to the back of the queue.[177] The SLC has been vocal in pressing the Scottish Government to give more attention to their proposals, in an attempt

> to instil an awareness of the need for law reform, and to encourage the Parliament to embrace fully a sense of responsibility for the statute book for Scotland; and to introduce closer working with and within Government, so as to ensure business planning for law reform implementation in addition to the priorities of the current administration.[178]

The problem of a lack of parliamentary time (or the prioritisation of their work within that time) is a recurring theme for the Commissions. As we will see later, measures have been taken to ameliorate this problem for SLC proposals in devolved areas. Coupled with the initial excitement of the Scottish Parliament having subsided, the disappointing implementation rate has already begun to rise.[179]

III. The Importance of Being Implemented

A. The Commissions' 'Only raison d'etre'?

Opinions vary as to how important implementation is as a way of evaluating the Commissions' output. The first Chairman of the LCEW, Lord Scarman, felt that

of State for Scotland rather than Scottish Ministers. In practice, however, such reports are usually presented to both the appropriate Scottish Minister and the Secretary of State for Scotland, as can be seen from the *Unincorporated Associations* report at v and, eg, *Criminal Liability of Partnerships* (Scot Law Com No 224 (2011)) v: G Gretton, 'Of Law Commissioning' (2013) 17 *Edinburgh Law Review* 119, 130. It is the text of the 1965 Act, and not the SLC's practice, which requires amendment and such amendment is proposed in ch 7, section II.

[174] McMillan, 'The Role of Law Reform' 3.

[175] ibid 4.

[176] ibid.

[177] *cf* A Ross, H Nash and CT Reid, 'The Implementation of EU Environmental Law in Scotland' (2009) 13 *Edinburgh Law Review* 224. Environmental law may not lie as low down the list of the Scottish Government's priorities as the authors might have imagined. Reducing environmental damage is, after all, one of the Scottish Government's National Outcomes: see section IV.C.i.

[178] McMillan, 'The Role of Law Reform' 5.

[179] ibid.

its reputation would 'stand or fall by the contributions it makes to enacted law'.[180] Another former LCEW Chairman, Sir Henry Brooke, believed that because making the law 'simpler, fairer and cheaper to use' is the Commissions' 'only raison d'etre', implementation rates provide a useful measure of their success.[181] A subsequent Chairman, Sir Terence Etherton, noted that, although the Commissions enjoy a good reputation, admiration alone is not enough, 'particularly if based upon a distant record of success'.[182] He clarified, however, that he did not equate 'success' with legislative implementation—implementation was one very important factor, but not the only consideration. A law commission is, after all, 'an advisory body and not an implementation agency'.[183] Nevertheless, it has been argued that non-implementation adversely affects Commissioners and other staff, who suffer 'wastage and frustration' if their proposals are ignored by government.[184] Individuals who have worked on projects (which can take a great deal of time and effort) can feel demoralised if their labours come to nothing. In the inimitable words of Richard Oerton, a lawyer at the LCEW during the 1970s and 1980s: 'I think I might have been willing in the end to work happily on a project to prescribe the size of the wire mesh on chicken runs if only its implementation had been guaranteed'.[185] As outsiders, however, we would probably prefer the Commissions to work on important projects in the hope that they might be implemented, rather than frivolous projects where implementation is guaranteed. That said, the Commissions are also reliant on consultees and advisory groups who offer their time voluntarily—and who may not be so keen to devote their time to future projects if their labours do not result in any change.[186] Furthermore, because the Commissions are publicly funded bodies, Brotchie has argued that unimplemented reports are not only a waste of work but a waste of public resources.[187]

The Commissions frequently take the opportunity in their annual reports to highlight their implementation successes and the need for measures to assist the implementation of other projects.[188] They undoubtedly feel pressurised to demonstrate success in terms of implementation and may see non-legislative results as a 'consolation prize'.[189] They do increasingly, however, draw attention to their

[180] L Scarman, *Law Reform: The New Pattern (The Lindsay Memorial Lectures)* (London, Routledge & Kegan Paul, 1968) 17.

[181] H Brooke, 'The Role of the Law Commission in Simplifying Statute Law' (1995) 16 *Statute Law Review* 1, 1.

[182] Etherton, 'A Shattered Dream?' 24.

[183] ibid.

[184] M Kerr, 'Law Reform in Changing Times' (1980) 96 *LQR* 515, 531.

[185] Oerton, *A Lament*, 106.

[186] DJ Cusine, 'Law Reform—Who Cares?' (1993) 38(3) *Journal of the Law Society of Scotland* 101, 101.

[187] Brotchie, 'The Scottish Law Commission' 31.

[188] See, eg, LCEW, *Annual Report 2013–14* (Law Com No 352 (2014)) Chairman's introduction.

[189] N Paines, 'Reflections on Statutory Implementation in the Law Commission' in Dyson, Lee and Stark, *Fifty Years of the Law Commissions*, 199.

other successes, such as citation in court judgments, Hansard, academic journals and the media.[190] It is to those 'value added'[191] benefits that we now turn.

B. 'Never Work Wasted'

Certain commentators, such as Lord Rodger, have claimed that a correlation between implementation and law reform success is 'crude'.[192] The Commissions' values can also be measured in other ways. For example, Commission proposals may be 'accepted by government, even if not implemented immediately',[193] or they may contribute to a debate which may be reignited in future.[194] Commission papers are used by legal students, academics, practitioners, MPs and the judiciary.[195] It has been observed in Scotland that, particularly

> [i]n the early days, when there was still a dearth of reliable textbooks on Scots law, the SLC's reports were eagerly awaited and carefully read by practitioners, seeking to bring themselves up-to-date as to what the law actually was, let alone how it might be reformed.[196]

Despite the increase in available textbooks, such use undoubtedly continues today in relation to both Commissions, and extends from students to practitioners and academics, and even the judiciary[197] and government. For example, a reference from the Lord Advocate to the SLC to examine the law on liability for antenatal injury included the question 'What is the present law of Scotland ... ?' in the area.[198] Clarifying what the current law is should not be the main target of the Commissions' work because it is not one of their tasks under the 1965 Act, but it can be a useful side effect of their projects.[199]

One former SLC Chairman, Lady Clark, has expressed the view that Commission work, even if unimplemented by legislation, is 'never work wasted' due to its use by the judiciary in particular.[200] To substantiate and expand on Lady Clark's

[190] eg, LCEW, *Annual Report 2015–16* (Law Com No 367 (2016)) 10; SLC, *Annual Report 2014* (Scot Law Com No 241 (2015)) 12.

[191] L Dunlop, 'A Good Name, a Long Game' in Dyson, Lee and Stark, *Fifty Years of the Law Commissions*, 168 ('A Good Name, a Long Game').

[192] A Rodger, 'The Bell of Law Reform' 1993 *Scots Law Times (News)* 339, 339 ('The Bell of Law Reform').

[193] Etherton, 'A Shattered Dream?' 24.

[194] B Hale, 'A Justice of the Supreme Court in Conversation' (JUSTICE Student Human Rights Network Lecture, 16 November 2011) (unpublished attendance notes).

[195] Etherton, 'A Shattered Dream?' 24–25.

[196] D Hope, 'Do We Still Need a Scottish Law Commission?' (2006) 10 *Edinburgh Law Review* 10, 21.

[197] J Drummond Young, 'Introduction' in Dyson, Lee and Stark, *Fifty Years of the Law Commissions*, 273.

[198] SLC, *Report on Liability for Antenatal Injury* (Scot Law Com No 30 (1973)) para 1. See also *McWilliams v Lord Advocate* 1992 SLT 1045 and, for discussion, Dunlop, 'A Good Name, a Long Game' 161.

[199] D Johnston, 'How Law Commissions Work: Some Lessons from the Past' in Dyson, Lee and Stark, *Fifty Years of the Law Commissions*, 241.

[200] 'Interview: Lady Clark, First Female Chairman of the SLC' *The Scotsman* (24 September 2012).

view, the use of Commission material (both implemented and unimplemented) in different contexts requires examination, starting with the use of Commission material by the courts. Such use may, in certain instances, even constitute implementation without the need for legislation.

i. Use and Implementation by the Courts

Lord Rodger reasoned that simply equating the implementation of a Commission proposal with successful law reform was too narrow an approach.[201] The Commissions must take and keep under review all the law, but they cannot, due to their sizes, examine all the law. Some law must therefore be reformed by other means. Implementation cannot be ignored. But due to the Commissions' finite ability to reform the law, instead of looking solely at how many Commission reports have been implemented by legislation, we should be concerned with whether a jurisdiction is, overall, keeping the law in a respectable state, including through the work of the Commissions. Lord Rodger was particularly eager that the Commissions should not relieve the judges of 'any of their responsibility for reforming our common law'.[202] Indeed, the Commissions and the common law can work hand-in-hand. As Lord Rodger noted, there is a 'growing importance' of the Commissions' proposals in 'informing debate in our courts'.[203] The Commissions' judicial members increase the likelihood of Commission material being used in court when they return to the bench. For example, three of our current Supreme Court Justices have previously held roles at the Commissions.[204] They, and the other Justices, make reasonably frequent use of materials published by both the LCEW and the SLC.[205] Lady Hale in particular has mentioned how useful Commission material can be for the Supreme Court.[206] In addition, the Court often recommends that certain areas of law are examined by the Commissions.[207] Nothing prevents judges, individually or in a group, from making a specific suggestion for a project to the Commissions under the current terms of section 3(1)(a) of the 1965 Act. According to current Commission practice, however, ministerial approval

[201] Rodger, 'The Bell of Law Reform' 340.

[202] ibid 345.

[203] ibid.

[204] Lady Hale (LCEW Commissioner 1984–93); Lord Hodge (SLC Commissioner 1997–2003); and Lord Carnwath (LCEW Chairman 1999–2002). Lord Toulson (LCEW Chairman 2002–06) was a Justice of the Supreme Court from 2013–16.

[205] See, eg, *Radmacher v Granatino* [2010] UKSC 42, [2011] 1 AC 534; *HM Advocate v P* [2011] UKSC 44, 2012 SC (UKSC) 108; *Gow v Grant* [2012] UKSC 29, 2013 SC (UKSC) 1. See too, in the Court of Appeal, former Chairman Sir Henry Brooke's use of LCEW material in the infamous conjoined twins case: *Re A (Children)* [2001] Fam 147. See also J Lee, 'The Etiquette of Law Reform' in Dyson, Lee and Stark, *Fifty Years of the Law Commissions*, ch 29 ('The Etiquette of Law Reform').

[206] B Hale, 'Legislation or Judicial Law Reform: Where Should Judges Fear to Tread?' (Society of Legal Scholars Annual Conference, 2016).

[207] See, eg, *Joseph v Spiller* [2010] UKSC 53, [2011] 1 AC 852; *Jones v Kaney* [2011] UKSC 13, [2011] 2 AC 398. See also former LCEW Chairman, Sir James Munby, in the High Court: *Re X (A Child)* [2016] EWHC 2271 (Fam) [74].

would be required to insert such a recommendation into a programme.[208] Dickson has suggested that the Commissions should keep a record of all judicial calls for legislative action—not just those mentioning the Commissions themselves—and make a 'public response regarding the desirability and possible shape of the required reforms'.[209] Such a suggestion would be relatively simple to implement by the Commissions keeping abreast of judicial decisions, or by the courts (for example, the judicial assistants at the Supreme Court) alerting the Commissions to relevant judgments. One Commissioner has suggested that such a 'formal mechanism', however, would be 'superfluous' given the informal responsiveness the LCEW already demonstrates.[210]

There has been a 'growing use of Scottish Law Commission publications in the courts'.[211] The courts have found it 'legitimate' to refer to SLC materials to assist with the interpretation of statutes emanating from SLC proposals.[212] Thus, SLC reports can be used in the same way as Hansard where a statutory provision is unclear—and, in fact, even when there is no such lack of clarity.[213] Judges may, however, disagree as to the extent to which such references can be made, particularly where no draft Bill was included in the report.[214] The courts have also been guided by SLC proposals in making their decisions,[215] and have praised the SLC, stating, for example, that it is 'known and respected for the thoroughness of its work'.[216]

The LCEW has been cited on occasion by the European Court of Human Rights,[217] the Court of Justice of the European Union,[218] and frequently by the

[208] House of Commons Justice Committee, 'The Work of the Law Commission', Oral Evidence, HC 858 (2 March 2016) Q6 (Sir David Bean).

[209] B Dickson, 'Judicial Activism in the House of Lords 1995–2007' in B Dickson (ed), *Judicial Activism in Common Law Supreme Courts* (Oxford, OUP, 2007) 398.

[210] D Ormerod, 'Reflections on the Courts and the Commission' in Dyson, Lee and Stark, *Fifty Years of the Law Commissions*, 327.

[211] HL MacQueen, 'Judicial Reform of Private Law' (1998) 3 *Scottish Law and Practice Quarterly* 134, 144.

[212] *Rehman v Ahmad* 1993 SLT 741, 745. See also, eg, *A v HM Advocate* [2012] HCJAC 29, 2012 JC 343, where the High Court of Justiciary made reference to the SLC's *Report on Hearsay Evidence in Criminal Proceedings* (Scot Law Com No 149 (1995)) in order to interpret the intention behind the Criminal Procedure (Scotland) Act 1995, s 260 (on the admissibility of prior statements of witnesses) which implemented that report. For a summary of such references until 1992, see G Maher, 'Statutory Interpretation and Scottish Law Commission Reports' 1992 *Scots Law Times (News)* 277.

[213] Maher, ibid 281–82. The liberal use of Commission publications may be controversial considering the more restrictive terms of *Pepper v Hart* [1993] AC 593 (which is discussed in ch 5, section IV.A.iii).

[214] *David T Morrison & Co Ltd v ICL Plastics Ltd* [2014] UKSC 48, 2014 SC (UKSC) 222, discussing SLC, *Reform of the Law Relating to Prescription and Limitation of Actions* (Scot Law Com No 15 (1970)).

[215] eg, in *HM Advocate v Cowie* [2011] HCJAC 111, 2012 JC 203, the High Court of Justiciary found the SLC's views on bodily samples being taken with force (in *Report on Evidence: Blood Group Tests, DNA Tests and Related Matters* (Scot Law Com No 120 (1989))) 'very instructive' at [15].

[216] *Monteith v Cape Insulation Ltd* 1998 SC 903, 906.

[217] For discussion of *Al-Khawaja and Tahery v UK* (2012) 54 EHRR 23 see Lee, 'The Etiquette of Law Reform' 292–96. See also, eg, *Ali v UK* (2016) 62 EHRR 7 and *Dallas v UK* (2016) 63 EHRR 13.

[218] Although such mentions are rare, and brief: see, eg, C-518/13 *R (on the application of Eventech Ltd) v Parking Adjudicator* [2015] 1 WLR 3881.

English courts. Like the SLC, the LCEW's reports can be used as an interpretative device for legislation emanating from its proposals. The courts have decided that it is 'both appropriate and permissible' for such references to be made, even though a report cannot provide conclusive proof of a statute's meaning.[219] Indeed previous LCEW Chairman, Dame Mary Arden, described one report as 'some of the best material a court could have for purposive statutory interpretation'.[220] Praise for the LCEW can be seen in, for example, *Woolwich Equitable Building Society v Inland Revenue Commissioners*,[221] where the House of Lords described the LCEW's consultation paper on *Restitution of Payments Made under a Mistake of Law*,[222] as 'most valuable'.[223] Indeed, the work was considered 'of such importance that it [had] a powerful bearing upon the consideration … of the central question in the case'.[224] LCEW research was also found useful in *Prince Jefri Bolkiah v KPMG*,[225] where the definition of 'Chinese Walls' was lifted from a consultation paper on *Fiduciary Duties and Regulatory Rules*.[226] The eventual report in that project was rejected by government.[227] In *Radmacher v Granatino*,[228] Lady Hale praised the LCEW's project on marital property agreements, stating that it was 'just the sort of task for which the Law Commission was established … and in which it has had such success'.[229] She applauded the LCEW for being 'the democratic way of achieving comprehensive and principled reform' due, in particular, to the extensive consultation it carries out before its proposals are put before Parliament.[230]

In *Radmacher v Granatino*, Lady Hale envisaged that legislation inspired by Commission recommendations was the 'democratic way' of achieving law reform. More recently, however, she has praised the idea of Commission material 'stimulat[ing] judicial law reform, by providing a fully researched, reasoned and consulted upon policy case for developing the law in a particular area in a particular way'.[231] Halliday's Review of the LCEW in 2003,[232] noted the possibility of LCEW proposals that had not been picked up by the executive being partially

[219] *Yaxley v Gotts* [2000] Ch 162, 182.

[220] *R (on the application of Best) v Chief Land Registrar* [2015] EWCA Civ 17, [2016] QB 23 [106], discussing LCEW, *Land Registration for the Twenty-First Century: A Conveyancing Revolution* (Law Com No 271 (2001)) and its preceding consultation paper which led to the Land Registration Act 2002. For a case study on the 2002 Act, see C Harpum, 'The Refiner's Fire' in Dyson, Lee and Stark, *Fifty Years of the Law Commissions*, ch 31.

[221] *Woolwich Equitable Building Society v Inland Revenue Commissioners* [1993] AC 70.

[222] LCEW, *Restitution of Payments Made under a Mistake of Law* (Law Com CP No 120 (1991)).

[223] *Woolwich Equitable Building Society*, 163.

[224] ibid 164.

[225] *Prince Jefri Bolkiah v KPMG* [1999] 2 AC 222.

[226] LCEW, *Fiduciary Duties and Regulatory Rules* (Law Com CP No 124 (1992)); *Prince Jefri Bolkiah*, 238.

[227] LCEW, *Fiduciary Duties and Regulatory Rules* (Law Com No 236 (1995)).

[228] *Radmacher v Granatino* [2010] UKSC 42, [2011] 1 AC 534.

[229] ibid [134].

[230] ibid [135].

[231] B Hale, 'Fifty Years of the Law Commissions: The Dynamics of Law Reform Now, Then and Next' in Dyson, Lee and Stark, *Fifty Years of the Law Commissions*, 24.

[232] Discussed further at section IV.B.ii below.

implemented by the courts.[233] Indeed, the courts have occasionally implemented reforms that have been proposed by the LCEW, thus negating the need for legislation. For example, the House of Lords in *Kleinwort Benson Ltd v Lincoln City Council*[234] implemented the main recommendations in the LCEW's *Restitution: Mistakes of Law and Ultra Vires Public Authority Receipts and Payments* report;[235] *Heil v Rankin*[236] partially implemented *Damages for Personal Injury: Non-Pecuniary Loss*;[237] and *Kuddus v Chief Constable of Leicestershire Constabulary*[238] partially implemented *Aggravated, Exemplary and Restitutionary Damages*.[239] The Commissions themselves have occasionally decided that legislation would be inappropriate and have left an area of law for the courts to develop. For example, in *The Illegality Defence*,[240] the LCEW recommended that 'no legislative reform is needed in relation to the illegality defence as it applies to claims other than those arising under a trust'.[241] Instead, the LCEW recommended it should be 'open to the courts to develop the law in ways that would render it considerably clearer, more certain and less arbitrary'.[242] Unfortunately, the Supreme Court's development of the law in the area has not achieved the clarity the LCEW hoped for.[243] A draft Bill was included in *Claims for Wrongful Death*,[244] but the LCEW also said, in relation to one particular issue, that 'legislation is probably neither necessary nor appropriate'.[245] The draft Bill remains unimplemented, but the Supreme Court cited the LCEW's invitation to reform the law when invoking the Practice Statement in *Knauer v Ministry of Justice*.[246]

[233] J Halliday, *Quinquennial Review of the Law Commission* (2003) annex 4, para 16.

[234] *Kleinwort Benson Ltd v Lincoln City Council* [1999] 2 AC 349.

[235] LCEW, *Restitution: Mistakes of Law and Ultra Vires Public Authority Receipts and Payments* (Law Com No 227 (1994)). See LCEW, *Thirty-Fourth Annual Report: 1999* (Law Com No 265 (2000)) para 1.10.

[236] *Heil v Rankin* [2001] QB 272.

[237] LCEW, *Damages for Personal Injury: Non-Pecuniary Loss* (Law Com No 257 (1999)). The LCEW specifically recommended that legislative reform of certain aspects should be postponed pending judicial development: see paras 3.165, 3.170, 3.176 and 3.188.

[238] *Kuddus v Chief Constable of Leicestershire Constabulary* [2001] UKHL 29, [2002] 2 AC 122.

[239] LCEW, *Aggravated, Exemplary and Restitutionary Damages* (Law Com No 247 (1997)).

[240] LCEW, *The Illegality Defence* (Law Com No 320 (2010)).

[241] ibid para 1.18.

[242] ibid para 3.37. See also *ParkingEye Ltd v Somerfield Stores Ltd* [2012] EWCA Civ 1338, [2013] QB 840.

[243] See *Hounga v Allen* [2014] UKSC 47, [2014] 1 WLR 2889; *Les Laboratoires Servier v Apotex Inc* [2014] UKSC 55, [2015] AC 430; *Jetivia SA v Bilta (UK) Ltd* [2015] UKSC 23, [2016] AC 1; and *Patel v Mirza* [2016] UKSC 42, [2016] 3 WLR 399. For discussion, see J Beatson, 'Challenges for Independent Law Reformers from Changing External Priorities and Shorter Timescales' in Dyson, Lee and Stark, *Fifty Years of the Law Commissions*, 252 ('Challenges for Independent Law Reformers') and Lee, 'The Etiquette of Law Reform' 286–92.

[244] LCEW, *Claims for Wrongful Death* (Law Com No 263 (1999)).

[245] The issue being whether the multiplier for damages under the Fatal Accidents Act 1976 should be applied at the date of injury or the date of trial: ibid para 4.19.

[246] *Knauer v Ministry of Justice* [2016] UKSC 9, [2016] AC 908.

Precedent also exists for SLC proposals shaping judicial opinions and being partially implemented through the common law.[247] For example, the Inner House of the Court of Session in *Morgan Guaranty Trust Company of New York v Lothian Regional Council*[248] reached substantially the same conclusion as the SLC's *Discussion Paper on Recovery of Benefits Conferred under Error of Law*,[249] thus negating the need for the project to proceed to report stage. The Court did not cite the SLC, but the discussion paper had been cited in the lower court,[250] and the SLC claimed the appellate court was 'assisted by [the SLC's] research and the discussion set out in that Paper'.[251] It may be that explicit mentions are just the tip of the iceberg in terms of when Commission reports assist the courts. As Laura Dunlop, a previous SLC Commissioner and QC at the Scottish bar, has said, counsel may be reluctant to expressly cite a Commission report because it will naturally set out 'both sides of an argument'.[252]

As established above, Commission proposals at least partially implemented by the courts (but not where reports have simply been referred to as, for example, a guide to legislative interpretation) are classed in this book as implemented because they have contributed to law reform. The Commissions already class certain projects as implemented by the courts.[253] The approach adopted in this book, as well as endorsing a realistic demonstration of the effect the Commissions have had on our law, allows for judicial implementation to be recorded openly and consistently. Although primarily established to reform the law by legislation, the Commissions are not, and should not be, limited to proposing reforms either to, or by way of, enacted law. Indeed, as we have seen, their duty under section 3(1) of the 1965 Act is to keep under review '*all* the law'. As Beale has noted, section 3(1)(c) specifically allows the Commissions to propose reform by draft Bills 'or otherwise', allowing for the possibility of judicial, as well as statutory, reform.[254] Although projects that have been implemented by the common law are rare, their exclusion would do the Commissions an injustice by fixating only on their contribution to enacted law. Commission proposals can improve common law reform by providing independent and thoroughly researched proposals reflecting 'informed professional opinion'.[255] Those who doubt that such research is enough to sanction judicial law-making may find it comforting to know that the courts have shown reluctance to implement Commission proposals which have been specifically rejected

[247] For further examples, see L Dunlop, 'A Good Name, a Long Game' in Dyson, Lee and Stark, *Fifty Years of the Law Commissions*, ch 17 ('A Good Name, a Long Game').

[248] *Morgan Guaranty Trust Company of New York v Lothian Regional Council* 1995 SC 151.

[249] SLC, *Recovery of Benefits Conferred under Error of Law* (Scot Law Com DP No 95 (1993)).

[250] *Morgan Guaranty Trust Company of New York v Lothian Regional Council* 1994 SCLR 213.

[251] SLC, *Report on Unjustified Enrichment, Error of Law and Public Authority Receipts and Disbursements* (Scot Law Com No 169 (1999)) para 1.3.

[252] Dunlop, 'A Good Name, a Long Game' 168.

[253] LCEW, *Annual Report 2015–16* (Law Com No 367 (2016)) app A and above n 23.

[254] H Beale, 'The Law Commission and Judicial Law Reform' (2001) 35 *The Law Teacher* 323, 335 ('The Law Commission and Judicial Law Reform').

[255] ibid 341.

by government, as opposed to those which have 'merely not been implemented'.[256] Commission proposals may therefore help to cure 'judicial hesitation' in certain appropriate areas,[257] by reducing (albeit not eradicating) the democratic deficit inherent in judicial law-making.

ii. Pushing the Boundaries of Legal Thinking

Away from the courts, academic discussion of Commission proposals, both before and after implementation and both for and against the Commissions' views, is commonplace and examples are too numerous to cite.[258] Academic endorsement of a Commission proposal can show its utility, even if it is not implemented—or at least not implemented quickly. Such proposals can generate debate and inform legal thinking. For example, a European Court of Human Rights ruling in relation to a lack of Swedish privacy law led one author to argue that the UK may be compelled to enact a privacy law.[259] Despite the time since its publication, James Michael argued that there was a 'ready-made bill' for this purpose in the form of an unimplemented LCEW report published in 1981.[260] This example demonstrates that Commission work, even if not immediately (or ever) implemented, may stand the test of time and be used in academic discourse, in this case some three decades later. Eventually, proposals may become more palatable for implementation after such discourse. The longest gap between publication and implementation for either Commission was the LCEW's recommendation to abolish the crime of blasphemy, which took almost 23 years to be implemented.[261] By concentrating solely on immediate implementation, the Commissions could lose this valuable function of pushing the boundaries of legal thinking.

C. Assessing Output as a Whole

Gretton has remarked that the second (and now defunct) Law Commission of Canada sought 'to educate, to challenge, to provoke'.[262] Gretton wonders whether law commissions are 'wiser [...to] aspire to be merely useful'.[263] A choice need not be made, however, between educating, challenging and provoking on the one hand

256 ibid 338, comparing *President of India v La Pintada Compania Navigacion SA* [1985] AC 104 with *Darlington Borough Council v Wiltshier Northern Ltd* [1995] 1 WLR 68.

257 Beale, 'The Law Commission and Judicial Law Reform' 340.

258 See, however, section V below for some critical commentary on the Commissions.

259 J Michael, 'UK May Need Law against Secret Filming and Photography after European Court Ruling', UK Human Rights Blog, 21 November 2013 ukhumanrightsblog.com/2013/11/21/uk-may-need-law-against-secret-filming-and-photography-after-european-court-ruling-james-michael/. I am grateful to Neil Faris for referring me to this piece.

260 ibid; LCEW, *Breach of Confidence* (Law Com No 110 (1981)).

261 LCEW, *Criminal Law: Offences against Religion and Public Worship* (Law Com No 145 (1985)), implemented by the Criminal Justice and Immigration Act 2008.

262 G Gretton, 'Of Law Commissioning' (2013) 17 *Edinburgh Law Review* 119, 129.

263 ibid.

and utility on the other if the Commissions' output is assessed as a whole. When selecting a project, all three chapter three criteria: (i) the availability and economical use of resources; (ii) the suitability of the project; and (iii) the importance of the project must be taken into account. A project will often be judged to be more viable on one criterion than the others. Sometimes, for example, the examination of a certain area of law will be important enough to justify the risk that implementation is uncertain (ostensibly a poor use of resources). Another project may be less important, but may be a good use of resources and also highly suitable for the Commissions to examine, such as a consolidation or repeals project. The criteria therefore often pull in different directions. A mixture of projects weighing more heavily in different categories will result in a Commission's balanced output. In addition, a parallel between the Law Commission of Canada's remit and its demise should not necessarily be drawn given that an earlier Law Reform Commission of Canada with a more traditional remit was also abolished.[264]

Although implementation cannot be ignored, it should not be assumed to be the main hallmark of a project's success. Implementation is only one potential measure of a successful project, together with its quality and any other impact—for example, judicial, parliamentary, or academic consideration. Nor should implementation be expected immediately. Implementation can take time—especially if we value the Commissions' ability to push at the boundaries of reform. Furthermore, implementation should be defined broadly, to include, for example, recommendations implemented by the judiciary, but to exclude reports published within the past two years. Such a definition reflects more accurately the impact the Commissions have had on the law. Consequently, the pressure to achieve even higher implementation rates being caused by the current figures could be partially alleviated, because those figures are artificially low. In addition, as even the SLC itself has noted, mere implementation does not equate with successful law reform, because it is the *quality* and not just the *quantity* of the measures enacted which is important.[265] The Commissions' independence is important in allowing them to propose reforms that appear to be the best solution after extensive research and consultation—and not necessarily the reforms the government wants to see. Nevertheless, implementation cannot be ignored and certainly all Commission projects cannot be allowed to go unimplemented. Reform of the law (mainly, but not exclusively, by legislation) is the reason for the Commissions' existence and it would be dangerous to allow implementation to falter lest the Commissions face abolition. Such abolition would rob the British jurisdictions of the valuable function the Commissions provide by way of independent law reform proposals, based on wide consultation, in oft-neglected areas.

[264] Y Le Bouthillier, 'The Former Law Commission of Canada: The Road Less Travelled' in Dyson, Lee and Stark, *Fifty Years of the Law Commissions*, 98.

[265] SLC, *Eighth Annual Report: 1972–73* (Scot Law Com No 33 (1974)) para 6.

IV. Attempts to Improve Implementation

Concern as to the extent of implementation has led to various attempts being made to improve implementation rates. Such attempts have, due to the different reasons for non-implementation, sometimes differed in England and Scotland, causing the two Commissions to drift apart from their shared constitution under the 1965 Act. Certain measures to improve implementation have been positive developments, whereas other measures have put too much emphasis on implementation at the expense of independence.

A. Attempts Affecting Both Commissions

i. Second Reading Committee

Since the Commissions' establishment, many attempts have been made to streamline parliamentary procedures so that Commission Bills can be more easily accommodated. It was originally envisaged that all Commission Bills would be heard in select committees, akin to the Scottish Grand Committee.[266] A Second Reading Committee along these lines was established in 1965 to be used for Commission Bills, among other things.[267] The Second Reading Committee was, however, not used frequently for Commission Bills for various reasons, including indecision as to whether a Bill was non-contentious enough to use the procedure.[268] Nevertheless, during the ensuing decades, the Commissions' implementation rates were perceived to be relatively healthy,[269] and finding methods of improving implementation was not therefore high on the agenda. As implementation rates fell, however, concerns grew and attempts to increase implementation of Commission proposals gained pace.

ii. Jellicoe Report

In the early 1990s, a recommendation was made in the *Report from the Select Committee on the Committee Work of the House*, chaired by Lord Jellicoe (the Jellicoe Report),[270] which aimed to allow more Commission proposals to be heard in Parliament. Concern had been expressed by the then Lord Chancellor, Lord Mackay, that space was not being found for Commission proposals in the

[266] See, eg, HC Deb vol 706 col 57 (8 February 1965) (Sir Eric Fletcher); HL Deb vol 264 col 1220 (1 April 1965) (Lord Gardiner).

[267] House of Commons Select Committee on Procedure, *First Report* (1964–65, HC 149).

[268] P Hopkins, *Parliamentary Procedures and the Law Commission: A Research Study* (1994) paras 2.5–2.6.

[269] See above n 1.

[270] House of Lords Select Committee, *Report from the Select Committee on the Committee Work of the House* (1991–92, HL 35-I).

parliamentary process.[271] The Jellicoe Report therefore proposed the introduction of special standing committees in the House of Lords. Certain Commission Bills would be introduced in the Lords and would then be considered by the standing committee, off the floor of the House.[272] The procedure would be appropriate for Commission Bills,[273] which were 'not … contentious in party-political terms' even if 'the technical details might be contentious'.[274] The Commissions 'enthusiastically' supported this proposal.[275] It was eventually decided that 'as an experiment, one or two' such Bills should be introduced.[276] The procedure was, however, relatively unsuccessful, and resulted in the enactment of only two pieces of legislation based on Commission proposals.[277] Another Bill was introduced but was later withdrawn and subsumed into a new Bill which completed its process through Parliament without the special procedure.[278] The controversy of that final failed Bill may have contributed towards the demise of the procedure.[279] The Jellicoe procedure has now been overtaken by a new House of Lords procedure, which is described below.

iii. Legislative Reform Orders

In addition to various methods of aiding the implementation of Commission proposals by primary legislation, certain attempts have also been made to increase implementation by finding alternative avenues for law reform. One such attempt was made by increasing the ability to implement Commission proposals by statutory instrument, initially by way of Regulatory Reform Order under the Regulatory Reform Act 2001 and now by way of Legislative Reform Order (LRO) under the Legislative and Regulatory Reform Act 2006 (the 2006 Act).

The utility of this method of implementation is limited by three things. First, only the most technical and uncontroversial Commission recommendations qualify for the procedure, and so it does not cover all Commission work.[280] Second,

[271] ibid para 56.
[272] ibid para 183.
[273] And other Bills which were 'legal and technical': ibid para 184.
[274] ibid para 57. See also para 132.
[275] ibid para 58.
[276] ibid para 132(i).
[277] The Law of Property (Miscellaneous Provisions) Act 1994, which resulted from LCEW, *Transfer of Land: Implied Covenants for Title* (Law Com No 199 (1991)) and LCEW, *Title on Death* (Law Com No 184 (1989)); and the Private International Law (Miscellaneous Provisions) Act 1995, which implemented LCEW, *Private International Law: Foreign Money Liabilities* (Law Com No 124 (1983)); LCEW and SLC, *Private International Law: Polygamous Marriages* (Law Com No 146 and Scot Law Com No 96 (1985)); and LCEW and SLC, *Private International Law: Choice of Law in Tort and Delict* (Law Com No 193 and Scot Law Com No 129 (1990)).
[278] The Family Homes and Domestic Violence Bill, which was based on LCEW, *Domestic Violence and Occupation of the Family Home* (Law Com No 207 (1992)), and which was incorporated into the Family Law Act 1996.
[279] Beatson, 'Challenges for Independent Law Reformers' 247.
[280] LCEW, *Thirty-Sixth Annual Report: 2001* (Law Com No 275 (2002)) para 2.15.

LROs can only make amendments to existing legislation, not the common law.[281] Third and finally, the LRO must have the effect of removing or reducing a 'burden' rather than simply removing inconsistencies or anomalies.[282] Consequently, few Regulatory Reform Orders or LROs have been made.[283]

As originally drafted, the Legislative and Regulatory Reform Bill gave ministers the power to implement Commission[284] recommendations by order 'with or without changes'.[285] This power, however, proved highly controversial, because it would have allowed any non-contentious Commission proposal to be implemented without parliamentary scrutiny.[286] The provision was removed before the legislation was enacted, because Parliament ultimately felt that it could not 'leave it to the Law Commission, good though it undoubtedly is, to legislate on our behalf'.[287] The Commissions are advisory bodies and, although their recommendations should never be completely ignored, they should not be implemented without some degree of scrutiny either. As well as the fact that it cannot be assumed that all Commission proposals are good, a total lack of scrutiny propagates the myth, dispelled in chapter three, that the Commissions only examine uncontroversial and technical areas. The possibility of implementing Commission proposals by LRO has therefore only made a modest impact on implementation.

iv. House of Lords Procedure

Another 'modest glimmer of hope'[288] to solve the perennial problem of a shortage of parliamentary time came with a change in House of Lords procedure, piloted in 2008 and made a permanent feature in 2010. Technical and uncontroversial Commission Bills may be introduced in the House of Lords and the second reading debated by a Second Reading Committee rather than on the floor of the

[281] 2006 Act, s 1(2); *Thirty-Sixth Annual Report*, para 2.16.

[282] 2006 Act, s 1(2); *Thirty-Sixth Annual Report*, para 2.16.

[283] The Regulatory Reform (Business Tenancies) (England and Wales) Order 2003 implemented LCEW, *Landlord and Tenant: Business Tenancies—A Periodic Review of the Landlord and Tenant Act 1954 Part II* (Law Com No 208 (1992)); the Regulatory Reform (Execution of Deeds and Documents) Order 2005 implemented LCEW, *The Execution of Deeds and Documents by or on behalf of Bodies Corporate* (Law Com No 253 (1998)); and the Legislative Reform (Limited Partnerships) Order 2009 implemented part of LCEW and SLC, *Partnership Law* (Law Com No 283 and Scot Law Com No 192 (2003)).

[284] Either the LCEW, SLC or the Northern Ireland Law Commission.

[285] Legislative and Regulatory Reform Bill (as introduced), cl 1(1)(b).

[286] The Bill itself made no distinction between 'contentious' and 'non-contentious' Commission proposals, but parliamentary debates confirmed that the procedure was not intended to be used for contentious proposals. See, eg, HC Deb vol 442 cols 1048–49 (9 February 2006) (Jim Murphy and David Howarth).

[287] HL Deb vol 683 col 146 (13 June 2006) (Lord Lloyd of Berwick). See also, eg, JR Spencer et al, 'Legislative Reform' *The Times* (16 February 2006) and D Howarth, 'Who Wants the Abolition of Parliament Bill?' *The Times* (21 February 2006).

[288] T Etherton, 'Law Reform in England and Wales: A Shattered Dream or Triumph of Political Vision?' (Bar Law Reform Committee Lecture, 2007) 30 ('A Shattered Dream?').

House. Subsequently, a Special Public Bill Committee takes oral and written evidence (including from the Commissions) and considers the Bill clause by clause. The report and third reading stages remain unchanged, as does the House of Commons procedure.[289] The procedure from introduction to Royal Assent still takes some months, and the resultant Act may differ from the Commission's draft Bill. Starting in the Lords, however, gives the Bill a greater chance of being introduced and thereafter it does not have to jostle for time on the floor of the House at every stage. The involvement required from the Commissions in terms of giving evidence on Bills using this procedure could be seen as an extra burden which takes the Commissions away from current projects, although any such burden is deemed necessary in improving implementation rates, and is carried out effectively by the Commissions.[290] The procedure is working well. Two Acts were passed during the trial period: the Perpetuities and Accumulations Act 2009 and the Third Parties (Rights against Insurers) Act 2010. Since the procedure became permanent, five further Acts (the Consumer Insurance (Disclosure and Representations) Act 2012, the Trusts (Capital and Income) Act 2013, the Partnerships (Prosecution) (Scotland) Act 2013, the Inheritance and Trustees' Powers Act 2014 and the Insurance Act 2015) were passed.[291]

The procedure benefits both Commissions, although the SLC less so because only reserved matters are now implemented by Westminster. Three of the Acts passed using the procedure so far (the Third Parties (Rights against Insurers) Act 2010, the Consumer Insurance (Disclosure and Representations) Act 2012 and the Insurance Act 2015) were based on collaborative projects.[292] The House of Lords procedure has also been used for a draft Bill published by the SLC alone. The Partnerships (Prosecution) (Scotland) Act 2013 (the 2013 Act) implemented an SLC report on *Criminal Liability of Partnerships*.[293] The subject matter was an odd choice for the new procedure, which was designed specifically for 'unspectacular but worthy'[294] Commission Bills. The SLC report, and the 2013 Act, were designed to close a 'loophole' which meant that it was previously impossible to prosecute dissolved partnerships.[295] The other Acts passed using this procedure

[289] For background to the procedure, see House of Lords Procedure Committee, *First Report, Law Commission Bills* (2008, HL 63) and *Second Report* (2010, HL 30) and HL Deb vol 721 col 224 (7 October 2010) (Lord Brabazon of Tara).

[290] SLC internal memo, 'Implementation of Scottish Law Commission Recommendations: Update' (February 2012), SLC file, para 13.

[291] At the time of writing, the Intellectual Property (Unjustified Threats) Bill was proceeding through Parliament. Assuming it completes its passage, it will be the eighth Commission Bill to use the procedure.

[292] LCEW and SLC, *Third Parties—Rights against Insurers* (Law Com No 272 and Scot Law Com No 184 (2001)); LCEW and SLC, *Consumer Insurance Law: Pre-Contract Disclosure and Misrepresentation* (Law Com No 319 and Scot Law Com No 219 (2009)); and LCEW and SLC, *Insurance Contract Law* (Law Com No 353 and Scot Law Com No 238 (2014)) respectively.

[293] SLC, *Criminal Liability of Partnerships* (Scot Law Com No 224 (2011)).

[294] HL Deb vol 710 col GC2 (28 April 2009) (Lord Bach).

[295] HL Deb vol 741 col GC173 (4 December 2012) (Lord Wallace of Tankerness).

involve highly technical matters that struggled to find time in the parliamentary process without the new procedure. That struggle is evidenced by the fact that the two Acts passed during the trial period (2008 to 2010) emanated from Commission reports published as far back as 1998[296] and 2001.[297] Despite the fact that the government had accepted the reforms in principle soon after their publication, the reforms were not exciting enough to 'fire the busy politician's imagination'.[298] The same cannot be said about an Act ascribing criminal liability, as the 2013 Act does. Although it did not happen on this occasion, if a Bill is, after introduction, found to contain 'controversial provisions', then the new procedure can be 'halted' and a decision can be taken as to whether the Bill should instead proceed in the orthodox way.[299] Care should be taken so that the House of Lords procedure does not meet the same fate as the Jellicoe procedure.

The new procedure bolsters the Commissions' implementation rates and aids the speedy reform of technical law. It levels the playing field for technical reforms that might otherwise be unlikely to be implemented. If, however, too much emphasis is put on achieving high implementation rates, the Commissions could be discouraged from undertaking less technical reforms because they do not benefit from an increased likelihood of implementation under the House of Lords procedure. More controversial reforms are now more of a gamble in the implementation stakes. The 2013 Act does indicate, however, that the subject matter caught under the new procedure is being interpreted broadly. By altering the definition of implementation and the importance placed on it, and by viewing the Commissions' output as a whole, less technical Commission proposals would not be discouraged.

B. Attempts Affecting the LCEW

i. Ministerial Committee

While he was Lord Chancellor, Lord Irvine set up the Ministerial Committee on the Law Commission. He was motivated by concerns about the relationship between the LCEW and government and intended to bring them closer together and to bring the LCEW's work to the government's attention. The Ministerial Committee was also to advise the Lord Chancellor on the appropriate disposal of LCEW recommendations. The Committee, however, had little effect.

The Ministerial Committee's lack of success was directly attributable to government apathy. Members routinely failed to attach any importance to its meetings and, consequently, 18 months elapsed between sittings, proxies were frequently

[296] LCEW, *The Rules against Perpetuities and Excessive Accumulations* (Law Com No 251 (1998)).

[297] *Third Parties—Rights against Insurers.*

[298] P Gibson, 'Law Reform Now: The Law Commission 25 Years On' (Denning Lecture, 1991) 27.

[299] House of Lords Procedure Committee, *First Report, Law Commission Bills* (2008, HL 63) para 5.

sent in place of members, and one meeting was abandoned as inquorate after only three members turned up.[300] The Ministerial Committee no longer exists, a need for it having been negated by the 2010 Protocol.[301]

ii. Quinquennial Reviews

Quinquennial reviews were introduced in the 1990s. Government departments were obliged to have the bodies for which they were responsible reviewed at five-yearly intervals. The procedure was abolished in 2003 after a government report found such reviews to be 'bureaucratic and inflexible'.[302] Two Quinquennial Reviews of the LCEW were carried out. The first, completed in 1997, received little attention, despite discussing potential measures to improve the LCEW's performance.[303] The second review, completed by Halliday in 2003 just before the system was abolished, was more notable.[304] In his *Quinquennial Review of the Law Commission* (the *Quinquennial Review*), Halliday had some praise for the LCEW. He found that it was 'held in high esteem' and had 'many strengths'.[305] The *Quinquennial Review* did, however, recommend closer interaction between the LCEW and government, stating that such closeness did not automatically prejudice the LCEW's independence.[306] The *Quinquennial Review* praised the establishment of the Ministerial Committee described above to help achieve this aim.[307] More could be done, however, and the *Quinquennial Review* led to a renewed attempt to build the LCEW's relationship with government.

The LCEW is now the subject of triennial reviews. The first of those took place in 2013–14.[308] That review made no specific recommendations to improve implementation, being designed 'to provide robust challenge to the continuing need' for the LCEW and to ensure 'good corporate governance'.[309] For example, the review made the recommendation that non-departmental board members should be appointed to the LCEW,[310] and that a framework document should be agreed between the Ministry of Justice and the LCEW.[311] It was decided that the relationship between the LCEW and government 'operates well in practice',[312] but that

300 Etherton, 'A Shattered Dream?' 22.

301 Discussed at section IV.B.iv below. I am grateful to Phil Golding for this information.

302 Office of Public Services Reform and HM Treasury, *Better Government Services: Executive Agencies in the 21st Century* (2002) 36.

303 LCEW, *Thirty-Second Annual Report: 1997* (Law Com No 250 (1998)) para 1.29.

304 J Halliday, *Quinquennial Review of the Law Commission* (2003).

305 ibid paras 0.1 and 0.5.

306 ibid recommendation 1.

307 ibid ch 8.

308 Ministry of Justice, *Triennial Review: Law Commission, Report of Stage One* (2013) and *Report of Stage Two* (2014).

309 *Report of Stage One*, para 7; *Report of Stage Two*, para 7.

310 *Report of Stage Two*, para 47. Two non-departmental board members have since been appointed: see ch 2, section IV.D.

311 ibid, and see now Ministry of Justice and LCEW, *Framework Document* (2015).

312 *Report of Stage Two*, para 22.

greater clarity was required in terms of each party's role.[313] Improving implementation is therefore not squarely within the scope of triennial reviews. The earlier *Quinquennial Review* can be seen to have had some success—the relationship between the LCEW and government is evidently better than it once was, given the generally positive findings of the *Triennial Review*.

iii. 2004 Protocol

To further encourage the closer cooperation recommended in the *Quinquennial Review*, a protocol was drawn up, which set out how the LCEW and government could work together to achieve a better implementation rate.[314] Despite being hailed as 'a detailed, and thoroughly worthy and appropriate document' by a previous Chairman,[315] the 2004 Protocol was unsuccessful, because government departments did not follow the procedures it established.[316] Under the 2004 Protocol, government departments were required to provide an initial response to LCEW proposals within six months of their publication,[317] and a final decision on implementation 'as soon as is practicable'.[318] These deadlines were, however, routinely ignored. The 2004 Protocol recommended that, before the LCEW embarked on a project, the relevant government department should express its commitment to reforming the law in that area, because there is 'little point' in the LCEW embarking on a project if there is no prospect of its implementation.[319] The Protocol added, however, that this recommendation should not be a complete bar to any project going ahead, because even if implementation is less certain, there might 'nevertheless [be] a case for simplifying or clarifying the law'.[320] This provision should be contrasted with the provisions of a more recent protocol, which will be discussed next. The 2004 Protocol also restated the three criteria for project selection developed in chapter three: availability (and economical use) of resources; suitability of the project; and importance of the project.[321] The 2004 Protocol's main legacy was that it paved the way for a more formal Protocol, made under the Law Commission Act 2009.

iv. Law Commission Act 2009 and the Protocol

The biggest change to the LCEW since 1965 has been made by the Law Commission Act 2009 (the 2009 Act), which amended the 1965 Act. The 2009 Act

313 ibid para 47.
314 LCEW, *The Law Commission and Government—Working Together to Deliver the Benefits of Clear, Simple, Modern Law* (2004) (2004 Protocol).
315 Etherton, 'A Shattered Dream?' 23.
316 ibid.
317 2004 Protocol, para 1.11.
318 ibid.
319 ibid para 1.7.
320 ibid.
321 ibid para 1.6.

demonstrates how too much emphasis, and too narrow a focus, on immediate implementation can be dangerous in threatening the Commissions' independence from government. Such independence is required for the Commissions to fulfil their valuable function of pursuing law reform in neglected areas, consulting widely and proposing independently chosen reforms. The effect of the 2009 Act in reducing this independence demonstrates why it is preferable to adopt the approach to implementation advanced in this chapter.

The 2009 Act can be mainly credited to previous LCEW Chairman, Sir Terence Etherton. In 2007, Etherton campaigned for the Lord Chancellor to be more accountable to Parliament for the LCEW's proposals and for the 2004 Protocol to be put on a more formal footing.[322] He pointed out that although, in theory, the provisions would only give statutory effect to what could already happen, in practice relations were so frosty that statutory duties seemed necessary.[323] In response to increasing concerns about falling implementation rates, therefore, the 2009 Act made two significant changes.

First, the Lord Chancellor must now report annually to Parliament on how she is dealing, or intends to deal, with LCEW proposals, giving reasons for any decisions taken not to implement LCEW reports.[324] The fact that the original text of the 1965 Act did not require the government to give a response to Commission recommendations has been criticised as a 'gap' in the Act.[325] The 2009 Act attempts to fill that gap in relation to LCEW proposals. Once rejected, LCEW proposals need not be referred to in future Lord Chancellor's reports.[326] Blom-Cooper correctly criticised the fact that rejected proposals need not be reconsidered, saying that '[r]eminders of unpaid bills are the order of all creditors'.[327] Rejected projects may later become suitable for implementation and so should be reconsidered periodically (unless superseded by subsequent reform or proposals). Such reconsideration would remove the expectation of immediate implementation.

Section 3A(6) of the 1965 Act (as inserted by the 2009 Act) requires the Lord Chancellor to report only on the LCEW's programme work under section 3(1)(c) of the 1965 Act and consolidation and repeals work under section 3(1)(d). In other words, items referred to the LCEW by government need not be reported on, although in practice they are.[328] As we saw in chapter three, the implementation rate for references is not substantially greater than the projects the LCEW itself chooses and all projects should therefore be subject officially to the reporting duty.

[322] Etherton, 'A Shattered Dream?' 28.

[323] ibid 29.

[324] 2009 Act, s 1, which inserted s 3A into the 1965 Act.

[325] N Brotchie, 'The Scottish Law Commission: Promoting Law Reform in Scotland' (2009) 9 *Legal Information Management* 30, 31.

[326] 1965 Act, s 3A(4).

[327] L Blom-Cooper, 'Reform? Reform? Aren't Things Bad Enough Already?' [2010] *PL* 441, 441.

[328] 1965 Act, s 3(1)(e). There is also no mention of references from other parties under the 1965 Act, s 3(1)(a), although as we have seen such proposals are nowadays incorporated into programmes.

The idea that the Lord Chancellor should make public the government's thinking on LCEW proposals is to be welcomed.[329] North, a previous LCEW Commissioner, had opined that the inability to assess the reasons for rejection of law reform proposals would be likely to 'agitate' both law reformers and the public alike.[330] By forcing the Lord Chancellor to give reasons for the rejection of Commission proposals, her decision-making is transparent and it should ensure that Commission proposals do not 'gather dust' without at least being considered.[331] So far the reports have appeared fairly regularly since the first report in 2011, although the report for January 2015–January 2016 was not published until January 2017.

Etherton's successor as Chairman of the LCEW, Sir James Munby, was originally optimistic about the changes the 2009 Act would make, heralding it a 'landmark' in bringing the LCEW and the government closer together.[332] The following year, he was, despite the 2009 Act 'generally extremely concerned' about implementation,[333] and some months later, he had the opportunity to voice his full fears.[334] The Lord Chancellor's first report was published in January 2011,[335] and was described by Munby as 'disappointing'.[336] In many instances, a full reply indicating the government's response to the LCEW's proposed reform was merely deferred and, in certain cases, the LCEW still awaited a decision almost a year later.[337] In other cases, vague statements such as '[l]egislation is to be introduced when Parliamentary time permits' were used.[338] Where proposals were rejected, the explanations were typically short and simply stated that the topic was not a government priority.[339] Later Lord Chancellor's reports follow much the same pattern.[340]

Second, under the terms of the 2009 Act, the Lord Chancellor and the LCEW were obliged to prepare jointly a Protocol which would detail how they could work together in their shared interest of law reform to ensure 'a more productive relationship, with improved rates of implementation'.[341] The Protocol was published

[329] On the New Zealand equivalent, see G Hammond, 'The Legislative Implementation of Law Reform Proposals' in Dyson, Lee and Stark, *Fifty Years of the Law Commissions*, 182–83.

[330] P North, 'Law Reform: Processes and Problems' (1985) 101 *LQR* 338, 353.

[331] S Cretney, 'The Politics of Law Reform—A View from the Inside' (1985) 48 *MLR* 493, 498.

[332] LCEW, *Annual Report 2009–10* (Law Com No 323 (2010)) Chairman's introduction.

[333] LCEW, *Annual Report 2010–11* (Law Com No 328 (2011)) Chairman's introduction.

[334] J Munby, 'Shaping the Law—The Law Commission at the Crossroads' (Denning Lecture, 2011) ('Shaping the Law').

[335] Ministry of Justice, *Report on the Implementation of Law Commission Proposals* (2011, HC 719) (Lord Chancellor's Report).

[336] Munby, 'Shaping the Law' 7.

[337] ibid.

[338] Lord Chancellor's Report, para 33.

[339] ibid paras 50 and 56.

[340] Ministry of Justice, *Report on the Implementation of Law Commission Proposals* (2012, HC 1900); (2013, HC 908); (2014, HC 1237); (2015, HC 1062); and (2017, HC 613).

[341] 2009 Act, s 2, which inserted s 3B into the 1965 Act; LCEW and Ministry of Justice, *Protocol between the Lord Chancellor (on behalf of the Government) and the Law Commission* (Law Com No 321 (2010)) (the Protocol) introduction.

in 2010, and must be revised from time to time, although no revisions have yet been made.[342] The LCEW views the Protocol as a 'wholly positive' step.[343] Former LCEW Commissioner Elizabeth Cooke has guessed that of the various law reform agencies worldwide, the ones which have more free rein in terms of project selection are the ones most in danger of abolition. She has suggested that the development of the Protocol was essential to the LCEW's survival, a view shared by Lady Hale.[344] Former Northern Ireland Law Commissioner Neil Faris has similarly queried whether the Protocol was a case of 'surrender or be abolished'.[345] While he sees some sensible elements in the Protocol, he has expressed concern at the potential chilling effect of the Protocol in putting further power into the hands of senior civil servants and for that reason he would have 'resisted the imposition of any such Protocol' on the Northern Ireland Law Commission.

The Protocol is worrying for a number of reasons. The main reason is the effect it has on the selection of new projects. Cooke argues that the LCEW has not sacrificed its independence by virtue of the Protocol. She notes that the LCEW never enjoyed complete independence in the selection of projects anyway due to the requirement that the Lord Chancellor must approve programme projects,[346] but that the Protocol 'certainly … changes things'.[347] In the past, Commissioners have spoken of 'calling the shots' in relation to the projects selected for LCEW programmes.[348] Former LCEW Commissioner, Andrew Burrows, has remarked that although projects may have been 'fine-tuned' between the Chairman, the Secretary (now Chief Executive) and the relevant department, ministerial approval tended to be 'a mere formality'. Indeed, he recalls that when applying to be Commissioner, he was specifically asked about which new projects he would want to embark on, which he was then able to undertake. Now, by contrast, the government (the Minister in the relevant area with the support of the relevant Permanent Secretary) must express its 'serious intention' to reform the law in an area before the LCEW can start work.[349] The LCEW has stated that ministerial approval is 'ultimately'

342 1965 Act, s 3B(3).

343 I am grateful to former LCEW Commissioner Elizabeth Cooke for discussing her views on the Protocol with me in March 2015 while she was still a Commissioner. The comment above reflects her opinion on the general attitude within the LCEW at that time. What follows hereafter are her personal views as stated during the same discussion.

344 B Hale, 'Fifty Years of the Law Commissions: The Dynamics of Law Reform Now, Then and Next' in Dyson, Lee and Stark, *Fifty Years of the Law Commissions*, 23 ('The Dynamics of Law Reform').

345 I am grateful to Neil Faris for supplying me with a note of his comments on the Protocol in January 2015.

346 1965 Act, s 3(1)(b). See also D Lloyd Jones, 'The Law Commission and the Implementation of Law Reform' (2013) 15 *European Journal of Law Reform* 333, 343.

347 E Cooke and HL MacQueen, 'Law Reform in a Political Environment: The Work of the Law Commissions' in D Feldman (ed), *Law in Politics, Politics in Law* (Oxford, Hart Publishing, 2013) 143 ('Law Reform in a Political Environment').

348 I am grateful to former LCEW Commissioners, certain of whom wish to remain anonymous, for their comments on pre-Protocol project selection. The comments, which follow in this section, result from discussions I had with those Commissioners between January and March 2015. The immediate quotation is from a previous Commissioner who wished to remain anonymous.

349 Protocol, para 6(2).

required before a project can be undertaken.[350] If a Minister/Permanent Secretary refuses to give a 'serious intention' to take forward law reform in that area, Cooke has observed that the LCEW would be 'unwise and irresponsible' to proceed with the project anyway. Elsewhere, Cooke has argued that the LCEW '*cannot* take on a project in which the relevant department is not able to express a commitment to reform'.[351] Further, Cooke has questioned why the government should pay for a Commission project in which it is not interested and which it knows it will not implement. The Protocol ultimately has resulted in a 'very different relationship' between the LCEW and government.[352] The terms of the Protocol should be compared with the 2004 Protocol, discussed earlier, where a lack of governmental commitment was not to stand in the way of otherwise worthy projects going ahead. This begs the question—is the current Protocol preventing the LCEW from examining worthy projects?

In its *Eleventh Programme of Law Reform*,[353] the first to be compiled post-Protocol, the LCEW chose to list the projects which it considered but which ultimately did not feature in the programme. Such listing is not new—a similar list, for example, was provided in the *Tenth Programme*.[354] A comparison of the *Tenth* and *Eleventh* programmes, however, reveals significant differences. The *Tenth Programme* lists six projects which were not taken forward, all of which were rejected 'in part simply [as] a result of the relative suitability and importance of competing projects' and in part because of the LCEW's own concerns about each project, for example, that the project was too political, or that its consideration would be premature.[355] Discussion of governmental views is limited and, where such views are mentioned, the LCEW makes it clear that it was ultimately the LCEW's decision not to embark on a particular project.[356] By contrast, the *Eleventh Programme* lists 18 projects which were not taken forward.[357] Of those 18 projects, ten projects across a range of areas of law were not taken forward because of a lack of governmental support, as opposed to being based on the LCEW's own choice.[358] For example, a project on the simplification of sentencing law was not included in the *Eleventh Programme* because the Lord Chancellor 'would not support' the project 'at this time';[359] a project on the age of criminal responsibility was not included because the Ministry of Justice did 'not support' the project;[360] and a

[350] I am grateful to Catherine Vine of the LCEW for providing me with this information in March 2015.

[351] Cooke and MacQueen, 'Law Reform in a Political Environment' 143, emphasis in original.

[352] Hale, 'The Dynamics of Law Reform' 23.

[353] LCEW, *Eleventh Programme of Law Reform* (Law Com No 330 (2011)).

[354] LCEW, *Tenth Programme of Law Reform* (Law Com No 311 (2008)) part 5.

[355] ibid part 5 generally, and paras 5.3 and 5.6 specifically.

[356] See, eg, ibid paras 5.7 and 5.9.

[357] *Eleventh Programme*, paras 3.12–3.85.

[358] ibid.

[359] ibid para 3.21. The project was subsequently included in LCEW, *Twelfth Programme of Law Reform* (Law Com No 354 (2014)) paras 2.27–2.29.

[360] *Eleventh Programme*, para 3.28.

project on mortgage law was not included because of a lack of 'sufficient Government support'.[361] Cooke has opined that many 'good' suggestions for the *Eleventh Programme* 'fell at the first fence because they were not ones in which a department had an interest'.[362] The LCEW had, before the 2009 Act, been refused permission to examine certain areas of law.[363] Such refusal is, however, now more frequent and occurs after the LCEW has undoubtedly already deselected projects which it suspected were unlikely to be given governmental approval.

The *Twelfth Programme* provides another interesting contrast with earlier programmes.[364] In that programme, only five rejected projects are discussed,[365] only one of which was rejected because of a lack of ministerial support—and even then, because no decision had been reached timeously, not because of an outright veto.[366] The *Twelfth Programme* may indicate that project negotiations are becoming easier as the LCEW and government adjust to the new Protocol. The concern (the truth of which cannot be ascertained) is whether the LCEW no longer suggests certain appropriate projects for fear that they will not be approved by government.

On the other hand, Cooke argues that the Protocol prevents the 'kicking into the long grass' approach where the government refers a project to the LCEW simply to be seen to do something about an issue, but with no commitment to actually taking it forward.[367] Proper use, however, of the project-selection criteria developed in chapter three should remove any possibility of undeserving projects being undertaken, either at a Commissioner or a Minister's request.

At first sight, the Protocol appears to benefit the LCEW in improving implementation rates—one of the Protocol's explicit aims.[368] The LCEW's view is that the Protocol 'provides … a helpful template to structure our case for reform and a useful basis for further discussion with Government'.[369] Cooke observes that, because the LCEW has finite resources, the Protocol provides a useful 'filter' so that only those projects with a genuine possibility of implementation are embarked on. By moving implementation considerations to the start of a project, the aim is to

[361] ibid para 3.82.

[362] Cooke and MacQueen, 'Law Reform in a Political Environment' 143.

[363] See S Cretney, 'The Law Commission: True Dawns and False Dawns' (1996) 59 *MLR* 631, 650, fn 131; S Cretney, 'The Politics of Law Reform—A View from the Inside' (1985) 48 *MLR* 493, 497, fn 18; S Cretney, 'The Programmes: Milestones or Millstones?' in G Zellick (ed), *The Law Commission and Law Reform* (London, Sweet & Maxwell, 1988) 4; and ch 3, section V.A.ii. No record of the SLC ever being so denied has been found.

[364] LCEW, *Twelfth Programme* (Law Com No 354 (2014)).

[365] ibid part 3.

[366] A project on 'criminal law in the digital age': ibid paras 3.6–3.9. See also, however, the Lord Chancellor's veto of a project on environmental law in Wales: para 1.13.

[367] See too J Beatson, 'Challenges for Independent Law Reformers from Changing External Priorities and Shorter Timescales' in Dyson, Lee and Stark, *Fifty Years of the Law Commissions*, 256 ('Challenges for Independent Law Reformers').

[368] Protocol, introduction.

[369] I am grateful to Catherine Vine for this information.

remove the 'frustration' caused at the end of a project when government does not implement—or does not even consider—a report.

Implementation can never be guaranteed, and the Protocol does not attempt to provide such a guarantee. Commission projects are (necessarily) lengthy endeavours. A government may no longer have the same priorities or personnel or even be comprised of the same political party (or parties) at the end of a project. In addition, because the law continues to develop through other means such as case law and non-Commission legislation, the need for Commission intervention could be negated during the life of a project. Alternatively, the Commission might present a proposal which government simply does not like. As Cooke stresses, the LCEW still retains ultimate independence in the substantive reforms which it proposes.

There is a risk that a Minister or a Permanent Secretary might be reluctant to confirm a serious intention to take forward law reform in an area, despite seeing the benefits of the project, if he or she thinks that there is any possibility of non-implementation, for example, because of a topic not being headline worthy, or because of a fear that the eventual recommendations will not be liked. Cooke has argued that 'it is very hard to imagine' certain types of project being viable post-Protocol, including particularly large projects.[370] Even if it has not yet been the case that a project has been unfairly vetoed, it is certainly possible that one may be so vetoed in the future. A particularly risk-averse Minister or Permanent Secretary may be overcautious—independent law reform always entails a risk of non-implementation. As we saw in chapter three, many Commission projects concern topics that the government has little interest in reforming itself. It is possible that such lack of interest could influence ministerial decisions to allow or veto Commission projects. We also know of the severe difficulty in finding parliamentary time for Commission proposals. It is possible that such difficulty could lead to a Minister not being willing to give his or her 'serious intention' to implement an otherwise deserving project. Previous Commissioner Sir Stephen Silber has commented that no Minister or Permanent Secretary will be keen to express any intention to take forward law reform in a particular area before a project is finished because of 'various unknowns'. Because of the very nature of politics, civil servants and ministers are likely to be more cautious than law reformers who should, by nature, be less willing to accept the status quo. The Protocol may therefore result in a project which fulfils the project-selection criteria being vetoed by government without good reason. The Commissions are not (and should not be) able to select projects without ministerial approval. As well as such approval being required by the terms of the 1965 Act,[371] the Commissions must use their public funding wisely and would be foolhardy to embark on a project of which government disapproves. But ministerial support should be guided by the project-selection criteria, not solely by the prospects of implementation. The project-selection criteria were

[370] Cooke and MacQueen, 'Law Reform in a Political Environment' 144.
[371] 1965 Act, s 3(1)(b).

developed because of a concern over falling implementation rates. They risk being undermined by the Protocol.

As we have already seen, implementation should not only be viewed in terms of primary legislation, and the Commissions' work may have uses beyond legislative implementation, such as judicial implementation, or academic or parliamentary debate. Those other uses cannot be known before the project is undertaken. As Cooke has stated, '[l]aw reform is a bigger process than the enactment of statutes; statutory implementation is often the best way forward, but if that fails the work is not wasted'.[372] A Minister (or Permanent Secretary) having no immediate commitment to an issue should not be an automatic bar to a project going ahead, provided it satisfies the project-selection criteria.

Beyond project selection, the Protocol also attempts to ensure cooperation throughout a project. Cooperation between the LCEW and government may seem like a positive step because of previous difficult relations. The terms of the Protocol, however, may again compromise too much of the LCEW's independence. For example, the Protocol requires meetings between the LCEW and government 'at least every quarter while the project is live'.[373] Although there is no direct evidence of governmental hijacking of a Commission project, such regular meetings risk too much governmental involvement in what should be independent law reform, and could exhaust the LCEW's finite time. As one former Commissioner (who wished to remain anonymous) put it: 'there is a difference between going with the grain and the government getting too involved'. Furthermore, the Protocol requires 'review points' during the currency of a project and, although the Minister 'may not require the Commission to stop working on an ongoing project' the LCEW must 'take full account of the Minister's views' in deciding whether to continue a project.[374] Although no projects appear to have been abandoned due to such review points as yet, the Protocol puts too much power into the hands of the Minister. The LCEW cannot be compelled to cease work on a project, but it is possible that it would give great weight to the Minister's views—and worryingly, such views can be based on a project's 'prospects for implementation'.[375] More promising recognition of the parties' respective roles can be found in the 2015 *Framework Document* which states that, although the Ministry of Justice 'monitors the Law Commission's activities' it 'has no involvement in the exercise of the Commissioners' judgment in relation to the exercise of their functions'.[376]

The Protocol also requires government departments to give responses to completed LCEW projects speedily, to address the problem noted above that, in the past, Commission proposals were frequently not examined at all. Government departments are now therefore required to respond to the LCEW with an 'interim response' within

[372] Cooke and MacQueen, 'Law Reform in a Political Environment' 153.
[373] Protocol, para 11.
[374] ibid para 15.
[375] ibid.
[376] Ministry of Justice and LCEW, *Framework Document* (2015) para 3.15.

six months of publication of an LCEW report, and a 'full response' within one year of publication.[377] The government does not always, however, fulfil its duty under the Protocol to respond to the LCEW. After the first six months of the Protocol's operation, none of the reports due an interim response received one within the time limit.[378]

Even though the LCEW itself does not feel constrained by the Protocol (or at least claims not to), outsiders (such as lawyers, parliamentarians or the general public) may feel aggrieved if the LCEW's remit is increasingly restricted. The LCEW is, after all, a publicly funded body, with a remit to keep 'all the law' under review.[379] Additionally, because Commissioners are only appointed for five-yearly terms, they may have no experience of how the LCEW operated pre-Protocol and may not realise that they are more constrained (more so than is necessary) than their predecessors. A critical analysis of the Commissions' history and role, such as the one provided in this book, is required in order to observe whether the LCEW is, objectively speaking, now being unduly constrained by the Protocol.

In addition, the Commissions themselves are often their own harshest critics when it comes to implementation rates.[380] Speedy implementation of projects is of great importance to the Commissions because of the turnover of Commissioners and staff. It is preferable, from the Commissions' perspective, for a project to be picked up by government while the expertise still exists at the Commission to offer a helpful after-sales service. Once a length of time passes, such expertise may no longer be readily available and therefore the report may struggle without its Commission pilot, unless he or she is willing to continue to assist.[381] Such pragmatic concerns are obviously important to the Commissions, and having a project picked up by government quickly may well increase its chance of implementation, especially if it otherwise becomes outdated. As outsiders, however, we can (and should) view the Commissions more objectively, and as continuing entities, separate from their individual Commissioners and staff. Just because a project is not picked up quickly, it does not necessarily follow that that project is a failure.

During its process through Parliament, the 2009 Act was described as being not the 'gem' that Etherton envisaged, but rather mere 'costume jewellery' that would serve no real purpose.[382] The effect of the Protocol, however, is more insidious than this. Sir James Munby pointed out that the Protocol 'raises wider issues … that go to the soul of the Law Commission', the main issue being independence from government.[383] From the beginning, Gardiner emphasised that the Commissions should enjoy 'a high degree of independence'.[384] It has been noted that if the structure of the Commissions had been different and if they had been part of

[377] Protocol, paras 18–19. On the 2004 Protocol, see section IV.B.iii above.

[378] Munby, 'Shaping the Law' 8.

[379] 1965 Act, s 3(1).

[380] See above n 13.

[381] See, eg, Beatson, 'Challenges for Independent Law Reformers' 250.

[382] HC Deb vol 497 col 583 (16 October 2009) (Christopher Chope).

[383] Munby, 'Shaping the Law' 17.

[384] G Gardiner and A Martin, 'The Machinery of Law Reform' in G Gardiner and A Martin (eds), *Law Reform Now* (London, Victor Gollancz, 1963) 9. It must be acknowledged, however, that the

government, 'there would no doubt have been closer co-operation with ministers and administrators' which might have led to 'an easier route for the reforms which they proposed onto the statute book'.[385] Gardiner, however, chose to make the Commissions 'quite deliberately more detached'.[386] The 2009 Act jeopardises this detachment by forcing the LCEW to only examine things which please the government and, even more worryingly, by refusing it permission to examine things which the government does not wish to be examined.

The Commissions should not be allowed to waste public money on entirely futile projects. Indeed, the LCEW itself has observed that it is 'always mindful of the need to spend public money effectively'.[387] As Cooke adds, the Commissions are not academic institutions, but publicly funded bodies. But the project-selection criteria have been designed to guide the Commissions to the most deserving projects. The Commissions should be able to choose projects which have merit and which, importantly, the government could not, or would not, examine itself—the highly suitable but technical projects that may very well be a good use of public money, even if the government does not see them as a priority. Mere implementation alone is not necessarily an indication of public money being well spent because it takes no account of the quality of the reforms proposed, or of the need for studying a particular project in the first place. There is little public good in an implemented but unimportant or flawed Commission project.

The Commissions' independence is not an end in itself. The Commissions can examine areas of law that are unfair, unclear, inefficient, unduly complex or outdated and that no other body plans to consider. As Cooke put it, 'Our independence is not for our own benefit ... it is so we can be of benefit as a public service'. Cooke has admitted that the Protocol 'carries obvious risks for independent law reform'.[388] Although it is desirable that there is a dialogue between the Commissions and government, that dialogue should be restricted to cooperation and not a power of veto over unpopular projects. Using immediate implementation as, in effect, the only desirable outcome of a Commission project will lead to very many valuable projects not being given the go-ahead, whether that is because they are too technical or too controversial. Both types of project might struggle, for different reasons, in their likelihood of implementation—the former because they are unlikely to sparkle enough to attract attention, and the latter because they might prove too contentious. A prediction of likely implementation at a project's outset is not even conclusive because no government can ever guarantee that implementation will definitely occur in the years between the selection of the

independence enjoyed by the Commissions is less than Gardiner envisaged and 'should not [be] overestimate[d]': H Beale, 'The Law Commission and Judicial Law Reform' (2001) 35 *The Law Teacher* 323, 330.

[385] D Hope, 'Do We Still Need a Scottish Law Commission?' (2006) 10 *Edinburgh Law Review* 10, 19.
[386] ibid.
[387] I am grateful to Catherine Vine for this information.
[388] Cooke and MacQueen, 'Law Reform in a Political Environment' 144.

project and the eventual report. The Protocol should therefore be amended so as to remove the need for a serious intention to take forward law reform in that area to be expressed, and to restrict government's involvement throughout the course of a project.

C. Attempts Affecting the SLC

The 2009 Act has changed the LCEW so dramatically that the LCEW and the SLC are much more different now than they have ever been. Different measures have been taken to address falling SLC implementation rates, which reflect the different relationship the SLC has with government.

i. Scottish Ministers' Undertaking

The SLC's relationship with Scottish Ministers benefits from being less formal, and less fraught, than the LCEW's relationship with the Lord Chancellor. It was observed from the Commissions' outset that, because of the smaller size of the jurisdiction, bodies 'are all nearer and friendlier to each other in Scotland'.[389] The SLC did raise for consideration whether similar legislation to the 2009 Act should be introduced in Scotland. In 2009, the Scottish Government was invited to consider whether to have corresponding legislation by the then Subordinate Legislation Committee of the Scottish Parliament.[390] The then Cabinet Secretary for Justice, Kenny MacAskill, did not favour this approach, and instead put in place a non-statutory undertaking. Instead of the 2009 Act, therefore, the SLC benefits from an agreement, also introduced in 2009, whereby Scottish Ministers are expected to respond to SLC proposals within three months of their publication.[391] The undertaking initially appeared to be working well, with the SLC being satisfied that Scottish Ministers had 'put into practice their agreement' by diligently responding to SLC proposals within the agreed time frame.[392] More recently, however, the current Chairman of the SLC, Lord Pentland, has expressed concern that the system is 'not working adequately' because the three-month time period is 'too short to allow for a properly considered response to be provided'.[393] A period of six months, as Lord Pentland has suggested, would be more appropriate.

The Lord Chancellor has also undertaken to write to the Chairman of the SLC each year to report on the implementation of SLC reports on reserved matters.[394]

389 W Murrie to RH Law (Scottish Office), 27 November 1964, NRS HH41/2048.

390 Subordinate Legislation Committee of the Scottish Parliament, 51st Report, 2009 (SL/S3/09/R51) para 308. As noted below, this committee is now the Delegated Powers and Law Reform Committee.

391 Scottish Parliament Official Report, Written Answer, 12 February 2010 (S3W-31752) (Kenny MacAskill).

392 SLC, *Annual Report 2010* (Scot Law Com No 223 (2011)) Chairman's foreword.

393 Lord Pentland, 'The Scottish Law Commission and the Future of Law Reform in Scotland' 2016 *Juridical Review* 169, 175 ('The Future of Law Reform').

394 SLC internal memo, 'Implementation of Scottish Law Commission Recommendations: Update' (February 2012), SLC file, para 6.

This undertaking should more sensibly be carried out by the Secretary of State for Scotland, as the person who receives SLC reports on reserved matters.[395] Furthermore, both Ministers currently discharge their duties by writing directly to the SLC. Although the letters are published on the SLC's website,[396] the Ministers' duties would be more openly and publicly discharged if their reports were, like the Lord Chancellor's reports on the LCEW, made annually to their respective parliaments. Lord Pentland has suggested that reports should be made to Parliament whenever the government rejects an SLC proposal,[397] but in fact a separate report would not be needed if the changes recommended here were made. In addition, setting out these requirements of both the Scottish Ministers and the Secretary of State for Scotland in statutory form could reduce the risk of any future disappointment of responses not being received, although, as has been demonstrated by the 2009 Act, nothing can absolutely guarantee cooperation. Recent suggestions that the SLC would benefit from a more 'concrete assurance of government support' of its proposals at an earlier stage sounds too much like the LCEW's Protocol, and should be resisted, with the substitution of the suggestions made here.[398]

No equivalent to the Protocol exists in Scotland, although the SLC does endeavour to follow the Scottish Government's National Outcomes.[399] These National Outcomes were introduced in 2007 to encapsulate the Scottish Government's aims for the next ten years to 'make Scotland a better place to live and a more prosperous and successful country'.[400] Under the Public Services Reform (Scotland) Act 2010, the SLC is, as a public body, obliged to state annually what it has done to 'promote and increase sustainable growth ... [and] improve efficiency, effectiveness and economy in the exercise of its functions', as well as to provide financial information.[401] Since 2012, the SLC has used these annual statements as an opportunity to demonstrate how each of its projects contributes to the National Outcomes,[402] in the hope, perhaps, of improving a project's chance of implementation. The SLC is not, however, obliged to take the National Outcomes into account when selecting projects, nor do Scottish Ministers need to express any 'serious intention' to implement SLC projects at their outset. Therefore, the SLC benefits from similar advantages to the 2009 Act without having to suffer the drawbacks. The SLC faces

[395] See above n 173.

[396] And the Lord Chancellor's response is placed in the libraries of the House of Commons and the House of Lords.

[397] Pentland, 'The Future of Law Reform' 175.

[398] ibid 173.

[399] Such as making Scotland a more attractive place to do business; reducing crime in Scotland; reducing inequality; and reducing environmental damage. For information on all 16 Scottish Government National Outcomes, see Scottish Government website, 'National Outcomes' www.gov.scot/About/Performance/scotPerforms/outcome.

[400] ibid.

[401] Public Services Reform (Scotland) Act 2010, s 32 and see also ss 31, 33–35 and sch 8.

[402] See SLC, *Public Services Reform (Scotland) Act 2010: Statement for 2011–12* (2012); *Statement for 2012–13* (2013); *Statement for 2013–14* (2014); *Statement for 2014–15* (2015); and *Statement for 2015–16* (2016).

bigger challenges than the LCEW in certain ways by virtue of its smaller size. It does, however, benefit from friendlier relations with Parliament and government than the LCEW enjoys. Implementation rates are slightly better,[403] and the SLC retains more freedom than the LCEW because of these closer relations, with the result that there is no need for an exact equivalent of the 2009 Act or Protocol.

ii. New Parliamentary Procedure

In 2009, after the SLC expressed increasing concern at the then apparent slowing implementation rate of its reports (particularly its more technical recommendations),[404] a working group was set up to determine how this concern could be addressed. The Law Reform Working Group comprised officials from the Scottish Parliament, Scottish Government and the Office of Scottish Parliamentary Counsel, with input from the SLC. It recommended that non-controversial SLC Bills could be referred to the Subordinate Legislation Committee (now the Delegated Powers and Law Reform Committee) to ensure that such Bills find time in Holyrood's busy schedule.[405] Essentially the recommendation was for a particular procedure for non-controversial SLC Bills, similar to the House of Lords procedure described above,[406] but adapted for a unicameral Parliament. The Working Group recommended a test run of the procedure. In July 2010, the Scottish Government consulted on a draft Penalty Clauses (Scotland) Bill based closely on an SLC report.[407] This Bill would have piloted the new procedure, but it was withdrawn after it proved not to be as uncontroversial as is required for the procedure. The proposals did not have unanimous support, although there were no criticisms of the pilot procedure itself.[408] Despite the lack of criticism of the procedure itself, after the 2011 election, a further working group was set up to reconsider the parliamentary procedure. The SLC fully supported the attempts being made to improve implementation rates,[409] although the delay must have been somewhat frustrating given that the second Law Reform Working Group reported with much the same conclusions as its predecessor in July 2012.[410] The experience provides further evidence, alongside the Jellicoe Committee experience, of the need to tread carefully with new parliamentary procedures.

[403] See section I.A.

[404] SLC, *Annual Report 2008* (Scot Law Com No 214 (2009)) Chairman's foreword.

[405] Scottish Parliamentary Bureau, 'Parliamentary Scrutiny of Bills Arising from Scottish Law Commission Reports' (PB/S3/10/60, March 2010) para 5.

[406] Section IV.A.iv.

[407] SLC, *Report on Penalty Clauses* (Scot Law Com No 171 (1999)).

[408] The SLC is currently reconsidering the same issues as part of a large project on contract law generally: SLC website, 'Contract Law in Light of the Draft Common Frame of Reference (DCFR)' www.scotlawcom.gov.uk/law-reform/law-reform-projects/contract-law-light-draft-common-frame-reference-dcf/.

[409] SLC internal memo, 'Implementation of Scottish Law Commission Recommendations: Update' (February 2012), SLC file, para 22.

[410] Law Reform Working Group, *Final Report* (2012).

Eventually, in May 2013, the Standards, Procedures and Public Appointments Committee of the Scottish Parliament decided to allow certain SLC Bills to be referred to the Delegated Powers and Law Reform Committee for Stage One scrutiny. The introduction of the new procedure prompted the Committee's name change from the Subordinate Legislation Committee. Such structural changes reflect the Scottish Government and Parliament's commitment to the new procedure. The Bills which qualify for the procedure are Bills where 'the need for reform is widely agreed but no major or contentious political or financial issues arise', which is expected to be only a 'minority' of SLC Bills.[411] We saw earlier that the House of Lords procedure was used to pass the Partnerships (Prosecution) (Scotland) Act 2013, which deals with the criminal liability of dissolved partnerships and previous partners of dissolved or extant partnerships. In contrast, SLC proposals that 'relate directly to criminal law reform' will not qualify for the new Scottish Parliament procedure.[412] The exclusion of criminal matters from the Holyrood procedure was partly motivated by the need not to effectively create a second Justice Committee,[413] as well as by the typically 'sensitive' nature of such reforms.[414] The criteria for establishing which SLC Bills are suitable for the new procedure could possibly be adjusted in future,[415] although such adjustment has been seen as premature for now.[416] Unless or until such adjustment is made, the selection of a new criminal project has not been rendered impossible, but such projects may not be as attractive given that the SLC now considers whether a project would be appropriate for the new procedure as part of its 'suitability' project-selection criterion.[417]

The plan is for the procedure to generally be used for one SLC Bill per year.[418] It has already been used to pass two Acts: the Legal Writings (Counterparts and Delivery) (Scotland) Act 2015;[419] and the Succession (Scotland) Act 2016.[420]

[411] Scottish Parliament Official Report, 28 May 2013, cols 20374 (Dave Thompson) and 20378 (Nigel Don).

[412] Scottish Parliament Official Report, 28 May 2013, col 20377 (Nigel Don); Scottish Parliament Business Bulletin (93/2013) 1.

[413] Scottish Parliament Official Report, 28 May 2013, col 20375 (Dave Thompson); M McMillan, 'Implementation of Law Reform Reports: Developments in Scotland' in Dyson, Lee and Stark, *Fifty Years of the Law Commissions*, 374 ('Implementation of Law Reform Reports').

[414] McMillan, 'Implementation of Law Reform Reports' 375.

[415] Such adjustment could be made relatively easily since the criteria are not found in a Standing Order but in a determination of the Presiding Officer: see McMillan, 'Implementation of Law Reform Reports' 376–77.

[416] Standards, Procedures and Public Appointments Committee of the Scottish Parliament, 'Scottish Law Commission Bill Procedures—Review, Note of Outcome of Review' (2015) para 33.

[417] See ch 3, section IV.C. The current lack of a Commissioner with criminal expertise also makes criminal law reform difficult: J Chalmers, F Leverick and SW Stark, 'The Process of Criminal Evidence Law Reform in Scotland: What Can We Learn?' in P Duff and P Ferguson (eds), *Current Developments in Scottish Criminal Evidence Law* (Edinburgh, EUP, forthcoming 2017).

[418] Standards, Procedures and Public Appointments Committee of the Scottish Parliament, 'Scottish Law Commission Bill Procedures—Review, Note of Outcome of Review' (2015) para 17.

[419] Which implemented SLC, *Review of Contract Law—Report on Formation of Contract: Execution in Counterpart* (Scot Law Com No 231 (2013)).

[420] Which partially implemented SLC, *Report on Succession* (Scot Law Com No 215 (2009)).

The procedure was to be reviewed after two Bills or two years, whichever came first.[421] The review, by the Scottish Parliament's Standards, Procedures and Public Appointments Committee, took place two years after the procedure came into effect and was completed in December 2015.[422] It concluded that the procedure had so far 'worked well' and did not propose any changes.[423] The third Bill to use the procedure looks set to be a Bill based on the SLC's *Review of Contract Law—Report on Third Party Rights*.[424] The procedure is off to an impressive start, but the SLC must be mindful not to neglect its more controversial projects.

V. Conclusion: Quality Over Quantity

Implementation can be regarded as *one* useful measure of the Commissions' success. Equating implementation with success, however, risks the Commissions' independence by making certain projects that are more of a gamble in the implementation stakes less likely to be undertaken, despite the fact that the law in that area is unfair, unclear, inefficient, unduly complex or outdated. It also endangers the substantive recommendations made by the Commissions in the projects they do undertake. As North argued, the Commissions should not make proposals for reform that are known not to be able to be implemented.[425] Proposals for reform should, however, be based on extensive independent consultation, not necessarily what government wants to hear. The LCEW has already compromised some of its independence for implementation. It is unrealistic, however, to suggest that implementation is irrelevant—the Commissions could be abolished if implementation rates plummeted, depriving the British legal systems of independent law reform in areas neglected by government. In any event, there are other reasons why implementation must remain at a certain level—consultees might stop engaging with purely academic commissions, their reports might lose esteem, and the Commissions are publicly funded law reform bodies, not academic institutions. The trend for dropping implementation rates had to therefore be curtailed and certain measures, such as the new House of Lords and Scottish Parliament procedures, contribute well to achieving that aim.

[421] Scottish Parliament Official Report, 28 May 2013, col 20375 (Dave Thompson).

[422] Standards, Procedures and Public Appointments Committee of the Scottish Parliament, 'Scottish Law Commission Bill Procedures—Review, Note of Outcome of Review' (2015).

[423] ibid paras 31–33.

[424] SLC, *Review of Contract Law—Report on Third Party Rights* (Scot Law Com No 245 (2016)); A Ewing MSP (Minister for Community Safety and Legal Affairs) to Lord Pentland, 'Review of Contract Law: Report on Third Party Rights' (29 September 2016) www.scotlawcom.gov.uk/news/contract-third-party-rights-bill/.

[425] eg, SLC, *Discussion Paper on Moveable Transactions* (Scot Law Com DP No 151 (2011)) is highly critical of the floating charge, but does not recommend its abolition because, inter alia, '[a]s a practical matter, that seems not to be a real policy option, at least at the present time' (para 22.26).

A broad definition of implementation should be employed. That definition should explicitly take into account Commission proposals which have been partially implemented or implemented by non-orthodox means, such as by the courts. Reports should not be included in implementation rates until two years have passed from the date of publication. Calculating implementation rates in the way advanced in this chapter more accurately reflects the Commissions' contribution to law reform—the current figures do not reflect the Commissions' true contribution. As well as satisfying the government's need to feel like the Commissions are providing value for money, more accurate implementation figures would also allow the Commissions to feel more satisfied with their achievements. The Commissions frequently feel demoralised when their recommendations are not implemented and, even if others are satisfied with their performance,[426] the Commissions too must feel content with the work that they are doing. Even if the implementation 'problem ... lie[s] largely or wholly in the eye of the beholder ... that does not mean that it is illusory'.[427]

The government's role in LCEW project selection and involvement during the life of a project under the Protocol should be softened. On the other hand, requirements for government to make open and published decisions about Commission proposals should be strengthened. The government should continue to have an obligation at least to consider Commission proposals. If the government decides that a proposal should not be implemented (which it must be able to do, as a democratic entity), it should give reasons. Furthermore, decisions taken not to implement Commission proposals should be revisited annually (unless superseded by subsequent proposals or reform) in case the situation changes sufficiently to make the proposal more appealing. By reassessing Commission proposals, the notion of scoring quick implementation points would be removed, thereby allowing the Commissions the ability to undertake projects less certain of being immediately acted upon. Such an undertaking is not unduly onerous because the Commissions only produce an average of three (in the SLC's case) or five (in the LCEW's case) reports per year.[428] Although the governmental response may simply be that the reform is still 'not a priority', the government would be reminded of previous Commission work that may become more suitable for implementation over time. A requirement for periodic reconsideration ensures that valuable Commission work does not go to waste simply because there was no governmental time to implement a proposal shortly after its publication. The government should not be

[426] Reid, for example, has remarked that despite 'periodic lamentation to the contrary', the SLC 'has been remarkably successful in guiding its proposals on to the statute book': KGC Reid, 'Smoothing the Rugged Parts of the Passage: Scots Law and its Edinburgh Chair' (2014) 18 *Edinburgh Law Review* 315, 338.

[427] G Drewry, 'The Legislative Implementation of Law Reform Proposals' (1986) 7 *Statute Law Review* 161, 168.

[428] Calculated from the number of reports (excluding consolidation and repeals) published between 1 January 2006 and 31 December 2015 inclusive. Admittedly, there have been some particularly productive years, such as 2014 when the LCEW produced 14 reports.

able to discharge its duty to consider a Commission proposal so swiftly by simply saying there is no time to implement it. If a proposal is thought to have some merit, it should be reconsidered until such time is found. Annual reconsideration could also ensure that the government does not need to have an immediate legislative plan in relation to that particular project, thus negating the need for the Protocol's 'serious intention' to take forward law reform in that area. Projects should be selected and approved according to proper consideration of the project-selection criteria—not solely or mainly on the basis of the likelihood of immediate implementation. The independence of the Commissions would thereby be secured.

Implementation by primary legislation is one, but only one, measure of the Commissions' success. Other measures include implementation by other means (such as secondary legislation or the courts) and contribution to academic, public or parliamentary debate. In particular, it is important that the reforms proposed by the Commissions are good ones. Implementation figures do not take the quality of the reforms into account—a project that is implemented should not automatically be counted as a success regardless of its quality. Assessing quality is, of course, more difficult than assessing quantity, but it is not impossible.[429] In the context of criminal law reform, LCEW Commissioner David Ormerod has suggested five criteria for measuring the quality of a piece of legislation: academic views; number of appeals generated; judicial views; ratio of convictions to prosecutions; and cost-effectiveness.[430] Of course, these criteria are not all suitable for non-criminal reforms, but they provide a useful starting point for the consideration of quality as well as quantity. Another useful innovation could be following New Zealand's lead in having statutes with inbuilt provisions for post-legislative review, where the Commission is obliged to review its own implemented legislation periodically.[431]

Too much emphasis should not be placed on implementation (and especially on immediate implementation) for three reasons. First, project selection should always be based on application of all the chapter three criteria—availability and economical use of resources; suitability of the project; and importance of the project—and certain projects fulfilling the criteria will not necessarily be implemented immediately, if ever. Although it is an unjustifiably poor use of resources to embark on a project that it is known will never be implemented, such a certainty can rarely be known and, in most cases, implementation is merely uncertain. Often the criteria will be in conflict and projects will be viable by scoring more highly on one criterion than another. A project that is unimplemented may

[429] See A Burrows, 'Post-legislative Scrutiny, Legislative Drafting and the "Elusive Boundary"' in Dyson, Lee and Stark, *Fifty Years of the Law Commissions*, ch 20.

[430] D Ormerod, 'Reflections on the Courts and the Commission' in Dyson, Lee and Stark, *Fifty Years of the Law Commissions*, 335.

[431] See the discussion of the Evidence Act 2006 (New Zealand) in G Hammond, 'The Legislative Implementation of Law Reform Proposals' in Dyson, Lee and Stark, *Fifty Years of the Law Commissions*, 180–81. See also the discussion of the LCEW and SLC's approach to reviewing previous work in ch 7, section III.

not have been the best use of resources, but that might sometimes be outweighed, in a particular context, by the importance of the examination of its subject matter and the suitability of its examination by a commission. An implemented project—ostensibly a good use of resources—may not have been quite as important, or indeed may be downright unnecessary or undesirable. The Commissions' output must therefore be assessed as a whole. If such an assessment were to be made, the Commissions would be more able to examine a selection of projects, with differing likelihoods of implementation. Second, focusing too much on implementation risks eroding the Commissions' independence. Projects may be chosen, and recommendations made, based on what will be implemented, not what is the best solution, arrived at after extensive research and consultation. A lack of independence in project selection could lead to the neglect of certain areas of law that are suitable for the Commissions' examination partly because of an absence of another source of reform. Third and finally, implementation cannot be the only measure of the Commissions' success because it does not reflect the quality of the reform made. Although criticism of the very notion of the Commissions as law reform bodies is extremely rare,[432] criticism of specific Commission proposals is ubiquitous in academia[433] and, to a lesser extent, Parliament[434] and the courts.[435] It cannot be assumed that a Commission proposal is good and that implementation of that proposal is therefore automatically a good thing. Particularly when implementation is overemphasised, the Commissions may pander to government in order to increase their chances of a proposal being implemented. The objective quality of that proposal may therefore suffer. In short, the extent or *quantity* of implementation alone cannot be the main measure of success when it reveals nothing about, and in fact may negatively impact, the *quality* of those reforms.

[432] Although see, eg, Melanie Phillips, who has criticised the LCEW for being 'institutionally liberal': 'Hallelujah! A Family Court Judge Has Told the Truth About the Damage Divorce Wreaks on Children' *Daily Mail* (30 April 2012). Phillips has been particularly outspoken about the LCEW's family law projects, and about previous Commissioner Lady Hale in particular. See, eg, M Phillips, 'The Marriage Wrecker' *Daily Mail* (13 November 2003). See also above n 121.

[433] Examples are too numerous to provide a comprehensive list, but include P Cane, 'The Law Commission on Judicial Review' (1993) 56 *MLR* 887, which criticises the LCEW's consultation paper on *Administrative Law: Judicial Review and Statutory Appeals* (Law Com CP No 126 (1993)); WW McBryde, 'Law Reform: The Scottish Experience' (1998) 3 *Scottish Law and Practice Quarterly* 86, which describes how the SLC's *Report on Bankruptcy and Related Aspects of Insolvency and Liquidation* (Scot Law Com No 68 (1981)) 'contained an error which cost taxpayers millions of pounds' (93); and F Stark, 'Wiping the Slate Clean: Reforming Scots Law's Approach to Evidence of the Accused's Bad Character' (2013) 76 *MLR* 346, which argues against the SLC's proposals in its *Report on Similar Fact Evidence and the Moorov Doctrine* (Scot Law Com No 229 (2012)).

[434] See, eg, above n 20.

[435] See, eg, *Rimmer v Liverpool City Council* [1985] QB 1, which described one provision of the Bill attached to LCEW, *Civil Liability of Vendors and Lessors for Defective Premises* (Law Com No 40 (1970)) and the Defective Premises Act 1972 which implemented it as being 'imperfectly' drafted (15); and *N v HM Advocate* 2003 JC 140, [25] where Lord Justice Clerk Gill had 'strong reservations about the policy recommendation' of the SLC in *Evidence: Report on Hearsay Evidence in Criminal Proceedings* (Scot Law Com No 149 (1995)) which led to the Criminal Justice (Scotland) Act 1995, s 17, re-enacted in the Criminal Procedure (Scotland) Act 1995, s 259.

5

The Codification Task

Striving for codification is one of the Commissions' tasks under the Law Commissions Act 1965 (the 1965 Act).[1] In 1966, the first Chairman of the Law Commission for England and Wales (LCEW), Lord Scarman, predicted that this task marked the end of 'an era of reliance upon judicial decision and spasmodic law reform' and inaugurated 'an era of law reform by planned legislative process'.[2] In the same year, Lord Devlin felt that the establishment of the Commissions, with their codification task, indicated that the importance of the common law would 'almost entirely vanish'.[3] In their early years, the Commissions were credited with 'taking the law reform bull by the horns by embarking upon an extensive scheme of codification'.[4] The ambitious aims set out by both Commissions in their *First Programmes of Law Reform* are outlined later in this chapter.[5] So great were their aims that they have been criticised in hindsight as being naive.[6] The Commissions have, in fact, been criticised for having a 'disastrous record' of codification.[7] In this chapter, it will be argued that the Commissions should not be expected to codify the law and that such criticism is therefore undeserved. Aside from hostility towards codification in the British jurisdictions, the Commissions have struggled with their codification task because 'codification' has more than one meaning, and its intended meaning for the Commissions is unclear. Another obstacle to codification is the Commissions' own limited resources. Recently, siren calls have been heard for codification to be 'salvage[d] from the original vision' and put firmly back on the Commissions' agendas.[8] The current Lord Chief Justice, Lord Thomas of Cwmgiedd, has

[1] 1965 Act, s 3(1).

[2] L Scarman, 'A Code of English Law?' (lecture, University of Hull, 1966) 3 ('A Code of English Law?').

[3] P Devlin, 'The Process of Law Reform' (1966) 63 *Law Society's Gazette* 453, 461.

[4] HR Hahlo, 'Here Lies the Common Law: Rest in Peace' (1967) 30 *MLR* 241, 242.

[5] LCEW, *First Programme of Law Reform* (Law Com No 1 (1965)) is described at section V.A and SLC, *First Programme of Law Reform* (Scot Law Com No 1 (1965)) is described at section V.B.

[6] JH Farrar, *Law Reform and the Law Commission* (London, Sweet & Maxwell, 1974) 124 (*Law Reform and the Law Commission*); A Rodger, 'The Bell of Law Reform' 1993 *Scots Law Times (News)* 339, 342.

[7] F Bennion, 'Additional Comments' in G Zellick (ed), *The Law Commission and Law Reform* (London, Sweet & Maxwell, 1988) 63.

[8] G Palmer, 'The Law Reform Enterprise: Evaluating the Past and Charting the Future' (2015) 131 *LQR* 402, 411. See also D Neuberger, 'General, Equal and Certain: Law Reform Today and Tomorrow' (2012) 33 *Statute Law Review* 323, 337–38; E Clive, 'Law Reform and Social Policy' in M Dyson, J Lee and SW Stark (eds), *Fifty Years of the Law Commissions: The Dynamics of Law Reform* (Oxford,

spoken of the need for a 'modern code' of criminal law, and suggested that the LCEW might undertake that task.[9] This chapter takes a different view. The chapter three project-selection criteria will be used to argue why codification projects are less likely than certain other projects to deserve prioritisation in the allocation of the Commissions' limited resources. In addition to pre-existing obstacles, developments since 1965 have reduced the perceived need for codification by the Commissions. In particular, reliance on the common law did not 'vanish' as Lord Devlin predicted. The 1965 Act should be amended to reflect the reality of what the Commissions can, and should, achieve.

I. Definition of Codification

First, 'codification' must be defined, because there are different (but related)[10] understandings of what it means and it is not defined in the 1965 Act. It is essential to define codification before the Commissions' codification record can be appraised. Furthermore, a lack of clear definition has hindered that record. For example, one reason for the collapse of a joint LCEW and Scottish Law Commission (SLC) project to draft a harmonised contract code was apparently that there was 'no agreement on what "codification" implies'.[11]

A. Two Traditional Definitions

There are two traditional definitions of codification, at least in Great Britain. First, and most commonly, codification can mean that the entirety of a broad area of law (for example, the entire civil or criminal law) is contained in one comprehensive enactment of the sort found in continental Europe (referred to subsequently as 'continental-style' codification). Such codes are very general in their terms and their 'essential characteristic' is that they are intended to be, at least when they are brought into force, the exclusive source of law in a wide area.[12] Continental-style

Hart Publishing, 2016) 72 (Dyson, Lee and Stark, *Fifty Years of the Law Commissions*); GL Gretton, 'The Duty to Make the Law More Accessible?: The Two C-Words' in Dyson, Lee and Stark, ibid 93–96 ('The Two C-Words'); and D Lloyd Jones, 'Looking to the Future' in Dyson, Lee and Stark, ibid 357.

[9] J Thomas, 'Speech Given at the Dinner for Her Majesty's Judges' (Mansion House, 6 July 2016) paras 14–20.

[10] See JR Spencer, 'The Codification of Criminal Procedure' in J Chalmers, F Leverick and L Farmer (eds), *Essays in Criminal Law in Honour of Sir Gerald Gordon* (Edinburgh, EUP, 2010) 306 ('The Codification of Criminal Procedure').

[11] HRM Macdonald, JC Mullin, TB Smith and JF Wallace, *The Laws of Scotland: Stair Memorial Encyclopaedia*, vol 22 (Edinburgh, Law Society of Scotland, 1987) para 626.

[12] Scarman, 'A Code of English Law?' 5.

codes 'must necessarily exclude reference to pre-code case law'.[13] They have had certain supporters but little success in both England[14] and, despite its mixed civilian and common law heritage, in Scotland.[15]

Second, and less ambitiously, codification can refer to enactments which bring together various sources on one particular, narrower branch of an area of law (referred to subsequently as 'codifying statutes'). In the UK jurisdictions, codification exercises often concentrate on the bringing together of common law sources (as distinct from consolidation—the bringing together of statutory sources). Codifying statutes may, however, bring together both common law and statutory provisions. For example, the Criminal Attempts Act 1981 has been described as a codifying statute in relation to the law of criminal attempts.[16] This type of codification has been more successful in Britain, and a particular trend for codifying statutes was seen in the late-nineteenth century.[17] As well as not covering as large an area of law as continental-style codes, codifying statutes do not necessarily purport to be an exclusive source of law in that area. Such statutes may provide expressly that the common law rules continue in force where not covered by, or inconsistent with, the Act,[18] a technique which would not be used in a continental-style code.

B. The Commissions' Definitions

The lack of definition in the 1965 Act has contributed to the Commissions' confusion in determining what their codification function is. As noted above, a lack of agreement between the LCEW and the SLC as to what codification implied was

[13] TB Smith, 'Law Reform in a Mixed "Civil Law" and "Common Law" Jurisdiction' (1974–75) 35 *Louisiana Law Review* 927, 946.

[14] Codification of the civil law (in a style similar to what could later be termed continental-style codification) was first mooted in England during the reign of Henry VIII: see GA Weiss, 'The Enchantment of Codification in the Common-Law World' (2000) 25 *Yale Journal of International Law* 435, 471. Centuries later, Bentham argued strongly for continental-style codification and, in fact, coined the expression 'codification' (Weiss, ibid 448–49; L Scarman, 'Codification and Judge-made Law: A Problem of Co-Existence' (lecture, University of Birmingham, 1966) 3–4) ('A Problem of Co-Existence'). Codification was popular with a few others in nineteenth-century England, and two failed attempts to codify the criminal law both reached the stage of being introduced as Bills in Parliament. Despite the failure to codify its own laws, England exported codes to numerous countries. For a brief history, see: Scarman, 'A Code of English Law?' 4–8; T Bingham, 'A Criminal Code: Must We Wait for Ever?' in *The Business of Judging: Selected Essays and Speeches* (Oxford, OUP, 2011) 295 (*The Business of Judging*); Spencer, 'The Codification of Criminal Procedure' 310–14; and Farrar, *Law Reform and the Law Commission*, 8.

[15] For Scottish attitudes to codification, see section V.B below.

[16] See below n 321.

[17] eg, the Offences against the Person Act 1861, the Accessories and Abettors Act 1861 (both English Acts), the Bills of Exchange Act 1882 and the Sale of Goods Act 1893 (both UK-wide Acts). On the UK-wide Acts, see A Rodger, 'The Codification of Commercial Law in Victorian Britain' (1992) 108 *LQR* 570.

[18] See, eg, the Bills of Exchange Act 1882, s 97 and further AE Anton, 'Obstacles to Codification' 1982 *Juridical Review* 15, 18 ('Obstacles to Codification').

one reason for the faltering of the contract code.[19] As well as the two Commissions disagreeing as to the meaning of codification, that definition has not been consistent within each Commission over time, as we will see later. Scarman noted the problem of defining codification, because it is not 'a term of art'.[20] He thought that the 1965 Act envisaged a series of codifying statutes rather than continental-style codes, with no complete supersession of the common law.[21] He was clear, however, that codification implied something more than a collection of normal statutes.[22] Some years later, Lord Bingham agreed. He hoped that the LCEW would succeed in its plan to codify the criminal law,[23] but also that the common law would 'survive and flourish'.[24] He felt that the relationship between enacted law and the common law was not like 'oil and water', but that the two could mix.[25] Bingham's view necessitates preferring codifying statutes to continental-style codes, because the latter supplant the common law completely, and subsequent cases only interpret the codes. Anton, a former SLC Commissioner, was also of the opinion that codifying statutes were the sort of work that was in mind for the Commissions, based on the references to the mainly nineteenth-century work of that type in the course of the debates on the Law Commissions Bill.[26] These codifying statutes were also mentioned in the White Paper.[27] One former LCEW Chairman, however, expressed the view that continental-style codification was 'no doubt' what was intended by the 1965 Act.[28] Gretton has concluded that 'there probably was no definite policy' either way.[29] It is unlikely that the drafters of the 1965 Act had true continental-style codification in mind for the Commissions. Continental-style codification would be extremely difficult to achieve in the British jurisdictions because it would go against the common law tradition and, to be possible at all, would require many more resources than the Commissions alone. For example, a recent new Civil Code for Argentina took 138 people three years to complete.[30] It is far more likely, therefore, that codifying statutes were the Commissions' intended output, but a lack of clarity as to that fact may have hindered its realisation.

[19] See the text accompanying n 11 above.

[20] Scarman, 'A Code of English Law?' 4; Scarman, 'A Problem of Co-Existence' 3.

[21] Scarman, 'A Problem of Co-Existence' 5.

[22] Scarman, 'A Code of English Law?' 4.

[23] Discussed at section V.A below.

[24] Bingham, *The Business of Judging*, 353.

[25] T Bingham, 'The Future of the Common Law' in *The Business of Judging*, 386. Beatson used the oil/water analogy originally: J Beatson, 'Has the Common Law a Future?' (1997) 56 *CLJ* 291, 301, 308, 310 and 312.

[26] See Anton, 'Obstacles to Codification' 19–20 and HC Deb vol 706 col 53 (8 February 1965) (Sir Eric Fletcher); col 68 (Sir John Hobson); and col 146 (Norman Wylie).

[27] Lord Chancellor's Department, *Proposals for English and Scottish Law Commissions* (Cmnd 2573, 1965) 2.

[28] M Kerr, 'Law Reform in Changing Times' (1980) 96 *LQR* 515, 527.

[29] Gretton, 'The Two C Words' 93, fn 23.

[30] Código Civil y Comercial Argentino (Buenos Aires, Infojus, 2014). I am grateful to Andrew Steven for referring me to this statistic.

The Commissions have used the term 'codification' inconsistently. While there are examples of the term 'codification' being used to mean one comprehensive code on a broad area of the law (for example, criminal law),[31] there are also examples of the term being used to mean no more than putting smaller pockets of common law (either with or without prior reform) on a statutory footing.[32]

C. The Codification Spectrum

As we will see later, the Commissions have sometimes endorsed meanings of codification which do not fit neatly into either category (continental-style codification or codifying statutes), but which fit somewhere between them. As opposed to its two traditional meanings, therefore, codification is better viewed as being on a spectrum without bright lines as follows in Figure 1.

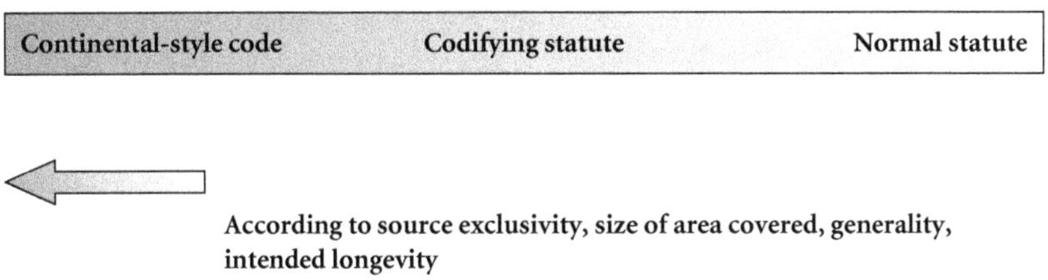

Figure 1: The codification spectrum

There are four interrelated features to be considered in deciding where an instrument fits onto the spectrum: (1) whether it is the exclusive source of an area of law; (2) the size of the area of law it covers; (3) its generality; and (4) its intended longevity. First, it must be considered whether an instrument is the exclusive source of law in an area. As time passes, a code will be supplemented by other sources, including judicial decisions on how the code should be interpreted. Hahlo argued that, far from providing an exclusive account of an area of law, a code is still dependent on 'a thick encrustation of case law' for interpretation.[33] At its outset, however, the more an instrument provides the entire body of law in an area, the closer it is to a continental-style code. If other previous sources of law are not superseded, particularly if those sources include the common law, the

[31] See sections V.A (LCEW) and V.B (SLC) below.

[32] eg, LCEW, *Report on Personal Injury Litigation: Assessment of Damages* (Law Com No 56 (1973)) talks about its Draft Law Reform (Personal Injuries etc) Bill codifying 'the present law' (para 159 and app 4, para 12). The SLC's *Report on Double Jeopardy* (Scot Law Com No 218 (2009)) uses the notion of codifying the law on double jeopardy interchangeably with merely placing it on a statutory footing (paras 2.4–2.7).

[33] HR Hahlo, 'Here Lies the Common Law: Rest in Peace' (1967) 30 *MLR* 241, 249 ('Here Lies the Common Law').

instrument lies towards the middle or right of the spectrum.[34] Second, the size of the area of law covered is important. The larger the area covered, the closer that instrument is to being a continental-style code. For example, compare a code on obligations to an Act imposing civil liability for animals.[35] The former covers a much greater area of law than the latter and is more akin to a continental-style code. The latter is narrower in its focus—more like a codifying statute at most. Third, the more general the provisions of an instrument, the further left it will fit on the codification spectrum; the more specific they are, the further right on the spectrum it will be. At least partially as a result of the intended longevity of continental-style codes, they must be kept general so as not to become obsolete quickly, particularly in areas which develop quickly, such as commercial law.[36] Furthermore, because of the size of areas covered, there is no room for specificity. To take one example, the sexual offences part of the *Draft Criminal Code for Scotland* (published under the auspices of the SLC) comprises 15 (mainly short) sections.[37] The brevity of the *Draft Criminal Code* can be compared with the corresponding current law in the area. The Sexual Offences (Scotland) Act 2009 (which, as will be highlighted below, has been considered to contain an element of codification) comprises 62 sections plus six schedules. A comparison of each instrument's definition of rape, for example, demonstrates how little detail is contained in a code as opposed to a codifying statute.[38] Fourth and finally, the intended longevity of the instrument should be considered. Codes are designed to endure, even though they will be amended from time to time. Acts can also be relatively permanent. They may equally, however, be replaced partially or completely by new legislation after a relatively short amount of time. Certain pieces of legislation, often drafted to deal with specific events or emergencies, even have sunset clauses, which provide that the Act expires after a certain date.[39]

[34] See above n 18.

[35] The SLC set out to codify the entire 'law of obligations arising by force of law, voluntary obligations, and delictual obligations' in its *First Programme of Law Reform* (Scot Law Com No 1 (1965)) paras 10–14. For the fate of this project, see section V.B below. More modest reforms to impose civil liability for animals were carried out by both Commissions: SLC, *Obligations: Report on Civil Liability in Relation to Animals* (Scot Law Com No 97 (1985)) implemented by the Animals (Scotland) Act 1987; LCEW, *Civil Liability for Animals* (Law Com No 13 (1967)) implemented by the Animals Act 1971.

[36] Anton, 'Obstacles to Codification' 17. See also R Wright, 'Precedents' (1942–44) 8 *CLJ* 118, 130. The need for a code's longevity has been used by the Commissions as a reason not to codify areas of rapidly developing law. See, eg, LCEW, *The Execution of Deeds or Documents by or on behalf of Bodies Corporate* (Law Com No 253 (1998)) para 1.15.

[37] E Clive, P Ferguson, C Gane and A McCall Smith, *A Draft Criminal Code for Scotland with Commentary* (2003) part 3 (*Draft Criminal Code for Scotland*).

[38] The *Draft Criminal Code for Scotland* provides succinctly that 'A person who (a) has sexual intercourse with another person without the consent of that person; and (b) knows that, or is reckless as to whether, the other person does not consent, is guilty of the offence of rape' (s 61). The Sexual Offences (Scotland) Act 2009, s 1 consists of four much more detailed subsections.

[39] eg, the Scottish Independence Referendum (Franchise) Act 2013 was enacted to make provision as to voting entitlement in the September 2014 referendum on Scottish independence. The Act provided, at s 14, that it was repealed on 1 January 2015. The Criminal Evidence (Witness Anonymity) Act 2008, a piece of emergency legislation passed to overturn a House of Lords decision, provided that the powers it conferred expired on a certain date (s 14).

Because of the ambiguity in the meaning of codification (as well as for other reasons which will become apparent later) it would be wiser to remove the term from the 1965 Act altogether.

II. Reasons for Tasking the Commissions with Codification

Codification is a controversial subject in common law jurisdictions like England and even in mixed civil and common law systems like Scotland. Many people are against the idea of codification in principle, and even those in its favour recognise significant practical problems. Those in support of codification argue that it simplifies law for practitioners,[40] makes law more accessible to the public,[41] modernises the law,[42] allows the law to be updated more easily and quickly,[43] encourages certainty,[44] and reduces the body of law to a manageable size.[45] It is also argued that codification (or legislation more generally) puts the control of law-making into the hands of the correct body—the legislature. The courts' 'primary function' should not be to make law.[46] Opponents of codification argue that, as well as being a dauntingly huge task, codification does not necessarily offer any of its supposed benefits.[47] Codification is certainly one way of attempting to ensure a clear and efficient system of law. Continental-style codification would, however, be extremely difficult to achieve in the British jurisdictions and, despite its supposed benefits, codification should not be one of the Commissions' specific aims.

It is important to consider the reasons why, in the light of the division of opinion as to its merits, the Commissions were tasked with codification as one of their aims, and whether those reasons endure today. Gardiner placed little emphasis on codification in his pre-1965 writings. He saw its benefits, but was mainly concerned with the reform of the existing law first, and opposed enacting codes based on the current 'obsolete or unjust law'.[48] Although he argued that codification was

[40] A Diamond, 'Codification of the Law of Contract' (1968) 31 *MLR* 361, 361 ('Codification of the Law of Contract'); M Arden, 'Time for an English Commercial Code?' (1997) 56 *CLJ* 516, 533.

[41] Diamond, ibid 370; Arden, ibid 532; JH Farrar, *Law Reform and the Law Commission* (London, Sweet & Maxwell, 1974) 60 (*Law Reform and the Law Commission*).

[42] Arden, ibid 533.

[43] Diamond, 'Codification of the Law of Contract' 372; Arden, ibid 533–34; Farrar, *Law Reform and the Law Commission*, 60.

[44] Arden, ibid 534; Farrar, ibid.

[45] Arden, ibid; Farrar, ibid.

[46] L Scarman, 'A Code of English Law?' (lecture, University of Hull, 1966) 11 ('A Code of English Law?').

[47] See in particular Hahlo, 'Here Lies the Common Law'.

[48] G Gardiner and A Martin, 'The Machinery of Law Reform' in G Gardiner and A Martin (eds), *Law Reform Now* (London, Victor Gollancz, 1963) 12.

'overdue', he felt it should not be given 'high priority'.[49] Gardiner had pointed out on several occasions the unwieldy amount of law,[50] and he was in favour of eventual codification, but prioritised reform. He did, however, indicate that codification could be pursued by the Commissions 'where appropriate',[51] and extolled the values of codification by comparing the neat set of Dutch codes with the scattered sources of English law.[52] Instructions to Parliamentary Counsel to draft the Law Commissions Bill made no reference to any codification function.[53] It had, however, become commonly understood that the Commissions would attempt to codify the law.[54] Codification was made a distinct aim of the Commissions under the 1965 Act,[55] although there appears to have been little discussion at the time as to why such a duty was created. Three broad reasons can, however, be discerned.

A. Dissatisfaction with the Common Law and Legislation

Scarman claimed that one reason for the Commissions' establishment in 1965 was the gradual decline of the common law.[56] Bingham reflected in hindsight that, by the mid-twentieth century, the common law could no longer survive on its own due to 'the complexity and range of modern government, the increasing sophistication of legal issues and relationships, the demands of representative democracy, the growth of regulation and the ever-growing interdependence of national communities'.[57] Complaints about the common law were not new; it had been criticised for centuries.[58] It was the factors outlined in chapter two, however—changes to the social, legal and political landscapes—which eventually led to the creation of bodies to reduce reliance on the common law through comprehensive legislative reform.

Cross observed that the dissatisfaction with the common law was an argument for legislation, but not necessarily codification.[59] But as the law became more statute based, observations were made that such piecemeal, patchwork statutory

[49] ibid 11.

[50] eg, in HL Deb vol 258 col 1080 (11 June 1964), Gardiner noted that English law comprised: '4,000 extant Statutes … 358 volumes [of Acts still in force] … 99 volumes of delegated legislation and about 350,000 reported cases'. He lamented, '[w]hat sort of system of law is this?'.

[51] Draft Law Reform (Miscellaneous Provisions) Bill 1964, National Archives (NA) T330/18. This draft Bill was the precursor to the eventual Law Commissions Bill. It was drafted, under Gardiner's instruction, by his *Law Reform Now* co-editor Andrew Martin.

[52] HL Deb vol 264 cols 1141–46 (1 April 1965).

[53] 'Law Commission Bill: Instructions to Parliamentary Counsel', 16 December 1964, NA T330/18.

[54] eg, HL Deb vol 258 col 1037 (11 June 1964) (Viscount Colville of Culross).

[55] 1965 Act, s 3(1).

[56] See ch 2, section II.B.

[57] T Bingham, 'The Future of the Common Law' in *The Business of Judging*, 383.

[58] See Diamond, 'Codification of the Law of Contract' 364 for a summary.

[59] R Cross, 'The Reports of the Criminal Law Commissioners (1833–1849) and the Abortive Bills of 1853' in PR Glazebrook (ed), *Reshaping the Criminal Law: Essays in Honour of Glanville Williams* (London, Stevens & Sons, 1978) 11.

reforms created 'little island[s] of statute in an ocean of common law'.[60] The mixture of common law and statute further complicated the issue of where to find the law, as opposed to alleviating it. Certain commentators, therefore, saw codification as a way of making the law more accessible, because it was 'extremely difficult for anyone without special training to discover what the law is on any given topic, and sometimes, indeed, to know where to find it'.[61] The White Paper accompanying the 1965 Act proposed ambitiously that people without special training should be able to find out what the law is on any topic.[62]

Hahlo argued that codification does not make the law any clearer for laypersons because '[i]n a highly stratified and complicated society, law cannot be anything but intricate and difficult'.[63] Scarman felt that a code should never be too simple, for it would then 'in eschewing detail attract so much subsequent case law that it will rapidly lose any practical importance'.[64] He argued that the complexity of a code should depend on its subject matter and how likely it would be that an average citizen would need or want to consult it. Certain areas of law, he argued, should be accessible to the public so that the average person can 'regulate his dealings and his conduct in the knowledge of its requirements'.[65] Other areas are 'concerned more to provide a remedy than to chart a course', in which case the public have less need to consult them.[66] It is unconvincing, however, to suggest that citizens are not at all interested in the remedies available to them as compared with the course that they should follow. In any event, accessibility to the law, and for that law to be 'so far as possible intelligible, clear and predictable' is usually thought to be a necessary component of the rule of law.[67] That said, certain areas of law are particularly complex and it is overly ambitious to hope that the entirety of the law is always fully understood by the public. Codification would, however, allow for a greater ability to at least *find* the relevant provisions. Furthermore, lawyers could more easily show their clients the relevant provisions for their information, with an explanation if necessary.[68]

Sir Roger Toulson, a previous LCEW Chairman, has suggested that the real public advantage of a code is not that laypersons can access it themselves, but that lawyers and other officials can provide a better service. He illustrated his point

[60] A Rodger, 'The Bell of Law Reform' 1993 *Scots Law Times (News)* 339, 342. See also DM Walker, 'The Scottish Law Commission under Review' (1987) 8 *Statute Law Review* 115, 122.

[61] HC Deb vol 706 col 48 (8 February 1965) (Sir Eric Fletcher).

[62] Lord Chancellor's Department, *Proposals for English and Scottish Law Commissions* (Cmnd 2573, 1965) 2.

[63] Hahlo, 'Here Lies the Common Law' 245.

[64] L Scarman, 'Codification and Judge-made Law: A Problem of Co-Existence' (lecture, University of Birmingham, 1966) 15 ('A Problem of Co-Existence').

[65] eg, the law of contract or the criminal law: Scarman, 'A Code of English Law?' 6; Scarman, 'A Problem of Co-Existence' 15–16.

[66] eg, the law of tort: Scarman, 'A Code of English Law?' 6; Scarman, 'A Problem of Co-Existence' 16.

[67] T Bingham, *The Rule of Law* (London, Penguin Books, 2011) 37.

[68] Diamond, 'Codification of the Law of Contract' 370.

using a real (unnamed) criminal case where he allowed an appeal on the basis of a recent unreported judicial decision which the prosecution was not aware of:

> If the police or Crown Prosecution Service had known that this would be the ruling, I doubt whether the defendant would ever have been charged with any offence. The result has been a waste of public time and costs and a human cost to the people involved. There would have been no room for uncertainty if the Act had provided the answer.[69]

The public benefit of codification is not only, therefore, accessibility to the code itself. It is also, and more importantly, accessibility to a more efficient and predictable legal system with increased certainty and consequent savings in cost and time.[70] The law should be more accessible in a code (even if it is not necessarily more comprehensible), as opposed to the 'impenetrable maze of distinctions and qualifications' when the law is scattered throughout judicial decisions and separate legislative enactments.[71]

Hahlo admitted that codification 'wipes out the past' and 'generally obviates the need for historical research going back in time'.[72] He argued, however, that this supposed advantage may not have much practical significance, because there are few legal cases anyway 'in which deep historical research is required'.[73] He claimed that even without a code, one must rarely look 'beyond the last thirty years of law reports' for a solution.[74] Even proponents of codification, such as former LCEW Commissioner, Aubrey Diamond, have admitted that practitioners in common law jurisdictions rarely have to look too far back into historical cases.[75] Diamond carried out research into the number of cases cited by the English courts in judgments reported in 1965.[76] The average number of authorities cited in a case was 8.9 and almost half of those authorities were from the previous 20 years.[77] These statistics suggest that case law may not be quite as unwieldy as is usually thought. Diamond's research, however, ignored the vast number of cases the parties undoubtedly had to sift through before they found the manageable number of cases relevant to the pertinent issue, plus the further challenge in finding relevant legislative provisions. Moreover, while fewer authorities were cited in

[69] R Toulson, 'Forty Years On: What Progress in Delivering Accessible and Principled Criminal Law?' (2006) 27 *Statute Law Review* 61, 71. On the similar problems which can be posed by legislation, see Toulson's discussion of *R v Chambers* [2008] EWCA Crim 2467: R Toulson, 'Democracy, Law Reform and the Rule of Law' in Dyson, Lee and Stark, *Fifty Years of the Law Commissions*, 130–31.

[70] See also MR Topping and JPM Vandenlinden, '*Ibi Renascit Jus Commune*' (1970) 33 *MLR* 170, 171–72; MD Chalmers, 'Codification of Mercantile Law' (1903) 19 *LQR* 10, 16–17 and LCB Gower, 'Reflections on Law Reform' (1973) 23 *University of Toronto Law Journal* 257, 257 ('Reflections on Law Reform').

[71] J Reid, 'The Judge as Law Maker' (1972–73) 12 *Journal of the Society of Public Teachers of Law* 22, 24.

[72] Hahlo, 'Here Lies the Common Law' 248–49.

[73] ibid 249.

[74] ibid.

[75] Diamond, 'Codification of the Law of Contract' 364.

[76] Diamond examined all 434 reported cases from the *All England Law Reports* for that year.

[77] Diamond, 'Codification of the Law of Contract' 365–66.

certain cases, an unwieldy amount of case law would have been cited in others. In a later example highlighted by Gower, 108 cases were cited.[78] Further, with more and more cases being heard and reported in modern times, together with the average length of judgments growing,[79] Diamond's research has lost some of its relevance.[80] Diamond conceded, despite his findings, that a statute gives 'statements of law laid down in simple language, uncluttered by the detailed facts of particular cases. Handling a case is much more complicated'.[81] A code is even more user-friendly than case law, or separate legislative enactments.

As the Commissions were established, certain commentators hoped that codification could overhaul the statute book, which was full of 'deadwood' and 'cluttered' with ancient, obsolete Acts.[82] Some opposition was heard, however, from the 'most ancient common law lawyers' who thought codification was 'a Continental invention of the worst type'.[83] Despite this opposition to the Commissions' codification role, no attempt was made to remove it from the Law Commissions Bill during its progress through Parliament.[84] Due to the wording of the legislation, it would have been easy (in theory) to attempt to do so.[85] Those who were dissatisfied with the prevailing system of law were therefore in the majority—at least in 1965. We shall see later that certain of the criticisms levelled at judge-made law at the time of the Commissions' creation have since been at least partially addressed. The statute book is ever more cluttered, but technological developments have made it easier to find the relevant law in an area than it once was.[86] The case for codification, therefore, is not as strong as it was in 1965. Furthermore, despite certain values (particularly the accessibility argument), codification projects are less likely than certain other projects to warrant the use of the Commissions' resources. If codification is to be pursued, it should not be the Commissions' responsibility.

B. Desire for Simultaneous Reform and Codification

Farrar has said that it is 'axiomatic' that reform should precede codification.[87] The draftsman of the 1965 Act, however, disagreed. Codification was added to

[78] *Karak Rubber Co Ltd v Burden (No 2)* [1972] 1 WLR 602; Gower, 'Reflections on Law Reform' 257.
[79] See section IV.B.i.
[80] See also C Stoddart, 'Educating the Judiciary' (2000) 45(6) *Journal of the Law Society of Scotland* 23, 25.
[81] Diamond, 'Codification of the Law of Contract' 361.
[82] HL Deb vol 258 cols 1048–49 (11 June 1964) (Lord Silkin). See also, eg, HC Deb vol 706 cols 112–13 (8 February 1965) (David Weitzman).
[83] HC Deb vol 706 cols 108–09 (8 February 1965) (Charles Fletcher-Cooke).
[84] Diamond, 'Codification of the Law of Contract' 385.
[85] See section V.A below.
[86] Although admittedly this may only be a 'partial answer' to the accessibility problem: I Dennis, 'The Law Commission and the Criminal Law: Reflections on the Codification Project' in Dyson, Lee and Stark, *Fifty Years of the Law Commissions*, 116.
[87] JH Farrar, *Law Reform and the Law Commission* (London, Sweet & Maxwell, 1974) 39.

the Commissions' duties because it was thought that it could be carried out simultaneously with reform. As we have seen, Gardiner had not opposed the idea of codification. He was simply concerned that the law was in such desperate need of change that reform had to come first—there would be no point in codifying bad law. Prior to the Commissions' introduction, the view was advanced that reform need not precede codification—both could happen simultaneously.[88] In its early days, the LCEW planned to present brand new sets of principles in codes, reforming as it went,[89] despite warnings about the 'tremendous task' codification posed.[90]

The SLC, however, soon employed a different approach. During its first decade, it stated that it found it 'wasteful … to embark on the codification of any area of law before the defects in that area have been identified and corrected and the necessary decisions reached on questions of principle'.[91] The SLC still favours shying away from codifying an area of law where extensive reform is needed.[92] The LCEW also now adopts this approach, as we will see later. This cautious approach acknowledges that, because of a code's longevity, the new law should be tried and tested before being enshrined in a code. Previous codifying statutes generally followed the same method—they were only drafted once the principles of an area of law had 'already stood the test of time'.[93] The idea that reform and codification could occur simultaneously in the British jurisdictions was overly ambitious, as well as undesirable. Areas of law not in need of prior reform could, in theory, be codified immediately. Such projects are, however, less likely to be viable than projects proposing substantive reform when judged against the project-selection criteria.

C. Joining the European Union (EU)

The Commissions were also tasked with codification because it was hoped that harmonisation and codification could aid the UK's entry into what is now the EU.[94] Hahlo observed that the main motivation behind the Commissions' codification task was 'the strongly felt need to bring order into the "superabundance of

[88] HL Deb vol 258 col 1063 (11 June 1964) (Lord Chorley). *cf* HC Deb vol 706 col 68 (8 February 1965) (Sir John Hobson), who thought that codification should only be attempted when the law in an area was settled.

[89] See, eg, LCEW, *First Annual Report: 1965–66* (Law Com No 4 (1966)) para 31.

[90] HC Deb vol 706 col 146 (8 February 1965) (Norman Wylie).

[91] SLC, *Seventh Annual Report: 1971–72* (Scot Law Com No 28 (1973)) para 10. See also WW McBryde, 'Law Reform: The Scottish Experience' (1998) 3 *Scottish Law and Practice Quarterly* 86, 91.

[92] See, eg, below n 303.

[93] MD Chalmers, 'Codification of Mercantile Law' (1903) 19 *LQR* 10, 11. *cf*, on the Sale of Goods Act 1893 in Scotland, GL Gretton, 'The Duty to Make the Law More Accessible?: The Two C-Words' in Dyson, Lee and Stark, *Fifty Years of the Law Commissions*, 93, fn 24.

[94] LCB Gower, 'A Comment' (1967) 30 *MLR* 259, 260 ('A Comment'). Harmonisation is discussed separately in ch 6.

materials"' and that a convenient side effect would be the harmonisation of English and Scots law.[95] One of the first LCEW Commissioners disagreed. Gower stated that the harmonisation of Scots and English law was not a by-product, but one of the main motivations for codification. The harmonisation of the two jurisdictions, with their 'fundamental' differences, was thought to be 'an essential pre-requisite to harmonisation with the laws of the Continental countries', itself an 'essential' precursor to joining the (then) European Economic Community.[96] Commissioners felt that it should be 'easier to explain our law to our continental partners'.[97] In relation to the attempted drafting of a contract code by both Commissions, the LCEW explicitly stated that it was 'mindful of the importance of achieving harmonisation with continental systems, the relevance of which has been enhanced by the Government's application to join the Common Market'.[98] It was thought desirable in particular that the contract laws of 'our small island' should be unified in readiness for Europe.[99] Scarman felt it was 'urgent' that the laws of Scotland and England should be harmonised, noting that such a task could only fall to Parliament, not judges.[100] It is clear from the context that he had Europe on his mind.[101]

The SLC also noted the European dimension, but instead of intending to mould its proposed reforms to fit a continental system, it believed that Scots law, with its mixed civilian and common law heritage, could act as a useful link between England and Europe.[102] This belief was undoubtedly influenced by then Commissioner, TB Smith, who had earlier written that Scotland 'came out of Europe to go into Britain' and therefore had 'an invaluable contribution' to make in bridging the gap between English law and the civilian tradition in mainland Europe.[103] One previous SLC Chairman thought that the harmonisation of English and Scots law 'in isolation from a wider process of harmonisation among all member states of the Community' would be positively dangerous because Scots law's 'special advantages as a bridge jurisdiction into continental Europe' could be lost if Scots law was Anglicised.[104]

Separate jurisdictions and a lack of codification were therefore seen by certain critics as potential barriers to the UK entering Europe. The aim to harmonise and codify the British (or UK) legal systems was a hugely ambitious one. Even

95 Hahlo, 'Here Lies the Common Law' 244.
96 Gower, 'A Comment' 260.
97 Diamond, 'Codification of the Law of Contract' 374.
98 LCEW, *Second Annual Report: 1966–67* (Law Com No 12 (1967)) para 29.
99 LCB Gower, 'Reflections on Law Reform' (1973) 23 *University of Toronto Law Journal* 257, 264.
100 L Scarman, 'A Code of English Law?' (lecture, University of Hull, 1966) 9 ('A Code of English Law?').
101 ibid.
102 SLC, *Second Annual Report: 1966–67* (Scot Law Com No 7 (1967)) para 11.
103 TB Smith, *British Justice: The Scottish Contribution (The Hamlyn Lectures)* (London, Stevens & Sons Ltd, 1961) 228 (*British Justice: The Scottish Contribution*). See also 'Scots Lawyers Loth to Give up Independence' *The Guardian* (8 January 1965).
104 C Davidson, 'Law Reform—Who Cares?' (1992) 37(4) *Journal of the Law Society of Scotland* 130, 131.

once much European harmonisation took place and despite the supremacy of EU law,[105] countries retain specific rules of domestic law. To harmonise completely would be 'wildly impractical'[106] and the idea that Europe could have one uniform jurisdiction has been said to be as unlikely as it having one uniform language.[107] As it turned out, the UK became a part of what is now the EU in 1973, failed attempts at codification notwithstanding. And, as the UK prepares for its probable departure from the EU, this reason to task the Commissions with codification is now redundant—if it was ever convincing in the first place. Given the Euroscepticism prevalent in large parts of British society, it is almost certainly the case that codification was rejected by some as too un-British a prospect.

It is clear that certain reasons for tasking the Commissions with codification are no longer as compelling today as they were in 1965. Despite the strength of surviving reasons such as greater accessibility, the Commissions are not well suited to pursue codification.

III. Pre-Existing Obstacles to Codification

Codification is likely to be a huge task, and the Commissions' limited resources have often prevented them from completing a codification exercise. Where, however, codification has been attempted, it has often been met with hostility because of both parliamentary and common law traditions. Ultimately, despite the reasons just advanced, there has been a lack of perceived need for such an extreme shift in our legal culture.

A. The Commissions' Resources

Sir Geoffrey Palmer has said that bodies like the Commissions are 'ideal' for drafting codes.[108] But the Commissions simply do not have the resources to undertake the frequently large task of codification. The Commissions are small bodies. Each consists of only five Commissioners, plus supporting staff. They rely on Parliamentary Counsel (another limited resource) to draft Bills that are usually attached to their reports. On occasion, such Bills have been omitted in order to speed up publication.[109] Such an approach is not feasible where codification is involved. Furthermore, codification projects are likely to be large when a large

[105] See section IV.C.i below.

[106] A Rodger, 'The Bell of Law Reform' 1993 *Scots Law Times (News)* 339, 343.

[107] Smith, *British Justice: The Scottish Contribution*, 216.

[108] G Palmer, 'The Law Reform Enterprise: Evaluating the Past and Charting the Future' (2015) 131 *LQR* 402, 413.

[109] See, eg, LCEW and SLC, *Liability for Defective Products* (Law Com No 82 and Scot Law Com No 45 (1977)) para 18.

area of law (such as the entire criminal law) must be examined. The size of such projects has resulted in them frequently being broken up into smaller projects.

Because of the Commissions' small sizes, they cannot examine all the law. In chapter three, we saw that Commission projects are selected according to three criteria: (i) the availability and economical use of resources; (ii) the suitability of the project; and (iii) the importance of the project. Particularly large projects need not be out of bounds, but must be sufficiently suitable and important to justify being a drain on a Commission's resources. When considering the 'resources' criterion before embarking on a codification project, the potentially vast resources required must be taken into account, including ensuring the availability of Parliamentary Counsel. Even where the resources are found (including where government supplies additional resources), a project must still meet the other selection criteria. Projects which do not reform (or reform only incidentally) the substance of the law (such as consolidation and repeals work) are unlikely to be as important as projects which make substantive changes to laws. We saw earlier that both Commissions now prefer to reform an area of law first, prior to a second codification stage. If no prior reform is needed, then the Commissions would skip straight to the second stage. Therefore codification projects, during their second stage (after reform has already occurred), will not (or will only incidentally) reform the law—they will merely change its style.[110] Furthermore, Lord Rodger, a 'noted opponent of codification',[111] reflected that codification requires solving both the actual problems which have infiltrated the law, and also what does not (yet) cause difficulty in practice, but must still be included in any comprehensive code.[112] The Commissions' resources are better used to examine what actually causes problems in practice, rather than pondering hypotheticals. Changes of style and reforming law that has not caused difficulty in practice are less likely to score highly in the 'importance' criterion for project selection than changes of substance which are critically needed. The task of codification should consequently not be a general priority for the Commissions. It is entirely proper that their limited resources have prevented much codification from being undertaken.

B. Parliamentary Problems

A lack of parliamentary time (or will) for Commission proposals is a huge problem for the Commissions generally, and in relation to codification in particular.[113]

[110] No such codification projects have yet reached a second, post-reform stage, but see below for a discussion of the LCEW's current endeavour to simplify the criminal law, as preparatory work for later potential codification.

[111] A Steven, 'Codification: A Perspective from a Scottish Law Commissioner' (Seminar Series on Codification, All Souls College, Oxford, 2014) 15 ('Codification').

[112] A Rodger, 'The Bell of Law Reform' 1993 *Scots Law Times (News)* 339, 342 ('The Bell of Law Reform').

[113] AE Anton, 'Obstacles to Codification' 1982 *Juridical Review* 15, 27–29 ('Obstacles to Codification').

The larger, and even more technical, undertaking of codification does not sit well with a lack of prioritisation of apolitical law reform. One of the nineteenth-century Bills attempting to codify English criminal law[114] was abandoned due to a lack of parliamentary time.[115] Smaller projects with smaller Bills may have a better chance of being accommodated in Parliament's busy programme. Codes are, therefore, less likely to be so accommodated. Furthermore, Steven, a current SLC Commissioner, has noted that any 'major' codification project would not be 'non-controversial' enough to benefit from the new House of Lords and Holyrood procedures discussed in chapter four.[116]

Sir Roger Toulson, however, remarked that '[t]he problem is not so much one of lack of parliamentary time as lack of departmental time and commitment'.[117] Even Scarman, one of the main proponents of codification, was realistic about the problems posed by the lack of prioritisation of such work by government and Parliament. Giving a lecture in 1966 entitled 'A Code of English Law?' he stated that '[u]ntil one sees what Parliament … can do, the question mark cannot be removed from the title of this address'.[118] Bingham noted that the LCEW's criminal code was not implemented due to a lack of parliamentary time, 'a powerful but not, surely, an insuperable obstacle'.[119] As with implementation generally, the real problem is not a lack of parliamentary *time*, but a lack of executive and parliamentary *interest*.

Codification is simply not a priority for government or Parliament. The political drive towards codification that has been seen in certain other countries has never been evident in the UK. In France, for example, Napoleon's Civil Code of 1804 followed the French Revolution. German codification was part of a distinct attempt to systematise a legal system fragmented by various historical developments.[120] Numerous Eastern European countries have enacted civil codes in the decades since the end of communism. By comparison, we have never had the sort of political developments in the UK that have necessitated a code. Evidently entry into the EU was not enough of an impetus. Politicians will be reluctant to try to find parliamentary time for codes when there is no public clamour for change.

[114] See above n 14.

[115] For a discussion, see JR Spencer, 'The Codification of Criminal Procedure' in J Chalmers, F Leverick and L Farmer (eds), *Essays in Criminal Law in Honour of Sir Gerald Gordon* (Edinburgh, EUP, 2010) 310 and 313.

[116] Steven, 'Codification' 14.

[117] R Toulson, 'Forty Years On: What Progress in Delivering Accessible and Principled Criminal Law?' (2006) 27 *Statute Law Review* 61, 66.

[118] Scarman, 'A Code of English Law?' 15–16, and see also 13, where Scarman noted that parliamentary time (or will) was the real 'practical obstacle' to codification.

[119] T Bingham, 'A Criminal Code: Must We Wait for Ever?' in *The Business of Judging: Selected Essays and Speeches* (Oxford, OUP, 2011) 296, and see also T Bingham 'The Future of the Common Law' in ibid 387.

[120] See JA Bargenda and SW Stark, 'In Search of the Legal Holy Grail: Critical Perspectives on Codification from Britain and Germany' (unpublished, 2016).

Lord Hunter, a former SLC Chairman, complained that codification 'in any proper sense of the term' would 'remain a pipe dream until new methods of drafting, new legislative approaches and machinery and new principles of interpretation' were introduced.[121] For him, the legislative machine was so geared up to churn out a certain model of statute that parliamentary draftsmen would only draft Bills in a very precise way to 'get them through the legislature with the least possible trouble and delay'.[122] Codes, with their higher degree of generality, would not fit this model. Lord Goff noted that there would have to be 'a change of heart among our Parliamentary draftsmen' for there to ever be any 'significant move' towards codification in Britain.[123] He noted that, contrary to the generality typical of codes, UK statutes tended to be worded 'as tightly as possible'.[124] Sir Michael Kerr, a former LCEW Chairman, has similarly said that a change from our 'highly detailed and complex' statutes, which purport to cover 'every foreseeable situation' to a much more general style, would be 'alien' to our traditional methods.[125] In the early 1970s, the SLC noted that for codification to be a success, parliamentary draftsmen would have to 'alter radically their style of presentation'.[126] Despite certain exceptions to this (such as the Human Rights Act 1998, discussed below), UK statutes still tend to be drafted without the generality typical of a code.[127] The redrafting of the joint contract code in a style that displeased the Scots (discussed later) is evidence of an antipathy towards codification among parliamentary draftsmen. Codes are shunned for the reason that they are alien to our parliamentary process and the Commissions are prevented from achieving their codification goal.

C. Common Law Tradition

Anton observed that the Commissions fight a losing battle in their codification task because codification is incompatible with the features of the English, and even the Scottish, legal systems.[128] For Anton (a Scottish Law Commissioner from 1966 until 1982), the 'principal obstacle' to codification in Britain is the common law tradition—to codify, particularly in a continental style, would be to reject 'the

[121] J Hunter, 'Law Reform: The Meanings and the Methods' in *Proceedings and Papers of the Fifth Commonwealth Law Conference* (Edinburgh, Fifth Commonwealth Law Conference, 1977) 7.

[122] ibid.

[123] R Goff, 'The Future of the Common Law' (1997) 46 *ICLQ* 745, 752 ('The Future of the Common Law').

[124] ibid.

[125] M Kerr, 'Law Reform in Changing Times' (1980) 96 *LQR* 515, 528. See also M Kerr, *As Far as I Remember* (Oxford, Hart Publishing, 2006) 294.

[126] SLC, *Seventh Annual Report: 1971–72* (Scot Law Com No 28 (1973)) para 10.

[127] For an illustration, see section I.C above.

[128] Anton, 'Obstacles to Codification' 16.

common law as the ultimate repository of legal principle'.[129] Anton cited Mackenzie Chalmers, the draftsman of codifying statutes such as the Bills of Exchange Act 1882 and the Sale of Goods Act 1893, to make it clear that even for those in favour of some degree of codification, the common law endures. Chalmers compared a code to a building, while the common law is 'the atmosphere which surrounds that building, and which penetrates every chink and crevice where the bricks and mortar are not'.[130] Lord Cooper had also lamented the fact that codification could never be a realistic prospect where the common law thrives, due to an 'instinctively hostile' reaction to codes.[131] It may also be observed that criticism of the common law (from, for example, Lord Scarman and Lord Devlin) was not unanimous. Others more keen to defend the common law took a 'less pessimistic view'.[132]

Opponents of codification argue that codes erode the immediacy of common law developments and require constant revision so as not to 'stultify' the progress of the law and 'destroy the spirit of the common law'.[133] Certain commentators have argued that lawyers in codified systems find that reform is impeded by their codes, and that they would prefer the flexibility of the British mixture of common law and statute.[134]

In support of codification, it has been argued that the perceived 'elasticity' of the common law is 'another name for uncertainty and obscurity'.[135] Furthermore, the flexibility of the common law is limited by judges having to wait until the right case comes along, with no ability to choose the areas of law they wish to reform.[136] As Lord Devlin put it, '[t]he trouble about judicial law reform was never, as it is with Parliament, lack of time but lack of opportunity'.[137] Eric Clive, a previous SLC Commissioner and the 'arch-advocate of codification in Scotland',[138] has observed that it is much easier to change a statute or code than it is to wait for another similar case to come along.[139] Dame Mary Arden, a previous LCEW Chairman, has added that not only must the right case come up, but the judge is

[129] ibid 23.

[130] MD Chalmers, 'Codification of Mercantile Law' (1903) 19 *LQR* 10, 10 ('Codification of Mercantile Law').

[131] TM Cooper, 'The Common and the Civil Law—A Scot's View' (1949–50) 63 *Harvard Law Review* 468, 471–72.

[132] eg, Goff, 'The Future of the Common Law' 745.

[133] HC Deb vol 706 col 146 (8 February 1965) (Norman Wylie). On the immediate effect of a rule developed by the courts compared with reform by legislation, see Lord Denning's dicta at n 248 below.

[134] Rodger, 'The Bell of Law Reform' 343. See also Anton, 'Obstacles to Codification', who notes that codes are rarely amended (30).

[135] Chalmers, 'Codification of Mercantile Law' 15.

[136] E Clive, 'Codification of the Criminal Law' in J Chalmers, F Leverick and L Farmer (eds), *Essays in Criminal Law in Honour of Sir Gerald Gordon* (Edinburgh, EUP, 2010) 65 ('Codification of the Criminal Law'); N Marsh, 'Law Reform in the United Kingdom: A New Institutional Approach' (1971) 13 *William & Mary Law Review* 263, 267.

[137] P Devlin, 'The Process of Law Reform' (1966) 63 *Law Society's Gazette* 453, 461.

[138] Steven, 'Codification' 14.

[139] Clive, 'Codification of the Criminal Law' 67. See also A Diamond, 'Codification of the Law of Contract' (1968) 31 *MLR* 361, 372 ('Codification of the Law of Contract').

reliant on counsel arguing the necessary point.[140] Furthermore, due to the time and the expense of litigation, many civil matters only reach the courts if the parties can afford to bring an action. Indeed, the inaccessibility of justice has been cited as the 'real reason' why codification was thought by certain commentators to be needed urgently in the 1960s.[141]

Clive has argued that there is both good and bad flexibility in the law.[142] 'Good flexibility', which can be provided equally by the common law or a code, comprises the use of deliberately 'open-ended terms such as "reasonable", "reckless", "serious" or "severe"'.[143] 'Bad flexibility' comes from 'unnoticed conflicts in the law' or 'insufficiently precise definition'.[144] To Clive, it is 'perverse' to 'praise the common law' for having the latter type of flexibility, because '[i]t is like saying a house is well ventilated without mentioning that the reason is a lot of broken windows'.[145] It must be acknowledged, however, that conflicts and imprecision can also be found in legislation, and indeed it has been argued that statutes can, in fact, be *more* prone to 'bad flexibility'.[146]

It has been observed that judges may be obliged to follow a badly drafted provision of a code 'with reluctance'.[147] Clive has suggested that this objection is a 'puzzling' argument against codification.[148] He argues that such a claim could also apply to any statute and 'underestimate[s] the power of a court to interpret a statutory provision', as well as implying that the courts can simply 'refuse to follow common law rules' where they are deemed unfair.[149] In short, the flexibility of the common law is often overestimated.

A code, as the exclusive source of law in an area, is commonly thought to provide better legal certainty than the common law. Proponents of the common law, however, argue that judge-made law provides more certainty than a code, or indeed any enacted law. The uncertainty caused by enacted law is said to occur because 'there is more room for difference of opinion with regard to the words of a Statute, however carefully they may have been framed, than there is in interpreting a line of legal decision moving from precedent to precedent'.[150] British legislation has been criticised for its 'obscurity and uncertainty', caused by long Acts, drafted to cover 'all eventualities', contrary to the ethos of more general codes.[151] This argument reveals, however, that judges play an important role in interpreting

140 M Arden, 'Time for an English Commercial Code?' (1997) 56 *CLJ* 516, 534.
141 HL Deb vol 264 cols 1174–75 (1 April 1965) (Lord Wilberforce).
142 Clive, 'Codification of the Criminal Law' 58–59.
143 ibid 58.
144 ibid 59.
145 ibid.
146 See below nn 150 and 151.
147 JC Smith, 'Codification of the Criminal Law' (lecture, Inns of Court School of Law, 1986) 10.
148 Clive, 'Codification of the Criminal Law' 58.
149 ibid.
150 HL Deb vol 264 col 1203 (1 April 1965) (Lord Tangley).
151 K Miller, 'Legal Change: The Social Dimension' (1998) 3 *Scottish Law and Practice Quarterly* 117, 122.

statutes—and that statutes do, in fact, have a certain degree of flexibility to allow such interpretation.

Judges themselves have been said to be one of the main obstacles to codification in the British jurisdictions. One of the nineteenth-century attempts at codification of the criminal law[152] failed due to being 'condemned by the judiciary' when circulated for comment.[153] Diamond contended that the main argument against codification was judicial conservatism and a difficulty in preventing 'judges from applying the law they know, and have learnt to love, instead of the new and strange statute'.[154] Common law judges, it was argued in the 1960s, had an 'undoubted prejudice against legislation'.[155] Such a view was not unanimous, given the views of Lord Scarman and Lord Devlin. And if such a view prevails today, it still cannot be unanimous given the pro-codification views cited in this chapter from, for example, Lord Thomas of Cwmgiedd and Arden LJ. In the 1980s, Anton mooted that such 'disfavour' of codes extended to the legal profession as a whole.[156] Views today may be more 'mixed'.[157] But even at the turn of the twenty-first century, it was queried whether judges might struggle to adapt to a new method, having been 'reared on a diet of case law'.[158] As Lord Goff argued:

> Common lawyers tend to proceed by analogy, moving gradually from case to case. We tend to avoid large, abstract, generalisations, preferring limited, temporary formulations, the principles gradually emerging from concrete cases as they are decided. In other words, we tend to reason *upwards* from the facts of the cases before us, whereas our continental colleagues tend to reason *downwards* from abstract principles embodied in a code.[159]

It has been argued that it is 'surprising' that it is thought that judges should be the *primary* law-makers in the light of the notion of parliamentary sovereignty.[160] Codification (or statute law generally) puts the law-making power firmly in the hands of the democratically elected legislature. The strength of the common law tradition, however, has made the Commissions' codification task extremely difficult.

[152] Mentioned above at n 14.

[153] R Cross, 'The Reports of the Criminal Law Commissioners (1833–1849) and the Abortive Bills of 1853' in PR Glazebrook (ed), *Reshaping the Criminal Law: Essays in Honour of Glanville Williams* (London, Stevens & Sons, 1978) 9–10.

[154] Diamond, 'Codification of the Law of Contract' 377. See also L Blom-Cooper, 'Reform? Reform? Aren't Things Bad Enough Already?' [2010] *PL* 441, 442.

[155] Diamond, ibid 379.

[156] Anton, 'Obstacles to Codification' 25.

[157] E Clive, 'The Scottish Civil Code Project' in HL MacQueen, A Vauer and S Espiau Espiau (eds), *Regional Private Laws and Codification in Europe* (Cambridge, CUP, 2003) 85 ('The Scottish Civil Code Project').

[158] R Goff, 'The Future of the Common Law' (1997) 46 *ICLQ* 745, 753.

[159] ibid, emphasis in original. See also M Kirby, 'Judicial Dissent—Common Law and Civil Law Traditions' (2007) 123 *LQR* 379.

[160] Clive, 'Codification of the Criminal Law' 63. An element of judicial law-making, secondary to that of the legislature, is more commonly accepted (section IV.A.ii), although not uncontroversial (below n 293).

IV. Developments Reducing the Need for Codification

In addition to the pre-existing obstacles to codification, developments since 1965 have reduced the need for codification. One reason codification fell out of fashion is because there is no longer the pressure to codify which was perceived when the UK was preparing for entry into the Common Market. Another reason is that certain of the criticisms levelled at the law around the time of the Commissions' establishment are no longer as convincing today. For example, both the bulging statute book and the increasing number of cases are less troublesome because technological developments have made it easier to locate legal sources. The number of separate enactments and cases have increased rather than decreased. Such increase now appears, however, to be both inevitable and to pose less of a practical challenge, and so it is more tolerated.[161] Furthermore, certain criticisms levelled at judge-made law are no longer as convincing as they were in the 1960s. Contrary to the views expressed by Lord Devlin that the importance of the common law would 'almost entirely vanish',[162] judge-made law has not only survived, but has in fact grown in importance for various reasons. As we have seen, the desire for codification in the 1960s was partially a reaction to certain criticisms of the common law. Neat, modern codes were seen as an appealing alternative to the sprawling mass of cases. The common law was not seen as a suitable tool for law reform in the early 1960s, but as the criticisms of judge-made law have become less convincing, so too has the case for codification. The courts are (and are perceived to be) a more suitable tool of law reform, with the result that comprehensive codes are no longer perceived to be needed. Piecemeal statutes supplemented by judge-made law can suffice. In addition, codes could impede the development of the common law—which may now be unnecessary as well as undesirable lest developing areas of law become ossified.[163]

A. The Practice Statement

i. The Making of the Practice Statement

When the Commissions were established, one of the problems noted with the common law was that it was not moving with the times. At that time, the House of Lords was bound by the principle of stare decisis to follow its own precedents; a rule 'of [its] own making'.[164] By having 'forged its own fetters' in this way, Scarman

[161] *cf* Clive, who moots that the number of 'undigested cases available at the click of a mouse' makes codification more, not less, appealing: 'The Scottish Civil Code Project' 84.

[162] P Devlin, 'The Process of Law Reform' (1966) 63 *Law Society's Gazette* 453, 461.

[163] See, eg, *Alfred McAlpine Construction Ltd v Panatown Ltd* [2001] 1 AC 518, 553 (Lord Goff).

[164] A Lester, 'English Judges as Law Makers' [1993] *PL* 269, 271.

reasoned that the common law was not flexible enough to be used as a tool of law reform, especially when society was developing more rapidly than ever before.[165] During its relatively short duration,[166] the stare decisis rule's application to the House of Lords was roundly criticised. One writer announced that he was 'unable to find … any wholehearted approval of the doctrine by anyone'—the judges were 'obviously squirming under the restraint' and '[t]he academics were uniformly hostile'.[167]

In 1966, however, the House of Lords declared that it would no longer be bound by stare decisis. The Commissions (and particularly the SLC) played a major part in the House of Lords' *Practice Statement (Judicial Precedent)* (the Practice Statement), which put an end to the doctrine's application to the House of Lords.[168] The Practice Statement was not, as certain critics thought, a competitive reaction by the Court to the creation of the Commissions.[169] The Practice Statement has been said to have resulted from the 'changing social and political climate of the 1960s', the 'innovatory activities' of certain judges such as Lord Denning and Lord Reid, and the academic criticism of the previous rule, with the SLC as the 'catalyst'.[170] The initiative came from TB Smith, who had previously written on judicial precedent, deriding the infiltration into Scots law of the rigid English rule.[171] Undoubtedly Smith was once again influenced by Lord Cooper, who bemoaned the fact that the doctrine of precedent 'crept … unobserved' into Scots law and now held it in its 'suffocating grip'.[172] The subject of precedent was then put in the SLC's *First Programme of Law Reform*,[173] and the LCEW later joined in with the project, having apparently regretted not putting the subject in its own *First Programme*.[174] The Commissions worked together until they were 'alerted to the Lord Chancellor's interest in the topic' who then concocted (with other House of Lords judges, notably Lord Reid) the Practice Statement on the back of the

[165] L Scarman, 'A Code of English Law?' (lecture, University of Hull, 1966) 10 ('A Code of English Law?').

[166] The House of Lords had only been bound by its own decisions since *Beamish v Beamish* (1861) 9 HL Cases 274, confirmed by *London Tramways Co v London County Council* [1898] AC 375. See L Blom-Cooper, '1966 and All That: The Story of the Practice Statement' in L Blom-Cooper, B Dickson and G Drewry (eds), *The Judicial House of Lords 1876–2009* (Oxford, OUP, 2009) 129 ('1966 and All That').

[167] WB Leach, 'Revisionism in the House of Lords: The Bastion of Rigid Stare Decisis Falls' (1966–67) 80 *Harvard Law Review* 797, 801.

[168] *Practice Statement (Judicial Precedent)* [1966] 1 WLR 1234.

[169] J Hunter, 'Law Reform: The Meanings and the Methods' in *Proceedings and Papers of the Fifth Commonwealth Law Conference* (Edinburgh, Fifth Commonwealth Law Conference, 1977) 1–2.

[170] A Paterson, *The Law Lords* (London, Palgrave McMillan, 1982) 146 and 149 (*The Law Lords*).

[171] TB Smith, *The Doctrines of Judicial Precedent in Scots Law* (Edinburgh, W Green & Son Ltd, 1952). See also TB Smith, *British Justice: The Scottish Contribution (The Hamlyn Lectures)* (London, Stevens & Sons Ltd, 1961) 84–85.

[172] TM Cooper, 'The Common and the Civil Law—A Scot's View' (1949–50) 63 *Harvard Law Review* 468, 472–73.

[173] SLC, *First Programme of Law Reform* (Scot Law Com No 1 (1965)) paras 16–19.

[174] Paterson, *The Law Lords*, 149.

'Scottish initiative'.[175] The Lord Chancellor at the time was Gardiner. It is therefore unsurprising that this additional law reform tool was introduced, despite Gardiner not being a fan of the common law. It had been noted (while the stare decisis rule was still in place) that the 'rigidities' of the rule would have to be removed for codification to work, because precedent could no longer be allowed to be 'sovereign'.[176] In fact, instead of clearing the path for codification, the Practice Statement allowed judge-made law to supplement statutory reform, making comprehensive codes less necessary as well as less desirable. The Practice Statement has been accepted and 'observed with a regularity of subsequent judicial behaviour'.[177]

ii. Use and Effect of the Practice Statement

The Practice Statement proved relatively popular with House of Lords judges, who found that it gave them more 'freedom of movement' in certain cases.[178] It allowed the House of Lords (and now allows the Supreme Court)[179] more flexibility in place of 'rigid adherence' to bad or old law.[180] This flexibility increases the capacity for judges to develop, rather than just restate, the law. Previously, the House of Lords may have endeavoured to distinguish a case, or else would have been obliged to follow a bad decision and 'perpetuate the erroneous and unjust rule'.[181] To allow the Court to depart from previous decisions recognises 'error as a natural and regular phenomenon'.[182] It removes the belief that judges only state, and do not develop, the law—a belief decried by Lord Reid as a 'fairy tale'.[183] Moreover, an old judgment may not be bad law, but just outmoded law.[184] The Supreme Court need not always wait for Parliament to intervene to correct (or update) the law, but can, where appropriate, be 'master of its own house',[185] making it a more valuable contributor to law reform.

Because of the Practice Statement, 'the legislature and the judiciary could … share the burden of law reform', albeit with the judiciary playing a secondary

[175] Blom-Cooper, '1966 and All That' 134.

[176] Scarman, 'A Code of English Law?' 14; L Scarman, 'Codification and Judge-made Law: A Problem of Co-Existence' (lecture, University of Birmingham, 1966) 17.

[177] Blom-Cooper, '1966 and All That' 133.

[178] J Reid, 'The Judge as Law Maker' (1972–73) 12 *Journal of the Society of Public Teachers of Law* 22, 25 ('The Judge as Law Maker').

[179] *Austin v Southwark London Borough Council* [2010] UKSC 28, [2011] 1 AC 355, where the Practice Statement was not used, but Lord Hope confirmed that the Supreme Court did have the power to use it if it so wished: [25]. See too Supreme Court Practice Directions, Direction 3.1.3.

[180] *Practice Statement (Judicial Precedent)* [1966] 1 WLR 1234.

[181] R Wright, 'Precedents' (1942–44) 8 *CLJ* 118, 122 ('Precedents').

[182] JH Langbein, 'Modern Jurisprudence in the House of Lords: The Passing of *London Tramways*' (1967–68) 53 *Cornell Law Review* 807, 811 ('Modern Jurisprudence').

[183] Reid, 'The Judge as Law Maker' 22. See also section III.C above. Note, however, more recent judicial comments to the effect that judges only 'discover', rather than 'make', the law, eg, House of Lords Select Committee on the Constitution, 'Judicial Appointments Process', Oral and Written Evidence, Lord Judge, Q162 (2011).

[184] A Lester, 'English Judges as Law Makers' [1993] *PL* 269, 272 ('English Judges as Law Makers').

[185] Langbein, 'Modern Jurisprudence' 812.

role.[186] The recognition of the courts' development of the law being subordinate to the legislature is essential in a system that recognises parliamentary sovereignty,[187] and separation of powers.[188] Above all, the Practice Statement ensures that judges, when making the law, have 'a more overt concern with the search for a more just rule'.[189] Indeed, the enduring conflict between certainty and justice is the 'raison d'etre' of the Practice Statement.[190] The judges can thus supplement Parliament's (and the Commissions') role in law reform. Since the loosening of the stare decisis shackles, judges are more able to be 'alive to the importance of actively developing the law in ways which accord with modern thinking' and which are based on being '"fair" or "reasonable"'.[191] Although judicial creativity is controversial, it has made certain criticisms of the common law's limitations as a tool of reform less convincing.[192] Since the Practice Statement, an increase in judicial law-making has taken place, importantly with increased 'candour' rather than secrecy.[193]

The Practice Statement's effect as a tool of law reform is, however, limited for three main reasons. First, it only applies to the Supreme Court vis-a-vis its own decisions or old House of Lords decisions.[194] All other normal rules of precedent remain in force.[195] Second, a case on the issue in point must still arrive at the Court in the first place.[196] It may be, however, that parties are not deterred from bringing cases which would, to be decided in their favour, require a previous House of Lords or Supreme Court decision to be overruled.[197] Third and finally, in order to ensure that the law remains certain, '[n]o Court will be anxious to repudiate a precedent. It will do so only if it is completely satisfied that the precedent is erroneous'.[198] The Practice Statement does require that decisions of the House of Lords (and now, the Supreme Court) should be treated as 'normally binding'.[199] There has been a general consensus among judges that the Practice Statement should be used 'sparingly'.[200] Blom-Cooper calculated 21 explicit uses

[186] Blom-Cooper, '1966 and All That' 135.

[187] B Dickson, 'Judicial Activism in the House of Lords 1995–2007' in B Dickson (ed), *Judicial Activism in Common Law Supreme Courts* (Oxford, OUP, 2007) 363 ('Judicial Activism'). See also above n 160.

[188] ibid 367; Lester, 'English Judges as Law Makers' 270.

[189] Blom-Cooper, '1966 and All That' 142.

[190] Paterson, *The Law Lords*, 126.

[191] Dickson, 'Judicial Activism' 411–12.

[192] See, eg, N Marsh, 'Law Reform in the United Kingdom: A New Institutional Approach' (1971) 13 *William & Mary Law Review* 263, 269.

[193] Paterson, *The Law Lords*, 154. Note, however, that certain judges evidently think a 'facade' is safer than candour: ibid 169.

[194] Since July 2016, the Privy Council can also depart from previous House of Lords, Supreme Court or Court of Appeal decisions: *Willers v Joyce* [2016] UKSC 44, [2016] 3 WLR 534.

[195] Despite Lord Denning's attempts to allow the Court of Appeal to be freer to depart from its own precedents, and those of the House of Lords: see, eg, *Broome v Cassell & Co Ltd* [1971] 2 QB 354.

[196] P Devlin, 'The Process of Law Reform' (1966) 63 *Law Society's Gazette* 453, 461–62.

[197] Langbein, 'Modern Jurisprudence' 810.

[198] Wright, 'Precedents' 144.

[199] *Practice Statement (Judicial Precedent)* [1966] 1 WLR 1234.

[200] Paterson, *The Law Lords*, 157. On Lord Reid's seven criteria for the use of the Practice Statement (of which 'use sparingly' is one) see ibid 156–57.

of the Practice Statement between 1966 and 2008, plus more probable instances of implicit usage.[201] Although it has been described as a 'modest' contribution to law reform, the effect of the Practice Statement is not insignificant, and it has been of particular use where 'the judiciary has sensed the disinclination of politicians to act promptly and in areas appropriate for judicial determination'.[202] Decisions to overrule previous judgments have occurred in a number of legal areas, although the Practice Statement makes reference to the 'especial need for certainty as to the criminal law',[203] and the Court has subsequently shown reluctance to use the Practice Statement as freely in that area.[204] Langbein noted that the Practice Statement would 'not of itself rescue English law from its century of petrification'.[205] It was, however, one contribution towards the resurgence of the courts as a vehicle for law reform. Beyond the cases in which the Practice Statement has been used it undoubtedly has a 'symbolic dimension', which has given judges more confidence even when they do not use it.[206] Wholesale codification has become less necessary—piecemeal statutes and judge-made law can be sufficient law reform tools.

iii. Interpretation of Statutes

The Practice Statement was used in a case which increased judicial discretion even further. In *Pepper v Hart*,[207] the House of Lords for the first time allowed parliamentary materials to be consulted by the courts where a piece of legislation is 'ambiguous, or obscure or the literal meaning of which leads to an absurdity'.[208] A move away from a more literal interpretation of statutes is now thought by many to be 'obvious common sense'.[209] It allows judges to develop the law through their interpretation of statutes. In the past, the courts' development of the law had been limited, until judges such as Lord Denning popularised a more 'creative' approach to legislative interpretation. The Lords may have been influenced by the UK's entry into the EU, where the Court of Justice regularly looks behind European legislation to discern its intended meaning.[210] In contrast to inspiring codification,

[201] Blom-Cooper, '1966 and All That' 136–37; 143–44. Paterson calculated 'almost 25' overt uses of the Practice Statement between 1966 and 2009: A Paterson, *Final Judgment: The Last Law Lords and the Supreme Court* (Oxford, Hart Publishing, 2013) 268 (*Final Judgment*).

[202] Blom-Cooper, '1966 and All That' 135. *cf* Dickson, who has described the use of the power as 'rare': 'Judicial Activism' 413.

[203] *Practice Statement (Judicial Precedent)* [1966] 1 WLR 1234.

[204] JR Spencer, 'Precedent and Criminal Cases in the House of Lords' (1986) 45 *CLJ* 361.

[205] Langbein, 'Modern Jurisprudence' 813.

[206] Paterson, *The Law Lords*, 167–68; Paterson, *Final Judgment*, 266–68.

[207] *Pepper v Hart* [1993] AC 593.

[208] ibid 616. The Commissions had been in favour of retaining the rule excluding such material: LCEW and SLC, *The Interpretation of Statutes* (Law Com No 21 and Scot Law Com No 11 (1969)), but the House of Lords preferred the approach of the New Zealand Law Commission (NZLC): see *Pepper v Hart*, 600–02; NZLC, *A New Interpretation Act: To Avoid 'Prolixity and Tautology'* (NZLC R17 (1990)); and, for discussion, KJ Keith, 'Making Law—Who, How and What?' in Dyson, Lee and Stark, *Fifty Years of the Law Commissions*, 408–09.

[209] A Lester, 'English Judges as Law Makers' [1993] *PL* 269, 272.

[210] ibid 274.

entry into the EU may have actually contributed to an increase in judicial development of the law. The Practice Statement allowed judges more freedom to develop the common law—and it led to them having more freedom to develop enacted law as well. Although such freedom can be contentious, the argument that the courts could no longer serve as a suitable vehicle of law reform has become less convincing. As Paterson has put it, the House of Lords and now the Supreme Court have 'shared the burden of law reform with Parliament on a significant number of occasions' since 1966.[211] The need for wholesale codification of the law has therefore been reduced.

B. Other Judicial Changes

Beyond the Practice Statement, other judicial changes have also reduced the need for comprehensive codes. The judiciary's reputation has improved since the Commissions were established. Judge-made law is therefore not only a more vital tool of law reform, it is also, equally importantly, *perceived* as such. With judge-made law thriving, the attractiveness of codification has been reduced.

i. Judgments

Although one would have to go back centuries to find British cases where little or no reasoning was reported,[212] modern judgments are more detailed, well reasoned and (thanks to electronic databases) accessible than even in the recent past. In fact, certain commentators have argued that the problems caused by too brief judgments have now been replaced by judgments of the other extreme. Judgments have been criticised as being 'longer and longer' with 'tedious and unnecessary repetition', due to technological developments making such duplication much easier.[213] Modern English judges have, however, been praised for their 'literary style'[214] and more detailed judgments, which allow judge-made law to be more attractive as a source of law. Especially when the Practice Statement is used, and considering its terms and the House of Lords/Supreme Court's innate reluctance to overrule its precedents, judges undoubtedly feel like they must go to 'some lengths to justify their conclusions'.[215]

[211] Paterson, *Final Judgment*, 268.

[212] See further J Reid, 'The Judge as Law Maker' (1972–73) 12 *Journal of the Society of Public Teachers of Law* 22, 24.

[213] LCB Gower, 'Reflections on Law Reform' (1973) 23 *University of Toronto Law Journal* 257, 257–58. See also L Blom-Cooper, 'Style of Judgments' in L Blom-Cooper, B Dickson and G Drewry (eds), *The Judicial House of Lords 1876–2009* (Oxford, OUP, 2009) 159–63 ('Style of Judgments').

[214] Blom-Cooper, ibid 145.

[215] Dickson, 'Judicial Activism' 412.

In addition, the courts are increasingly eager (and able) to look to foreign jurisprudence and academic writing to carry out considered reform of the law.[216] The increasing interaction with academic writing may be partially attributable to the number of judges who have spent time at the Commissions, thereby coming into greater contact with academics,[217] as well as the increasing number of judges who have been academics themselves.[218] The demise of the 'better read when dead' rule (which dictated that a living author should not be cited in case he later changed his mind) has also contributed greatly to the increase in the use of academic works in the courts.[219]

As well as the quality of judgments arguably improving, the capacity for judicial law reform has increased. It has been observed that judges are increasingly writing collective judgments, which were first trialled (albeit without much success) in the 1960s.[220] In the 1970s varying trends could be seen in this regard. On the one hand, Paterson found in his extensive research into the House of Lords that certain Law Lords had 'reservations about introducing the single judgment with greater frequency in the Lords'.[221] On the other hand, he found that most other Law Lords wanted to avoid an 'unnecessary multiplication of opinions' and that a 'general willingness' to present a 'common front', albeit only in certain cases, was on the rise.[222] That rise has continued,[223] and an increase in single, or at least joint or plurality,[224] opinions has been observed since the creation of the Supreme Court.[225] A trend has also been observed for the Court of Appeal to give 'single or collective' judgments,[226] and indeed it is obliged to do so (with rare exceptions) in criminal cases.[227] The more this 'collegiate' system is used, the more 'clarity of expression,

[216] See, eg, on the use of foreign jurisprudence in the Supreme Court, J Bell, 'Comparative Law in the Supreme Court 2010–11' (2012) 1(2) *Cambridge Journal of International and Comparative Law* 20 and on the use of academic writing in the courts, H Beale, 'The Law Commission and Judicial Law Reform' (2001) 35 *The Law Teacher* 323, 323. For a Scottish perspective, see HL MacQueen, 'Judicial Reform of Private Law' (1998) 3 *Scottish Law and Practice Quarterly* 134, 150–51 (on the use of foreign jurisprudence) and 154–56 (on the use of academic writing).

[217] Paterson, *Final Judgment*, 215. As noted in ch 4, three of the current Supreme Court Justices have been Commissioners or Chairmen.

[218] Such as Lady Hale, Lord Goff and Lord Rodger: Paterson, ibid.

[219] Paterson, *Final Judgment*, 216.

[220] Blom-Cooper, 'Style of Judgments' 153.

[221] Paterson, *The Law Lords*, 98.

[222] ibid 97 and 100. That rise has been linked to Lord Reid's death in 1975, since he was 'strongly in favour' of multiple judgments: ibid 184 and 187.

[223] Although the rise was not a steady one. For the varying popularity of single judgments and the personalities that caused such trends, see Paterson, *Final Judgment*, 99–110.

[224] Joint opinions are written by more than one judge; plurality opinions are written by one judge with whom other judges are listed as agreeing—the latter were not permitted in the House of Lords: Paterson, *Final Judgment*, 144.

[225] ibid 106 (table 3.5).

[226] P Darbyshire, *Sitting in Judgment: The Working Lives of Judges* (Oxford, Hart Publishing, 2011) 324 (*Sitting in Judgment*).

[227] Senior Courts Act 1981, s 59.

certainty in the legal ruling and … brevity' there is in judgments, making them a more attractive source of law.[228] It also frees up judges to hear more cases, which is reflected in the Supreme Court, for example, processing a larger number of cases than the House of Lords did.[229] Although dangers of single judgments have been raised,[230] they do allow judge-made law to be more accessible and speedier, addressing concerns which had been expressed in the recent past.[231] Single majority judgments send 'clearer messages to other courts and the profession as to what the law is',[232] as well as allowing greater access to the courts, thus increasing the quality and quantity of judicial law reform.

ii. Reforming Judges

In addition to the common law in general being derided for being outmoded and not fit for purpose, specific judges and judgments were also under attack in the mid-twentieth century. The House of Lords was accused of falling into 'burgeoning disrepute'.[233] Certain of its decisions were so unpopular,[234] that they led Gardiner to call for the abolition of its judicial function.[235] Besides questionable decisions, there was a general attitude among the judiciary in the period immediately preceding the creation of the Commissions that '[l]aw reform was for the legislature'.[236]

Later, however, at least partially as a result of developments such as the Practice Statement, a number of the same judges who were under attack were said to have 'recovered their self-confidence' and '[f]rom the early 1960s … Lord Reid, Lord

[228] Blom-Cooper, 'Style of Judgments' 154.

[229] Dickson observed that 'about 60 cases per year' were being heard in the House of Lords in 2007: Dickson, 'Judicial Activism' 366. Seventy-nine cases were heard by the Supreme Court in 2015: Supreme Court website, 'Decided Cases' www.supremecourt.uk/decided-cases/2015.html. Note, however, the general increase in judgments heard by the House of Lords over time: Paterson, *Final Judgment*, 17. Note too other reasons for the greater number of cases being heard, such as time constraints on oral advocacy: Paterson, ibid 39.

[230] See, eg, R Munday, '"All for One and One for All": The Rise to Prominence of the Composite Judgment within the Civil Division of the Court of Appeal' (2002) 61 *CLJ* 321, who speculates on the unintended consequences of collegiate decisions which go 'entirely against the English legal grain' where a judge usually speaks 'entirely as an individual, even when sitting with colleagues' (321–22). See too Paterson's criticisms that single judgments 'remove the humanity of individual difference and potentially undermine transparency': *Final Judgment*, 315. See also M Kirby, 'Judicial Dissent—Common Law and Civil Law Traditions' (2007) 123 *LQR* 379.

[231] See, eg, L Scarman, 'Codification and Judge-made Law: A Problem of Co-Existence' (lecture, University of Birmingham, 1966) 2: 'Speed, accessibility, and convenience are … powerfully demanded of the law'.

[232] Paterson, *Final Judgment*, 322.

[233] JH Langbein, 'Modern Jurisprudence in the House of Lords: The Passing of *London Tramways*' (1967–68) 53 *Cornell Law Review* 807, 813.

[234] Particularly in relation to criminal law: for a discussion, see JR Spencer, 'Precedent and Criminal Cases in the House of Lords' (1986) 45 *CLJ* 361.

[235] G Gardiner and F Elwyn Jones, 'The Administration of Justice' in G Gardiner and A Martin (eds), *Law Reform Now* (London, Victor Gollancz, 1963) 16.

[236] Paterson, *Final Judgment*, 263.

Denning and Lord Wilberforce … breathed new life' into non-statutory law.[237] They were particularly 'wise and courageous' in protecting the rights of the citizen against the misuse of public powers and protecting civil rights and freedoms.[238] Through 'their own attitudes and performance', the negative image of judges and judge-made law was somewhat alleviated.[239] Paterson has observed that this trend began even before the Practice Statement, with Lord Denning and Lord Reid putting more emphasis on fairness over consistency from the early 1960s.[240] Indeed, for Paterson, the Practice Statement was only the 'culmination of a period of increasing willingness' of the House of Lords to reform the law given that there had been 'considerable judicial law-making' since 1962.[241] Lord Reid, Paterson notes, believed strongly in the House of Lords' role in 'developing the common law to meet changing economic and social conditions'.[242] Moving into the 1970s, Reid's view was shared by other judges, the majority of whom saw themselves as having an 'obligation to develop the common law to meet changing social conditions', which was 'a considerable shift from the dominant orthodoxy' of the 1950s.[243] The clear limits to judicial law-making 'derived from common sense, legal principle … and public policy' espoused by Reid may have afforded enough 'democratic legitimacy' to justify an increase in judicial law-making.[244]

Lord Bingham observed that Lord Denning also led an 'agenda of reform',[245] which, coupled with the Practice Statement, allowed judge-made law to move away from a 'slavish' adherence to precedent.[246] In addition, Denning's purposive approach to statutory interpretation led to judicial decision-making being 'aroused from its torpor'.[247] In one case, for example, Denning explicitly elected to reform the law himself, rather than recommending that the LCEW should examine the issue, noting that latter approach would lead to:

> [A] reference to the Law Commission; then a report by them; and eventually a Bill before Parliament. It would be quite a long time before the law could be set right. Even then the law would only be set right for future cases. Nothing could be done to set right this present case.[248]

[237] A Lester, 'English Judges as Law Makers' [1993] *PL* 269, 278. Although not all criticism ended in the 1960s. See, eg, G Williams, 'Recklessness Redefined' (1981) 40 *CLJ* 252.

[238] Lester, ibid 278–79 and the cases cited there.

[239] Darbyshire, *Sitting in Judgment*, 35.

[240] Paterson, *The Law Lords*, 137.

[241] ibid 143–44. But that law-making had to take place behind a facade until 1966: Paterson, *Final Judgment*, 264.

[242] Paterson, *The Law Lords*, 170.

[243] ibid 173.

[244] ibid 198.

[245] T Bingham, 'The Judge as Lawmaker: An English Perspective' in *The Business of Judging: Selected Essays and Speeches* (Oxford, OUP, 2011) 28.

[246] T Bingham, 'Address at the Service of Thanksgiving for the Rt Hon Lord Denning OM' in *The Business of Judging*, ibid 410.

[247] ibid.

[248] *R v Bow Road Justices (Domestic Proceedings Court), ex parte Adedigba* [1968] 2 QB 572, 579. See also, on the divided views of Law Lords to the Commissions' effect on their role, Paterson, *The Law Lords*, 183.

More recently, as we have already seen, there has been a rise in the number of judges with an academic background. This rise has been cited by Lord Hope as a reason for judicial law reform being on the increase.[249] Although such judicial activism can be highly controversial, particularly among politicians,[250] certain judges have been keen to take law reform into their own hands, even when the Commissions plan to propose reforms in that area.[251] The gap in judicial law reform that was identified in the 1960s is therefore not as large as it was, and the case for wholesale codification is therefore less compelling.

iii. Diversification of the Judiciary and Judicial Training

In the 1960s and 1970s, complaints were heard that the judiciary was not diverse enough to speak for modern British society.[252] Darbyshire noted that from around the second half of the twentieth century, judges were routinely subject to criticism for their 'narrow social background'.[253] Her comprehensive study of the modern judiciary published in 2011 showed that the influx of 'Baby Boomer' judges has improved diversity.[254] Far from all being from one set of society, of her sample of English judges across a range of courts, only around half were privately educated,[255] and around half went to Oxbridge.[256] Such increased diversity is partly due to the more accessible tertiary education opportunities that emerged in Britain in the second half of the twentieth century.[257] Darbyshire found that the 'era of expanding legal education' resulted in 66 of 77 judges in her sample being first-generation lawyers.[258] Darbyshire was not, however, completely content with judicial diversity. She conceded that the stereotype of judges being 'old, white and male' was true in the main—it was only the further cliché of judges being 'privileged, elitist, insensitive and out-of-touch' which was no longer accurate.[259] Similar changes to legal education in Scotland have resulted in similar diversification.[260] Although there is a long way to go in terms of securing a fully diverse judiciary,[261] it is much

[249] D Hope, 'Law Reform: Alternative Strategies to Legislation' in *Law Reform: Catching the Eye of Government* (papers from a joint seminar presented by the Law Commission and UCL Faculty of Laws, 2001) 36–37.

[250] See below n 293.

[251] *Radmacher v Granatino* [2010] UKSC 42, [2011] 1 AC 534 (Lady Hale dissenting). *cf Smith v Chief Constable of Sussex Police* [2008] UKHL 50, [2009] 1 AC 225 [102] (Lord Phillips), where the Court elected not to reform the law, preferring to await the outcome of a forthcoming LCEW project.

[252] See ch 2, section II.B.

[253] Darbyshire, *Sitting in Judgment*, 34–35.

[254] ibid 7.

[255] 40 out of 77: ibid 45.

[256] 35 out of 77: ibid.

[257] Noted in ch 2, section II.B. See also ibid 49.

[258] ibid 51.

[259] ibid 42.

[260] D Hope, 'Do We Still Need a Scottish Law Commission?' (2006) 10 *Edinburgh Law Review* 10, 23–24.

[261] S Wilson, 'Judiciary Diversity: Where Do We Go From Here?' (2013) 2(1) *Cambridge Journal of International and Comparative Law* 7.

less homogenous than it was when the Commissions were established. Diversity at the highest reaches of the judiciary is, however, still problematic. Paterson has argued convincingly that greater diversity would increase the legitimacy of judicial law-making.[262] The diversification that has occurred, however, has made the argument that judges do not represent today's 'wide-ranging social structure' less convincing.[263]

In Scotland, the Judicial Appointments Board for Scotland was introduced in 2002 'to create a more open and accessible system for judicial appointments in Scotland that could be readily understood and so command the respect of the legal profession and the general public'.[264] In England, the Constitutional Reform Act 2005 (the 2005 Act) established the Judicial Appointments Commission,[265] which is now responsible for recommending judges (except Supreme Court judges)[266] for appointment. The selection of new judges was previously within the remit of the Lord Chancellor, who made his decisions based on the 'soundings' of existing judges.[267] The old system of selection was subject to a lot of criticism from the mid-twentieth century onwards for its 'systemic bias'[268] whereby it was often perceived that 'white Oxbridge males selected white Oxbridge males'.[269] The 2005 Act specifically enshrines in law that appointments must now be made solely on merit,[270] but that regard should also be had to the need for diversity in the pool of available applicants.[271] The new selection process has not been immune from criticism,[272] but it is preferable to the previous model.

As well as judicial selection now being more transparent, training is also prioritised so as to set standards for modern judges. Formal judicial training in England was the responsibility of the Judicial Studies Board from 1979, and since 2011 has been provided by the Judicial College. The Judicial Institute provides ongoing training for Scottish judges. In short, more transparent hiring procedures and training requirements in both jurisdictions have partially addressed concerns about the judiciary and their ability to contribute to law reform.

262 Paterson, *Final Judgment*, 286; A Paterson and C Paterson, *Guarding the Guardians? Towards an Independent, Accountable and Diverse Senior Judiciary* (London, CentreForum, 2012) 37 and 39 (*Guarding the Guardians*).

263 L Scarman, 'Codification and Judge-made Law: A Problem of Co-Existence' (lecture, University of Birmingham, 1966) 18.

264 Judicial Appointments Board for Scotland website, 'History' www.judicialappointments.scot/about-us/history.

265 2005 Act, s 61.

266 On the lack of accountability of the appointment of Supreme Court judges see Paterson, *Final Judgment*, 309. Elsewhere, Paterson and another have argued that the system is 'not fit for purpose' because it is dominated by the senior judiciary themselves: Paterson and Paterson, *Guarding the Guardians*, 33.

267 Darbyshire, *Sitting in Judgment*, 97.

268 ibid 21.

269 N Phillips, 'Constitutional Reform: One Year On' (Judicial Studies Board Annual Lecture, 2007) 8.

270 2005 Act, s 63.

271 2005 Act, s 64.

272 See, eg, Darbyshire, *Sitting in Judgment*, 100–01.

iv. The Supreme Court

In 2009, the judicial function of the House of Lords was replaced by a new Supreme Court.[273] The Supreme Court is now more obviously independent than the House of Lords was, having broken its 'historic link with Parliament' and thereby adhering more obviously to the doctrine of separation of powers.[274] Dickson has noted that the House of Lords typically took a 'cautious' approach to reform and was generally 'unwilling to tread on the toes of the legislature' except when absolutely necessary.[275] Dickson ponders whether this deference to Parliament was because of the Law Lords' own membership of the House of Lords, which made them 'all the more conscious of the appropriate division of responsibilities between elected representatives and judges'.[276] If Dickson is correct, the inability of serving Supreme Court Justices to sit or vote in the House of Lords[277] should cause a surge in judicial activism. It must be acknowledged, however, that the House of Lords did not always shy away from judicial activism or controversial decisions.[278] Dickson himself has noted the House of Lords' particular activism in the areas of equality and human rights.[279] Indeed Paterson has observed a trend for the Supreme Court to be 'less overt' in judicial law-making than the post-1966 House of Lords, its 'coyness' caused by a combination of factors such as an acute awareness of the importance of the separation of powers, its control over its caseload and its increasingly politicised subject matter.[280]

The more important consideration for present purposes is that the public perception of judicial independence has been improved by the Supreme Court's physical separation from Parliament, thereby refuting previous criticisms of the House of Lords' judicial function.[281] Greater transparency and accessibility through televised hearings and press releases may also have increased the Court's status in the eyes of the public.[282] That increase in status could be one reason for there being less of a clamour for codification than there was in 1965.

[273] 2005 Act, pt 3.

[274] Darbyshire, *Sitting in Judgment*, 361.

[275] B Dickson, 'Judicial Activism in the House of Lords 1995–2007' in B Dickson (ed), *Judicial Activism in Common Law Supreme Courts* (Oxford, OUP, 2007) 367 ('Judicial Activism').

[276] ibid 368.

[277] 2005 Act, s 137(3).

[278] Consider, eg, the famous example of judicial ingenuity in *Anisminic Ltd v Foreign Compensation Commission* [1969] 2 AC 147.

[279] Dickson, 'Judicial Activism' 379–80.

[280] Paterson, *Final Judgment*, 272–73.

[281] The Select Committee on the Constitutional Reform Bill was told by Diana Woodhouse that 'seeing the final and top court in its own building is very important psychologically for public confidence and perception about judicial independence': House of Lords Select Committee, *First Report, Constitutional Reform Bill* (2004, HL 125) para 103.

[282] Lord Phillips, the first President of the Supreme Court, was deliberately chosen as a 'moderniser': Paterson, *Final Judgment*, 158.

C. European Dimensions

Two separate European developments have, despite causing controversy, also added to the judiciary's ability to contribute to law reform.

i. European Union

We have already seen that the UK's proposed entry into what is now the European Union was one important motivation for codification. When the UK joined the EU in 1973, domestic legislative autonomy was curtailed where EU law took priority. As a consequence, judicial power over the UK legislature increased. For Member States, EU law 'reigns supreme'.[283] British judges were therefore obliged to interpret domestic legislation 'subject to' EU law.[284] In the infamous *Factortame* series of cases, a domestic statute was disapplied when it could not be reconciled with EU law.[285] The courts' controversial power to disapply primary legislation 'profoundly alter[ed]' the status of our judges as the ultimate arbiters of European integration.[286] Thus, one purported reason for codification actually led to an increased role for the judges on occasion to disapply provisions of primary legislation.

When the UK voted to leave the EU in June 2016, any remaining thoughts that codification was necessary for EU integration were perhaps laid to rest. Indeed, the Euroscepticism which has ultimately prevailed in the UK is surely one additional reason for the failure of codification—a distinctly European import.

ii. European Convention on Human Rights

The incorporation of the European Convention on Human Rights (the ECHR) into our domestic law provided a further reason for the increased importance of judge-made law. When Parliament passed the Human Rights Act 1998 (the HRA) to 'bring rights home',[287] domestic courts were given powers to uphold Convention rights, albeit that the parameters of those powers were prescribed by Parliament to preserve its sovereignty. The courts are required to interpret domestic legislation compatibly with Convention rights '[s]o far as it is possible to do so',[288] a much stronger power than their previous powers of interpretation. Where reconciliation is not possible, certain courts may declare domestic legislation to be

[283] A Lester, 'English Judges as Law Makers' [1993] *PL* 269, 288 ('English Judges as Law Makers').

[284] European Communities Act 1972 (ECA), s 2(4).

[285] *R v Secretary of State for Transport ex p Factortame (No 1)* [1990] 2 AC 85; *R v Secretary of State for Transport ex p Factortame (No 2)* [1991] 1 AC 603.

[286] Lester, 'English Judges as Law Makers' 288.

[287] Home Office, *Rights Brought Home: The Human Rights Bill* (Cm 3782, 1997).

[288] Human Rights Act 1998 (HRA), s 3(1).

incompatible with Convention rights.[289] The ability to make such declarations has been described as an 'immense power',[290] despite the fact that it stops short of allowing the courts to 'strike down' legislation and the legislation continues in force until governmental action is taken. A modest number of declarations have been made,[291] and the courts will sometimes go to great lengths to use the interpretation power rather than declaration power.[292] The House of Lords had already showed particular judicial activism with regard to human rights and equality law, and the HRA provided the impetus for even further development by it and the Supreme Court.[293] In addition, the Supreme Court now also has a mechanism for departing from earlier decisions without the need for recourse to the Practice Statement where precedent is not in line with the ECHR.[294]

Both the European Communities Act 1972 (ECA) and the HRA are code-like in their generality. It is for the courts to interpret what the EU instruments and the broad rights contained in the ECHR mean. The courts are now therefore dealing with codification-style generality, but as part of an increased law reform role. The 1960s plea for law reform by systematic legislation, and codification by the Commissions, is no longer essential because the courts are more able to reform the law than they were at that time. The Supreme Court's position as a quasi-constitutional court, looking frequently at human rights cases, does, however, result in less private law and 'lawyers' law' being settled by our highest court.[295] A particular need exists, therefore, for the Commissions to carry out such work. When developing the criteria for project selection in chapter three, it was noted that the 'suitability' of a project includes the likelihood of other bodies carrying out work in that area. The greater ability of judges to develop the law has made the case for codification less compelling. It has not, however, made the need for the Commissions obsolete because judicial law reform is still limited. Especially in small jurisdictions such as Scotland, we cannot expect a large amount of reform to come from the courts.[296] Of course law reform by legislation is still needed and the

[289] HRA, s 4. The courts with the power to make such declarations are listed in HRA, s 4(5).

[290] Darbyshire, *Sitting in Judgment*, 359.

[291] 22 declarations had become final as at November 2016: Ministry of Justice, *Responding to Human Rights Judgments: Report to the Joint Committee on Human Rights on the Government's Response to Human Rights Judgments 2014–16* (Cm 9360, 2016) annex A.

[292] See, eg, *Ghaidan v Godin-Mendoza* [2004] UKHL 30, [2004] 2 AC 557.

[293] Dickson, 'Judicial Activism' 379–80. Such judicial activism is not uncontroversial. See, eg, T May, '"It is Not for Judges to be Legislators": Home Secretary's Public Attack on Rebel Judges' *Mail on Sunday* (17 February 2013).

[294] Dickson, 'Judicial Activism' 414, and the examples cited there.

[295] Paterson estimated in 2013 that 47% of the Supreme Court's case load comprised public law and human rights cases, because of the HRA and the growth in judicial review: Paterson, *Final Judgment*, 285. Unfortunately, the reduction in tax law cases from 30% to 4% of the Court's output is not a gap the Commissions can plug: ibid 285 and 289, and see ch 3 on the Commissions' lack of tax law remit.

[296] Lord Pentland, 'The Scottish Law Commission and the Future of Law Reform in Scotland' 2016 *Juridical Review* 169, 172. *cf* Lord Carloway, 'To "Mend the Laws, That Neids Mendement": A Scottish Perspective on Lawyers as Law Reformers' (speech at the Commonwealth Association of Law Reform Agencies Conference, Edinburgh, 2015) 20.

Commissions fulfil the important function of examining areas that do not reach the courts, and that government departments do not have the time or expertise to examine.[297] But Lady Hale has remarked that Commission proposals to reform the common law are less likely to be implemented than those which propose to reform statutory law, and so the courts thus fulfil a valuable role in reforming the common law.[298] As Paterson has argued, law reform is now a shared partnership between all three branches of government and the Commissions.[299]

V. The Commissions' Codification Track Records

The 'naivety'[300] of the Commissions' early codification plans is evidenced by the fact that they have, due to the factors we have already considered, achieved little codification. The 1965 Act has been interpreted as implying that the Commissions should at least consider codification,[301] although views on whether it is a 'duty' as such vary.[302] Different Commissioners take different views as to whether they should at least consider codification as an option in their proposed reforms,[303] with one current SLC Commissioner stating that he considers it his 'responsibility to keep codification under active consideration'.[304] Codification projects tend not to fare well in the implementation stakes. For example, the LCEW's second attempt to codify criminal law had to be broken up into much smaller pieces in order to achieve even partial implementation.[305] The Commissions' poor codification record, however, has not only been caused by a lack of implementation, but by the Commissions' own limited resources and decreasing inclination to undertake such work. The Commissions should not be criticised on that basis—codification was never an ideal task for them and the reasons for codification have become less

[297] Pentland, ibid.

[298] B Hale, 'Legislation or Judicial Law Reform: Where Should Judges Fear to Tread?' (Society of Legal Scholars Annual Conference, 2016) 13–15.

[299] Paterson, *Final Judgment*, 311. On the need to establish who does what within that partnership, see J Lee, 'The Etiquette of Law Reform' in Dyson, Lee and Stark, *Fifty Years of the Law Commissions*, ch 29.

[300] JH Farrar, *Law Reform and the Law Commission* (London, Sweet & Maxwell, 1974) 124; A Rodger, 'The Bell of Law Reform' 1993 *Scots Law Times (News)* 339, 342.

[301] Farrar, ibid 59.

[302] Compare ibid 28 with A Steven, 'Codification: A Perspective from a Scottish Law Commissioner' (Seminar Series on Codification, All Souls College, Oxford, 2014) 9 ('Codification').

[303] eg, compare two SLC discussion papers: *Discussion Paper on Moveable Transactions* (Scot Law Com DP No 151 (2011)) and *Discussion Paper on Adults with Incapacity* (Scot Law Com DP No 156 (2012)). The former states that, due to the extensive reforms needed in the area: 'for the present we are not thinking of the codification of these areas of law. In the longer term such codification might well be desirable' (para 1.18). The latter makes no mention of codification.

[304] Steven, 'Codification' 20.

[305] See section V.A.

convincing. Instead, the 1965 Act should be amended to remove the expectation of codification.

A. LCEW

The LCEW has not settled on any one definition of codification. A lack of clarity as to the meaning of codification can be problematic—a joint project to devise a unified contract code in the 1960s and 1970s collapsed, partly due to a lack of agreement between the SLC and the LCEW as to what codification involved. On one occasion, the LCEW favoured Bennion's definition of the 'useful reduction of scattered enactments and judgments on a particular topic to coherent expression within a single formulation'.[306] This definition could mean a continental-style code, or equally a codifying statute, depending on the size of the 'particular topic'. Bennion's definition does not mention the necessity for any reform. Because of the LCEW's previous tendency to combine reform and codification,[307] it added to the definition that a code would make 'any changes considered necessary'.[308] Equally, the LCEW has used the term 'codification' when the proposed reform seems more like normal legislation.[309] It has been argued that, since 1965, the LCEW's 'conception of what codification means has shrunk to very modest proportions'.[310] Where codification is expressly considered (and in many reports it is not) it has often been rejected.[311]

In its *First Programme of Law Reform*, the LCEW set out ambitious plans for a contract code, a code of landlord and tenant law and a code of family law,[312] followed in its *Second Programme* by a criminal code.[313] Apart from a later attempt to revive the criminal code, and an unsuccessful attempt to codify the law relating to compulsory purchase,[314] there have been no other major codification projects.[315] Some quasi-codification has been achieved through codifying statutes,

[306] F Bennion, *Statutory Interpretation*, 3rd edn (London, Butterworths, 1997) 466, cited in LCEW, *Seventh Programme of Law Reform* (Law Com No 259 (1999)) 18, fn 84.

[307] See above n 89.

[308] *Seventh Programme*, 18, fn 84.

[309] See, eg: LCEW, *Report on Personal Injury Litigation: Assessment of Damages* (Law Com No 56 (1973)) paras 20 and 159, app 4, para 12 and explanatory notes cl 1; and LCEW, *Double Jeopardy and Prosecution Appeals* (Law Com No 267 (2001)) pt VI.

[310] I Dennis, 'RIP: The Criminal Code (1968–2008)' [2009] *Crim LR* 1, 1.

[311] eg: LCEW, *Law of Contract: Minors' Contracts* (Law Com No 134 (1984)) para 3.4; LCEW, *Fiduciary Duties and Regulatory Rules* (Law Com No 236 (1995)) para 12.2; and LCEW, *The Execution of Deeds or Documents by or on behalf of Bodies Corporate* (Law Com No 253 (1998)) para 1.15.

[312] LCEW, *First Programme of Law Reform* (Law Com No 1 (1965)) items I, VIII and X respectively.

[313] LCEW, *Second Programme of Law Reform* (Law Com No 14 (1968)) item XVIII.

[314] LCEW, *Towards a Compulsory Purchase Code: (1) Compensation* (Law Com No 286 (2003)) and LCEW, *Towards a Compulsory Purchase Code: (2) Procedure* (Law Com No 291 (2004)).

[315] A commercial code was mooted in the 1990s, but never got under way. See *Seventh Programme*, paras 1.14–1.15; M Arden, 'Time for an English Commercial Code?' (1997) 56 *CLJ* 516.

for example, the Unfair Contract Terms Act 1977[316] (and later the Consumer Rights Act 2015)[317] and various family law Acts.[318]

In relation to the ill-fated contract code drafted with the SLC, the LCEW started out optimistically:

> We are very conscious of the desirability of producing a code which will, so far as possible, be common to both England and Scotland and which, in due course, will facilitate a closer association between the United Kingdom and the Continent of Europe … The two Commissions have exchanged ideas regarding the nature and arrangement of the proposed code.[319]

This optimism soon faded, and the demise of the contract code, instigated by the Scots, is discussed below. The family law, landlord and tenant and criminal codes also faltered. In contrast to the grand plans to codify, piecemeal chunks of reform were presented over the years.[320] Most (but not all) of these projects resulted in discrete statutes, and occasionally codifying statutes. For example, the Criminal Attempts Act 1981 (the result of a report emanating from the criminal code project) has been described as a codifying statute because it 'amends and sets out completely the law relating to attempts'.[321] More continental-style codification, however, is a huge undertaking, and has proved too much for a body as small as the LCEW to undertake. Dissecting the work into more manageable pieces has been essential for the LCEW to be able to make any progress at all in codifying the law.[322]

Another attempt to codify the criminal law was made in the 1980s. This attempt (acknowledging the LCEW's limited resources) began as research undertaken by

[316] Resulting from a joint project between the two Commissions: LCEW and SLC, *Exemption Clauses: Second Report* (Law Com No 69 and Scot Law Com No 39 (1975)).

[317] Resulting from three joint projects: LCEW and SLC, *Unfair Terms in Contracts* (Law Com No 292 and Scot Law Com No 199 (2005)); *Consumer Remedies for Faulty Goods* (Law Com No 317 and Scot Law Com No 216 (2009)); and *Consumer Redress for Misleading and Aggressive Practices* (Law Com No 332 and Scot Law Com No 226 (2012)).

[318] eg: the Family Law Reform Act 1987 (LCEW, *Family Law: Illegitimacy* (Law Com No 118 (1982)) and LCEW, *Family Law: Illegitimacy (Second Report)* (Law Com No 157 (1986))); the Children Act 1989 (LCEW, *Review of Child Law: Guardianship* (Law Com No 172 (1988))); and the Family Law Act 1996 (LCEW, *The Ground for Divorce* (Law Com No 192 (1990)) and LCEW, *Domestic Violence and Occupation of the Family Home* (Law Com No 207 (1992))).

[319] LCEW, *First Annual Report: 1965–66* (Law Com No 4 (1966)) para 32.

[320] To take just a few examples: LCEW, *Landlord and Tenant: Report on the Landlord and Tenant Act 1954 Part II* (Law Com No 17 (1969)); LCEW, *Proposal for the Abolition of the Matrimonial Remedy of Restitution of Conjugal Rights* (Law Com No 23 (1969)); LCEW, *Criminal Law: Report on Offences of Damage to Property* (Law Com No 29 (1970)); and LCEW, *Criminal Law: Report on Conspiracy and Criminal Law Reform* (Law Com No 76 (1976)).

[321] *R v Jones* [1990] 1 WLR 1057, 1060. The 1981 Act implemented LCEW, *Criminal Law: Attempt and Impossibility in Relation to Attempt, Conspiracy and Incitement* (Law Com No 102 (1980)). The court in *Jones* also claimed (1060) that the 1981 Act is a complete code on conspiracy, but see the Criminal Law Act 1977, ss 1–5 (as partially amended by the 1981 Act). The 1977 Act is, however, also based on LCEW recommendations: LCEW, *Criminal Law: Report on Conspiracy and Criminal Law Reform* (Law Com No 76 (1976)).

[322] Such reform allegedly paves the way for future codification by consolidation: see below n 340.

an external group chaired by JC Smith and carried out under the auspices of the LCEW,[323] before a final report with the LCEW's additions was published.[324] Smith admitted that he was not a fan of codification 'for its own sake' and, in fact, 'did not support' the Commissions' earlier endeavours to codify contract law.[325] Codification of the law of contract, he felt, had 'no practical advantage' because the law in that area was 'generally consistent, coherent and logical'.[326] Criminal law, on the other hand, required codification because it was 'incoherent and inconsistent'.[327] The criminal code, therefore, was intended to reform the law, not just restate it. Apparently the then LCEW Chairman, Sir Ralph Gibson, would have preferred restatement of the current law. Such restatement, Smith felt 'would not have been worthy of the name Code. The essence of a code is that it should be a consistent and coherent whole. A mere restatement of the present law would necessarily have lacked that essential quality'.[328] Smith believed that his code embodied the main advantages of codification: accessibility, comprehensibility and certainty.[329] He also argued that the effect on the common law would be negligible, because most of the law was currently found in statute anyway.[330] As for the areas of criminal law (for example, murder and manslaughter) still covered by the common law, Smith had contempt for their piecemeal progress, asking rhetorically 'is there anything in their development over the last thirty years in which we can take any pride?'.[331]

In devising the criminal code, Smith also attacked the slow progress of the common law. Lord Reid had previously endorsed the slower progress of the common law, musing 'more haste less speed'.[332] For Smith, such slow progress in the field of criminal law was unacceptable, as he noted in relation to the unsettled mens rea of murder, '[t]he common law develops slowly; but 700 years to determine the mental element required for our gravest crime is too long'.[333] Although the criminal

[323] LCEW, *Criminal Law: Codification of the Criminal Law—A Report to the Law Commission* (Law Com No 143 (1985)). For more detail on this project from one of its members, see I Dennis, 'The Law Commission and the Criminal Law: Reflections on the Codification Project' in Dyson, Lee and Stark, *Fifty Years of the Law Commissions*, ch 12.

[324] LCEW, *Criminal Law: A Criminal Code for England and Wales* (Law Com No 177 (1989)).

[325] JC Smith, 'Codification of the Criminal Law' (lecture, Inns of Court School of Law, 1986) 2 ('Codification of the Criminal Law').

[326] ibid.

[327] ibid. Such 'incoherence and inconsistency' was heavily criticised in the 1980s: see, eg, G Williams, 'Recklessness Redefined' (1981) 40 *CLJ* 252. See further T Bingham, 'A Criminal Code: Must We Wait for Ever?' in *The Business of Judging: Selected Essays and Speeches* (Oxford, OUP, 2011) 296 ('Must We Wait for Ever?'), where it was argued that 'arguments for incremental development of the law, persuasive elsewhere, have no application' in criminal law, due to the likelihood of unjust punishment.

[328] Smith, 'Codification of the Criminal Law' 3.

[329] ibid 6–7.

[330] ibid 11.

[331] ibid.

[332] J Reid, 'The Judge as Law Maker' (1972–73) 12 *Journal of the Society of Public Teachers of Law* 22, 28.

[333] Smith, 'Codification of the Criminal Law' 12. See also Bingham, 'Must We Wait for Ever?' 296–97. The same argument has been made in relation to Scotland: E Clive, 'Codification of the Criminal Law' in J Chalmers, F Leverick and L Farmer (eds), *Essays in Criminal Law in Honour of Sir Gerald Gordon* (Edinburgh, EUP, 2010) 60–63 (*Essays in Criminal Law in Honour of Sir Gerald Gordon*).

code is the closest thing to a continental-style code published by the LCEW, it does make reference to certain rules of the common law still applying except insofar as they are covered by, or inconsistent with, the code.[334]

Despite apparently piquing the government's interest,[335] and generally having 'commanded respect and support',[336] the criminal code was never implemented, apparently due to a lack of parliamentary time (or, more accurately, lack of prioritisation of that time).[337] The fact that the criminal code was not implemented was described by one former LCEW Chairman as being 'very disappointing'.[338] Several parts of the code were divided up into more manageable reforms, most (but not all) of which were implemented, at least partially.[339] The intention behind this division was that the Acts could later be 'welded together into a Code' and the resultant work could find time in Parliament more easily by qualifying for the streamlined procedure for consolidation Bills.[340] Such consolidation has not been attempted and, because of the patchwork nature of the reforms, the resultant code would lack comprehensiveness—particularly because certain of the reports were implemented in small parts only.[341] Given that Parliamentary Counsel are 'very reluctant to codify existing rules of law',[342] it seems unlikely that the gaps left by the LCEW would be closed by an eventual codifying Bill. One solution could be for the new statute to have 'flags' to other existing provisions,[343] but that solution cannot work where the rules are found in the common law, and in any event is not as user-friendly as a comprehensive code.

[334] LCEW, *Criminal Law: A Criminal Code for England and Wales* (Law Com No 177 (1989)) draft Bill, cl 4(4). *cf* The Scottish *Draft Criminal Code* (discussed at section V.B below) which, by contrast, provides that 'Nothing done after the commencement of this Act is an offence under the law of Scotland unless so provided by legislation' (cl 1).

[335] W Bach, 'Law Reform: Servant or Master of Government Policy?' in *Law Reform: Catching the Eye of Government* (papers from a joint seminar presented by the Law Commission and UCL Faculty of Laws, 2001) 8 ('Servant or Master?').

[336] Bingham, 'Must We Wait for Ever?' 295.

[337] Bach, 'Servant or Master?' 9; JR Spencer, 'The Codification of Criminal Procedure' in Chalmers, Leverick and Farmer, *Essays in Criminal Law in Honour of Sir Gerald Gordon*, 316; GA Weiss, 'The Enchantment of Codification in the Common-Law World' (2000) 25 *Yale Journal of International Law* 435, 495; M Arden, 'Time for an English Commercial Code?' (1997) 56 *CLJ* 516, 524; LCEW, *Seventh Programme of Law Reform* (Law Com No 259 (1999)) 19.

[338] Arden, ibid 536.

[339] See, eg, LCEW, *Legislating the Criminal Code: Offences against the Person and General Principles* (Law Com No 218 (1993)); and LCEW, *Legislating the Criminal Code: Involuntary Manslaughter* (Law Com No 237 (1996)).

[340] *Seventh Programme*, 19. For a description of the streamlined consolidation procedure, see ch 4, section I.B.

[341] For example, LCEW, *Legislating the Criminal Code: Offences against the Person and General Principles* (Law Com No 218 (1993)) (only one recommendation implemented by the Domestic Violence, Crime and Victims Act 2004) and LCEW, *Legislating the Criminal Code: Involuntary Manslaughter* (Law Com No 237 (1996)) (partially implemented by the Corporate Manslaughter and Corporate Homicide Act 2007).

[342] C Harpum, 'The Refiner's Fire' in Dyson, Lee and Stark, *Fifty Years of the Law Commissions*, 312.

[343] D Ormerod, 'Reflections on the Courts and the Commission' in Dyson, Lee and Stark, *Fifty Years of the Law Commissions*, 331.

The difficulty of the LCEW's codification task has been openly acknowledged by many of its personnel. In 1980, while still Chairman, Sir Michael Kerr referred to the 'failure' of codification, and opined that it was 'unattainable in this country'.[344] In relation to the LCEW's attempt to codify the law of landlord and tenant, he lamented that it had 'no realistic prospect' of success.[345] In 1997, successful codification was described as being 'unlikely',[346] a remark which was derided as being 'depressing',[347] coming as it did from a former LCEW Commissioner (Sir Jack Beatson). In 2007, the then LCEW Chairman, Sir Terence Etherton, stated that there had been a 'downgrading of codification as an explicit objective of [the LCEW's] programmes of reform'.[348] The subsequent Chairman, Sir James Munby, agreed, adding that not only was there no 'political will' for codification, but that there was 'indeed little enthusiasm for any kind of systematic law reform'.[349] In 2008, the LCEW noted in its *Tenth Programme of Law Reform* that, despite codification being 'desirable', its 'main priority' would be to 'reform an area of the law sufficiently to enable it to return and codify the law at a subsequent stage'.[350] In the same year, the LCEW also formally ended its endeavour to codify the criminal law,[351] something that has been described as 'dispiriting and frustrating'.[352] Munby reiterated his view that codification was not to be prioritised in 2011 when he said that the LCEW's codification function is now 'little more than a distant memory'.[353] Munby's view was radical in that, while LCEW Chairman, he consciously disregarded one of the LCEW's tasks under its founding legislation. His approach is to be praised, however, in directing the LCEW's resources to endeavours which better satisfy the project-selection criteria. More recently, however, a resurgence in codification is evident, albeit that the plans of what can be achieved are more realistic. The process of codification in the UK, in contrast to the norm in most other countries, may have to be a gradual one—a 'decidedly British model of codification'.[354]

The LCEW has been working on a broad project on the simplification of criminal law, which it notes is 'not the same as codification, but includes work that

[344] M Kerr, 'Law Reform in Changing Times' (1980) 96 *LQR* 515, 527.

[345] ibid 529.

[346] J Beatson, 'Has the Common Law a Future?' (1997) 56 *CLJ* 291, 301.

[347] T Bingham, 'The Future of the Common Law' in *The Business of Judging: Selected Essays and Speeches* (Oxford, OUP, 2011) 387.

[348] T Etherton, 'Law Reform in England and Wales: A Shattered Dream or Triumph of Political Vision?' (Bar Law Reform Committee Lecture, 2007) 35.

[349] J Munby, 'Shaping the Law—The Law Commission at the Crossroads' (Denning Lecture, 2011) 12 ('Shaping the Law').

[350] LCEW, *Tenth Programme of Law Reform* (Law Com No 311 (2008)) para 1.5.

[351] ibid para 1.6.

[352] I Dennis, 'RIP: The Criminal Code (1968–2008)' [2009] *Crim LR* 1, 1 ('RIP: The Criminal Code').

[353] Munby, 'Shaping the Law' 11.

[354] M Dyson, J Lee and SW Stark, 'Introduction' in Dyson, Lee and Stark, *Fifty Years of the Law Commissions*, 13–14.

could be preparatory to later codification'.[355] Projects on kidnapping and public nuisance have already been completed.[356] In addition, the LCEW is working on a sentencing code project.[357] The LCEW has changed the way it approaches codification, favouring a more piecemeal approach, which is infinitely more achievable than its earlier plans. It may even be that by working in a more piecemeal fashion, 'codification values' become normalised and thus more can be achieved.[358]

Even the closest attempt to codify English law in a continental style did not plan to oust the common law completely. The LCEW has achieved little codification (however defined) yet still perseveres towards it as an ultimate goal. Reforming the substance of the law is now prioritised, with the view that it can then be codified at a later date. If codification is ultimately to be achieved, the LCEW has admirably done a great deal of preparatory work. If the codification stage is to be proceeded to, however, the Commissions are not necessarily the right bodies to undertake it.[359] The LCEW should not be attacked for its lack of codification success. Instead, it should be protected from such attack by amending the 1965 Act to remove the expectation to codify. Such removal would not prevent the Commissions from codifying when it might be appropriate (or undertaking its useful preparatory work) considering the wording of section 3(1) of the 1965 Act:

> It shall be the duty of each of the Commissions to take and keep under review all the law with which they are respectively concerned with a view to its systematic development and reform, including in particular *the codification of such law*, the elimination of anomalies, the repeal of obsolete and unnecessary enactments, the reduction of the number of separate enactments and generally the simplification and modernisation of the law.

Emphasis has been added to the provision to demonstrate how the specific codification task could be removed. The remainder of section 3(1) would allow codification to take place where appropriate without putting too much emphasis on the codification task, or causing any ambiguity as to what 'codification' means.

B. SLC

The SLC has sometimes been clear that codification should mean something between continental-style codes and codifying statutes. Like the LCEW, however,

[355] LCEW, *Annual Report 2011–12* (Law Com No 334 (2012)) para 2.34. Although, as Dennis notes, '[n]o one will be holding their breath': Dennis, 'RIP: The Criminal Code' 1. Simplification of the criminal law was an item in the LCEW's *Tenth Programme*.

[356] LCEW, *Kidnapping and Related Offences* (Law Com No 355 (2014)); *Public Nuisance and Outraging Public Decency* (Law Com No 358 (2015)).

[357] LCEW, *A New Sentencing Code for England and Wales* (Law Com No 365 (2016)).

[358] I Dennis, 'The Law Commission and the Criminal Law: Reflections on the Codification Project' in Dyson, Lee and Stark, *Fifty Years of the Law Commissions*, 120.

[359] If codification is to be pursued, Hogg's suggestion of the establishment of a 'Civil Code Commission' is worth investigating and adapting to other areas of law: M Hogg, 'Codification of Private Law:

the SLC has occasionally used the term 'codification' to apply to something more like normal statutory reform.[360] When codification has even been considered as an option (and, like the LCEW, many reports do not mention codification at all) it has frequently been rejected by the SLC across many areas of law.[361]

Scotland was, despite being a legal system with mixed common and civil law roots, generally not eager for codification in 1965. Like other aspects of the Commissions' foundation, the codification function was already established before the enterprise was extended to Scotland. As with law reform machinery generally, relatively few calls for codification were heard in Scotland. William Ross, the Secretary of State for Scotland in 1965, acknowledged that codification was a difficult task, but he felt that the time was ripe to attempt it.[362] But even Lord Cooper, who strongly favoured a civil code,[363] opposed the codification of criminal law to avoid 'premature rigidity'.[364] Gane has argued that a 'preference for judge-made law as opposed to legislation is undoubtedly one of the hallmarks of Scottish criminal law'.[365] A distinction between civil and criminal law has also been drawn in England, but the opposite conclusion (that codification of the criminal law is more, not less, important) is usually reached.[366] Certain Scots feared that codification would condemn the once flexible law to a 'straitjacket'.[367] In criminal law in particular, it has been noted that Scots lawyers dislike 'abstract theory', and instead have 'a preference for proceeding by way of concrete example', thus creating an antipathy towards codification.[368] Furthermore, concern was expressed at the Commissions' outset about codification being a vehicle for the harmonisation of the laws of Scotland and England. TB Smith had written in the early 1960s about the possibility of 'a small committee directed by a master mind' to oversee the codification of 'British' law. Far from recommending its creation, he felt that such a body could only be supported by 'sky-blue idealists' who were 'not aware of the facts of life'.[369] Despite being the Commissioner responsible for the joint contract code, Smith had opined that harmonisation of British law by codification would

Scots Law at the Crossroads of Common and Civil Law' in K Barker, K Fairweather and R Grantham (eds), *Private Law in the 21st Century* (Oxford, Hart Publishing, 2017) 121–22.

[360] See, eg, SLC, *Report on Double Jeopardy* (Scot Law Com No 218 (2009)) paras 2.6 and 2.82.

[361] See, eg: SLC, *The Mental Element in Crime* (Scot Law Com No 80 (1983)) para 2.2; SLC, *Evidence: Report on Corroboration, Hearsay and Related Matters in Civil Proceedings* (Scot Law Com No 100 (1986)) para 3.30; and SLC, *Discussion Paper on Moveable Transactions* (Scot Law Com DP No 151 (2011)) para 1.18.

[362] HC Deb vol 706 col 152 (8 February 1965) (William Ross).

[363] See, eg, TM Cooper, 'The Common and the Civil Law—A Scot's View' (1949–50) 63 *Harvard Law Review* 468.

[364] TB Smith, *British Justice: The Scottish Contribution (The Hamlyn Lectures)* (London, Stevens & Sons Ltd, 1961) 96 (*British Justice: The Scottish Contribution*).

[365] CHW Gane, 'Criminal Law Reform in Scotland' (1998) 3 *Scottish Law and Practice Quarterly* 101, 106.

[366] See section V.A above.

[367] HL Deb vol 264 col 1192 (1 April 1965) (Earl of Selkirk).

[368] Gane, 'Criminal Law Reform in Scotland' 109.

[369] Smith, *British Justice: The Scottish Contribution*, 222–23.

be 'premature' and would pose 'formidable problems'.[370] Even those in favour of codification have recognised that the parliamentary will is not there for codification to work.[371]

Nevertheless, in its *First Programme of Law Reform*,[372] the SLC set out with 'enthusiastic innocence',[373] to codify the law of evidence and the law of obligations.[374] Realising how bold these plans were, these projects were, as in England, soon broken up and presented in various reports over the ensuing years.[375] Codification 'for the sake of codification' was soon expressly rejected.[376] So gradual was their completion that a project stemming from the evidence code project, which was embarked on in 1965, was published in 1995.[377]

As we have already seen, the two Commissions acted together on an abortive contract code. Anton (one of the SLC Commissioners at the time) noted that a joint meeting of the Commissions decided that the style of the code would be something between the two traditional types of codification—more general than a codifying statute, but less general than a continental-style code.[378] The project reached the stage of a first draft in that style. When it was passed by the LCEW to Parliamentary Counsel, however, the code was reworked in 'an entirely different manner, more in keeping with the traditional style of United Kingdom statutes'.[379] The codification spectrum employed above can be used to illustrate this shift.

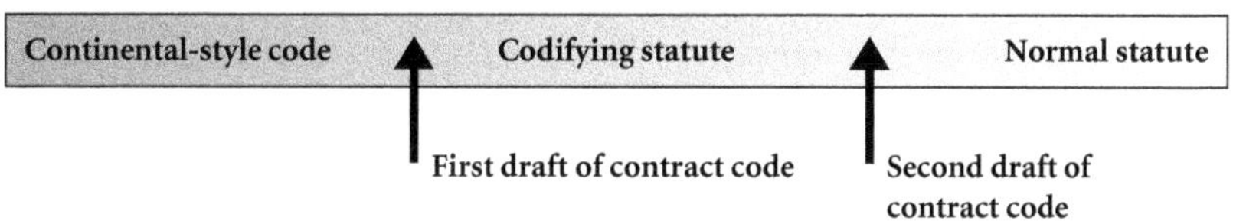

Figure 2: The Commissions' draft contract code on the codification spectrum

This reworking, together with 'areas of disagreement ... on fundamental issues' of substance as well as style, caused the SLC's withdrawal from the project.[380] The negative reaction to codification from practitioners was apparently also taken into

[370] TB Smith, 'Little Sympathy for its Ideas' *The Scotsman* (16 January 1965).
[371] DM Walker, 'The Scottish Law Commission under Review' (1987) 8 *Statute Law Review* 115, 117.
[372] SLC, *First Programme of Law Reform* (Scot Law Com No 1 (1965)).
[373] TB Smith, 'Law Reform in a Mixed "Civil Law" and "Common Law" Jurisdiction' (1974–75) 35 *Louisiana Law Review* 927, 942 ('Law Reform in a Mixed Jurisdiction').
[374] The obligations code was intended to cover both contractual and delictual obligations. It was later split into these two parts—and, later still, was broken up even further.
[375] eg, SLC, *Proposal for Reform of the Law of Evidence Relating to Corroboration* (Scot Law Com No 4 (1967)).
[376] SLC, *First Annual Report* (Scot Law Com No 3 (1966)) para 11.
[377] SLC, *Report on Hearsay Evidence in Criminal Proceedings* (Scot Law Com No 149 (1995)).
[378] AE Anton, 'Obstacles to Codification' 1982 *Juridical Review* 15, 20 ('Obstacles to Codification').
[379] ibid 21. On which, see section III.B above.
[380] SLC, *Seventh Annual Report: 1971–72* (Scot Law Com No 28 (1973)) para 16.

account.[381] The opinion of the then Chairman of the SLC, Lord Hunter, was also undoubtedly influential. Some years later he admitted that he was 'not sure that the enthusiasm in some quarters for unification and harmonisation, although currently much the vogue, is in all circumstances and in all its aspects sound'.[382]

The SLC's (also ill-fated) attempted codification of the law of evidence gives a further insight into the SLC's definition of codification. In the first part of the draft code produced under this topic, the SLC said:

> A code … is designed to set out the whole law relating to a particular subject in a comprehensive and systematic way, and to form the basic source of legal principle in that field … it is designed … to supplant the existing law completely.[383]

Here, the SLC made clear that it envisaged something more akin to continental-style codes than codifying statutes when it strove for codification. The SLC's views, however, were again not popular with practitioners,[384] and codification of the law of evidence was formally abandoned at the same time as the SLC withdrew from the contract code.[385]

By the early 1980s, the SLC admitted that codification was 'just not a practical proposition in the foreseeable future' due to its 'limited resources'.[386] It sensibly decided that it was preferable to concentrate on areas of the law where there was 'a real need for change'.[387] An attempted resurgence of codification took place, however, a decade later.[388] The SLC acknowledged that previous attempts at codification had been 'too ambitious',[389] but remained committed to the desirability of codification in theory. The SLC also recognised codification as a 'duty' under the 1965 Act.[390] It therefore embarked on a 'feasibility study' to ascertain

[381] Smith, 'Law Reform in a Mixed Jurisdiction' 953.

[382] J Hunter, 'Law Reform: The Meanings and the Methods' in *Proceedings and Papers of the Fifth Commonwealth Law Conference* (Edinburgh, Fifth Commonwealth Law Conference, 1977) 7. See also the views of the lead Scottish Commissioner on the project, TB Smith, discussed above. Harmonisation is discussed separately in ch 6.

[383] SLC, *Draft Evidence Code: First Part* (Scot Law Com Memorandum No 8 (1968)) 3–4. This memorandum did not proceed to report stage and, as mentioned above, progress on the evidence code was much more piecemeal.

[384] See Anton, 'Obstacles to Codification' 22–23 for a summary of the reaction to the draft evidence code. In a later evidence project, the SLC noted that the reception to their evidence code 'was not such as to suggest that the time is yet ripe for a Code of Evidence'. Therefore, although codification remained 'an eventual objective', the instant project was 'more limited': SLC, *Law of Evidence*, vol 1 (Scot Law Com Memorandum No 46 (1980)) para A.02. More recently, the SLC has published a draft Bill which could provide the first sections of an evidence code: SLC, *Report on Similar Fact Evidence and the Moorov Doctrine* (Scot Law Com No 229 (2012)) draft Criminal Evidence (Scotland) Bill.

[385] Although projects to reform the law of evidence would still be pursued: SLC, *Seventh Annual Report: 1971–72* (Scot Law Com No 28 (1973)) para 14.

[386] SLC, *Eighteenth Annual Report: 1982–83* (Scot Law Com No 81 (1983)) para 2.3.

[387] ibid.

[388] SLC, *Fifth Programme of Law Reform* (Scot Law Com No 159 (1997)) paras 2.14–2.16.

[389] ibid para 2.15.

[390] SLC, *Thirty-Second Annual Report: 1996–97* (Scot Law Com No 161 (1997)) para 2.10. See also F Bennion, 'Additional Comments' in G Zellick (ed), *The Law Commission and Law Reform* (London, Sweet & Maxwell, 1988) 63.

whether codification was possible.[391] It soon became apparent, however, that the SLC simply did not have the resources to undertake any significant codification of the law.[392]

In 2003, *A Draft Criminal Code for Scotland* was published under the auspices of the SLC, although, because of a lack of resources, it was carried out completely independently.[393] The *Draft Criminal Code* neither 'simply restate[d] the law' nor provided 'a fresh start'.[394] Instead, it reformed certain areas of the law, such as rape, while leaving many provisions 'firmly based on the existing law'.[395] Like the similar English effort, it remains unimplemented, apparently due to a lack of political will.[396] It has been claimed that the work was carried out despite the fact that there was 'not a great clamour for codification' in Scotland.[397] Clive, one of the authors of the *Draft Criminal Code* and also a former SLC Commissioner, noted that only two objections were raised to codification from consultees to the project. First, it was argued that codification would result in less flexibility in the law, and second, that the law should be capable of judicial development.[398] Clive dismissed these objections as being arguments against legislation generally, rather than codification.[399] Unfortunately for him and the other authors of the *Draft Criminal Code*, however, the objections came from persuasive figures such as the Lord President and the Law Society of Scotland.

The SLC embarked, in its *Eighth Programme of Law Reform*, on a project to review contract law based on the Draft Common Frame of Reference.[400] The SLC stressed that its project was not necessarily 'leading to the codification of the Scots law of contract'.[401] Instead, in line with the project-selection criteria, the SLC would focus on areas that are 'lacking or … out of synch with the modern world and commercial/legal practice'.[402] Expectations are not high, therefore, for any imminent codification of Scots law by the SLC. One current SLC Commissioner has admitted that 'the likelihood of codification is low'.[403] The Scottish legal

[391] SLC, *Fifth Programme of Law Reform* (Scot Law Com No 159 (1997)) para 2.16.

[392] SLC, *Thirty-Third Annual Report: 1997–98* (Scot Law Com No 167 (1998)) para 2.11; SLC, *Thirty-Fourth Annual Report: 1998–99* (Scot Law Com No 179 (2000)) paras 2.9–2.11.

[393] E Clive, P Ferguson, C Gane and A McCall Smith, *A Draft Criminal Code for Scotland with Commentary* (2003) (*Draft Criminal Code for Scotland*). See also *Thirty-Fourth Annual Report*, ibid paras 2.10–2.11.

[394] *Draft Criminal Code for Scotland*, 3.

[395] ibid.

[396] E Clive, 'Codification of the Criminal Law' in J Chalmers, F Leverick and L Farmer (eds), *Essays in Criminal Law in Honour of Sir Gerald Gordon* (Edinburgh, EUP, 2010) 67 and 69 ('Codification of the Criminal Law').

[397] ibid 55, although Clive thought that the reception was more favourable to codification than it had been at the beginning of the SLC's existence.

[398] ibid 54 and 57–65.

[399] ibid 65.

[400] SLC, *Eighth Programme of Law Reform* (Scot Law Com No 220 (2010)) paras 2.16–2.21.

[401] ibid para 2.21.

[402] ibid.

[403] A Steven, 'Codification: A Perspective from a Scottish Law Commissioner' (Seminar Series on Codification, All Souls College, Oxford, 2014) 11.

community's attitude towards codification, historically hostile as we have seen, is at best still 'mixed'.[404] Since devolution, Holyrood has proved to be unreceptive to codification, at least partly because of being overwhelmed by 'other legislative priorities'.[405] It has been pondered, however, whether the surge in Scottish nationalism could increase the chances of codification 'to celebrate and bolster national identity and legal culture'.[406]

So as not to be in breach of its codification 'duty', the SLC has highlighted projects it has completed which 'involved a measure of codification'.[407] The SLC has undoubtedly achieved some codification in the codifying statute sense, for example in bankruptcy,[408] and prescription and limitation.[409] The Sexual Offences (Scotland) Act 2009 has been described as a 'mini-code' and something which could never have been achieved by the common law.[410] The Commissioner who led that project has, however, explicitly stated that he did not think he was codifying the law because the project was 'clearly' not intended to cover all the law in the area.[411] Reid has described the SLC's contribution to putting much of Scots law onto a legislative footing as 'virtually codification by stealth'.[412]

In summary, the SLC's usual vision of codification has been a little closer to continental-style codes than the LCEW has been comfortable with. The SLC has, however, like the LCEW, achieved little codification. Also like the LCEW, the SLC has increasingly chosen to prioritise its resources to reform the substance of the law, rather than presenting reforms in a fully codified style. In contrast, however, to the LCEW, the SLC evidently does not even feel the need to be working towards codification as a long-term goal—neither its recent annual reports nor its

[404] E Clive, 'The Scottish Civil Code Project' in HL MacQueen, A Vauer and S Espiau Espiau (eds), *Regional Private Laws and Codification in Europe* (Cambridge, CUP, 2003) 85.

[405] M Hogg, 'Codification of Private Law: Scots Law at the Crossroads of Common and Civil Law' in K Barker, K Fairweather and R Grantham (eds), *Private Law in the 21st Century* (Oxford, Hart Publishing, 2017) 120.

[406] Hogg, ibid 129, where it is also noted that a 'growing sense of national self-identity' led to codification in France, Italy and Germany (108). See also Wales: LCEW website, 'Should we Include These Projects in the 13th Programme?' www.lawcom.gov.uk/13th-programme-potential-projects/.

[407] SLC, *Thirty-Fourth Annual Report: 1998–99* (Scot Law Com No 179 (2000)) para 2.9, citing projects on the law of the tenement, directors' duties and real burdens. See also the Unfair Contract Terms Act 1977, the result of a joint project with the LCEW: LCEW and SLC, *Exemption Clauses: Second Report* (Law Com No 69 and Scot Law Com No 39 (1975)).

[408] The Bankruptcy (Scotland) Act 1985 implemented SLC, *Report on Bankruptcy and Related Aspects of Insolvency and Liquidation* (Scot Law Com No 68 (1981)) and the Bankruptcy (Scotland) Act 2016 implemented SLC, *Report on the Consolidation of Bankruptcy Legislation in Scotland* (Scot Law Com No 232 (2013)).

[409] The Prescription and Limitation (Scotland) Act 1973 implemented SLC, *Reform of the Law Relating to Prescription and Limitation of Actions* (Scot Law Com No 15 (1970)).

[410] Clive, 'Codification of the Criminal Law' 66–67. The Sexual Offences (Scotland) Act 2009 implemented SLC, *Report on Rape and Other Sexual Offences* (Scot Law Com No 209 (2007)).

[411] G Maher, 'Principles and Politics in Law Reform: Sexual Offences in Scots Law' 2013 *Juridical Review* 563, 566, and see also 583. For example, the report and the implementing legislation do not cover the law of incest: *Report on Rape*, ibid para 5.3.

[412] KGC Reid, 'Smoothing the Rugged Parts of the Passage: Scots Law and its Edinburgh Chair' (2014) 18 *Edinburgh Law Review* 315, 339.

latest programme of law reform make any mention of codification.[413] An ongoing project on compulsory purchase does, however, contain an element of codification, or at least consolidation. It ultimately aims 'to replace the diverse, overlapping and confusing layers of primary legislation … with a modern, comprehensive, statutory restatement'.[414] In the light of the consideration of the chapter three project-selection criteria, the shift in the Commissions' attitudes to codification is entirely proper.

VI. Conclusion: Substance Over Style

Although the English and Scottish legal traditions are quite different, there has been a dearth of codification by the Commissions in both jurisdictions. The lack of definition of codification in the 1965 Act caused problems for the Commissions in understanding what they were actually setting out to achieve by their codification task. The Commissions have shown a 'lack of decision', both as to whether they should codify and, if so, what form those codes should take.[415] Furthermore, various factors have made codification difficult for the Commissions. They do not have the resources for the huge task it poses and they have faced opposition from jurisdictions generally not ready to turn their backs on tightly drafted statutes or the common law, even when EU membership could have signalled a move towards codification. Our impending likely departure from the EU removes any motivation for codification that our membership may once have provided. Various other developments negated certain criticisms of judicial development of the law, making codification, as opposed to piecemeal legislation, less desirable. Furthermore, legal databases make searching for legal sources easier, with the result that the continued growth in the number of cases and separate pieces of enacted law is more tolerated. Despite a lack of success, codification remains an aim under the 1965 Act. It is now over two decades since Lord Rodger urged that if, as he argued, we no longer expect our law reform bodies to codify the law, we must 'alter our thinking about what we are seeking to achieve through the work of the Law Commissions'.[416] Rodger's request remains as cogent as ever—the reasons for codification, and consequently its popularity, have waned since 1965. Our altered thinking should be reflected in changes to the 1965 Act.

The criteria for project selection developed in chapter three (availability and economical use of resources, suitability, and importance) should be used to determine whether any project, including one to codify, is viable. The resources needed

[413] SLC, *Annual Report 2015* (Scot Law Com No 244 (2016)); *Ninth Programme of Law Reform* (Scot Law Com No 242 (2015)).

[414] SLC, *Discussion Paper on Compulsory Purchase* (Scot Law Com DP No 159 (2014)) para 1.13.

[415] JH Farrar, *Law Reform and the Law Commission* (London, Sweet & Maxwell, 1974) 62.

[416] A Rodger, 'The Bell of Law Reform' 1993 *Scots Law Times (News)* 339, 342.

for codification projects are likely to be great because of their size. The idea that smaller statutes can simply be welded together to form a code is unlikely to result in codes which have the desired comprehensiveness. Draft Bills are essential for codification projects and the availability of Parliamentary Counsel must therefore be guaranteed when considering the 'resources' criterion. Although it was concluded in chapters three and four that importance should not be based on a project's likelihood of implementation, it must be acknowledged that codification projects suffer doubly in terms of such likelihood. As well as there being no guarantee that government will find the *substance* to be palatable, the *style* may also prove controversial. Nevertheless, where it is sufficiently important that an area of law is examined, implementation need not be certain. Importance of the subject matter, however, is likely to be the main stumbling block for codification projects. The Commissions have conceded that it is impossible to reform and codify simultaneously. Codification projects therefore necessarily involve two stages—reform then codification—the second of which will suggest little (if any) reform of the substance of the law.[417] Alternatively, the existing law might not require prior reform, and instead be ready to be enshrined in a code. Furthermore, as Rodger observed, codes in their truest sense (as one comprehensive source of the law in an area) necessarily require the consideration of issues that are not posing problems in practice. The Commissions' importance criterion should lead to substance taking precedence over style. That is, it will typically be more important to examine law which is unfair, unclear, inefficient, unduly complex or outdated than it will be to consolidate or codify existing laws, or laws which are not causing problems in practice. The Commissions' limited resources should be targeted at the content of the law, before its format. Gardiner and Martin's argument, therefore, that codification was not a priority in the 1960s still rings true today.

Dennis has lamented that the Commissions 'may now be realistic in finally conceding that codification is never going to happen, but this is nonetheless a sad end for a noble ideal'.[418] It need not be the complete end, however. The Commissions can use their continuing existence to recommend that codification should be carried out by another body,[419] or that they should be allocated extra resources where a codification project is sufficiently suitable and important. Codification does have certain merits. If it is to be pursued seriously, however, it should not be the Commissions' responsibility.

The specific codification task should therefore be removed from the 1965 Act as part of a wider rethink of the Commissions' proper role today. Its removal would

[417] Substantive reforms may be necessary if, for example, a long time elapses between stages one and two.

[418] I Dennis, 'RIP: The Criminal Code (1968–2008)' [2009] *Crim LR* 1, 2.

[419] The Commissions can use their power under the 1965 Act, s 3(1)(b) to recommend to the Ministers that codification should be pursued by another body, or indeed by government itself. See too GL Gretton, 'The Duty to Make the Law More Accessible?: The Two C-Words' in Dyson, Lee and Stark, *Fifty Years of the Law Commissions*, 96.

not prevent the Commissions from carrying out codification if appropriate, because codification can be included in the Commissions' broader responsibility for the 'systematic development and reform of the law', including the 'elimination of anomalies, the repeal of obsolete and unnecessary enactments, the reduction of the number of separate enactments and generally the simplification and modernisation of the law'.[420] Nor would its removal prevent the Commissions from carrying out important simplification work. The LCEW sees such work as preparation for an eventual code, but even if no code is forthcoming, the work is still worthwhile and valuable. The removal of the explicit codification function would remove any ambiguity as to its intended meaning, alleviate the unrealistic expectation of codification, accord more with the reality of how the modern-day Commissions correctly allocate their resources, and prevent codification from being given disproportionate weight when assessing the Commissions' performance. We should assess the Commissions on the substance of their reforms. We should not require those reforms to be presented in a style which has proved difficult to achieve, is less likely to satisfy the project-selection criteria than substantive reform, and is no longer as necessary as it was perceived to be in 1965.

[420] 1965 Act, s 3(1).

6

From Harmonisation to Devolution and Brexit

When the Commissions were established, impending entry into what is now the European Union (EU) was an impetus for the harmonisation of the UK's different legal systems. Lord Scarman went so far as to argue that the Commissions were the perfect bodies to facilitate a complete 'unifying process' of English and Scots law.[1] At the turn of the twenty-first century, however, devolution signified a trend towards the increased fragmentation of the UK and its respective legal systems. Although the Scots legal tradition has always been staunchly defended to one extent or another, claims of English 'cultural imperialism' which had died down in the late-twentieth century resurfaced after devolution.[2] Both Commissions have faced challenges because of the pressure to harmonise on the one hand, and the consequences of devolution on the other. By examining the issues of harmonisation and devolution we can reveal further reasons why the project-selection criteria developed in chapter three are needed, more than ever, to clarify the scope of the Commissions' activity. In addition, the UK's impending likely departure from the EU removes any European pressure that was felt to harmonise.

The Commissions have a duty under the Law Commissions Act 1965 (the 1965 Act) to act 'in consultation' with each other.[3] This duty includes working together on collaborative projects. Because considerations may differ between jurisdictions, transparent use of the project-selection criteria would ensure that the Commissions select projects in a consistent manner, and that they can communicate effectively to understand that selection. Consistent application of the project-selection criteria would ensure that the Commissions select the most appropriate new projects when acting both individually and collaboratively. Appropriate project selection ensures that their resources are allocated correctly.

As the Commissions were established, public comments were made that 'no complete assimilation' of English and Scots law was intended,[4] yet the Commissions

[1] L Scarman, 'A Code of English Law?' (lecture, University of Hull, 1966) 9.

[2] A Paterson, *Final Judgment: The Last Law Lords and the Supreme Court* (Oxford, Hart Publishing, 2013) 236, in the context of Scots appeals to the House of Lords (now Supreme Court).

[3] And with the Northern Ireland Law Commission, if it still exists (see below): 1965 Act, s 3(4).

[4] HC Deb vol 706 col 153 (8 February 1965) (William Ross). See also 'No Complete Assimilation with English Law: Mr Ross Gives Assurance' *The Scotsman* (9 February 1965).

believed that they should strive to harmonise the law 'wherever possible'.[5] The likelihood of harmonisation need not now be given as much weight when assessing a potential project's viability as it was in the past, because the goal of harmonisation is not as relevant, or as achievable, as it was in 1965. The importance of recommending improvement to the law (one of the criteria advanced in chapter three) is the overarching criterion under which harmonisation will, in certain cases, be relevant.

Far from the harmonised system anticipated at the Commissions' inception, the UK has become increasingly fragmented with devolution for Scotland, Wales and Northern Ireland.[6] Devolution raises two separate issues: the effect on the substance of reforms proposed (and on the Commissions' harmonisation goal in particular); and the practical problems posed by the new constitutional arrangements. In particular, working with both the UK and the devolved Scottish and Welsh governments has increased the number of parties interacting with the Scottish Law Commission (SLC) and the Law Commission for England and Wales (LCEW) respectively. Because of that increase, a clear, and ideally statutory, framework of how Commission projects are selected is now needed urgently to ensure consistency and clarity as to the scope of the Commissions' activity.

I. Collaborative Projects

Collaborative projects require compromise and an understanding of the needs of each Commission and jurisdiction. Despite the Commissions having generally worked in 'good harmony',[7] improvements can be suggested to better ensure that the Commissions communicate effectively and use their resources wisely.

A. The Commissions' Statutory Duty to Consult Each Other

The Commissions have a duty to 'act in consultation with each other' under section 3(4) of the 1965 Act. The Commissions therefore do not always operate in isolation. Consequently, it is important for there to be a certain degree of consistency between them. It is particularly important for the Commissions to agree

[5] AG Brand (SLC) to HHA Whitworth (Scottish Office), 'Full-time Commissioner', 29 September 1967, National Records of Scotland (NRS) HH83/702; 'Draft Memorandum by the SLC Seeking a Second Full-Time Commissioner', 20 July 1967, NRS HH83/702.

[6] See, primarily, the Scotland Act 1998, the Northern Ireland Act 1998 and the Government of Wales Acts 1998 and 2006.

[7] R Toulson, 'Democracy, Law Reform and the Rule of Law' in M Dyson, J Lee and SW Stark (eds), *Fifty Years of the Law Commissions: The Dynamics of Law Reform* (Oxford, Hart Publishing, 2016) 127 (Dyson, Lee and Stark, *Fifty Years of the Law Commissions*). See also Lord Pentland, 'The Scottish Law Commission and the Future of Law Reform in Scotland' in Dyson, Lee and Stark, ibid 345–46.

on what their proper scope of activity is when they collaborate, and the project-selection criteria developed in chapter three should aid such agreement.

Even if not provided for by statute, it is likely that the two Commissions would be required to consult each other and even to work together on certain projects. Certain areas of law examined by the Commissions are the same (or substantially similar) in England and Scotland (and indeed throughout the EU), such as the law relating to consumer rights.[8] Other areas of law physically span the border, as demonstrated by a joint Commission project that proposed reform of the law relating to level crossings and dealt with the 'national network' of railways.[9] Other areas of law might be different, but the jurisdictions might seek to learn from each other. The Commissions have a duty under section 3(1)(f) of the 1965 Act to survey the laws of other jurisdictions, and it is natural that a Commission's first port of call might be its neighbouring jurisdiction. Even TB Smith, despite seeking to protect Scots law from Anglicisation, remarked in 1965 that '[o]ne would hope that the Scottish and English Commissioners would exchange views and often act together'.[10]

The consultation duty was taken particularly seriously in the Commissions' formative years, with both Commissions viewing it as implying that they were obliged to review everything the other Commission wrote.[11] Furthermore, both Commissions shared the view that the laws of their respective jurisdictions should 'wherever possible ... be brought into harmony with each other'.[12] Happily, neither view persists today. Reasons for the Commissions to collaborate and harmonise more selectively are advanced in this chapter.

Many joint projects are consolidation or repeals projects.[13] Even excluding such work, the implementation rate for joint projects is extremely high.[14] Because the SLC is smaller than the LCEW and produces fewer reports, joint projects will naturally comprise a higher proportion of the overall number of SLC projects. Given that the LCEW will usually take the lead, however, joint projects will not take up that same proportion of the SLC's *time*. Nevertheless, it is important, because of the resources devoted to them, that joint projects are selected based on proper consideration of the selection criteria.

[8] See, eg, LCEW and SLC, *Consumer Remedies for Faulty Goods* (Law Com No 317 and Scot Law Com No 216 (2009)).

[9] LCEW and SLC, *Level Crossings* (Law Com No 339 and Scot Law Com No 234 (2013)) para 1.11.

[10] TB Smith, 'Legal Imperialism and Legal Parochialism' 1965 *Juridical Review* 39, 55.

[11] HHA Whitworth (Scottish Office) to Pittam (Treasury), 22 November 1967, NRS HH83/702.

[12] AG Brand (SLC) to HHA Whitworth (Scottish Office), 'Full-time Commissioner', 29 September 1967, NRS HH83/702; 'Draft Memorandum by the SLC Seeking a Second Full-Time Commissioner', 20 July 1967, NRS HH83/702.

[13] The Commissions worked together on 74 joint projects between June 1965 and December 2015, 46 of which (62%) concerned consolidation/repeals.

[14] As at December 2016, 88% of joint projects published between 1965 and 2014 were implemented either fully or substantially, or partially. Consolidation and repeals projects have been excluded because a significant number joint projects are consolidation/repeals projects (above n 13) and, as was seen in ch 4, such projects have a 100% implementation rate.

B. Practical Difficulties

i. The Difference in the Commissions' Sizes

Because the Commissions sometimes work together on projects, consistently applied project-selection criteria are needed. The criteria could be used by one Commission to persuade another Commission to collaborate on a worthwhile project. Equally, they could be used by a Commission to refuse to collaborate on a project which it does not believe satisfies the criteria and which diverts it from more important and suitable projects that are a better use of its resources. Because of the SLC's smaller size, it is especially important to ensure that it does not become overwhelmed by undeserving joint projects. More consistent and more transparent use of the chapter three project-selection criteria would ensure that only the most deserving projects are embarked on.

The 'practical difficulties' caused by the need for the two differently sized Commissions to work together on joint projects have 'called for the evolution of particular processes … which respect the working methods and the autonomy of two sets of Commissioners and each Commission'.[15] Such methods include the presumption that the better-resourced LCEW will usually 'shoulder the burden of preparing the research … and so take the lead in the project'.[16] Exceptions to this presumption have occurred, however, such as a report on the law of partnerships, which was led by previous SLC Commissioner, Patrick Hodge (now Lord Hodge).[17] At the Commissions' outset, one commentator expected that, in matters where the two bodies worked in collaboration, the LCEW would 'assume final responsibility'.[18] The 1965 Act makes no such provision,[19] although in practice the LCEW's larger size necessitates it often taking a leading role. The LCEW must be careful, however, not to dictate the SLC's workload, or the substance of the reforms proposed. McBryde has argued that the SLC has, at least in the past, suffered 'disruption, caused by responding to the demands of the English Law Commission'.[20] The need for all Commissioners to sign off on a report should ensure that all ten Commissioners are happy with the substantive proposals. But the SLC may feel under pressure to agree to undertake a joint project in order for Scots law implications to be properly considered. The LCEW has in recent years been careful

[15] M McMillan, 'The Role of Law Reform in Constitutionalism, Rule of Law and Democratic Governance: Reflections by the Scottish Law Commission' (Association of Law Reform Agencies of Eastern and Southern Africa Lecture, 2011) 7.

[16] ibid 8.

[17] LCEW and SLC, *Partnership Law* (Law Com No 283 and Scot Law Com No 192 (2003)) para 1.21.

[18] HC Deb vol 706 col 56 (8 February 1965) (Sir Eric Fletcher).

[19] See the 1965 Act itself and, for discussion, JH Farrar, *Law Reform and the Law Commission* (London, Sweet & Maxwell, 1974) 27 (*Law Reform and the Law Commission*).

[20] WW McBryde, 'Law Reform: The Scottish Experience' (1998) 3 *Scottish Law and Practice Quarterly* 86, 88.

to consult the SLC on potential projects and to share emerging views on project and programme consultations to facilitate good dialogue between the two bodies. The SLC will often have to face the difficult balancing exercise of the availability and use of its own resources with the desire to see adequate consideration of Scots law.[21] Proper use of the project-selection criteria would ensure that the SLC only embarks on projects which it feels are truly deserving. The criteria should provide a shield for the SLC to refuse to collaborate on projects where a lack of resources would prevent it from making a contribution, or projects which are deemed not suitable or important enough to warrant examination.

The SLC was smaller than the LCEW when the two bodies were created,[22] and it remains smaller to this day. A lack of ability to keep pace with the LCEW when the two Commissions collaborated soon posed problems. As soon as February 1966, AG Brand, the first Secretary[23] of the SLC wrote to the Solicitor of the Secretary of State for Scotland, saying that recent meetings with the LCEW had 'very strongly confirmed the view, towards which we were already tending, that we shall require more legal staff to enable the Commission to carry out its functions adequately and within a reasonable time'.[24] Later, Brand advanced three compelling reasons (compiled at Lord Kilbrandon (the first Chairman of the SLC)'s request[25] and with the Lord Advocate's support)[26] why constituting a smaller SLC was a mistake from the outset and which still ring true today.[27] First, although there are more legal sources in England (for example, a greater number of court judgments) leading frequently to more complexity in the law, 'it cannot be said that there is less law in Scotland than in England'.[28] Each jurisdiction, after all, has a system of criminal law, of family law, of property law, of contract law and so on. Second, although it might have been true that English law was more desperately in need of reform than Scots law in 1965, where a particular branch of the law is examined, just as much work needs to be done on the Scottish branch as the English branch. The number of legal authorities might be greater in England, but in both jurisdictions the same research has to be done to formulate reforms, including, for example,

[21] I am grateful to Malcolm McMillan for sharing his views on this subject in a discussion in December 2014.

[22] Three part-time Commissioners and a full-time Chairman at the SLC, compared with four full-time Commissioners and a full-time Chairman at the LCEW.

[23] The role (for both Commissions) is now entitled 'Chief Executive'. The position is held by a senior government lawyer.

[24] AG Brand (SLC) to JS Dalgetty (Solicitor to the Secretary of State for Scotland), 1 February 1966, National Archives (NA) BA25/24.

[25] Lord Kilbrandon (SLC) to G Stott (Lord Advocate) and W Ross (Secretary of State for Scotland), 28 September 1967, NRS HH83/702.

[26] JH Gibson (Lord Advocate's Office) to HHA Whitworth (Scottish Office), 'Scottish Law Commission', 5 October 1967, NRS HH83/702.

[27] AG Brand (SLC) to HHA Whitworth (Scottish Office), 'Full-time Commissioner', 29 September 1967, NRS HH83/702.

[28] 'Draft Memorandum by the SLC Seeking a Second Full-Time Commissioner', 20 July 1967, NRS HH83/702.

analysing the law of other jurisdictions. Third and finally, where changes are proposed which affect both jurisdictions, a constant comparative process is required where the pace is set by the larger LCEW, and the SLC struggles to keep up. Such projects involve the 'added burden' of the SLC usually travelling to London, rather than the LCEW travelling to Edinburgh, because more people are based in London.[29] The LCEW has in the past expressed frustration with the SLC's smaller size and its resultant inability to keep pace. For example, the LCEW Commissioner leading the joint contract code project,[30] LCB Gower, remarked that the difficulties the project faced were 'further aggravated ... by the difference in pace of the two bodies and by the inevitable fear that the legal system of the majority would swamp that of the minority'.[31] The Scottish Office, however, decided it would not be tactful to lead evidence of the LCEW's 'grumbles' to support its case for expanding the SLC.[32]

In 1968, Brand called the discrepancy in staffing levels between the Commissions 'ludicrous'.[33] That discrepancy is now less manifest, but has never been completely redressed. Most (but not all) SLC Commissioners are now appointed on a full-time basis.[34] As the number of Scottish Commissioners has grown, however, the rest of the SLC has not. The LCEW has four full-time Commissioners (plus a full-time Chairman), each heading up a team supported by (in general): (i) a team manager; (ii) between three and five qualified lawyers; and (iii) between three and six research assistants.[35] In contrast, the SLC has four Commissioners (currently three full-time and one part-time, plus a part-time Chairman), each heading up a team supported by (in general): (i) one project manager; and (ii) one legal assistant.

Since its establishment, therefore, the SLC has struggled to keep pace with the LCEW.[36] The SLC continues to face the 'perennial task of matching resources to workload'.[37] A comparison of the latest SLC and LCEW annual reports reveals that the LCEW costs almost three times as much to run as the SLC—the running costs for 2015 were approximately £1.6 million for the SLC and £4.6 million for

[29] AG Brand (SLC) to HHA Whitworth (Scottish Office), 'Full-time Commissioner', 29 September 1967, NRS HH83/702. This burden has been somewhat alleviated by the increased ability to communicate electronically.

[30] See ch 5, particularly sections V.A and V.B.

[31] LCB Gower, 'Reflections on Law Reform' (1973) 23 *University of Toronto Law Journal* 257, 264–65.

[32] Scottish Office Filenote, HHA Whitworth to JM Fearn, 1 August 1967, NRS HH83/702.

[33] AG Brand (SLC) to DS Mackenzie (Scottish Office), 'Full-Time Commissioner', 5 February 1968, NRS HH83/702.

[34] Currently only the Chairman and one Commissioner are part-time. The remaining three Commissioners are full-time.

[35] See LCEW website, 'Law Commission Organisation Chart' www.lawcom.gov.uk/wp-content/uploads/2016/09/WhosWho_senior-staff-names_latest.pdf.

[36] CC Lucas (Treasury) Memorandum, 'Scottish Law Commission', 25 March 1966, NA BA25/24. See also Farrar, *Law Reform and the Law Commission*, 37–40.

[37] N Brotchie, 'The Scottish Law Commission: Promoting Law Reform in Scotland' (2009) 9 *Legal Information Management* 30, 30.

the LCEW.[38] Even taking into account the fact that London premises are exponentially more expensive,[39] the difference is marked. Notably there is little difference between the money required to fund the Commissioners.[40] It is in the cost of other staff members where the difference is most apparent.[41] It must be acknowledged, however, that the LCEW has struggled to operate with fewer resources in recent years after being a target of government spending cuts. Recent annual running costs are almost £2 million less than just over a decade ago.[42] The SLC, however, faces the additional problem of being the smaller of two bodies that must sometimes work together. In the light of spending cuts, it is unrealistic to recommend increasing the size of the SLC. Achieving parity by shrinking the LCEW would be unwise when its limited resources are already restrictive. Instead, we need a way to ensure that collaborative projects work as smoothly as possible, despite the current size discrepancy.

One particular problem the SLC has experienced, at least historically, is when it has found itself 'having to take on work which [it] might not otherwise do' because such areas are being examined by the LCEW.[43] Occasionally, instead of proposing a fully joint project, the LCEW may only ask for input from the SLC when considering areas which may affect (or be influenced by) Scots law,[44] or where harmonisation is a goal.[45] For example, in a report on *Shareholder Remedies*,[46] the LCEW consulted with the SLC. The SLC agreed with most of the LCEW's proposals, stating that it was 'highly desirable that there should be consistency in policy between English law and Scots law'.[47] Such consultation is necessary because the terms of the 1965 Act give the LCEW no power to propose reform of Scots law (and the SLC no power to propose reform of English law).[48] The government,

[38] LCEW, *Annual Report 2015–16* (Law Com No 367 (2016)) app B; SLC, *Annual Report 2015* (Scot Law Com No 244 (2016)) 29. The Commissions have different year ends and so the LCEW figure relates to 1 April 2015 to 31 March 2016, whereas the SLC figure relates to 1 January to 31 December 2015. Note also that the LCEW's funding comprises a mixture of core Ministry of Justice funding and funding from governmental departments on a project-by-project basis.

[39] The LCEW's accommodation cost for 2015 (met directly by the Ministry of Justice) was £663,500 whereas the SLC's was £77,411: ibid.

[40] In fact, the SLC spent more on Commissioners (£599,008) than the LCEW (£507,900) in 2015: ibid.

[41] In 2015, other staff costs were over £3.2 million at the LCEW and just £740,378 at the SLC: ibid.

[42] The running cost for the LCEW for 2002–03 was almost £6.3 million: LCEW, *Annual Report 2002–03* (Law Com No 280 (2003)) app F.

[43] SLC, *Seventeenth Annual Report 1981–82* (Scot Law Com No 73 (1982)) para 2.9.

[44] See, eg, LCEW, *Proposals to Abolish Certain Ancient Criminal Offences* (Law Com No 3 (1966)); LCEW, *Administrative Law* (Law Com No 20 (1969)); and LCEW, *Criminal Law: Report on Forgery and Counterfeit Currency* (Law Com No 55 (1973)).

[45] eg, LCEW, *Restitution: Mistakes of Law and Ultra Vires Public Authority Receipts and Payments* (Law Com No 227 (1994)).

[46] LCEW, *Shareholder Remedies* (Law Com No 246 (1997)).

[47] ibid app D, para 40. The eventual implementing legislation, the Companies Act 2006, covers the entire UK.

[48] The 1965 Act provides that the LCEW should promote the reform of 'the law of England and Wales' and that the SLC should promote the reform of 'the law of Scotland': ss 1(1) and 2(1).

however, can choose to extend draft Bills to Great Britain or the UK.[49] In cases where any degree of collaboration is sought, the SLC faces the difficult decision of either using its scarcer resources to give Scottish input, or risking criticism for failing to get involved when the resultant legislation does not apply to Scotland, or does not consider sufficiently the Scots law tradition. Despite its greater resources, the LCEW may face similar difficulties and, as we will see later, may refuse an SLC request to collaborate on a project. The development of the project-selection criteria can assist the Commissions when making such difficult decisions.

ii. The Northern Ireland Law Commission

The Northern Ireland Law Commission (the NILC) became fully operational in 2008, with the result that tripartite law reform projects became a possibility. The LCEW, the SLC and the NILC examined together the regulation of health care professionals, a reference from the UK Department of Health.[50] A tripartite project dealing with electoral reform was also commenced.[51] The practicalities of these tripartite projects raised 'definite challenges', but the Commissions were optimistic about the increased opportunities they afforded.[52] With an extra Commission collaborating with the LCEW and the SLC it became even more important that all bodies were agreed on their proper scope of activity. Without clear and agreed project-selection criteria, the Commissions are less likely to select projects consistently or appropriately. Inappropriate projects are a waste of the Commissions' resources, and the use of inconsistent criteria in project-selection could result in communication between the Commissions being fraught.

The difficulties created by the NILC took a different turn, however, in early 2015 when the following message appeared on the NILC's website:

> The [Northern Ireland] Minister of Justice has decided to reduce significantly funding to the Northern Ireland Law Commission from April 2015 in response to budget pressures within the Department of Justice. This will allow only essential law reform to continue.[53]

The effect of the message is still unclear. The NILC is currently defunct—it has closed its doors and has no Commissioners. The question remains unanswered, however, as to whether it might be revived. In the meantime, the fate of the ongoing electoral law project is unclear given that Northern Ireland has no independent law reform body and the GB Commissions have no vires to deal with the law of Northern Ireland. These issues will be returned to later in this chapter.

[49] See, eg, the Bribery Act 2010, based on LCEW, *Reforming Bribery* (Law Com No 313 (2008)).

[50] LCEW, SLC and NILC, *Regulation of Health Care Professionals, Regulation of Social Care Professionals in England* (Law Com No 345, Scot Law Com No 237 and NILC No 18 (2014)).

[51] LCEW, SLC and NILC, *Electoral Law: An Interim Report* (2016).

[52] M McMillan, 'The Role of Law Reform in Constitutionalism, Rule of Law and Democratic Governance: Reflections by the Scottish Law Commission' (Association of Law Reform Agencies of Eastern and Southern Africa Lecture, 2011) 9–10 ('The Role of Law Reform').

[53] NILC website www.nilawcommission.gov.uk/.

C. Varying Degrees of Harmonisation

Hopes were expressed when the Commissions were established that they could harmonise English and Scots law. Collaborative projects in particular could help to achieve that aim. Harmonisation is, however, correctly no longer a goal in itself. A collaborative project's viability, therefore, is not contingent on its potential to harmonise the law. The prospect of harmonisation is instead one consideration which can be taken into account under the 'importance' project-selection criterion. In certain circumstances, the law can be improved by harmonisation—but the goal is improvement, not harmonisation as such, or for its own sake.

Certain joint projects, even concerning consolidation, have been able to promote harmonisation. For example, in the consolidation report *Amendment of the Companies Acts 1948–1983*, the intention 'to achieve the same result for Scotland' as for England and Wales was expressed.[54] One area where the two Commissions have frequently interacted is private international law. In that area, harmonisation has often been a distinct aim, with the Commissions saying in one joint project that it was 'more satisfactory to have one set of rules applicable to all countries', not just England and Scotland.[55] In certain instances, however, even the Commissions' belief that private international law rules should be 'essentially the same throughout the United Kingdom wherever possible' was not enough to overcome the intrinsic differences between the two systems and certain separate provisions were necessary.[56] Nevertheless, private international law implications are often kept in mind when the Commissions work together with the aim to 'unify the existing jurisdictional rules' in relation to aspects such as family law.[57] Commercial law is another area where the Commissions have occasionally worked together in more recent years with the aim of having a 'largely uniform law'.[58] Commercial law has long been an area where harmonisation has been rife due to pressure from 'the business community wishing the law to facilitate trading across the border'.[59]

[54] LCEW and SLC, *Amendment of the Companies Acts 1948–1983* (Law Com No 126 and Scot Law Com No 83 (1983)) amendments 35 and 51. See also LCEW and SLC, *Further Amendments of the Companies Acts 1948–1983* (Law Com No 136 and Scot Law Com No 87 (1984)).

[55] LCEW and SLC, *Hague Convention on Recognition of Divorces and Legal Separations* (Law Com No 34 and Scot Law Com No 16 (1970)) para 19. See also LCEW and SLC, *Private International Law: Report on Recognition of Foreign Nullity Decrees and Related Matters* (Law Com No 137 and Scot Law Com No 88 (1984)); LCEW and SLC, *Private International Law: Choice of Law Rules in Marriage* (Law Com No 165 and Scot Law Com No 105 (1987)); LCEW and SLC, *Private International Law: Report on the Law of Domicile* (Law Com No 168 and Scot Law Com No 107 (1987)); LCEW and SLC, *Private International Law: Choice of Law in Tort and Delict* (Law Com No 193 and Scot Law Com No 129 (1990)).

[56] LCEW and SLC, *Private International Law: Polygamous Marriages* (Law Com No 146 and Scot Law Com No 96 (1985)) para 1.1.

[57] See, eg, LCEW and SLC, *Family Law: Report on Custody of Children: Jurisdiction and Enforcement within the United Kingdom* (Law Com No 138 and Scot Law Com No 91 (1985)) para 1.14.

[58] LCEW and SLC, *Partnership Law* (Law Com No 283 and Scot Law Com No 192 (2003)) para 3.16.

[59] A Steven, 'Codification: A Perspective from a Scottish Law Commissioner' (Seminar Series on Codification, All Souls College, Oxford, 2014) 5.

A trend can therefore be discerned for greater cooperation and harmonisation in areas of law which were already similar to begin with, or where it makes sense for the UK (or at least Great Britain) to be 'one unit'.[60]

Although joint projects are commonly carried out in areas where it is felt that 'a common set of rules is required across the whole of the UK',[61] the resulting recommendations may not be precisely the same for Scotland and England. In certain joint projects, despite the Commissions working together, the resultant recommendations and draft Bill provisions differ slightly for England and Scotland.[62] In certain other cases, the differences are so great as to necessitate completely separate draft Bills.[63] Since 1999, separate provisions for Scotland are usually needed where the issue is devolved, even if the proposed reform is the same in both jurisdictions.[64] Occasionally the Commissions acknowledge that they agreed on 'most but not all aspects' of a joint report,[65] although such disagreement will not always be because of harmonisation concerns or jurisdictional differences, but rather a difference of opinion.[66] In other joint projects, 'significant differences' have been highlighted.[67]

In summary, harmonisation will frequently be the result of joint projects—but that is by no means always the case. Such a result follows logically from the fact that the Commissions correctly strive for improvement of the law—which will sometimes, but not always, comprise an element of harmonisation.

D. The Way Ahead

Sometimes joint projects fail to get underway because the participation of both (or potentially all three, if the NILC is to be revived) Commissions cannot be secured. In one instance, the SLC tried to interest the LCEW in a joint project on the postal rule in contracts, but was rebuffed.[68] The SLC nevertheless expressed

[60] LCB Gower, 'A Comment' (1967) 30 *MLR* 259, 260.

[61] McMillan, 'The Role of Law Reform' 8. See also N Brotchie, 'The Scottish Law Commission: Promoting Law Reform in Scotland' (2009) 9 *Legal Information Management* 30, 32.

[62] eg, LCEW and SLC, *Report on Sale and Supply of Goods* (Law Com No 160 and Scot Law Com No 104 (1987)); LCEW and SLC, *Third Parties—Rights against Insurers* (Law Com No 272 and Scot Law Com No 184 (2001)).

[63] eg, LCEW and SLC, *Exemption Clauses: Second Report* (Law Com No 69 and Scot Law Com No 39 (1975)). The eventual legislation, the Unfair Contract Terms Act 1977, has an England/Wales/Northern Ireland part, a Scotland part and a UK part.

[64] See, eg, LCEW and SLC, *Trustees' Powers and Duties* (Law Com No 260 and Scot Law Com No 172 (1999)). The Sewel Convention mandates that Westminster will not legislate for Scotland in devolved matters without Holyrood's consent: see below n 199.

[65] LCEW and SLC, *Liability for Defective Products* (Law Com No 82 and Scot Law Com No 45 (1977)) para 2.

[66] See, eg, Eric Clive's partial dissent in LCEW and SLC, *Rights of Suit in Respect of Carriage of Goods by Sea* (Law Com No 196 and Scot Law Com No 130 (1991)).

[67] LCEW and SLC, *Damages under the Human Rights Act 1998* (Law Com No 266 and Scot Law Com No 180 (2000)) para 1.8.

[68] SLC, *Report on the Formation of Contract: Scottish Law and the United Nations Convention on Contracts for the International Sale of Goods* (Scot Law Com No 144 (1993)) para 1.5.

its view on the 'desirability of having the same rule on [... formation of contract] throughout the United Kingdom, as well as throughout Europe and indeed the world'.[69] The ill-fated contract code[70] is evidence that sometimes a joint project will founder when the differences (in style or substance) are just too great between the jurisdictions. In a few areas, instead of working together on a joint project, the Commissions have worked on similar projects simultaneously or shortly after each other.[71] While it is clear that occasionally the Commissions consulted on the projects,[72] not having joint projects in certain instances may reflect the fact that the Commissions do not always feel that they can collaborate. Sometimes, however, the Commissions do not collaborate as much as they could. In a project examining illegitimacy, the LCEW revised its previous (recent) work in the area, issuing a whole new report to coincide with the SLC's view.[73] Such duplication of effort is wasteful in organisations like the Commissions with such limited resources. Sometimes working together will be beneficial, particularly when European dimensions necessitate UK-wide reform—although this will perhaps be less of a concern in the future. In certain other areas, the applicable law may be so different that there would be no benefit in a joint or tripartite project, but this should be confirmed before any project is selected. As we have seen, despite now having a roughly equal complement of Commissioners, the SLC does not have the same resources, in either a human or a financial sense, as the LCEW. The NILC was even smaller and its contribution to tripartite projects was appropriate to its size. The SLC, on the other hand, often needs to make a larger contribution to collaborative projects because Scots law varies from English law to a greater extent than Northern Ireland's law does. The SLC's resource limitations must therefore be borne in mind when the Commissions are considering a collaborative project—leading, in certain cases, to the conclusion that such collaboration cannot take place and, perhaps, that the project cannot therefore be undertaken. Selection of appropriate collaborative projects (and protection from feeling coerced to contribute to inappropriate projects) could be achieved by use of the chapter three project-selection criteria.

When considering whether to commence work on any project, a Commission will judge that project against the project-selection criteria: (i) the availability

[69] ibid para 4.7.

[70] See ch 5, sections V.A and V.B.

[71] See, eg, LCEW, *Family Law: Illegitimacy* (Law Com No 118 (1982) and *Family Law: Illegitimacy (Second Report)* Law Com No 157 (1986)) and SLC, *Family Law: Report on Illegitimacy* (Scot Law Com No 82 (1984)); LCEW, *Family Law: Financial Relief after Foreign Divorce* (Law Com No 117 (1982)) and SLC, *Report on Financial Provision after Foreign Divorce* (Scot Law Com No 72 (1982)); LCEW, *Company Security Interests* (Law Com No 296 (2005)) and SLC, *Registration of Rights in Security by Companies* (Scot Law Com No 197 (2004)).

[72] In one project, the Commissions specifically sought each other's advice (despite the project not being a joint one) in order to produce 'complementary' draft Bills: LCEW, *Family Law: Report on Jurisdiction in Matrimonial Causes* (Law Com No 48 (1972)) explanatory notes cl 4; SLC, *Family Law: Report on Jurisdiction in Consistorial Causes Affecting Matrimonial Status* (Scot Law Com No 25 (1972)).

[73] See below n 158.

and economical use of resources; (ii) the suitability of the project; and (iii) the importance of the project. We saw in chapter three that the use of the criteria is in need of development, in particular because it cannot be known whether the Commissions currently do judge potential projects in that manner, and because of inconsistent statements as to what the criteria are. Further reasons can now be advanced to justify the need for greater transparency. When considering availability of resources, a Commission should take into account whether it would be necessary, or beneficial, for that project to be a joint or tripartite project, or whether it at least requires some input from the other Commission(s).[74] If so, it should use the selection criteria to demonstrate why it believes that a project is particularly suitable and important and should allow the other Commission(s) to also consider the project against the same selection criteria. A Commission receiving a request to collaborate on a project (or at least have some input) should consider its own resources in conjunction with the resources the instigating Commission is proposing to devote to the project, as well as the project's importance and suitability. It is possible that one or more of the criteria will be better satisfied in one jurisdiction than the other(s). Where that is the case, a project might not be able to be pursued on a collaborative basis if another Commission does not agree to it based on a proper consideration of the criteria. In that instance, the instigating Commission will have to decide whether to embark on the project without such collaboration, or whether the project must be abandoned. On other occasions, one Commission might decide to assist on a project even if it means that its own individual workload suffers. The pressure to reach such an outcome is likely to be great when there is significant merit to a project because a Commission may wish to avoid exclusion from such reforms, having no input into the reforms, or being responsible for the abandoning of a compelling project. Where concern exists only as to a lack of resources rather than the substantive merits of a project, a Commission may wish to attempt to obtain additional resources,[75] or negotiate a smaller role in the project. The SLC may have to decide whether it is content to play a smaller role in line with its fewer resources, or whether a lack of ability to make a meaningful contribution makes it impossible to collaborate.

Difficult decisions have to be reached when the Commissions seek to collaborate with each other. Compromises have to be made and negotiations have to take place. The benefit of using the criteria in their developed (and, ideally, statutory) form is that increased certainty as to their meaning and increased transparency as

[74] Such a consideration is currently part of the Protocol's 'nine considerations' (see ch 3, section IV.B) but is not explicitly part of the project-selection criteria: LCEW and Ministry of Justice, *Protocol between the Lord Chancellor (on behalf of the Government) and the Law Commission* (Law Com No 321 (2010)) para 5 (see also para 9). See also LCEW and Welsh Ministers, *Protocol between the Welsh Ministers and the Law Commission/Protocol Rhwng Gweinidogion Cymru a Comisiwn y Gyfraith* (2015) para 7.

[75] As argued in ch 3, section V.A.i, resources must either be available or obtainable for a project to be viable.

to their use would better allow the Commissions to understand and test each other's decisions. The project-selection criteria, because of their focus on the substantive values of a project, allow the Commissions to allocate their resources correctly when they work individually. By each using the same criteria before embarking on collaborative projects, the Commissions could also allocate their resources correctly when they work together. Of course, it is entirely possible that the Commissions will disagree over how well a prospective project meets the criteria. As well as potentially differing as to whether they have the necessary resources, the Commissions may also have differing views as to the importance of a prospective project. The main strength of the use of the criteria, as developed in this book, is that it involves the structured and transparent exercise of the Commissions' discretion. The Commissions' decisions would therefore be more synchronised, but each would retain its own separate autonomy to embark on projects that are viable when judged against the criteria, or to refuse to embark on projects that are not.

II. Individual Projects

As well as when they collaborate, harmonisation can also be a consideration when the Commissions work individually.

A. European Pressure and Scottish Concerns

Attempts to harmonise the laws of England and Scotland did not begin with the Commissions' establishment in 1965. Harmonisation had been a 'sporadic aim' of those attempting law reform since the Union of the Crowns in 1603.[76] By the time the Commissions were established, however, the perceived pressure to harmonise was increasing. As we have already seen, the main motivation for such harmonisation (combined with codification) was impending entry into what is now the EU. Scarman opined that it was 'becoming daily more urgent that we should seek harmony, if not uniformity, between our law and the systems of our neighbours'.[77] His motivation for such harmonisation was 'the real possibility of entering into the common market'.[78] For Scarman, the 'unifying process' of the UK jurisdictions, ahead of European harmonisation, was a task which was ripe for the Commissions because it was 'beyond the power of the judges to command'.[79] Certain views on harmonisation from north of the border, however, were not as enthusiastic.

[76] MR Topping and JPM Vandenlinden, '*Ibi Renascit Jus Commune*' (1970) 33 *MLR* 170, 171.
[77] L Scarman, 'A Code of English Law?' (lecture, University of Hull, 1966) 9.
[78] L Scarman, *Law Reform: The New Pattern (The Lindsay Memorial Lectures)* (London, Routledge & Kegan Paul, 1968) 54.
[79] Scarman, 'A Code of English Law?' 9.

In 1965, concerns were rife in certain Scottish quarters about the Commissions' plan to harmonise the law of the UK jurisdictions, leading to the Secretary of State for Scotland having to assure Parliament and the public that 'there will be no complete assimilation of the Scottish and English law'.[80] These concerns were at least partially incited by TB Smith, who feared the harmonisation of Scots and English law.[81] Smith wrote that a loss of the distinct system of Scots law would infringe Article XVIII of the Acts of Union.[82] Despite his appointment as one of the first SLC Commissioners, those in government organising the introduction of the SLC emphatically blamed Smith for fostering a nationalistic suspicion that Scots law was to be '*gleichgeschaltet*' with English law.[83] The risk of Anglicisation would, however, have been greater had a separate Commission for Scotland not been established.[84] Scots law was not free from Anglicisation already,[85] and such Anglicisation could in fact be curbed by the creation of the SLC and its ability to propose distinctly Scottish law reform. The first SLC Chairman, Lord Kilbrandon, argued for the preservation of Scots law's distinctiveness, mentioning his distaste for the process of the 'tagging along' of Scottish provisions on English Bills—a process which the SLC helped to reduce.[86]

Certain other, less nationalistic, views were expressed that total assimilation was 'not a real danger' but that the two systems coming closer together in certain ways would be 'a success, not a failure' if Scots law (and English law) were to be changed for the better.[87] In fact, concern was expressed that the two Commissions would not cooperate enough to ensure assimilation where it could be beneficial.[88]

Kilbrandon urged that the SLC did not have the aim of assimilating Scots law with English law 'merely for the sake of assimilation'.[89] The fact that two Commissions and not one 'Great British' Commission had been created showed that

[80] HC Deb vol 706 col 153 (8 February 1965) (William Ross). See also 'No Complete Assimilation with English Law: Mr Ross Gives Assurance' *The Scotsman* (9 February 1965).

[81] See ch 2, section III.B.

[82] TB Smith, 'Little Sympathy for its Ideas' *The Scotsman* (16 January 1965). Article XVIII of both the Union with Scotland Act 1706 and the Union with England Act 1707 (the Acts of Union) provide for the continuation of the distinct rules of Scots law except those relating to trade, custom and excise which were to be Anglicised. It affords particular protection to 'private rights' which are to be altered only 'for evident utility of the subjects within Scotland'.

[83] RH Law (Scottish Office) to W Ross (Secretary of State for Scotland), 'Scottish Law Commission—Appointments', 18 March 1965, NRS HH41/1609. 'Gleichschaltung' is the process of 'making the same' or 'bringing into line'. Its origins are in Nazi Germany and so its use is emphatically pejorative. For further scepticism in relation to Smith's appointment, see ch 2, section III.B.

[84] 'Law Reform Commission—Mixed Welcome for Scheme' *The Scotsman* (15 February 1965), discussing the views of Gordon Wilson MP of the Scottish National Party.

[85] See, eg, TB Smith's concern that the lack of Scottish legal writing led to recourse to English texts and the subsequent Anglicisation of Scots law: 'The Scottish Universities Law Institute: The First Year' 1961 *Scots Law Times (News)* 97, 97.

[86] 'Aim Will be to Bring Law Up to Date' *The Scotsman* (17 June 1965). *cf* DM Walker, 'The Scottish Law Commission under Review' (1987) 8 *Statute Law Review* 115, 122.

[87] 'Reform of the Law' *The Scotsman* (17 June 1965).

[88] 'Law Reform' *The Scotsman* (8 February 1965).

[89] 'Aim Will be to Bring Law Up to Date' *The Scotsman* (17 June 1965).

the two legal systems were distinct, but it was possible that the Commissions might learn from each other. Hurlburt has expressed the view that the SLC has the 'unique' function of 'preserv[ing] the system of Scots law against pressure from the English common law'.[90] The SLC's statement, however, in its *First Annual Report* that it would be 'vigilant to preserve' certain aspects of Scots law must be read in conjunction with its wider aim to harmonise 'where this is appropriate'.[91] Indeed, the *First Annual Report* continues:

> There are also large areas of the law such, for example, as those relating to commercial contracts in which distinctions in this day and age may be unrealistic and, perhaps, positively harmful. It is in such areas that we feel that unification or harmonisation may prove to be particularly desirable.[92]

As we have seen, William Ross, the Secretary of State for Scotland at the time of the Commissions' creation, gave his assurance that no 'complete' assimilation with English law was intended.[93] But Ross's words were chosen carefully—although he spoke publicly of no *complete* assimilation, both Commissions soon began consciously attempting to harmonise their laws 'wherever possible' under ministerial orders.[94] A harmonised (and codified) law, certain commentators believed, would be 'easier to explain' to Europe.[95] For example, in relation to contract law, LCEW Commissioners pushed to end the 'absurd' differences between Scots and English law, because, in economic terms, the UK was 'one unit'.[96] Previous SLC Chairman Lord Davidson, however, worried that such harmonisation should not take place 'in isolation from a wider process of harmonisation among all member states of the Community' lest the advantages of Scotland's partially civilian roots be lost.[97] LCEW Commissioners such as Gower made clear their view that the harmonisation process was an 'essential pre-requisite' to harmonisation with Europe.[98]

Arguments which relied on the UK's pending accession to the EU are no longer applicable because of its impending likely departure. Indeed, those arguments have not been convincing for decades because the UK became a member of the EU notwithstanding it consisting of different jurisdictions. The UK's entry into the EU was evidently not contingent on our laws being either codified, or harmonised, or both. Despite the shift away from harmonisation, and despite the rise of devolution, certain projects continue to harmonise the law. Such harmonisation is, however, merely one possible aspect of improving the law, and not an end in itself.

[90] WH Hurlburt, *Law Reform Commissions in the United Kingdom, Australia and Canada* (Edmonton, Juriliber, 1986) 92.

[91] SLC, *First Annual Report* (Scot Law Com No 3 (1966)) para 41.

[92] ibid.

[93] See above n 80.

[94] AG Brand to HHA Whitworth, 'Full-time Commissioner', 29 September 1967, NRS HH83/702.

[95] A Diamond, 'Codification of the Law of Contract' (1968) 31 *MLR* 361, 374.

[96] LCB Gower, 'A Comment' (1967) 30 *MLR* 259, 260 ('A Comment').

[97] C Davidson, 'Law Reform—Who Cares?' (1992) 37(4) *Journal of the Law Society of Scotland* 130, 131.

[98] Gower, 'A Comment' 260.

B. Intentional and Incidental Harmonisation

The Commissions have achieved a certain degree of harmonisation, at least in overall effect, although not always by intent. In many relevant projects, there is no express mention of a desire to harmonise as such. Instead, the Commissions have simply selected the best aspects from another jurisdiction after examination (as they are obliged to do under section 3(1)(f) of the 1965 Act), and it just so happens that that jurisdiction is the other British jurisdiction. Further, in certain Commission projects, the laws of both jurisdictions were already similar and so no further harmonisation has been necessary.[99] In other projects, the law in an area has moved from being unified to being different, and the Commissions have attempted to harmonise the law again. For example, in relation to the private international law aspects of limitation periods for personal injuries, it was noted that the law in both jurisdictions diverged after English reforms. The SLC sought to restore the previous, more harmonised, situation with the adoption of certain English rules.[100] In other projects, the notion that the law should remain the same throughout Great Britain has been a reason to *not* recommend reform. For example, in an SLC project on *Insanity and Diminished Responsibility*, the defence of diminished responsibility was not renamed (despite having attracted some criticism) because, among other things, the expression was used and well known in England (as well as in other countries).[101] On one occasion, the SLC completed a project for Scotland alone that was later implemented (with modifications) as a UK-wide Act (although with certain provisions only for/excluding Scotland).[102] In certain instances, projects have demonstrated a clear compromise between English and Scots law, with strands of each legal tradition being woven together.[103]

Sometimes, however, the Commissions have recommended changing law which was unified (or similar) throughout Great Britain to being different. For example, in a report on *Personal Injury Actions: Limitation and Prescribed Claims*, the SLC recommended changing the limitation period for personal injury claims from three years (as it is in England) to five years.[104] In a project examining unincorporated

[99] See, eg, SLC, *Report on Financial Provision after Foreign Divorce* (Scot Law Com No 72 (1982)).

[100] eg, in the definition of 'injury': SLC, *Prescription and the Limitation of Actions: Report on Personal Injuries Actions and Private International Law Questions* (Scot Law Com No 74 (1983)) para 3.9.

[101] SLC, *Insanity and Diminished Responsibility* (Scot Law Com No 195 (2004)) para 3.12. The defence of diminished responsibility originated in Scotland and was imported into English law by the Homicide Act 1957, s 2, showing that harmonisation did not begin with the establishment of the Commissions, and did not always result in Scots law being Anglicised.

[102] SLC, *Report on Computer Crime* (Scot Law Com No 106 (1987)), implemented by the Computer Misuse Act 1990. The later LCEW project on the same area contained no draft Bill, mainly because of pressures of time (para 1.13), but the LCEW did note that it was 'desirable' that the law should be 'uniform throughout the United Kingdom': LCEW, *Computer Misuse* (Law Com No 186 (1989)) para 1.39.

[103] See, eg, LCEW, *Structured Settlements and Interim and Provisional Damages* (Law Com No 224 (1994)).

[104] SLC, *Personal Injury Actions: Limitation and Prescribed Claims* (Scot Law Com No 207 (2007)) paras 2.54–2.60.

associations, the SLC recommended another departure from the UK-wide position that such bodies do not have legal personality, proposing a reform that would have seen them being attributed with a legal personality in certain circumstances.[105] In one criminal law LCEW project, reforms were recommended which moved English law further away from Scots law.[106] The LCEW argued that this was not necessarily an 'undesirable inconsistency' because the rules were already 'quite different' between the two jurisdictions.[107] The fact that the LCEW felt obliged to justify its position demonstrates that harmonisation was still occasionally a consideration at the turn of the twenty-first century.

The Commissions have not achieved as much harmonisation as was anticipated in 1965. Even where no harmonisation is recommended, however, the Commissions have usually at least examined the law of the other jurisdiction. It is such examination, and selection of the most appropriate solution, which is important—not harmonisation for harmonisation's sake.

i. The SLC's Use of English Law

Under the 1965 Act, both Commissions have a duty to 'obtain such information as to the legal systems of other countries as appears to the Commissioners likely to facilitate the performance of any of their functions'.[108] Very occasionally, the terms of a reference to one of the Commissions may specifically require it to examine the law of its neighbouring jurisdictions. For example, in asking the SLC to consider the law of child abduction in 1984, because of 'cross-border implications', the Secretary of State for Scotland specifically asked the SLC to have 'regard to the laws applicable in England and Wales and Northern Ireland'.[109] Mostly, however, the Commissions choose to examine Scots/English law. As SLC Commissioner Hector MacQueen has observed, the SLC takes 'close account of English law. We have to because that is our nearest neighbour and obviously our largest comparator'.[110] For example, in relation to the SLC's extensive quasi-codification of bankruptcy law,[111] repeated references were made to English law, despite the 'distinctive' nature of Scots law in the area.[112] Section 3(1)(f) of the 1965 Act does not, however, confer a duty to always consult the law of the neighbouring jurisdiction if, for whatever reason, it is clear that it would not 'facilitate' the Commission's

105 SLC, *Unincorporated Associations* (Scot Law Com No 217 (2009)).

106 LCEW, *Legislating the Criminal Code: Corruption* (Law Com No 248 (1998)).

107 ibid para 4.75.

108 1965 Act, s 3(1)(f).

109 SLC, *Report on Child Abduction* (Scot Law Com No 102 (1987)) para 1.1.

110 E Cooke and HL MacQueen, 'Law Reform in a Political Environment: The Work of the Law Commissions' in D Feldman (ed), *Law in Politics, Politics in Law* (Oxford, Hart Publishing, 2013) 152.

111 SLC, *Report on Bankruptcy and Related Aspects of Insolvency and Liquidation* (Scot Law Com No 68 (1981)).

112 SLC, *Sixteenth Annual Report 1980–81* (Scot Law Com No 70 (1981)) para 2.3. See also SLC, *Seventeenth Annual Report 1981–82* (Scot Law Com No 73 (1982)) para 2.1; SLC, *Eighteenth Annual Report 1982–83* (Scot Law Com No 81 (1983)) para 2.5.

research. For example, in certain areas the legal systems may be so different that no real benefit could be derived.[113] Furthermore, in one SLC report, English law was of little use where it was also currently under review.[114] In almost all projects, however, the SLC does at least consider English law as an option, even where it is eventually (and sometimes swiftly) found not to be a suitable model for reform.[115] Consideration of English law is particularly prevalent where it has recently been reformed.[116] It is rare to find an SLC project where the equivalent English position is not referred to at all, even if that reference is brief.[117]

In its very first substantive report, the SLC recommended the abolition of the corroboration requirement in civil cases. No corroboration requirement existed (or exists) in England. The SLC was keen to stress, however, that Scots law should not be harmonised with English law 'just because'.[118] Other projects around the same time brought Scots law closer to English law (although not always necessarily in precisely identical terms), sometimes without any express mention of harmonisation, suggesting that the SLC was motivated by improvement rather than harmonisation.[119] In one later annual report, however, the SLC claimed to 'deplore the divergence in principle between the divorce laws of Scotland and England'.[120] In certain SLC projects, the borrowing from English law has been particularly explicit. For example, in its report on *The Companies (Floating Charges) (Scotland) Act 1961*,[121] the SLC recommended that 'the law of Scotland should be brought into conformity with that of England' in relation to the assets caught under floating charges,[122] and drew heavily on English law. English law was also adapted in a report on the presumption of death, where a seven-year period (before a missing person can be declared to be deceased) was chosen with the specific intention of Scots law being the same as in England.[123] The SLC has acknowledged that it has

[113] *cf* discussion on property law, below.

[114] SLC, *Report on the Law of Incest in Scotland* (Scot Law Com No 69 (1981)) para 3.4.

[115] See, eg, SLC, *Obligations: Report on Negligent Misrepresentation* (Scot Law Com No 92 (1985)), where the relevant English legislation (Misrepresentation Act 1967) was explicitly rejected; and SLC, *Evidence: Report on Corroboration, Hearsay and Related Matters in Civil Proceedings* (Scot Law Com No 100 (1986)), where the English Civil Evidence Act 1968 was found to be helpful, but did not 'provide a convenient model for reform of the law of Scotland' (para 3.34).

[116] Often by the LCEW: see, eg, SLC, *Report on Breach of Confidence* (Scot Law Com No 90 (1984)); SLC, *Report on Incapable Adults* (Scot Law Com No 151 (1995)); SLC, *Report on Three Bad Rules in Contract Law* (Scot Law Com No 152 (1996)); SLC, *Report on Double Jeopardy* (Scot Law Com No 218 (2009)).

[117] As in, for example, SLC, *Report on Boundary Walls* (Scot Law Com No 163 (1998)) para 1.6. See also below n 200.

[118] SLC, *Proposal for Reform of the Law of Evidence Relating to Corroboration* (Scot Law Com No 4 (1967)) para 22.

[119] eg, SLC, *Reform of the Law Relating to Legitimation per Subsequens Matrimonium* (Scot Law Com No 5 (1967)).

[120] SLC, *Sixth Annual Report 1970–71* (Scot Law Com No 23 (1971)) para 22.

[121] SLC, *The Companies (Floating Charges) (Scotland) Act 1961* (Scot Law Com No 14 (1970)).

[122] ibid para 13.

[123] SLC, *Report on Presumption of Death* (Scot Law Com No 34 (1974)) paras 37–39.

sometimes 'profited from the experience gained in England and Wales' in areas recently reformed south of the Tweed.[124]

In certain SLC projects, only selected parts of English law were borrowed, and others rejected.[125] In other projects, English law has been heavily drawn on, but modified. For example, in a project on prescription and limitation, it was noted that the harmonisation of Scots and English rules was a 'valuable immediate objective', but the eventual limitation periods proposed were not exactly the same.[126] In a project reforming the law on sexual offences, the SLC again described recent English reforms as 'influential' even if its eventual recommendations differed in much of the 'detail', again suggesting that perhaps harmonisation was not the motivation for the reforms.[127]

The English law examined (and sometimes adopted) by the SLC has frequently resulted from LCEW projects. For example, in a project examining civil liability for animals, the SLC admitted that recent LCEW reforms were 'very influential' although a wholesale adoption of the relevant legislation would 'not be satisfactory'.[128] In family law too, the SLC has followed some, but not all, of the LCEW's recent recommendations in the area, once commenting on the 'desirability of having similar rules on these matters in both England and Scotland'.[129] In a later family law project, the SLC noted that it was not 'of great importance' that the law was the same in the two jurisdictions, as long as they are 'broadly equal' and specifically decided not to postpone its report until after the LCEW reported on the same matter.[130] In most instances, however, the view that the SLC 'could not ignore' recent LCEW work in the same area has prevailed, even if not with a view to harmonisation, as opposed to improvement.[131]

Sometimes a Commission has examined the solution found in the other jurisdiction but, for whatever reason, found it unattractive or inappropriate. For example, the SLC has examined English law but found it 'not helpful'.[132]

[124] SLC, *Report on Occupancy Rights in the Matrimonial Home and Domestic Violence* (Scot Law Com No 60 (1980)) para 1.9.

[125] eg, SLC, *Report on Evidence: Blood Group Tests, DNA Tests and Related Matters* (Scot Law Com No 120 (1989)).

[126] SLC, *Reform of the Law Relating to Prescription and Limitation of Actions* (Scot Law Com No 15 (1970)) para 86. The English period of short negative prescription of six years was rejected in favour of a period of five years (para 68).

[127] SLC, *Report on Rape and Other Sexual Offences* (Scot Law Com No 209 (2007)) para 1.8.

[128] SLC, *Obligations: Report on Civil Liability in Relation to Animals* (Scot Law Com No 97 (1985)) para 1.10, discussing the English Animals Act 1971.

[129] SLC, *Family Law: Report on Illegitimacy* (Scot Law Com No 82 (1984)) para 8.15. See also SLC, *Family Law: Report on Aliment and Financial Provision* (Scot Law Com No 67 (1981)); SLC, *Report on Vulnerable Adults* (Scot Law Com No 158 (1997)), where 'much the same' approach as a recent LCEW project was taken but with 'many differences' due to the differing existing law (para 1.6).

[130] SLC, *Report on Reform of the Ground for Divorce* (Scot Law Com No 116 (1989)) paras 4.9–4.10.

[131] SLC, *Report on Unjustified Enrichment, Error of Law and Public Authority Receipts and Disbursements* (Scot Law Com No 169 (1999)) para 1.2.

[132] SLC, *Report on the Scottish Term and Quarter Days* (Scot Law Com No 108 (1987)) para 3.4.

In one example, the SLC was scathing of an LCEW project on mens rea,[133] pointing out that the solutions it proposed would be 'inappropriate and misleading' in Scotland.[134] Similarly, the SLC has sometimes specifically stressed that it has reached different conclusions from the LCEW where both Commissions have worked on similar projects.[135] The main reason for rejection has usually been that the English law would be too much of 'a major departure from Scottish practice' to recommend.[136] Occasionally, however, the substance of the English rules themselves has been criticised.[137] Even where English law has been rejected, it has usually been clear that it was for a considered reason and that the SLC has not endorsed 'legal isolationism'.[138]

In certain projects, the SLC has recommended reform where Scots law was thought to compare unfavourably with English law. In the 1970s, the Law Society of Scotland was 'deeply concerned' that Scots law could not provide for damages in certain circumstances where they were available in England.[139] The resultant SLC project borrowed from previous LCEW work in the area, although with certain important differences. In the same decade, the Law Society of Scotland referred another project to the SLC for similar reasons. The *Report on the Married Women's Policies of Assurance (Scotland) Act 1880*[140] resulted from a reference to bring Scots law into line with English law. Such harmonisation was thought to be necessary because Scots law was plagued with disadvantages, which caused the 'highly undesirable' result of people in Scotland attempting to have recourse to the equivalent English Act.[141] In other projects, even if no harmonisation is mentioned, the impetus for the project has been that recent English reform has left Scots law lagging behind.[142] In one project related to criminal evidence, the inspiration came from comments from the then Lord Justice General, Lord Hope, 'on the urgent need for statutory provisions for Scotland similar to those which [apply] in England and Wales'.[143] In the event, the English legislation was not adopted wholesale because

[133] LCEW, *Report on the Mental Element in Crime* (Law Com No 89 (1978)).

[134] SLC, *The Mental Element in Crime* (Scot Law Com No 80 (1983)) para 4.39.

[135] eg, SLC, *Report on Liability for Antenatal Injury* (Scot Law Com No 30 (1973)) para 2.

[136] SLC, *Evidence: Report on Hearsay Evidence in Criminal Proceedings* (Scot Law Com No 149 (1995)) para 4.46.

[137] As being, for example, 'brief and unhelpful' in relation to class actions: SLC, *Multi-Party Actions* (Scot Law Com No 154 (1996)) para 3.1. See also the SLC's view that there was 'virtually no support' for the adoption of certain English rules in SLC, *Poinding and Warrant Sale* (Scot Law Com No 177 (2000)) para 5.66.

[138] *Poinding and Warrant Sale*, ibid paras 2.44–2.46.

[139] SLC, *Damages for Personal Injuries: Report on (1) Admissibility of Claims for Services and (2) Admissible Deductions* (Scot Law Com No 51 (1978)) para 2.

[140] SLC, *Report on the Married Women's Policies of Assurance (Scotland) Act 1880* (Scot Law Com No 52 (1978)).

[141] ibid paras 1 and 12.

[142] See, eg, SLC, *Report on Evidence in Cases of Rape and Other Sexual Offences* (Scot Law Com No 78 (1983)) para 1.2.

[143] SLC, *Evidence: Report on Documentary Evidence and Proof of Undisputed Facts in Criminal Proceedings* (Scot Law Com No 137 (1992)) para 1.3.

in certain instances it would have constituted a 'major departure from Scottish practice', but the SLC was 'indebted' to English law for inspiration.[144] In a project on damages, it was acknowledged that the inspiration for the project was the concern that the English rules were better, and that Scottish claimants should not be disadvantaged.[145] Despite adopting certain of the English rules, the SLC had a 'strong aversion' to certain other English solutions, and it was noted that the jurisdictions need not have 'identical' provisions.[146] In another project, the SLC was keen that the Scottish courts should be 'at least as well equipped' as those in England, although the English provisions should not be 'merely copied'.[147] More recently, a project on execution of contracts in counterpart was inspired by evidence from practitioners that English law was being used in Scots transactions because of the lack of clarity of Scots law.[148] The SLC has, therefore, been keen to note where English law could be used to plug 'a gap', or rectify a flaw, in Scots law.[149]

In certain areas, developments in English law have forced a change of opinion at the SLC. For example, in relation to hearing evidence from vulnerable witnesses, the SLC previously indicated its opposition to the use of screens to shield certain witnesses.[150] In its final report, however, the SLC noted that it had to 'revise [its] earlier reservations', because it was '[f]aced with the reality of what is now happening in Scotland (and to an even greater extent in England and Wales)'.[151]

In summary, the SLC keeps an eye on its neighbour in order to improve Scots law, and has frequently found attractive solutions in English law—even after the perceived European pressure for harmonisation dissipated. Working in a smaller jurisdiction, Scots lawyers are accustomed to looking across borders in order to find authority where there is a dearth or a deficiency locally. Indeed, one previous SLC Chairman, Lord Drummond Young, has stated that '[a]t one time "comparative law" in Scotland largely consisted of looking at English law and adapting it'.[152] As the SLC has pointed out, however, it will not harmonise the law 'just because'. Any such harmonisation is not an end in itself, but merely one aspect of the SLC's attempt to improve Scots law. Indeed, the SLC may not be motivated by harmonisation at all, but may simply find, in its duty to examine the law of other jurisdictions, that a good solution can be found close to home.

[144] ibid para 2.63.

[145] SLC, *Report on the Effect of Death on Damages* (Scot Law Com No 134 (1992)) paras 4.2 and 4.7.

[146] ibid para 3.37.

[147] SLC, *Report on Confiscation and Forfeiture* (Scot Law Com No 147 (1994)) para 2.12.

[148] SLC, *Review of Contract Law—Report on Formation of Contract: Execution in Counterpart* (Scot Law Com No 231 (2013)) paras 1.1–1.7.

[149] See, eg, SLC, *Report on Diligence and Debtor Protection* (Scot Law Com No 95 (1985)) para 4.33, where the 'gap' related to debt arrangement schemes.

[150] SLC, *The Evidence of Children and Other Potentially Vulnerable Witnesses* (Scot Law Com DP No 75 (1988)) paras 5.60–5.65.

[151] SLC, *Report on the Evidence of Children and Other Potentially Vulnerable Witnesses* (Scot Law Com No 125 (1990)) para 4.19.

[152] SLC, *Annual Report 2011* (Scot Law Com No 225 (2012)) Chairman's foreword.

ii. The LCEW's Use of Scots Law

Although they are not quite as ubiquitous as SLC projects that cite English law, many LCEW projects since 1965 have examined Scots law.[153] Various LCEW projects have considered the work of the SLC,[154] and occasionally of its predecessor, the Law Reform Committee for Scotland.[155] Numerous LCEW projects have adopted solutions found in Scots law.[156] Such adoption follows Gardiner's praise of Scots law during the Commissions' establishment, and shows that TB Smith was unduly concerned that Great British law would really mean 'English' law. On one occasion, the LCEW conceded, in following an SLC recommendation, that 'it clearly seems desirable that the law should be the same throughout Great Britain'.[157] On another occasion in relation to illegitimacy, the LCEW revised its 1982 report with a new report and draft Bill recast in 1986 to follow the SLC's recent (1984) recommendations in the area, because 'so far as our different systems of law will allow, there should be consistency on such an important subject'.[158] In relation to guardianship, previous SLC work was cited approvingly and certain recommendations were made in the light of the Scottish reforms.[159] Furthermore, the LCEW praised the SLC's work on domestic violence and occupation of the family home. The LCEW noted the desirability of bringing English law 'into

[153] To take just certain examples spanning the LCEW's history and areas of examination: LCEW, *Blood Tests and the Proof of Paternity in Civil Proceedings* (Law Com No 16 (1968)); LCEW, *Report on Liability for Damage or Injury to Trespassers and Related Questions of Occupiers' Liability* (Law Com No 75 (1976)); LCEW, *Law of Contract: Report on Interest* (Law Com No 88 (1978)); LCEW, *Criminal Law: Attempt and Impossibility in Relation to Attempt, Conspiracy and Incitement* (Law Com No 102 (1980)); LCEW, *Administrative Law: Judicial Review and Statutory Appeals* (Law Com No 226 (1994)); LCEW, *The Forfeiture Rule and the Law of Succession* (Law Com No 295 (2005)); LCEW, *Capital and Income in Trusts: Classification and Apportionment* (Law Com No 315 (2009)).

[154] Examples are too numerous to cite, but include: LCEW, *Limitation Act 1963* (Law Com No 35 (1970)); LCEW, *Matrimonial Property* (Law Com No 175 (1988)); LCEW, *Damages for Personal Injury: Medical, Nursing and Other Expenses; Collateral Benefits* (Law Com No 262 (1999)); LCEW, *Sharing Homes* (Law Com No 278 (2002)); LCEW, *Company Security Interests* (Law Com No 296 (2005)).

[155] eg, LCEW, *Civil Liability for Animals* (Law Com No 13 (1967)).

[156] eg, suggested reforms to English divorce law were similar to (although not the same as) Scots law in LCEW, *Family Law: Time Restrictions on Presentation of Divorce and Nullity Proceedings* (Law Com No 116 (1982)); recent SLC work was examined and much the same conclusions were reached in LCEW, *The Effect of Divorce on Wills* (Law Com No 217 (1993)); the Scottish rules on the admission of implied hearsay were adopted in LCEW, *Evidence in Criminal Proceedings: Hearsay* (Law Com No 245 (1997)); the Scots limitation period for defamation claims (three years) was recommended to replace the English period (one year) to avoid forum shopping in LCEW, *Limitation of Actions* (Law Com No 270 (2001)).

[157] LCEW, *Limitation Act 1963* (Law Com No 35 (1970)) para 20 followed the SLC's view that the limitation period for living persons making personal injuries claims should be increased from 12 months to three years. See also the 'necessity for uniform rules' in LCEW, *Family Law: Report on Jurisdiction in Matrimonial Causes* (Law Com No 48 (1972)) para 81.

[158] LCEW, *Family Law: Illegitimacy (Second Report)* (Law Com No 157 (1986)) para 1.1. *cf* the previous reports, LCEW, *Family Law: Illegitimacy* (Law Com No 118 (1982)) and SLC, *Family Law: Report on Illegitimacy* (Scot Law Com No 82 (1984)). The Scottish provisions had already been influenced by English law and the LCEW's proposals: see above n 129.

[159] LCEW, *Review of Child Law: Guardianship* (Law Com No 172 (1988)).

line' with Scots law in the area,[160] because it was 'much clearer',[161] and admitted learning from the Scottish experience.[162] The LCEW consciously followed, so far as possible, recent SLC work in a project on mental incapacity so that there were 'mutually consistent principles, while taking into account differences in law and procedure on each side of the border'.[163] In relation to an aspect of homicide reform, the LCEW admitted that English law was 'out of step' with Scots law, and indeed the rest of Europe, necessitating change.[164]

Sometimes, after examination, it nevertheless has become clear that the potential solution found in Scots law is not appropriate:

> We have tried in the Report to eliminate any needless differences between the marriage law of England and Wales and that of Scotland but there are such differences of law, practice and tradition that uniformity has not proved possible … Having regard to these considerations we do not feel able to propose the adoption here of the Scottish system. The situation in the two parts of Great Britain is different both in regard to social habits and legal norms.[165]

In one family law project the LCEW noted that, although it was 'clearly desirable' that English and Scots law should be 'based on similar principles', it was not necessary for the two jurisdictions' rules to be 'couched in identical terms'.[166] The rejection of a Scottish provision may be due to jurisdictional differences or a divergence of opinion, even where the SLC's work is found to have been 'of great importance'.[167] Despite not surveying Scots law quite as routinely as the SLC surveys English law, the LCEW has frequently considered Scottish provisions, and has quite often found them to be appealing enough to adopt.

iii. The Harmonisation Track Record Across Different Areas of Law

In its *Eighteenth Annual Report*, the SLC acknowledged that the laws of England and Scotland should not be different 'simply for the sake of being different'.[168] It was also recognised, however, that sometimes the same solution simply will not work both north and south of the border.[169] In certain areas of law, the Commissions have found it 'desirable' to have 'a common set of rules and provisions

160 LCEW, *Domestic Violence and Occupation of the Family Home* (Law Com No 207 (1992)) para 4.5.

161 ibid para 4.16.

162 ibid para 4.37. See also LCEW, *Cohabitation: The Financial Consequences of Relationship Breakdown* (Law Com No 307 (2007)).

163 LCEW, *Mental Incapacity* (Law Com No 231 (1995)) para 2.30.

164 LCEW, *The Year and a Day Rule in Homicide* (Law Com No 230 (1995)) para 2.24.

165 LCEW, *Family Law: Report on Solemnisation of Marriage in England and Wales* (Law Com No 53 (1973)) annex, paras 2 and 112.

166 LCEW, *Family Law: The Financial Consequences of Divorce* (Law Com No 112 (1981)) para 35.

167 LCEW, *Report on Injuries to Unborn Children* (Law Com No 60 (1974)) para 9.

168 SLC, *Eighteenth Annual Report 1982–83* (Scot Law Com No 81 (1983)) para 2.9.

169 ibid.

applying throughout the UK'.[170] In other areas, the SLC has strongly shaped the distinctiveness of Scots law, and has opposed 'ill-considered attempts to unify the laws of England and Scotland by the application of principles which are not consistent with Scots law'.[171] Certain areas, therefore, have lent themselves better to the borrowing of legal rules from the other British jurisdiction (with or without the distinct aim of harmonisation) than others.

Unsurprisingly, because of the number of joint projects and the nature of the subject matter, the SLC has recognised that 'it is particularly important that the laws of the United Kingdom should, so far as possible, coincide' in relation to private international law.[172] In administrative law, the SLC was consulted on an LCEW project and expressed the view that it was 'essential that any examination of principles should be carried out upon a United Kingdom footing'.[173] In matters relating to procedural rules, it has also been noted that it is 'desirable to retain some uniformity within the United Kingdom' to avoid difficulties when cross-border issues arise.[174] Commercial law is another area where it has been said that there was 'no reason … why Scots law should continue to be out of line' with England and Europe.[175] Harmonisation has been more prevalent in areas where the UK is already perceived as a single unit, or where conflicts of law are likely to arise.

Conversely, property law is one area where it might be thought that Scots law is unlikely to have much recourse to English law and vice versa because of the differences in the legal traditions in the jurisdictions. For example, projects on company securities were undertaken simultaneously by both Commissions.[176] Potential harmonisation was limited by the 'radical differences between the law of rights in security, and the underlying law of property in Scotland and England and Wales respectively'.[177] The LCEW in particular, however, has been keen to examine Scots property law and has made recommendations modelled on Scots law.[178] Scots property law was examined in one conveyancing project because English

[170] M McMillan, 'The Role of Law Reform in Constitutionalism, Rule of Law and Democratic Governance: Reflections by the Scottish Law Commission' (Association of Law Reform Agencies of Eastern and Southern Africa Lecture, 2011) 7.

[171] SLC, *Seventh Annual Report 1971–72* (Scot Law Com No 28 (1973)) para 12.

[172] SLC, *Twenty-First Annual Report 1985–86* (Scot Law Com No 101 (1986)) para 1.18.

[173] LCEW, *Administrative Law* (Law Com No 20 (1969)) para 12.

[174] SLC, *Report on the Legal Capacity and Responsibility of Minors and Pupils* (Scot Law Com No 110 (1987)) para 3.90. See also SLC, *Report on Requirements of Writing* (Scot Law Com No 112 (1988)) (where a requirement for writing in insurance contracts was not introduced because there was no such requirement in English law: para 2.30); and the various examples of limitation periods cited above (eg, nn 156 and 157). *cf* SLC, *Prescription and Title to Moveable Property* (Scot Law Com No 228 (2012)) and above n 126.

[175] SLC, *Report on Diligence on the Dependence and Admiralty Arrestments* (Scot Law Com No 164 (1998)) para 4.14. See also above nn 58 and 59.

[176] SLC, *Registration of Rights in Security by Companies* (Scot Law Com No 197 (2004)); LCEW, *Company Security Interests* (Law Com No 296 (2005)).

[177] *Registration of Rights in Security by Companies*, ibid para 1.6.

[178] See, eg, LCEW, *Renting Homes: The Final Report* (Law Com No 297 (2006)); LCEW, *Making Land Work: Easements, Covenants and Profits a Prendre* (Law Com No 327 (2011)).

lawyers had 'often heard it said that the procedure for buying and selling houses in Scotland is simpler and better than it is in England and Wales'.[179] The Scottish solutions were, however, found to be unsuitable.[180] The SLC has likewise occasionally looked at English property law,[181] although there has more usually been a robust guarding of the unique features of Scots property law. The 'reluctance to allow English doctrines to displace Scottish doctrines' in Scots property law was one motivation behind a project which examined the House of Lords' decision in *Sharp v Thomson*.[182] Furthermore, in an SLC project in relation to lost and abandoned property, it was noted that English law in the area was so different that it 'would not be profitable to analyse it in detail'.[183] Certain SLC property law projects, however, have made use of English law. For example, in a project examining the recovery of possession of heritable property, the SLC was, in one area, 'attracted to a scheme along the lines of the English one'.[184] More recently, an SLC land registration project proposed a system of advance notices based (mainly) on a hybrid of English and German law.[185]

In certain areas, therefore, English and Scots law are sometimes (but not always) too different to be harmonised easily. There are other areas where harmonisation is more likely—for example, private international law. It is impossible, however, to draw hard lines as to where harmonisation will or will not occur. The Commissions more often than not examine the law of their neighbouring jurisdiction. Whether a Commission decides, however, to adopt, adapt or reject that law depends on various factors. These include: (1) how deficient the current law in one's own jurisdiction is, including, in particular, whether it is often compared unfavourably with, or ignored in favour of, the neighbouring law, or whether there is a need to follow the other jurisdiction's lead; (2) whether the legal tradition in that general area is sufficiently similar between the two jurisdictions; (3) whether harmonisation would be desirable because of, for example, clarity and simplicity, economic unity, cross-border issues, or (although perhaps less of a concern in the future) European dimensions; (4) whether the law in the other jurisdiction has been reformed recently (perhaps by the LCEW/SLC); and (5) whether that law is deemed to be sound. Such considerations reveal that the Commissions are, entirely properly, guided by the improvement of their jurisdiction's law, rather than harmonisation with their neighbours. Because of the Commissions' duty to

[179] LCEW, *Transfer of Land: Report on 'Subject to Contract' Agreements* (Law Com No 65 (1975)) app B, para 32.

[180] ibid app B, para 40.

[181] Even if briefly: see above n 117.

[182] *Sharp v Thomson* 1997 SC (HL) 66; SLC, *Report on Sharp v Thomson* (Scot Law Com No 208 (2007)) para 1.11.

[183] SLC, *Report on Lost and Abandoned Property* (Scot Law Com No 57 (1980)) para 1.11.

[184] SLC, *Recovery of Possession of Heritable Property* (Scot Law Com No 118 (1989)) para 4.34, discussing responses to notices to quit.

[185] SLC, *Report on Land Registration* (Scot Law Com No 222 (2010)) para 14.9.

examine the law of other jurisdictions under section 3(1)(f) of the 1965 Act, the Commissions may not be motivated by harmonisation at all—they simply examine and take influence from other legal systems, including the neighbouring one. Whether harmonisation is intentional or incidental, it is carried out on a more informed basis than it would have been without the Commissions.

C. The Overall Goal of Improvement

We have seen that both Commissions have shown a strong tendency to consider the other jurisdiction's law and the other Commission's work. As a result, some harmonisation has been achieved, but in certain other areas the solutions found across the border have been rejected. Despite being seen at their establishment as tools of harmonisation, it is probable that, without separate Commissions, *more* harmonisation would have been achieved.[186] Such harmonisation, however, would likely have been less well considered, and had less cross-border cooperation,[187] because it was observed above that the SLC has helped to reduce the 'tagging along' of Scottish legislative provisions.[188]

The main reason for harmonisation—the perception that it would aid entry into the EU—is no longer relevant. Perhaps it was never convincing because such entry took place notwithstanding the lack of a completely harmonised 'UK' legal system. Devolution, particularly in Wales, has made such harmonisation less likely. Yet the Commissions continue, entirely properly, to act as conduits for greater discussion between their jurisdictions, even if harmonisation does not always result. A combination of the Commissions' duties to consult each other and to examine the law in other jurisdictions maximises such discussion. Exchange of knowledge and improvement of the laws of each jurisdiction is, and should be, the Commissions' aim—which will sometimes, but not necessarily, result in the jurisdictions coming closer together. As such, before embarking on a new project, a project's likelihood of harmonising the law should be considered as one aspect of the 'importance' criterion, but it is not essential to its viability. Sometimes the benefits of having one system of law may be relevant, for example, when cross-border issues apply. The essential consideration, taken into account under the 'importance' criterion, is the extent to which the law in the instant jurisdiction is lacking. Such consideration will usually, in due course, necessitate research into how the law in other jurisdictions is superior.[189] In certain cases, that research may eventually lead to the adoption of the neighbouring jurisdiction's law, depending on consideration of the five factors established in section II.B.iii above. It may instead, however, lead

[186] 'Law Reform Commission—Mixed Welcome for Scheme' *The Scotsman* (15 February 1965).
[187] See G Gretton, 'Of Law Commissioning' (2013) 17 *Edinburgh Law Review* 119, 123.
[188] 'Aim Will be to Bring Law Up to Date' *The Scotsman* (17 June 1965).
[189] As required by the 1965 Act, s 3(1)(f).

to the adoption of a solution found in a jurisdiction further afield, or the crafting of a new solution based on an amalgam of different rules. The overall goal is improvement—not harmonisation.

III. Devolution

Contrary to the original plan to use the Commissions to harmonise the law, devolution has caused the increasing fragmentation of the UK. Although Scotland has always been a proudly separate jurisdiction, increased devolution for Wales has made achieving harmonisation less likely than ever. In addition to making harmonisation less achievable, the 'complexities of working within the rapidly changing devolution settlements' have raised new challenges for the Commissions.[190] These challenges include the increasing number of parties who interact with the Commissions—all of whom must be clear about the proper scope of the Commissions' activity to know what they might reasonably expect, or request, from the Commissions. Statutory embodiment of the project-selection criteria developed in this book would lessen those challenges by providing a basis for negotiation and agreement.

A. Scotland

Scottish devolution requires consideration of three main issues.[191] First, the SLC now faces the complexity of having to work with two governments. The SLC examines both devolved and reserved areas of law. Consequently, both the Scottish and UK governments have the power to refer projects to the SLC.[192] Programme projects are approved by the Scottish Ministers alone. It has been observed by former LCEW Chairman, Sir David Lloyd Jones, that because the Scottish Ministers fund the SLC, they might, when approving programme projects, 'have a natural inclination to favour projects in areas for which [they are] responsible'.[193] He goes on to say, however, that because the SLC has a duty to review 'all the law', 'a balance must be struck'.[194] Giving a UK government minister (presumably the Secretary of State for Scotland) an input into programme projects would be complex and would cause confusion (or at least disruption and delay) if the Scottish Ministers

[190] D Lloyd Jones, 'The Law Commission and Law Reform in a Devolved Wales' (Wales Governance Centre Annual Lecture, 2013) 7 ('The Law Commission and Law Reform in a Devolved Wales').

[191] In addition to the issues surrounding implementation discussed in ch 4, section II.F.

[192] 1965 Act, s 3(1)(e) as amended by the Scotland Act 1998 (Consequential Modifications) (No 2) Order 1999 SI 1999/1820, sch 2, pt I, para 36(3)(a).

[193] Lloyd Jones, 'The Law Commission and Law Reform in a Devolved Wales' 21.

[194] ibid.

did not agree with a particular choice. The current system allows for UK ministers to refer specific projects to the SLC should they wish, ensuring that the SLC fulfils its obligation to take and keep under review all the law, including reserved matters.

Because it receives references from two governments,[195] the SLC must be careful to give priority to the most deserving references, as well as ensuring resources remain for the projects it has undertaken to complete in its programmes. The majority of the SLC's work concerns areas of devolved law, largely because most of Scots law is devolved rather than reserved. The SLC does, however, continue to work with the UK Government and Parliament on a regular basis. Amendment to the 1965 Act is recommended to reflect the fact that the SLC presents reports on reserved matters to both the Scottish Ministers and the Secretary of State for Scotland.[196] Both the Scottish and UK governments should have regard to the project-selection criteria when referring projects to the SLC. Such references should be checked by the SLC against the same criteria. Because of the number of governmental actors interacting with the SLC, clear project-selection criteria based on sound considerations must be agreed to ensure consistent project selection and correct resource allocation.

Second, despite devolution, the Commissions still regularly work together on joint projects. Most joint projects undertaken post-devolution have related to reserved matters,[197] although certain projects have related to a combination of devolved and reserved matters.[198] Where a joint project is devolved, separate legislation will normally be required for Scotland, even if the recommendations are the same—unless the Scottish Parliament grants its consent for Westminster to legislate. This requirement is due to the Sewel Convention, whereby Westminster will not normally legislate on devolved matters without Holyrood's consent.[199] Collaborative projects make up a significant minority of the SLC's output. For example, between 2006 and 2015, it published 20 solo reports and 11 collaborative reports. Because the LCEW usually takes the leading role when the Commissions collaborate, a joint project may not take up as many resources as a solo project. Joint projects do, however, constitute a significant proportion of the SLC's

[195] In practice, however, most references are now received from the Scottish Government. Since devolution, the SLC has only received references from the UK Government where the issue is also to be considered by the LCEW. One reference did not result in a joint project (SLC, *Registration of Rights in Security by Companies* (Scot Law Com No 197 (2004))), but a concurrent project was carried out by the LCEW as a result of a similar reference.

[196] See ch 4, section II.F and ch 7, section II.

[197] eg, LCEW and SLC, *Company Directors: Regulating Conflicts of Interest and Formulating a Statement of Duties* (Law Com No 261 and Scot Law Com No 173 (1999)); LCEW and SLC, *Partnership Law* (Law Com No 283 and Scot Law Com No 192 (2003)).

[198] eg, LCEW and SLC, *Unfair Terms in Contracts* (Law Com No 292 and Scot Law Com No 199 (2005)).

[199] See *Devolution: Memorandum of Understanding and Supplementary Agreements between the United Kingdom Government, the Scottish Ministers, the Welsh Ministers and the Northern Ireland Executive Committee* (2012) para 14 and Scotland Act 2016, s 2.

workload, and so the need for a system of selection of joint projects based on the project-selection criteria still exists.

Third and finally, devolution marks a shift away from the harmonisation envisaged in 1965. Despite that shift, in the 34 SLC reports not conducted jointly with the LCEW published between the start of devolution and the end of 2015, almost all cited English law (even if briefly).[200] Certain projects actively endorsed harmonisation, at least in some proposals.[201] Other projects highlighted the differences between Scots and English law.[202] Devolution has not drastically impacted the SLC's tendencies to either examine, or recommend adopting, English rules. Nor has devolution had any real impact on the number of joint projects embarked on by both Commissions. It has, however, made the structure within which the SLC operates more complicated. Such complication makes the adoption of statutory project-selection criteria all the more important to ensure that the SLC and every government official it interacts with have the same expectations of the SLC's scope of activity.

B. Wales

Welsh devolution 'has come a very long way in a short time',[203] resulting in a steep learning curve for the LCEW. A separate Welsh Government and legislature (the National Assembly for Wales; referred to subsequently as the Welsh Assembly) now operate with more powers than when they were first established in 1999, when previously (compared with Scotland and Northern Ireland) fewer areas were subject to their devolved competence.[204] Former Chairman of the LCEW, Sir David Lloyd Jones, has said that 'for the first time in over 450 years' it can be said that Welsh law is 'a living system of law'.[205] Lloyd Jones predicts that devolution was only the start of 'an increasing divergence between English law and Welsh law' in devolved areas.[206] Instead, therefore, of having one harmonised 'British' jurisdiction, English and Welsh law have gone from being virtually identical to having certain distinct differences. For the LCEW, although Welsh devolution has 'brought

[200] Only one project did not mention English law at all: SLC, *Law of the Foreshore and Seabed* (Scot Law Com No 190 (2003)).

[201] Elements of harmonisation can be observed in, for example, SLC, *Insanity and Diminished Responsibility* (Scot Law Com No 195 (2004)); SLC, *Report on Rape and Other Sexual Offences* (Scot Law Com No 209 (2007)); and SLC, *Review of Contract Law—Report on Formation of Contract: Execution in Counterpart* (Scot Law Com No 231 (2013)).

[202] eg, SLC, *Registration of Rights in Security by Companies* (Scot Law Com No 197 (2004)).

[203] Lloyd Jones, 'The Law Commission and Law Reform in a Devolved Wales' 1.

[204] While the Scotland Act 1998, sch 5 and the Northern Ireland Act 1998, schs 2–3 outline the reserved and excepted matters *outside* those parliaments' powers, the Government of Wales Act 2006, sch 7 (now repealed) outlined the devolved areas which were *within* the Welsh Assembly's powers. The Wales Act 2017 moved Wales to a system of general devolved competence subject to a list of reserved matters, as in Scotland/Northern Ireland.

[205] Lloyd Jones, 'The Law Commission and Law Reform in a Devolved Wales' 1.

[206] ibid.

with [it] many new opportunities', it has 'also brought many new challenges'.[207] Such challenges could be eased by the adoption of the proposals advanced in this section, which add to the reforms made by the Wales Act 2014.

The LCEW has taken seriously its duty to 'ensure that, in these fundamentally changed circumstances, it remains an effective law reform body both for Wales and for England'.[208] The increased recognition of specifically Welsh matters corresponded with the appointment of a Welsh Chairman of the LCEW, Sir David Lloyd Jones, who was Chairman from 2012–15. In discussion with the Welsh Government, the LCEW had to consider how to put in place 'the appropriate machinery' to deal with the new Welsh dimension to its work.[209] The option of having a separate Welsh Law Commission has not been endorsed by either the Welsh Government[210] or the LCEW.[211] Because of the Welsh Assembly's previously smaller area of devolved competence compared with the other devolved legislatures, the Welsh Government and the LCEW agreed that a Welsh Commission was not necessary, despite the closer access to Welsh politicians and lawyers it would bring. That decision may eventually need to be revisited because the Wales Act 2017 has since moved Wales to a system of general devolved competence. In the meantime, the LCEW has had to address three main issues to ensure that devolved Wales is not neglected by the LCEW.

First, Lloyd Jones noted that a 'deficiency' existed in relation to the ability of the Welsh Government to refer projects to the LCEW.[212] The Welsh Government did not, historically, have the power to refer projects to the LCEW directly. Previously, the Welsh Government had to ask the Wales Office to refer a project to the LCEW on its behalf. Lloyd Jones did not consider that to be 'a satisfactory route'—Welsh Ministers needed direct access to the LCEW because the LCEW operates for both England and Wales.[213] Lloyd Jones initially rejected the idea that the 1965 Act could be amended to address this deficit, citing the perennial problem of a lack of parliamentary time.[214] Instead, a transfer of ministerial functions order under section 58 of the Government of Wales Act 2006 was considered appropriate. Under this section, the powers available to the Wales Office would be transferred to, or shared with, the Welsh Ministers. The Welsh Government, however, ultimately sought reform of the 1965 Act.[215] The 1965 Act was, after all, amended following Scottish devolution.[216] The Wales Act 2014 has granted the power to Welsh

[207] ibid.
[208] ibid 3.
[209] ibid 13.
[210] Welsh Government, 'Evidence Submitted by the Welsh Government to the Commission on Devolution in Wales', 18 February 2013, para 22 (Welsh Government Evidence).
[211] Lloyd Jones, 'The Law Commission and Law Reform in a Devolved Wales' 19–24.
[212] ibid 13.
[213] ibid 14; 1965 Act, s 1(1).
[214] Lloyd Jones, ibid 14–15.
[215] Welsh Government Evidence, para 22.
[216] See section III.A above.

Ministers to refer projects directly to the LCEW.[217] The Wales Act 2014 also obliges Welsh Ministers to report on LCEW proposals in Welsh devolved areas,[218] and mandated that a Protocol was to be established between Welsh Ministers and the LCEW.[219] The Protocol agreed between the LCEW and the Welsh Ministers (the Wales Protocol) is along much the same lines as the Protocol with the Lord Chancellor. It requires Welsh Ministers to demonstrate, when making a reference to the LCEW or suggesting a project for inclusion in a programme, why the area it wishes to have examined is unsatisfactory and how it would benefit from reform.[220] And like the Lord Chancellor's Protocol, it also requires the Welsh Ministers to 'give an undertaking that there is a serious intention by the Welsh Ministers to take forward law reform' in the area, which we have already seen may have undesirable consequences.[221] Instead, it is argued here that Welsh Ministers should be bound to take the project-selection criteria into account when referring projects to the LCEW.

In receiving a reference from either the Welsh Ministers or the UK Government, the LCEW should check to ensure that it agrees that the project is viable according to the criteria. Both the Wales Protocol and the Lord Chancellor's Protocol list several factors that should be taken into account when deciding whether to accept a reference.[222] Use of the project-selection criteria would be a neater solution since they can be used by all parties in all situations (selecting, approving or referring projects). Use of the same criteria in all situations would allow the criteria to be more consistently applied and well known. Although necessary to allow Welsh input into LCEW law reform, the Wales Act 2014 adds complexity to LCEW project selection. Such complexity would be relieved by the use of the project-selection criteria to ensure that both the UK Government and the Welsh Ministers have the same expectations of the LCEW, and that the LCEW's resources are allocated correctly.

Second, the LCEW was aware that the Welsh Government was disenfranchised from the selection of projects when LCEW programmes of law reform were being compiled. The Welsh Government suggested that, like the Lord Chancellor, the Welsh Ministers should be able to give their approval to programme projects which concern devolved matters.[223] The LCEW has undertaken to 'consult fully' with the

[217] Wales Act 2014, s 25(2), which inserted s 3(1)(ea) into the 1965 Act.

[218] Wales Act 2014, s 25(4), which inserted s 3C into the 1965 Act. The first report was Welsh Government, *Report on the Implementation of Law Commission Proposals* (2016).

[219] Wales Act 2014, s 25(4), which inserted s 3D into the 1965 Act; LCEW and Welsh Ministers, *Protocol between the Welsh Ministers and the Law Commission/Protocol Rhwng Gweinidogion Cymru a Comisiwn y Gyfraith* (2015) (Wales Protocol).

[220] Wales Protocol, para 6.

[221] ibid. See ch 4, section IV.B.iv.

[222] Wales Protocol, para 7; LCEW and Ministry of Justice, *Protocol between the Lord Chancellor (on behalf of the Government) and the Law Commission* (Law Com No 321 (2010)) para 9. In the Wales Protocol's case, these factors also apply to deciding whether a project on Welsh devolved issues should be included in a programme.

[223] Welsh Government Evidence, para 22.

Welsh Government on its programmes of law reform from now on.[224] The Wales Protocol envisages that the Welsh Ministers will make suggestions for inclusion in programmes as well as direct references,[225] but the Lord Chancellor must still approve all programme projects. Now that the Welsh Ministers have the power to refer projects directly to the LCEW, the need for input into the programmes is less important. Any projects not inserted into the programme can be referred directly by the Welsh Ministers to the LCEW for its consideration, like the current position for the SLC's examination of reserved matters. Potential difficulties can, however, arise from giving two sets of ministers input into project selection. For example, the LCEW's *Twelfth Programme of Law Reform* contains two Wales-specific projects,[226] but the programme reveals that the Lord Chancellor refused permission for a third project concerning environmental law in Wales.[227] Technically, there is nothing stopping the Welsh Ministers from getting around that veto by referring the project to the LCEW directly. Shared project-selection criteria are needed to ensure a healthy dialogue between all parties.

Third, the LCEW must bear Welsh devolution in mind not only when it proposes projects, but also when it drafts its reforms to consider whether separate provisions for Wales are necessary. In March 2013, through the initiative of former LCEW Chairman, Sir David Lloyd Jones, the LCEW appointed a Welsh Advisory Committee to 'promote Welsh-centred law reform' and to 'advise the Law Commission on the exercise of its statutory functions in relation to Wales', in both reserved and devolved matters.[228] This initiative is evidence of the LCEW's commitment to Welsh matters and the Welsh Government has been 'strongly supportive' of the development.[229] The advisory committee had the 'great advantage' of being established quickly because it was set up on a non-legislative basis.[230] Now that it is up and running and playing a valuable function, its continuing existence should be guaranteed by the 1965 Act.

The Welsh Government has the power to introduce LCEW proposals on devolved matters into the Welsh Assembly for implementation as Acts of the Assembly. Lloyd Jones has noted a tendency for LCEW proposals to be 'more positively received in Wales than in England',[231] and a trend in particular for a greater

224 Lloyd Jones, 'The Law Commission and Law Reform in a Devolved Wales' 15. See also, for the Welsh Advisory Committee's input into programmes, LCEW, *Annual Report 2015–16* (Law Com No 367 (2016)) 2 and 10.

225 Wales Protocol, para 6.

226 LCEW, *Twelfth Programme of Law Reform* (Law Com No 354 (2014)) paras 2.9–2.12 and 2.20–2.22; LCEW, *Form and Accessibility of the Law Applicable in Wales/Ffurf a Hygyrchedd y Gyfraith sy'n Gymwys yng Nghymru* (Law Com No 366 (2016)); and LCEW, *Planning Law in Wales: Scoping Paper/Cyfraith Cynllunio yng Nghymru: Papur Cwmpasu* (Law Com CP No 228 (2016)).

227 *Twelfth Programme*, ibid para 1.13.

228 Lloyd Jones, 'The Law Commission and Law Reform in a Devolved Wales' 16.

229 ibid.

230 ibid 17.

231 ibid 10.

'appetite' for consolidation.[232] Consequently, LCEW work may now be implemented differently in Wales than in England. For example, the Social Services and Well-being (Wales) Act 2014 received Royal Assent in May 2014. The Act 'draw[s] heavily' on the proposals found in the LCEW's *Adult Social Care* report.[233] Separate legislation for England, the Care Act 2014, received Royal Assent around the same time. Both Acts implemented the majority of the LCEW's recommendations, but in separate Acts, which were by no means identical. The LCEW recommended that separate legislation was needed for England and for Wales (no draft Bill was published with the report), saying that it would be 'constitutionally infelicitous' for Westminster to legislate for Wales in an area which was devolved.[234] The need for separate legislation is again the result of the devolution settlements and Westminster's promise to not normally legislate for Wales on devolved matters without the devolved legislature's consent.[235] The LCEW must now check carefully all its recommendations to ascertain whether any issues are devolved and, if necessary, ensure that separate legislation is drafted (or recommended, if there is no draft Bill). Such checking undoubtedly adds an extra burden onto the LCEW, and the existence of the Welsh Advisory Committee is essential in ensuring that no devolved provisions are overlooked.

Furthermore, a project on renting homes was rejected in England but '[a]ccepted in principle' in Wales.[236] This acceptance led to the LCEW publishing a separate report (published in both English and Welsh) for Wales only, which reviewed and updated its recommendations, and addressed devolution issues.[237] The Welsh Government then produced a White Paper,[238] and eventually the Renting Homes (Wales) Act 2016 was passed.[239] The successful implementation of the LCEW's proposals are the justifiable reward of the LCEW's 'strenuous efforts … to discharge its statutory duty to be an effective law reform body for Wales'.[240] The result, however, is that Welsh devolution (more than Scottish devolution) has started the process of the increasing fragmentation of the law in Great Britain,

[232] D Lloyd Jones, 'Looking to the Future' in Dyson, Lee and Stark, *Fifty Years of the Law Commissions*, 356.

[233] Lloyd Jones, 'The Law Commission and Law Reform in a Devolved Wales' 7; LCEW, *Adult Social Care* (Law Com No 326 (2011)).

[234] *Adult Social Care*, ibid para 3.9.

[235] *Devolution: Memorandum of Understanding and Supplementary Agreements between the United Kingdom Government, the Scottish Ministers, the Welsh Ministers and the Northern Ireland Executive Committee* (2012) para 14 and Wales Act 2017, s 2.

[236] LCEW, *Renting Homes: The Final Report* (Law Com No 297 (2006)); LCEW, *Annual Report 2015–16* (Law Com No 367 (2016)) app A.

[237] LCEW, *Renting Homes in Wales/Rhentu Cartrefi yng Nghymru* (Law Com No 337 (2013)). Certain LCEW publications had previously been translated into Welsh, but this report was the first 'formal report in a single bilingual volume': Lloyd Jones, 'The Law Commission and Law Reform in a Devolved Wales' 12.

[238] Welsh Government White Paper, *Renting Homes: A Better Way for Wales* (2013).

[239] For further examples of the Welsh Government's treatment of LCEW proposals, see Welsh Government, *Report on the Implementation of Law Commission Proposals* (2016).

[240] Lloyd Jones, 'The Law Commission and Law Reform in a Devolved Wales' 25.

rather than the harmonisation envisaged in 1965. Welsh devolution has also complicated the selection of new LCEW projects. The project-selection criteria must now be examined (since the Wales Act 2014 came into force) by three separate bodies in relation to the LCEW—the LCEW, the UK Government and the Welsh Ministers. Such increasingly complex relations make it essential for there to be a common understanding of how new projects should be selected. Without such understanding, valuable (and increasingly scarce) LCEW resources could be allocated improperly and relations could be fraught. The criteria developed in chapter three would facilitate such understanding.

C. Northern Ireland

Institutional law reform in Northern Ireland was a more recent development than in England and Scotland. The NILC was established by sections 50–52 of the Justice (Northern Ireland) Act 2002 (the 2002 Act), but those provisions did not come into force until 2007 and the first Commissioners were not appointed until 2008. The establishment of the NILC coincided with more stable devolution for Northern Ireland.[241] A detailed examination of the NILC is beyond the scope of this book.[242] The establishment and current status of the NILC are noted briefly, however, to acknowledge their effect on the LCEW and the SLC.

The establishment of the NILC added to the practical difficulties of collaborative projects. The NILC's establishment resulted in the three Commissions (the NILC, the SLC and the LCEW) acting in consultation with each other. The NILC, under the terms of its founding legislation, was obliged to consult the LCEW and the SLC (as well as the Law Reform Commission of the Republic of Ireland).[243] A reciprocal duty for the LCEW and the SLC to consult with the NILC was also established.[244] The expansion of the consultation duty added further pressures onto the Commissions when they undertook tripartite projects. As we saw earlier, when proposing to embark on a collaborative project, each Commission should consider the project-selection criteria. Such consideration may lead to the realisation that one Commission believes that the project is not viable. Clear, statutory criteria would allow for more consistent and appropriate project selection—which is more important than ever if there is a third Commission to deal with. If the

[241] The Northern Ireland Assembly had been suspended on numerous occasions after devolution, most notably from 2002 to 2007. For more detail, see SW Stark and N Faris, 'Law Reform in Northern Ireland: Cheshire Cat or Potemkin Commission?' [2016] *PL* 651, 659 ('Cheshire Cat or Potemkin Commission?').

[242] For more detail, including why a Law Commission for Northern Ireland was not established in 1965, see Stark and Faris, 'Cheshire Cat or Potemkin Commission?' and N Faris, 'Fifty Years of Law Reform—A Note on the Northern Ireland Style' in Dyson, Lee and Stark, *Fifty Years of the Law Commissions*, ch 5.

[243] 2002 Act, s 51(4).

[244] 1965 Act, s 3(4) as amended by the 2002 Act, sch 12, para 9.

project is embarked on, the Commissions may also struggle to agree on the substantive reforms proposed. In projects completed by one Commission alone, one Commissioner usually assumes the responsibility of leading a project. Projects are, however, scrutinised by all Commissioners before publication. Such scrutiny can lead to lengthy meetings where five Commissioners propose their views on, and amendments to, a project. Consensus is doubly difficult to reach in joint projects where ten Commissioners must have their say. The potential difficulties are again increased where tripartite projects are concerned, and there is a risk that the largest Commission will dictate the policy.[245] That risk is especially strong in projects where a Commission feels forced to collaborate despite being uncertain about having sufficient resources to make a meaningful contribution. Use of project-selection criteria would allow each Commission to ensure it has the resources to contribute to a project before it is embarked on—and would allow Commissions to decline offers to collaborate if such resources are not available (or obtainable), or if the suitability or importance of the project is in doubt.

But as we have seen, the NILC was barely in operation for seven years before its funding was withdrawn by the Northern Ireland Department of Justice. There currently is no NILC, and its ongoing projects have been passed back to governmental departments to proceed as appropriate.[246] Given that the tripartite electoral law project is still ongoing, this poses a problem because the creation of the NILC altered the remit of the LCEW. Previously, the LCEW was responsible for reserved matters of Northern Ireland law.[247] The NILC, like the SLC, examined both reserved/excepted and transferred (devolved) areas of law.[248] The NILC's creation, therefore, may have eased something of the burden on the LCEW, although it tended to 'keep off Ireland's green lawns' anyway.[249] It must be the case now that new tripartite projects are an impossibility, given the lack of an independent law reform body for Northern Ireland and the lack of vires of the GB Commissions to deal with the law of that jurisdiction. This state of affairs is a marked difference from the enthusiasm just a short time earlier that '[m]ore UK-wide projects [were] likely in the future'.[250] Previous LCEW Chairman, Sir David Lloyd Jones, apparently sought unsuccessfully a reprieve for the NILC until the completion of the electoral law project.[251] The NILC's contribution to the latest publication on

[245] Although the NILC's contribution to collaborative projects may not need to be as significant as the SLC's due to the greater similarities between Northern Ireland's law and English law.

[246] NILC, *Annual Report 2015* (2015) 9–10.

[247] 1965 Act, s 1(5) as enacted, now repealed.

[248] The 2002 Act, s 51(1) tasked the NILC with keeping under review 'the law of Northern Ireland'. Projects examining reserved/excepted matters, however, had to be sanctioned by the Secretary of State: s 51(3A). Reserved, excepted and transferred matters are defined by the Northern Ireland Act 1998, s 4(1) and schs 2–3.

[249] G Gretton, 'Of Law Commissioning' (2013) 17 *Edinburgh Law Review* 119, 122, fn 19.

[250] D Lloyd Jones, 'The Law Commission and the Implementation of Law Reform' (2013) 15 *European Journal of Law Reform* 333, 347.

[251] L Clarke, 'Law Reform Body's Axing "Could Make Northern Ireland a Legal Backwater"' *Belfast Telegraph* (15 November 2014).

the electoral law project was completed by its Chairman,[252] apparently appointed only for that purpose and working within the Department of Justice.[253] The fact that that report does not mention that the NILC does not exist in the form that most people would recognise as an independent law reform body is troubling.

In summary, devolution, and with it the establishment and subsequent dismantling of the NILC, has posed new challenges for the Commissions. Statutory embodiment of the project-selection criteria would assist with the increased practical difficulties collaborative projects pose, as well as the greater number of governmental actors having recourse to those criteria. The increased complexities of devolution necessitate the criteria being adopted in their developed form and ideally set out in statute in order that they can be used consistently. Such consistent use is necessary for the Commissions' proper scope of activity to be clear—which is in turn necessary for the proper allocation of the Commissions' limited resources.

IV. Conclusion: Separate Commissions Working in Sync

The Commissions were established in an era of domestic and European harmonisation but now exist in an increasingly devolved UK on the brink of probable Brexit. The criteria for project selection developed in chapter three would allow for better synchronicity when choosing and approving projects—a process now complicated by devolution. Statutory project-selection criteria are more essential than ever because of the increasing number of parties which may now, especially since the Wales Act 2014 came into force, refer projects to the Commissions.

The Commissions' obligations to consult each other and to survey the law of other jurisdictions under the 1965 Act assists an exchange of knowledge between the LCEW and the SLC,[254] so that the law in each jurisdiction may be improved—sometimes, but not necessarily, by harmonisation. Because there is less perceived pressure to harmonise and because of superseding devolution, harmonisation is, quite rightly, no longer pursued as an aim in itself. Examination of alternative solutions in other jurisdictions may sometimes result in harmonisation, although that may be intentional or incidental. In certain cases, harmonisation may be a motivating factor for the selection of the project as an aspect of its importance, in particular where legal differences across shared borders cause difficulty in practice. In any event, the goal is the improvement of the law by reform proposed after

[252] Mr Justice Maguire: LCEW, SLC and NILC, *Electoral Law: An Interim Report* (2016).
[253] Stark and Faris, 'Cheshire Cat or Potemkin Commission?' 666 and 668.
[254] And the NILC, if it exists.

extensive independent research and consultation, rather than harmonisation for harmonisation's sake.

Despite devolution, the Commissions continue to consult with each other. Even if Scotland one day were to become an independent country, the Commissions should still retain their duty to act together, just as the NILC had a duty to consult with the Law Reform Commission of Ireland. The countries would, after all, still share a land border with all the consequent issues that entails. By using the same project-selection criteria openly and consistently, the Commissions would be assisted when cooperation on a project is sought. On occasion, the criteria may not be satisfied equally across the jurisdictions. In such cases, each Commission must retain its discretion to choose whether to embark on a project by reference to the selection criteria. A Commission seeking to embark on a collaborative project should use the criteria to demonstrate to the other Commission(s) why, in its view, the project is viable, before the criteria are considered by the other Commission(s). Use of the criteria would simplify the complexity of cross-border project selection and would allow the Commissions to make transparent project-selection decisions on the same basis. The criteria would allow the Commissions to persuade each other why a project is considered viable—or why it is not. No Commission should be forced to embark on a project if it is not satisfied that it is viable when judged against the criteria and if it believes that its resources could be put to better use, or that it has insufficient resources, even taking into account those of the instigating Commission, to make a meaningful contribution. The Commissions must work in sync, but their separate autonomy must be retained. The project-selection criteria are essential in achieving those aims.

7

Law Reform… Now?

During the passage of the Law Commissions Bill, Lord Reid optimistically suggested that the Commissions could do 'five or ten years of really useful work' by which time 'lawyers' law ought to be in pretty good shape'.[1] It is apparent that '[t]he great expectations of 1965 have not been realised'.[2] Over 50 years later, there is still as much work to do as there ever was. We have not codified our laws, the statute book is untidier than ever, and many laws are still unfair, unclear, inefficient, unduly complex or outdated. But it is equally clear that the naive hopes of the 1960s should not lead us to see the Commissions as failures. In terms, for example, of the decluttering of the statute book, the Commissions have been 'swimming upstream' against a tide of increasing enactments.[3] The picture may be no better than it was in 1965, but it would certainly have been much worse without the Commissions. And in terms of their substantive work, lack of codification aside, the Commissions have left their mark on almost every area of the law, not just 'lawyers' law'. In contrast to the naivety of 1965, we need to adjust our expectations of the Commissions, and some updating of the Law Commissions Act 1965 (the 1965 Act) would facilitate that adjustment. Indeed, we may never have really thought about, or may have forgotten, what the exact terms of that Act are. After 'diligent' reflection by the first Commissioners, study of its precise wording has 'drifted to the back of the drawer'.[4] We must be cognisant of that Act and the Commissions' rich history, while simultaneously seizing the opportunity 'to grasp good change' when necessary.[5]

I. Servicing our Law Reform Machinery

There are four main issues left open by the 1965 Act, which the Commissions have had to resolve over the years. First, the scope of the Commissions' activity is left

[1] HL Deb vol 264 col 1201 (1 April 1965) (Lord Reid).

[2] G Palmer, 'The Law Reform Enterprise: Evaluating the Past and Charting the Future' (2015) 131 *LQR* 402, 420.

[3] GL Gretton, 'The Duty to Make the Law More Accessible?: The Two C-Words' in M Dyson, J Lee and SW Stark (eds), *Fifty Years of the Law Commissions: The Dynamics of Law Reform* (Oxford, Hart Publishing, 2016) 90 ('The Two C-Words'; and Dyson, Lee and Stark, *Fifty Years of the Law Commissions*).

[4] ibid 89.

[5] E Cooke, 'Introduction' in Dyson, Lee and Stark, *Fifty Years of the Law Commissions*, 339.

unclear because the 1965 Act establishes a duty to 'take and keep under review all the law', leaving it unclear how projects deemed worthy of examination are to be chosen.[6] Second, the 1965 Act does not address the question of how parliamentary time is to be found for the implementation of Commission proposals. Third, the 1965 Act establishes that the Commissions should work towards the codification of the law,[7] but does not establish, for example, what codification should entail. Fourth and finally, the 1965 Act tasks the Commissions with consulting with each other.[8] The aim of this task in 1965 was at least partially to harmonise 'British' law—an aim which is less necessary and less achievable today. Some clarification and updating of the 1965 Act could help to address certain of the ambiguities caused by its current form.

A way of clarifying and securing the scope of the Commissions' activity was advanced in chapter three. We saw that the 1965 Act, by mandating that the Commissions 'take and keep under review all the law',[9] implies that the Commissions, the Ministers and government have discretion to select, approve and refer suitable projects for examination. The exercise of Commission, ministerial and governmental discretion can be controlled, and the scope of the Commissions' activity can be determined, by developing the use of three criteria for project selection: (i) the availability and economical use of resources; (ii) the suitability of the project; and (iii) the importance of the project. Commissioners, the Ministers and the rest of government could determine the potential viability of a project by scoring it against each criterion.[10] The development of the project-selection criteria already used by the Commissions attempts to ensure that project selection is transparent, and that the Commissions' resources are directed to the most valuable projects.

Once we have determined the proper scope of Commission projects, we must then consider the assessment of their outcome. In chapter four, it was argued that too much emphasis should not be placed on implementation, and on implementation by enacted law in particular. While implementation cannot be ignored, projects should be selected based on consideration of the chapter three project-selection criteria, not merely on their likelihood of being implemented. Furthermore, putting too much emphasis on implementation risks undermining the Commissions' independence from government and does not take account of (and in fact may even negatively affect) the substantive quality of the reforms proposed.

We can alter our view of implementation in three ways. First, a clear definition of what it means for a project to be 'implemented' is needed. A realistic definition of implementation must embrace, for example, proposals implemented other than by primary legislation and partially implemented proposals. The Commissions

[6] 1965 Act, s 3(1).
[7] 1965 Act, s 3(1).
[8] 1965 Act, s 3(4).
[9] 1965 Act, s 3(1).
[10] See ch 3, section V.B.ii.

should be more transparent about how they calculate their implementation rates in order that they can be fully understood. Second, governmental duties to examine Commission proposals should not be extinguished upon the proposal's rejection. Rejected proposals should instead be reconsidered annually (unless they have been superseded by subsequent reform or subsequent proposals) to remove the expectation of immediate implementation. Third and finally, if the Commissions' output is viewed as a whole, pressure to implement can be alleviated. In particular, certain less important projects may have a high likelihood of implementation (such as consolidation and repeals), whereas other more important projects may be more of an implementation gamble. The project-selection criteria have been established by the Commissions, and developed in this book, to ensure that the most deserving projects are undertaken—those criteria should not be usurped by a value-neutral 'likelihood of implementation' criterion.

The Commissions were to strive for the codification of the law[11] because of the burgeoning disrepute of the common law, the overabundance of statutory materials and a perceived need to harmonise and codify British law before entry into the European Union (EU). Little codification has in fact been achieved successfully, and the Commissions have now accepted that piecemeal reform must take precedence. Three main reasons can be advanced for the removal of the Commissions' codification task. First, codification projects are less likely than certain other projects to be viable according to the chapter three project-selection criteria. Because codification projects now necessarily reform the law first, the second codificatory stage does not endeavour to reform the substance of the law, thus being less likely than projects proposing substantive reform to satisfy the 'importance' criterion. And given their limited resources, the huge task of codification was never ideal for the Commissions. Second, codification is no longer perceived to be as necessary as it was, at least by most commentators, in 1965. Codification did not prove to be essential for entry into the EU, which the UK will likely soon cease to be a member of anyway. Furthermore, the common law is, for various reasons advanced in chapter five, seen as a more suitable tool of law reform than it was in 1965. The common law merely requires support from piecemeal statutes, as opposed to being substituted by full codes. The statute book is more of a 'teenager's bedroom'[12] than ever, but decluttering is now even more unachievable due to the increasing amount of enacted law, and less essential due to electronic legal databases where one can locate a source of law relatively easily.[13] Third and finally, the removal of the word 'codification' from section 3(1) of the 1965 Act would

[11] 1965 Act, s 3(1).

[12] Gretton, 'The Two C-Words' 91.

[13] See, however, on problems with the accuracy and currency of such databases, ibid 91–92; J Beatson, 'Challenges for Independent Law Reformers from Changing External Priorities and Shorter Timescales' in Dyson, Lee and Stark, *Fifty Years of the Law Commissions*, 247 ('Challenges for Independent Law Reformers') and M Dyson, 'The Future is a Foreign Country, They Do Things Differently There' in Dyson, Lee and Stark, ibid 397–98.

eradicate any confusion over its meaning and prevent it from being given undue weight when assessing the Commissions' performance. The remaining provisions of the 1965 Act would still allow codification projects (or simplification projects preceding eventual codification) to proceed where appropriate. Removal of the explicit duty would, however, remove the unrealistic expectation that the Commissions should prioritise codification.

In chapter six, examination of the different challenges the Commissions have faced, from a UK eager for harmonisation in 1965 to a state increasingly fragmented by devolution decades later, revealed further reasons to necessitate the project-selection criteria. The Commissions have not proposed one harmonised 'British' law, but they have improved the law in their respective jurisdictions by choosing the best parts from each, as well as from further afield. Harmonisation is only one aspect to be considered when deciding how to improve the law.

Frequently, the Commissions work together on collaborative projects,[14] and such projects entail both practical and legal difficulties. When considering the 'resources' project-selection criterion, consideration should be given as to whether full cooperation, or at least some input, will be required from the other Commission(s). A Commission being asked to collaborate should also use the criteria to determine whether or not they wish to do so. By using the same criteria, the Commissions could work in sync to understand each other's decisions and only the most appropriate projects would be embarked on.

Devolution, including the reforms made by the Wales Act 2014, has increased the potential number of actors who interact with the Commissions. As well as the UK Government, now devolved governments and the Northern Ireland Law Commission (NILC) (if it still exists) all work with the Law Commission for England and Wales (LCEW) and the Scottish Law Commission (SLC). It is more important than ever that the proper scope of their activity is understood in order that all parties have the same expectations of the LCEW and the SLC. Use of the chapter three project-selection criteria would ensure such understanding.

II. Proposed Amendments to the 1965 Act

We have seen throughout this book that many of the problems facing the Commissions stem from the 1965 Act, notably because of its vagueness, and also because it requires updating. In appendix two, amendments to the 1965 Act are proposed. Those proposed amendments are explained here.

In section 3(1), the Commissions' specific task to codify the law should be removed, as was recommended in chapter five.

[14] And with the NILC, if it still exists: 1965 Act, s 3(4).

Section 3(1)(e) should be amended to clarify that references from government do not have to be embarked on by the Commissions. Such references should be considered against the project-selection criteria.[15] Section 3(1)(ea), which was added to the 1965 Act by the Wales Act 2014, allows references to be made by the Welsh Ministers to the LCEW. Amendments are proposed to that section to mirror the amendments proposed to section 3(1)(e).

A new section 3(1A) should set out the chapter three project-selection criteria in statutory form. In selecting, approving or referring new projects, the Commissions, the Ministers and government (the Welsh Ministers, the UK Government and the Scottish Government) should be obliged to take the three criteria—the availability and economical use of resources; the suitability of the project; and the importance of the project—into account. They should demonstrate, with reasons, why each project satisfies (or why certain rejected projects do not satisfy) the criteria. Section 3(1A) should not give further guidance as to the types of matters to be taken into consideration under each criterion. Instead, the sub-criteria proposed in chapter three, figure 2 should be listed in a more easily updated document, such as a memorandum of understanding between the Commissions and the Ministers.[16] Section 3(1A) should, however, make clear that 'importance' is to mean the importance of the *examination* of a certain area of law, not the importance of the *implementation* of the Commissions' proposals.[17]

Section 3(2) requires a simple amendment to deal with the fact that technically there is no duty at present for the Ministers to lay before Parliament proposals for reform generated by governmental references. The existing text of section 3(2) refers only to the laying of proposals for reform 'pursuant to … programmes'. Deletion of those words would ensure that all reports, no matter what their origin, are laid before Parliament. Although reports stemming from references are, in practice, laid before Parliament already, it is undesirable that there is no duty in law to do so, especially given that projects stemming from programmes and references have similar implementation rates.[18]

A new section 3(3B) should be added to allow all recommendations for law reform made by the SLC in (or partially in) reserved matters to be presented to both the Secretary of State for Scotland to be laid before Westminster, and to Scottish Ministers to be laid before Holyrood, as was recommended in chapters four and six.[19] Another new subsection, section 3(3C), should compel the LCEW to present all reports in (or partially in) Welsh devolved matters to both the Lord

[15] The factors the LCEW currently considers listed in the Protocol and the Wales Protocol should be amended to be consistent with the project-selection criteria: see ch 2, section IV.C.v.

[16] See ch 3, sections V.A.iv and V.B.iii.

[17] See ch 3, section V.A.iii.

[18] See ch 3, section V.B.i.

[19] As observed in ch 4, section II.F, this amendment merely reflects current practice. See also ch 6, section III.A.

Chancellor and Welsh Ministers to be laid before Westminster and the Welsh Assembly respectively.

Amendments to section 3A should be made to alter the duty to report on Commission proposals in various ways proposed in chapter four. Section 3A presently only applies to the Lord Chancellor in respect of certain LCEW proposals. The duty should be extended so that both Commissions' proposals are reported on. The Wales Act 2014 has added a new section 3C which obliges the Welsh Ministers to report on all Welsh devolved matters. A new section 3A(6B) would clarify that both the Secretary of State for Scotland and Scottish Ministers should report on the SLC's proposals in reserved and devolved areas respectively.[20] A new section 3A(6A) would confirm that reports from the Secretary of State for Scotland on reserved matters should be laid before Westminster and reports from Scottish Ministers on devolved matters should be laid before Holyrood. Sections 3A(4) and 3C(6) should be amended to require rejected proposals to be reconsidered annually (unless they have been superseded).[21] Section 3A(6) should be amended to clarify that the reporting duty extends to projects resulting from references from government or other bodies.[22]

Section 3B, which establishes the LCEW and Lord Chancellor's duty to devise a Protocol, need not be amended. The section provides for the Protocol to be reviewed 'from time to time',[23] and such revision should certainly take place to remove, in particular, the need in the Protocol for the government to express a serious intention to implement projects before they are embarked on. The degree of involvement the government has throughout the course of a project should also be toned down.[24] The Wales Act 2014 added section 3D to provide for a similar Protocol to be drawn up between the LCEW and Welsh Ministers and that Protocol should be similarly amended.

Finally, a new section 3E should assure the continued existence, on a statutory basis, of the Welsh Advisory Committee to the LCEW described in chapter six. The statutory provision should guarantee a Committee of not more than 15 members. At the time of writing, the Committee has 14 members plus the Chairman of the LCEW who acts as Chair of the Committee.[25] That size of Committee appears to work well. Given, however, the possible difficulty of finding enough volunteers, the legislation should not mandate that the Committee should always necessarily be that size.

[20] See ch 4, section IV.C.i. The proposed reforms would necessitate a change to the 1965 Act, s 6(2) to reflect the fact that 'Minister' will no longer always mean the Lord Chancellor for the LCEW and Scottish Ministers for the SLC.

[21] See ch 4, sections I.C, II.A and IV.B.iv.

[22] See ch 4, section IV.B.iv.

[23] 1965 Act, s 3B(3). See also 1965 Act, s 3D(3).

[24] See ch 4, section IV.B.iv.

[25] I am grateful to Phil Golding, LCEW Chief Executive, for this information.

III. Final Remarks for Great Britain and Beyond

Law reform bodies across the world regularly share ideas for potential working strategies. The Commonwealth Association of Law Reform Agencies (CALRAs) facilitates 'the sharing of experience between members on methods and best practice for carrying out law reform'.[26] Given the common roots many law reform bodies have with the GB Commissions,[27] it may be useful to highlight some particular lessons which could be considered beyond these shores, as well as possible transplants for our Commissions to consider.

Our Commissions are law reform bodies, but there is no clear consensus as to what 'law reform' means, either in the context of the Commissions or more generally. Does 'reform' mean any change to the law, or only changes that are positive and significant?[28] Is the 'defining feature' of reform that improvement has to be deliberately intended, and not an incidental consequence?[29] There is no clear answer. Law reform means 'different things to different people'.[30] The Law Reform Commission of Ireland (LRCI)'s founding legislation sets out a definition of reform. For the LRCI, reform means the law's 'development, its codification (including in particular its simplification and modernisation) and the revision and consolidation of statute law'.[31] That definition is inclusive, but it does not clarify much. The 1965 Act does not even attempt any such definition. It is therefore unsurprising that the Commissions' responsibilities cannot be 'neatly packaged'.[32] But we must attempt to define the Commissions' scope of activity in order for them to function and be tested properly. If we do not think about what 'reform' means for the Commissions, then we risk misunderstanding their role and unfairly appraising them in terms of the projects they select. Instead, however, of attempting to define 'reform' (which may be impossible) or attempting to restrict unduly the Commissions' scope of activity (which is undesirable), the project-selection criteria allow us to see more clearly why certain projects are viable Commission projects, and why others are not.

Not all law reform bodies have the power to choose their own projects.[33] For those that do, adoption of project-selection criteria is worth serious consideration.

[26] CALRAs Constitution, Art II para 2(f).

[27] Certain of the law commissions established as a result of the LCEW and the SLC are cited in ch 1, section II.

[28] WW McBryde, 'Law Reform: The Scottish Experience' (1998) 3 *Scottish Law and Practice Quarterly* 86, 86.

[29] Lord Carloway, 'To "Mend the Laws, That Neids Mendement": A Scottish Perspective on Lawyers as Law Reformers' (speech at the Commonwealth Association of Law Reform Agencies Conference, Edinburgh, 2015) 7 ('A Scottish Perspective').

[30] ibid 9.

[31] Law Reform Commission Act 1975 (Ireland) s 1.

[32] Carloway, 'A Scottish Perspective' 7–8.

[33] eg, the Australian Law Reform Commission has no such power: see ch 3, section V.A.ii.

In terms of the Commissions' scope of activity, the three project-selection criteria allow for sharper focus on the substantive qualities of a project—its suitability and importance—as well as its potential impact on the Commissions' resources. These three, simple criteria are self-evidently the considerations that any law reform body should be taking into account as a matter of course. Selection criteria are not a uniquely British phenomenon. The South African Law Reform Commission, for example, has two sets of criteria it uses in two different phases when sifting proposals for inclusion in its programmes.[34] The Law Reform Commission of Hong Kong also publishes the usual factors it takes into consideration in project selection on its website.[35] Both of those Commissions' criteria incorporate aspects of the GB Commissions' criteria. Certain Commissions have adopted the GB Commissions' criteria more closely, for example the LRCI,[36] and the Law Reform Commission of Mauritius.[37] By developing the criteria discussed in this book and by setting them out in statutory form, the GB Commissions (and other commissions which have adopted their criteria) would be better protected from arbitrary ministerial or governmental control—as well as from the whims of their own Commissioners. The scope of Commission activity would be clarified and their resources would be correctly allocated. It will by now be apparent to the reader that the Commissions are increasingly under pressure to operate within reduced budgets and under closer scrutiny.[38] Such problems are not limited to these shores. Financial pressure was the ostensible reason for the NILC's demise, and there have been threats to the existence of, and budget cuts made at, for example, the Australian Law Reform Commission (ALRC).[39] In truth, independent law reform commissions provide good value for money,[40] although reluctant governments may need to be persuaded of that fact. Careful use of project-selection criteria would ensure that the Commissions' projects were chosen transparently and that their resources were targeted at only the most viable projects. The Commissions would thus be protected from accusations (from government, parliamentarians, legal professionals, academics, or the public) of misuse of resources.

The importance of consultation is a universal concern. Wide and thorough consultation has been frequently cited throughout this book as an advantage of the

[34] South African Law Reform Commission website, 'Requesting an Investigation' www.justice.gov.za/salrc/request.html.

[35] Law Reform Commission of Hong Kong website, 'About Us: Referral of Subjects to the Commission' www.hkreform.gov.hk/en/about/referral.htm.

[36] Law Reform Commission of Ireland, *Fourth Programme of Law Reform* (LRC 110 (2013)) para 2.10.

[37] Law Reform Commission of Mauritius, *Brief on the Law Reform Commission* (September 2016) para 32.

[38] See in particular ch 1, section I and ch 4, section IV.B.ii.

[39] K Cronin, 'Working on the Larger Canvas—Law Reform in a Federal System: Thoughts on Forty Years of the Australian Law Reform Commission' in Dyson, Lee and Stark, *Fifty Years of the Law Commissions*, 62 ('Working on the Larger Canvas').

[40] For useful figures, see Beatson, 'Challenges for Independent Law Reformers' 254–55.

commission model of law reform. As former SLC Commissioner Lord Hodge has remarked, the 'principal source of authority' for the Commissions' proposals is 'the quality of the consultation'.[41] The Commissions must make continued efforts to find and nurture ways of reaching consultees. Relationships could be strained by over-consultation, failure to take consultees' views seriously, or by lack of implementation. If the Commissions' consultation process were subject to criticism, the legitimacy of their output would be seriously jeopardised. In particular, North's praise for public meetings to create a 'sense of involvement' should be borne in mind by the Commissions and other law reformers wherever appropriate.[42] A 'sense of involvement' can only really be achieved, however, if consultees' views are properly taken into account.[43] At the same time, the Commissions must be cognisant of the dangers of over-consultation.[44] In particular, when the government consults the same group on the same issue before it accepts a Commission proposal, the danger of consultee-fatigue and the 'frustration' of both consultees and law reformers is very real.[45] Innovations like social media and public gatherings make it more practical for consultees to respond, but they should not have to respond to the same question multiple times.[46]

As we have seen throughout this book, consultation is important not only for the Commissions' own fact finding, but to imbue their reports with an authority that reforms crafted solely by lawyers would not otherwise have. Where the input comes from will depend on the project—insurance companies, Land Registry, banks, the police, landlords, the general public and so on. Consultation needs to be carefully conducted, including the consideration of translating materials into different languages or different formats, to reach the members of society from whom input is most required. In countries with indigenous populations such as Canada, New Zealand and Australia, careful consultation can be particularly important to give proposals proper legitimacy.[47] To facilitate consultation, and to make it more user-friendly, concerns about the growing length and complexity of Commission publications and the option for publishing 'the necessary underpinning for the Commission's proposals' separately should be given consideration.[48] As has

[41] P Hodge, 'Introduction' in Dyson, Lee and Stark, *Fifty Years of the Law Commissions*, 29.

[42] P North, 'Law Reform: Processes and Problems' (1985) 101 *LQR* 338, 340 ('Processes and Problems'). He also recommended radio and television broadcasts, although these may not be suitable for all Commission projects.

[43] For criticism of the Carloway Review (a judge-led project)'s 'roadshows' see J Chalmers, F Leverick and SW Stark, 'The Process of Criminal Evidence Law Reform in Scotland: What Can We Learn?' in P Duff and P Ferguson (eds), *Current Developments in Scottish Criminal Evidence Law* (Edinburgh, EUP, forthcoming 2017).

[44] North, 'Processes and Problems' 344–46.

[45] M Arden, 'Introduction' in Dyson, Lee and Stark, *Fifty Years of the Law Commissions*, 174.

[46] ibid.

[47] See, eg, Cronin, 'Working on the Larger Canvas' 58–59.

[48] D Johnston, 'How Law Commissions Work: Some Lessons from the Past' in Dyson, Lee and Stark, *Fifty Years of the Law Commissions*, 241 ('How Law Commissions Work').

been said elsewhere, law reform must 'continually innovate in order to progress'.[49] That can include practical and simple changes such as harnessing social media to increase consultation responses,[50] and saving money by publishing reports online instead of printing hard copies.[51] In July 2016, the SLC announced that it would no longer print hard copies of its publications.[52] The LCEW still publishes in hard copy as well as digitally, although it is considering options for moving to a digital-only model. In so doing, it will need to explore with the Houses of Parliament options for laying digital-only papers in the House libraries.[53] Moving to digital-only publications will not be appropriate, however, for law reform bodies in countries without widespread internet access.

Commissions need to think carefully about what consultation is designed to achieve. Sometimes consultees' responses will influence a commission to change its mind, perhaps because its original plan is shown to be flawed,[54] or perhaps because a plan, although sound, proves to be controversial.[55] Sometimes, however, a commission may feel a responsibility to recommend a reform that challenges, but does not reflect, public sentiment. For example, the Law Commission of India (established before the GB Commissions, in 1955) recommended the abolition of the death penalty (except for terrorism-related offences) despite public support for its retention.[56] It decided that its role was to influence views, not to reflect them, especially in the light of experience from other countries (including the UK) which suggested that public opinion changes once the death penalty has been abolished.[57] Closer to home, the SLC 'marked out … [its] independence' in its very first report by proposing the abolition of the corroboration requirement in civil cases despite opposition from the Lord President (Scotland's most senior judge), the Scottish Bar and the Law Society of Scotland.[58] The recommendation was only partially implemented—it took 20 years and a subsequent SLC report for the proposal to be implemented in full.[59] But in this case, the symbolism of the proposals

[49] Carloway, 'A Scottish Perspective' 28.

[50] ibid 27. See too Lord Pentland, 'The Scottish Law Commission and the Future of Law Reform in Scotland' in Dyson, Lee and Stark, *Fifty Years of the Law Commissions*, 351 ('The Future of Law Reform').

[51] Carloway, 'A Scottish Perspective' 27.

[52] SLC Press Release, 'The Scottish Law Commission Goes Digital Only', 6 July 2016.

[53] I am grateful to Phil Golding for this information.

[54] See, eg, LCEW, *Blood Tests and the Proof of Paternity in Civil Proceedings* (Law Com No 16 (1968)) para 40, discussed in P Mitchell, 'Strategies of the Early Law Commission' in Dyson, Lee and Stark, *Fifty Years of the Law Commissions*, 42–43.

[55] See, eg, SLC, *Report on Succession* (Scot Law Com No 215 (2009)) paras 3.17–3.35.

[56] Law Commission of India, *The Death Penalty* (Report No 262 (2015)), discussed in W Binchy, 'Law Commissions, Courts and Society: A Sceptical View' in Dyson, Lee and Stark, *Fifty Years of the Law Commissions*, 154, fn 4.

[57] *The Death Penalty*, ibid para 3.10.4.

[58] SLC, *Proposal for Reform of the Law of Evidence Relating to Corroboration* (Scot Law Com No 4 (1967)) discussed in Pentland, 'The Future of Law Reform' 344–45.

[59] See Law Reform (Miscellaneous Provisions) (Scotland) Act 1968, s 9; SLC, *Evidence: Report on Corroboration, Hearsay and Related Matters in Civil Proceedings* (Scot Law Com No 100 (1986)) and Civil Evidence (Scotland) Act 1988, s 1.

may have outweighed the need for immediate implementation. Where the balance between independence and implementation should be struck will vary from project to project as well as from jurisdiction to jurisdiction. Compromises will be needed in many cases, but commissions should continue to be careful not to simply propose 'the minimum that all stakeholders involved are prepared to accept'.[60] Equally, commissions must be aware that criticism from a key stakeholder can negatively affect the likelihood of a project's implementation.[61] In all projects, a careful balance must be struck between 'intellectual purity' and 'pragmatic advantage',[62] although where that balance can be found will vary. Particularly in projects where opinions vary wildly, a commission must try to build 'a coalition' without sacrificing its own perspective.[63] That process will not necessarily be easy since 'all worthwhile law reform has winners and losers' and '[t]he losers will naturally resist reform'.[64]

In terms of assessing the outcome of a project, the Commissions' independence can be better protected by altering what we expect in terms of implementation. The Commissions, because of their independence, can select projects that might otherwise be neglected, especially by government. Indeed, the lack of another body able or willing to carry out a project is one aspect of the 'suitability' project-selection criterion. Once a project is selected, the Commissions undertake a 'wide canvassing of different viewpoints' in order to reach an informed and impartial conclusion.[65] Proper project selection and impartial conclusions are the benefits of the Commissions' independence, but they do mean that projects may not be attractive to government, because of the topic and/or because of the conclusion reached. Equally, implementation cannot be ignored. As we have seen in Canada and Northern Ireland, law commissions are vulnerable to abolition and a commission with a poor implementation rate could be highly vulnerable in any jurisdiction.[66]

Methods for increasing implementation have to be chosen carefully in order to preserve a commission's independence. Law reform bodies should be careful—despite increasing pressure to provide value for money—to strike a balance between speed and thoroughness. Their reputations may suffer if the quality of

[60] HL MacQueen, 'Implementation by Statute: What the Future Holds' in Dyson, Lee and Stark, *Fifty Years of the Law Commissions*, 209 ('What the Future Holds').

[61] See, eg, the discussion of the construction industry's objections to SLC, *Report on Prescription and Limitation of Actions (Latent Damage and other Related Issues)* (Scot Law Com No 122 (1989)) in Johnston, 'How Law Commissions Work' 238–39.

[62] J Munby, 'Introduction' in Dyson, Lee and Stark, *Fifty Years of the Law Commissions*, 217.

[63] ibid.

[64] Beatson, 'Challenges for Independent Law Reformers' 255.

[65] N Marsh, 'Law Reform in the United Kingdom: A New Institutional Approach' (1971) 13 *William & Mary Law Review* 263, 277.

[66] *cf* Y Le Bouthillier, 'The Former Law Commission of Canada: The Road Less Travelled' in Dyson, Lee and Stark, *Fifty Years of the Law Commissions*, 106, where it is argued that implementation rates provide 'no cover when the government of the day wants to put an end to the operation of a Law Commission'.

their product drops due to pressure to churn out a report more quickly.[67] Other jurisdictions should exercise caution before adopting something like the LCEW's Protocol, but other methods may be more attractive. The development of special parliamentary procedures to process more technical Commission Bills has been said to be something which could 'readily be adopted' by other jurisdictions by a former President of the New Zealand Law Commission (NZLC).[68] The British jurisdictions have already shown that such procedures can be adapted for bicameral or unicameral parliaments. Such procedures must be used carefully, however, given the stalling of the Jellicoe procedure partially due to its attempted use for a controversial Bill,[69] and the Holyrood procedure's false start.[70] Certain Bills may only be suitable after revision, so as not to jeopardise not only the passage of the Bill, but the existence of the entire procedure.[71] Certain other Bills will be completely unsuitable for these special procedures and care must be taken not to neglect more controversial projects, particularly in jurisdictions where controversial projects make up a large part of a commission's output. The ingenious innovation of preparing draft Bills in-house is integral to the success of these special parliamentary procedures. That innovation should be invoked in law reform bodies wherever possible to aid implementation in a way that does not, unlike other methods of aiding implementation, sacrifice independence. If special parliamentary procedures cannot be introduced then commissions should at least consider providing some sort of after-sales service to aid the implementation of their proposals because '[t]he work of the law reform body in this day and age does not end with the submission of a report'.[72] At the same time, alternative methods of implementation other than primary legislation should continue to be considered, including nurturing the relationship between the Commissions and the courts. Other jurisdictions with a common law basis may wish to do likewise.[73]

Small jurisdictions must think especially carefully about their law reform bodies. The unfortunate situation in Northern Ireland will by now be familiar.[74] The difficulties of finding suitable Commissioners in a small jurisdiction was apparently

[67] See the striking contrast between Commission Bills and government Bills in A Burrows, 'Some Reflections on Law Reform in England and Canada' (2003–04) 39 *Canadian Business Law Journal* 320, 329–30.

[68] G Hammond, 'The Legislative Implementation of Law Reform Proposals' in Dyson, Lee and Stark, *Fifty Years of the Law Commissions*, 185 ('The Legislative Implementation of Law Reform Proposals').

[69] Beatson, 'Challenges for Independent Law Reformers' 247.

[70] See ch 4, section IV.C.ii.

[71] On the compromises made to pass the Insurance Act 2015, see S Lewis, 'The Bill's Progress' in Dyson, Lee and Stark, *Fifty Years of the Law Commissions*, 268–69.

[72] M McMillan, 'Implementation of Law Reform Reports: Developments in Scotland' in Dyson, Lee and Stark, *Fifty Years of the Law Commissions*, 379.

[73] eg for an Australian perspective, see B McDonald, 'Law Reform in Private Law: The Role of Statutes in Supplementing or Supplanting the Common Law' in Dyson, Lee and Stark, *Fifty Years of the Law Commissions*, ch 30 ('Law Reform in Private Law'); and for a New Zealand perspective, see KJ Keith, 'Making Law—Who, How and What?' in Dyson, Lee and Stark, ibid ch 39 ('Making Law—Who, How and What?').

[74] See ch 6, section III.C.

one reason for a law commission not being established there in 1965.[75] Undoubtedly, that is a real problem, although the size of the jurisdiction is only one possible reason for the unhappy story of law reform in Northern Ireland. If anything, law reform agencies are even more important in small jurisdictions which lack the 'steady stream and quality of case law' of larger systems.[76] Small jurisdictions must therefore think carefully before transplanting law reform models from larger countries, and think carefully in particular about maximising resource use. Innovations like the SLC's agreement for academic secondments might be worth considering.[77]

Also in terms of resources, all jurisdictions, not only small ones, may wish to consider allowing their commissions to have a general oversight function whereby, like the GB Commissions, they can recommend other bodies who might reform the law.[78] A commission's founding legislation, even if it does not make explicit reference to such a function, may be sufficiently broad so as to include it.[79] The GB Commissions should make more use than they do at present of their function as the overseers, albeit not the reformers, of all the law. They are not single-handedly responsible for the systematic development and reform of the law, but they should take more responsibility for its oversight.

Our Commissions can also learn lessons from overseas commissions.[80] For example, the legislation which established the ALRC makes no mention of a codification duty.[81] Given that one reason for imposing the codification duty on the GB Commissions was entry into the EU, such an absence is unsurprising.[82] Nevertheless, the ALRC has conducted work which has successfully resulted in codifying statutes, such as the Personal Property Securities Act 2009 (Cth).[83] The same can be said about the NZLC.[84] Such success shows that the removal of the explicit duty to codify in the 1965 Act would not remove the possibility of the GB Commissions codifying where appropriate. Another useful lesson from New Zealand could be the innovation of inbuilt post-legislative scrutiny of statutes emanating from

[75] SW Stark and N Faris, 'Law Reform in Northern Ireland: Cheshire Cat or Potemkin Commission?' [2016] *PL* 651, 654.

[76] MacQueen, 'What the Future Holds' 202.

[77] See ch 2, section IV.D.

[78] Keith, 'Making Law—Who, How and What?' 410.

[79] See, eg, Law Commission Act 1985 (New Zealand) s 5.

[80] See generally M Dyson, 'The Future is a Foreign Country, They Do Things Differently There' in Dyson, Lee and Stark, *Fifty Years of the Law Commissions*, ch 38.

[81] Australian Law Reform Commission Act 1996 (Cth).

[82] Although like the GB Commissions' early harmonisation aims, the ALRC does have to consider the need for 'uniformity between State and Territory laws' and for 'complementary Commonwealth, State and Territory laws': Australian Law Reform Commission Act 1996 (Cth), ss 21(1)(d) and (e).

[83] ALRC, *Personal Property Securities* (ALRC 64 (1993)); McDonald, 'Law Reform in Private Law' 302.

[84] The Law Commission Act 1985 (New Zealand) makes no mention of codification, yet the Evidence Act 2006 (which implemented NZLC, *Evidence* (NZLC R55 (1999))) has been described as 'an evidence code in all but name': Hammond, 'The Legislative Implementation of Law Reform Proposals' 180.

Commission reports. In other words, the idea that the Commissions should revisit their implemented statutes periodically to report on whether any adjustment is required. That innovation would help us to focus on the quality of legislation over the mere quantity of implementation—a goal, surely, for any reform of the law. Given the obvious additional resources that would require, however, it could not be provided for in every Bill unless extra resources could be made available. Similar quality control can be seen in Great Britain, although without explicit review provisions in the Acts based on Commission proposals. For example, the LCEW is currently revisiting the Land Registration Act 2002, an Act which resulted from its recommendations and which is now thought to be in need of review.[85] Similarly, the SLC is revisiting the Prescription and Limitation (Scotland) Act 1973, an SLC-inspired statute.[86]

Over half a century after their creation, the Commissions' roles have changed much more than their founding legislation. They operate with increasingly tight budgets, and must operate more transparently than ever before. Clarity as to the project-selection criteria is now essential for both maximisation of resources and for ultimate accountability. The constitutional climate in the UK is also very different now compared with 1965. Our impending likely departure from the EU has put the final nail in codification's coffin. New pressures caused by Scottish and Welsh devolution and the establishment of the NILC (if it continues to exist) have altered the Commissions' duty to consult one another, and increased the potential for projects to be selected inconsistently unless selection criteria are clearly set out. The Commissions' collaboration allows for the exchange of knowledge between the jurisdictions, but requires clear criteria for project-selection in order for the Commissions to work in sync while retaining their independence—from government and each other.

Without the Commissions, the British jurisdictions would be deprived of institutions that propose independent and thoroughly researched reform in areas which would often be neglected by government and other bodies. The Commissions have developed in order to survive—this book has proposed how they can continue to develop in order to thrive.

[85] LCEW, *Twelfth Programme of Law Reform* (Law Com No 354 (2014)) paras 2.13–2.16.

[86] SLC, *Ninth Programme of Law Reform* (Scot Law Com No 242 (2015)) paras 2.26–2.31.

APPENDIX 1: GB CHAIRMEN AND COMMISSIONERS 1965–2016

Scottish Law Commission[1]

Chairmen

1965–71:	Lord Kilbrandon
1971–81:	Lord Hunter
1981–88:	Lord Maxwell
1988–96:	Lord Davidson
1996–2002:	Lord Gill
2002–06:	Lord Eassie
2007–12:	Lord Drummond Young
2012–13:	Lady Clark
2014–present:	Lord Pentland

Commissioners

1965–68:	GD Fairbairn
1965–74:	JM Halliday
1965–80:	TB Smith
1966–82:	AE Anton
1968–71:	AM Johnston
1971–75:	EGF Stewart
1974–77:	RB Jack
1976–79:	JPH Mackay
1978–86:	RDD Bertram
1979–88:	J Murray
1981–99:	EM Clive

[1] Names/judicial titles are given as they were at the time of appointment. Correct as at 31 December 2016.

1982–90:	Sheriff CGB Nicholson
1986–95:	PN Love
1988–96:	WA Nimmo Smith
1990–94:	Sheriff ID Macphail
1995–2005:	KGC Reid
1995–2000:	NR Whitty
1997–2003:	PS Hodge
2000–08:	G Maher
2000–09:	JM Thomson
2003–09:	C Tyre
2006–11:	GL Gretton
2008–14:	P Layden
2009–present:	HL MacQueen
2009–14:	LJ Dunlop
2011–present:	AJM Steven
2015–present:	D Johnston
2015–present:	C Drummond

Law Commission[2]

Chairmen

1965–73:	Mr Justice Scarman
1973–78:	Mr Justice Cooke
1978–81:	Mr Justice Kerr
1981–85:	Mr Justice R Gibson
1985–89:	Mr Justice Beldam
1990–92:	Mr Justice P Gibson
1993–95:	Mr Justice Brooke
1996–99:	Mrs Justice Arden
1999–2002:	Mr Justice Carnwath
2002–06:	Mr Justice Toulson
2006–09:	Mr Justice Etherton

[2] Names/judicial titles are given as they were at the time of appointment. Correct as at 31 December 2016.

2009–12:	Mr Justice Munby
2012–15:	Mr Justice Lloyd Jones
2015–present:	Lord Justice Bean

Commissioners

1965–71:	LCB Gower
1965–71:	N Lawson
1965–78:	NS Marsh
1965–70:	A Martin
1970–75:	C Bicknell
1971–76:	AL Diamond
1971–77:	D Hodgson
1975–83:	S Edell
1976–84:	PM North
1977–81:	WAB Forbes
1978–83:	SM Cretney
1981–88:	B Davenport
1984–93:	TM Aldridge
1984–88:	J Farrand
1984–93:	B Hoggett
1989–93:	R Buxton
1989–94:	J Beatson
1994–2000:	D Faber
1994–2001:	C Harpum
1994–99:	S Silber
1994–99:	A Burrows
2000–07:	H Beale
2000–04:	Judge A Wilkie
2001–05:	M Partington
2001–08:	SN Bridge
2005–10:	J Horder
2006–09:	K Parker
2007–14:	D Hertzell

2008–15:	E Cooke
2010–13:	F Patterson
2010–present:	D Ormerod
2013–present:	N Paines
2015–present:	S Lewis
2015–present:	N Hopkins

APPENDIX 2: LAW COMMISSIONS ACT 1965 WITH PROPOSED AMENDMENTS

Proposed changes are marked in boxed text and in strikethrough where appropriate.

1. The Law Commission

(1) For the purpose of promoting the reform of the law of England and Wales there shall be constituted in accordance with this section a body of Commissioners, to be known as the Law Commission, consisting (except during any temporary vacancy) of a Chairman and four other Commissioners appointed by the Lord Chancellor.

(1A) The person appointed to be the Chairman shall be a person who holds office as a judge of the High Court or Court of Appeal in England and Wales.

(2) The persons appointed to be the other Commissioners shall be persons appearing to the Lord Chancellor to be suitably qualified by the holding of judicial office or by experience as a person having a general qualification (within the meaning of section 71 of the Courts and Legal Services Act 1990) or as a teacher of law in a university.

(3) A person appointed to be a Commissioner shall be appointed for such term (not exceeding five years) and subject to such conditions as may be determined by the Lord Chancellor at the time of his appointment; but a Commissioner may at any time resign his office and a person who ceases to be a Commissioner shall be eligible for reappointment.

(4) A person who holds judicial office may be appointed as a Commissioner without relinquishing that office, but shall not (unless otherwise provided by the terms of his appointment) be required to perform his duties as the holder of that office while he remains a member of the Commission.

2. The Scottish Law Commission

(1) For the purpose of promoting the reform of the law of Scotland, there shall be constituted in accordance with this section a body of Commissioners, to be known

as the Scottish Law Commission, consisting of a Chairman and not more than four other Commissioners appointed by the Scottish Ministers.

(2) The persons appointed to be Commissioners shall be persons appearing to the Scottish Ministers to be suitably qualified by the holding of judicial office or by experience as an advocate or solicitor or as a teacher of law in a university.

(3) A person appointed to be a Commissioner shall be appointed for such term (not exceeding five years) and subject to such conditions as may be determined by the Scottish Ministers at the time of his appointment; but a Commissioner may at any time resign his office, and a person who ceases to be a Commissioner shall be eligible for reappointment.

(4) A person who holds judicial office may be appointed as a Commissioner without relinquishing that office, but shall not (unless otherwise provided by the terms of his appointment) be required to perform his duties as the holder of that office while he remains a member of the Commission.

3. Functions of the Commissions

(1) It shall be the duty of each of the Commissions to take and keep under review all the law with which they are respectively concerned with a view to its systematic development and reform, including in particular ~~the codification of such law,~~[1] the elimination of anomalies, the repeal of obsolete and unnecessary enactments, the reduction of the number of separate enactments and generally the simplification and modernisation of the law, and for that purpose—

(a) to receive and consider any proposals for the reform of the law which may be made or referred to them;
(b) to prepare and submit to the Minister from time to time programmes for the examination of different branches of the law with a view to reform, including recommendations as to the agency (whether the Commission or another body) by which any such examination should be carried out;
(c) to undertake, pursuant to any such recommendations approved by the Minister, the examination of particular branches of the law and the formulation, by means of draft Bills or otherwise, of proposals for reform therein;
(d) to prepare from time to time at the request of the Minister comprehensive programmes of consolidation and statute law revision, and to undertake the preparation of draft Bills pursuant to any such programme approved by the Minister;
(e) to ~~provide~~ receive and consider (by reference to section 3(1A)) requests for advice and information ~~to~~ from government departments and other authorities or bodies concerned at the instance of the Government of the

[1] See ch 5.

United Kingdom or the Scottish ~~Administration~~ Government and to respond, where appropriate, with proposals for the reform or amendment of any branch of the law;[2]

(ea) in the case of the Law Commission, to ~~provide~~ receive and consider (by reference to section 3(1A)) requests for advice and information ~~to~~ from the Welsh Ministers and to respond, where appropriate, with proposals for the reform or amendment of any branch of the law;[3]

(f) to obtain such information as to the legal systems of other countries as appears to the Commissioners likely to facilitate the performance of any of their functions.

(1A) In selecting, approving or referring areas of law to examine, the Commissions, the Ministers and government departments and other authorities or bodies as mentioned in sections 3(1)(e) and (ea) shall take into account—[4]

(a) The resources available to (or obtainable by) the Commission(s) and their economical use;
(b) The suitability of the Commission(s) as the body or bodies responsible for examining an area of law; and
(c) The importance of an area of law being examined.

(2) The Minister shall lay before Parliament any programmes prepared by the Commission and approved by him and any proposals for reform formulated by the Commission ~~pursuant to such programmes~~.[5]

(3) Each of the Commissions shall make an annual report to the Minister on their proceedings, and the Minister shall lay the report before Parliament with such comments (if any) as he thinks fit.

(3A) Subsections (2) and (3) of this section shall have effect in relation to the Scottish Law Commission with the substitution of 'the Scottish Parliament' for 'Parliament'.

(3B) The Scottish Law Commission shall present proposals for reform in (or partially in) reserved matters to the Scottish Ministers to be laid before the Scottish Parliament by them and to the Secretary of State for Scotland to be laid before the Parliament of the United Kingdom by him.[6]

[2] See ch 2, section IV.C.v.
[3] ibid.
[4] See ch 3, section V. Sub-criteria are left to be developed in a non-legislative document: see ch 3, sections V.A.iv and V.B.iii.
[5] See ch 7, section II.
[6] See ch 4, section II.F and ch 6, section III.A.

(3C) The Law Commission shall present proposals for reform in (or partially in) Welsh devolved matters to the Welsh Ministers to be laid before the National Assembly for Wales by them and to the Lord Chancellor to be laid before the Parliament of the United Kingdom by him.[7]

(4) In the exercise of their functions under this Act the Commissions shall act in consultation with each other and the Northern Ireland Law Commission.

3A. Reports on Implementation of ~~Law~~ Commission Proposals

(1) As soon as practicable after the end of each reporting year, the ~~Lord Chancellor~~ Minister must prepare a report on—

(a) ~~the Law~~ Commission proposals implemented (in whole or in part) during the year;
(b) ~~the Law~~ Commission proposals that have not been implemented (in whole or in part) as at the end of the year, including—
  (i) plans for dealing with any of those proposals;
  (ii) any decision not to implement any of those proposals (in whole or in part) taken during the year and the reasons for the decision.

(2) The ~~Lord Chancellor~~ Minister must lay the report before Parliament.

(3) The first reporting year is the year starting with the day on which section 1 of the Law Commission Act 2009 comes into force; and the second reporting year is the year after that and so on.

(4) If a decision not to implement a ~~Law~~ Commission proposal (in whole or in part) is taken in a reporting year, ~~subsection (1)(b) does not require a report for a later reporting year to deal with the proposal so far as it is covered by that decision.~~ that decision should be reconsidered in each subsequent reporting year, unless the proposal has been superseded by subsequent reform or a subsequent proposal.[8]

(5) If a decision not to implement a ~~Law~~ Commission proposal (in whole or in part) has been taken before the first reporting year, subsection (1)(b) does not require any report to deal with the proposal so far as it is covered by that decision.

(6) '~~Law~~ Commission proposal' means—

(a) a proposal formulated by the Law Commission or the Scottish Law Commission[9] as mentioned in section 3(1) (a), (c) or (e);[10]

[7] Necessitated by the changes made by the Wales Act 2014, discussed in ch 6, section III.B.
[8] See ch 4, sections I.C, II.A and IV.B.iv.
[9] See ch 4, section IV.C.i.
[10] See ch 4, section IV.B.iv.

(b) a proposal for consolidation or statute law revision for which a draft Bill has been prepared by the Law Commission or the Scottish Law Commission as mentioned in section 3(1)(d).

(6A) Subsection (2) of this section shall have effect in relation to the Scottish Law Commission with the substitution of 'the Scottish Parliament' for 'Parliament', except where the report is made by the Secretary of State for Scotland, where 'Parliament' means the Parliament of the United Kingdom.[11]

(6B) 'Minister' means—

(a) in relation to the Law Commission, the Lord Chancellor;
(b) in relation to the Scottish Law Commission, the Scottish Ministers in devolved matters and the Secretary of State for Scotland in reserved matters.[12]

(7) This section does not require the Lord Chancellor to prepare reports on Law Commission proposals on which the Welsh Ministers are required to report (see section 3C).

3B. Protocol about the Law Commission's Work

(1) The Lord Chancellor and the Law Commission may agree for the purposes of this section a statement (a 'protocol') about the Law Commission's work.

(2) The protocol may include (among other things) provision about—

(a) principles and methods to be applied in deciding the work to be carried out by the Law Commission and in the carrying out of that work;
(b) the assistance and information that Ministers of the Crown and the Law Commission are to give each other;
(c) the way in which Ministers of the Crown are to deal with the Law Commission's proposals for reform, consolidation or statute law revision.

(3) The Lord Chancellor and the Law Commission must from time to time review the protocol and may agree to revise it.

(4) The Lord Chancellor must lay the protocol (and any revision of it) before Parliament.

(5) Ministers of the Crown and the Law Commission must have regard to the protocol.

[11] See ch 4, section IV.C.i.
[12] ibid.

3C. Report on Implementation of Law Commission Proposals: Wales

(1) The Welsh Ministers must prepare a report each year on—

(a) the Law Commission proposals relating to Welsh devolved matters that have been implemented since the preparation of the previous report under this section;
(b) the Law Commission proposals relating to Welsh devolved matters that have not been implemented as at the preparation of the report.

(2) The report required under subsection (1)(b) must include—

(a) plans for dealing with any of the proposals described in that paragraph;
(b) any decision not to implement any of those proposals taken since the preparation of the previous report under this section;
(c) the reasons for any such decision.

(3) The Welsh Ministers must lay the report before the National Assembly for Wales.

(4) The Welsh Ministers must prepare a report under this section—

(a) before the first anniversary of the day on which this section comes into force, and
(b) thereafter, before each subsequent anniversary of that day.

(5) In the case of the first report, the references in subsections (1) and (2) to the period since the preparation of the previous report are to be read as references to the period since the coming into force of this section.

(6) If a decision not to implement a Law Commission proposal is dealt with in a report under this section, ~~subsection (1)(b) does not require a later report to deal with the proposal so far as it is covered by that decision~~ that decision should be reconsidered in each subsequent reporting year, unless the proposal has been superseded by subsequent reform or a subsequent proposal.[13]

(7) If a decision not to implement a Law Commission proposal has been taken before the coming into force of this section, subsection (1)(b) does not require any report to deal with the proposal so far as it is covered by that decision.

(8) In this section—

(a) 'Law Commission proposal' means any proposal or recommendation for the reform of the law that has been published in a report by the Law Commission, and

[13] See ch 4, sections I.C, II.A and IV.B.iv.

(b) references to the implementation of a Law Commission proposal are to its implementation in whole or in part.

(9) Whether a Law Commission proposal relates to Welsh devolved matters is to be determined in accordance with section 3D(8).

3D. Protocol about the Law Commission's Work: Wales

(1) The Welsh Ministers and the Law Commission may agree for the purposes of this section a statement (a 'protocol') about the Law Commission's work relating to Welsh devolved matters.

(2) The protocol may include (among other things) provision about—

(a) the principles and methods to be applied in deciding the work relating to such matters to be carried out by the Law Commission and in the carrying out of that work;
(b) the assistance and information that the Welsh Ministers and the Law Commission are to give to each other;
(c) the way in which the Welsh Ministers are to deal with Law Commission proposals so far as they relate to Welsh devolved matters.

(3) The Welsh Ministers and the Law Commission must from time to time review the protocol and may agree to revise it.

(4) The Law Commission must not agree the protocol (or any revision of it) without the Lord Chancellor's approval.

(5) The Welsh Ministers must lay the protocol (and any revision of it) before the National Assembly for Wales.

(6) The Welsh Ministers and the Law Commission must have regard to the protocol.

(7) 'Law Commission proposal' has the meaning given in section 3C(8)(a).

(8) In this section and section 3C, the Law Commission's work (including any of their proposals) relates to Welsh devolved matters so far as it relates to—

(a) any matter provision about which would be within the legislative competence of the National Assembly for Wales if it were contained in an Act of the Assembly, or
(b) (so far as it is not within paragraph (a)), any matter functions with respect to which are exercisable by the Welsh Ministers, the First Minister for Wales, the Counsel General to the Welsh Government or the National Assembly for Wales Commission.

3E. Welsh Advisory Committee[14]

There shall be a Welsh Advisory Committee, consisting of a Chairman and not more than fourteen other members, which shall advise the Law Commission on the exercise of its statutory functions in relation to Wales in both devolved and reserved matters.

4. Remuneration and Pensions of Commissioners

(1) There shall be paid to the Commissioners of the Law Commission, other than a Commissioner who holds high judicial office, such salaries or remuneration as may be determined, with the approval of the Treasury, by the Lord Chancellor.

(1A) There shall be paid to the Commissioners of the Scottish Law Commission, other than a Commissioner who holds high judicial office, such salaries or remuneration as may be determined by the Scottish Ministers.

(2) In the case of any such holder of the office of Commissioner as may be so determined, there shall be paid such pension, allowance or gratuity to or in respect of him on his retirement or death, or such contributions or other payments towards provision for such a pension, allowance or gratuity, as may be so determined.

(3) As soon as may be after the making of any determination under subsection (2) of this section,

(a) in the case of the Law Commission, the Lord Chancellor shall lay before each House of Parliament; and
(b) in the case of the Scottish Law Commission, the Scottish Ministers shall lay before the Scottish Parliament,

a statement of the amount of the pension, allowance or gratuity, or contributions or other payments towards the pension, allowance or gratuity, payable in pursuance of the determination.

(4) In the case of the Law Commission, the salaries or remuneration of the Commissioners, and any sums payable to or in respect of the Commissioners under subsection (2) of this section, shall be paid out of moneys provided by Parliament.

(5) In the case of the Scottish Law Commission, the salaries or remuneration of the Commissioners, and any sums payable to or in respect of the Commissioners under subsection (2) of this section, shall be paid by the Scottish Ministers.

[14] See ch 6, section III.B.

5. Staff and Expenses

(1) The Lord Chancellor may appoint such officers and servants of the Law Commission, as he may, with the approval of the Treasury as to number and conditions of service, determine.

(1A) The Scottish Ministers may appoint such officers and servants of the Scottish Law Commission as they may determine.

(2) The Treasury may make regulations providing for the counting of service as an officer or servant of either of the Commissions as pensionable service in any other capacity under the Crown and vice versa.

(3) The power of the Treasury to make regulations under subsection (2) of this section shall be exercisable by statutory instrument, and any statutory instrument made by virtue of that subsection shall be subject to annulment in pursuance of a resolution of either House of Parliament.

(4) The expenses of the Law Commission, including the remuneration of officers and servants appointed under this section, shall be defrayed out of moneys provided by Parliament (except to the extent that those expenses are met by the Welsh Ministers).

(5) The expenses of the Scottish Law Commission, including the remuneration of its officers and servants appointed under this section, shall be paid by the Scottish Ministers.

6. Supplemental

(1) [Repealed]

(2) In this Act 'high judicial office' means such office within the meaning of Part 3 of the Constitutional Reform Act 2005 or membership of the Judicial Committee of the Privy Council; and 'the Minister' means, except as otherwise provided,[15] in relation to the Law Commission the Lord Chancellor and in relation to the Scottish Law Commission the Scottish Ministers.

7. Short Title

This Act may be cited as the Law Commissions Act 1965.

[15] See ch 7, section II.

BIBLIOGRAPHY

Anon, 'Corroboration of Evidence in Scottish Criminal Law' 1958 *Scots Law Times (News)* 137.

—— 'The Law Commission Bill' 1965 *Scots Law Times (News)* 29.

—— 'Scottish Law Commission' 1965 *Scots Law Times (News)* 148.

Anton, AE, 'The Formal Validity of Wills' 1958 *Scots Law Times (News)* 217.

—— 'Obstacles to Codification' 1982 *Juridical Review* 15.

Arden, M, 'Time for an English Commercial Code?' (1997) 56 *CLJ* 516.

—— 'The Work of the Law Commission' (2000) 53 *Current Legal Problems* 559.

—— 'Introduction' in M Dyson, J Lee and SW Stark (eds), *Fifty Years of the Law Commissions: The Dynamics of Law Reform* (Oxford, Hart Publishing, 2016) 173–74.

Australian Law Reform Commission, *Human Tissue Transplants* (ALRC 7 (1977)).

—— *Multiculturalism and the Law* (ALRC 57 (1992)).

—— *Personal Property Securities* (ALRC 64 (1993)).

—— *Integrity: But Not By Trust Alone* (ALRC 82 (1996)).

Bach, W, 'Law Reform: Servant or Master of Government Policy?' in *Law Reform: Catching the Eye of Government* (papers from a joint seminar presented by the Law Commission and UCL Faculty of Laws, 2001) 3–9.

Bargenda, JA and Stark, SW, 'In Search of the Legal Holy Grail: Critical Perspectives on Codification from Britain and Germany' (unpublished, 2016).

Beale, H, 'The Law Commission and Judicial Law Reform' (2001) 35 *The Law Teacher* 323.

—— 'The Law Commission Method: Exportable to the EU?' in M Dyson, J Lee and SW Stark (eds), *Fifty Years of the Law Commissions: The Dynamics of Law Reform* (Oxford, Hart Publishing, 2016) 219–34.

Beatson, J, 'Has the Common Law a Future?' (1997) 56 *CLJ* 291.

—— 'Challenges for Independent Law Reformers from Changing External Priorities and Shorter Timescales' in M Dyson, J Lee and SW Stark (eds), *Fifty Years of the Law Commissions: The Dynamics of Law Reform* (Oxford, Hart Publishing, 2016) 245–65.

Beith, A, 'Introduction' in M Dyson, J Lee and SW Stark (eds), *Fifty Years of the Law Commissions: The Dynamics of Law Reform* (Oxford, Hart Publishing, 2016) 75.

Bell, J, 'Comparative Law in the Supreme Court 2010–11' (2012) 1(2) *Cambridge Journal of International and Comparative Law* 20.

Bennion, F, 'Additional Comments' in G Zellick (ed), *The Law Commission and Law Reform* (London, Sweet & Maxwell, 1988) 60–66.

—— *Statutory Interpretation*, 3rd edn (London, Butterworths, 1997).

Bentham, J (published under the superintendence of his executor, J Bowring), *The Works of Jeremy Bentham*, vol IX (Edinburgh, William Tait, 1843).

Bethell, R, 'Address on Vacating the Office of President of the Society, at the Anniversary Meeting, 21st February, 1859' (1859) 2 *Juridical Society Papers* 129.

Beynon, H, 'Mighty Bentham' (1981) 2 *Journal of Legal History* 62.

Binchy, W, 'Law Commissions, Courts and Society: A Sceptical View' in M Dyson, J Lee and SW Stark (eds), *Fifty Years of the Law Commissions: The Dynamics of Law Reform* (Oxford, Hart Publishing, 2016) 151–58.

Bingham, TH, 'The European Convention on Human Rights: Time to Incorporate' (1993) 109 *LQR* 390.

—— 'A Criminal Code: Must We Wait for Ever?' in *The Business of Judging: Selected Essays and Speeches* (Oxford, Oxford University Press, 2011) 295–97.

—— 'Address at the Service of Thanksgiving for the Rt Hon Lord Denning OM' in *The Business of Judging: Selected Essays and Speeches* (Oxford, Oxford University Press, 2011) 409–13.

—— *The Business of Judging: Selected Essays and Speeches* (Oxford, Oxford University Press, 2011).

—— 'The Future of the Common Law' in *The Business of Judging: Selected Essays and Speeches* (Oxford, Oxford University Press, 2011) 375–89.

—— 'The Judge as Lawmaker: An English Perspective' in *The Business of Judging: Selected Essays and Speeches* (Oxford, Oxford University Press, 2011) 25–34.

—— *The Rule of Law* (London, Penguin Books, 2011).

Blom-Cooper, L, '1966 and All That: The Story of the Practice Statement' in L Blom-Cooper, B Dickson and G Drewry (eds), *The Judicial House of Lords 1876–2009* (Oxford, Oxford University Press, 2009) 128–44.

—— 'Style of Judgments' in L Blom-Cooper, B Dickson and G Drewry (eds), *The Judicial House of Lords 1876–2009* (Oxford, Oxford University Press, 2009) 145–63.

—— 'Reform? Reform? Aren't Things Bad Enough Already?' [2010] *PL* 441.

Boon, A and Webb, J, 'Legal Education and Training in England and Wales: Back to the Future?' (2008) 58 *Journal of Legal Education* 79.

Borrie, GJ, 'Law Reform: A Damp Squib?' (Inaugural Lecture, University of Birmingham, 1970).

Box, M, *Rebel Advocate* (London, Victor Gollancz Ltd, 1983).

Brandeis, LD, *Other People's Money and How the Bankers Use it* (Mansfield Centre, Martino Publishing, 2009).

Brooke, H, 'The Role of the Law Commission in Simplifying Statute Law' (1995) 16 *Statute Law Review* 1.

Brotchie, N, 'The Scottish Law Commission: Promoting Law Reform in Scotland' (2009) 9 *Legal Information Management* 30.

Burrows, A, 'Some Reflections on Law Reform in England and Canada' (2003–04) 39 *Canadian Business Law Journal* 320.

—— 'Post-legislative Scrutiny, Legislative Drafting and the "Elusive Boundary"' in M Dyson, J Lee and SW Stark (eds), *Fifty Years of the Law Commissions: The Dynamics of Law Reform* (Oxford, Hart Publishing, 2016) 189–97.

Cam, H, *Law as it Looks to a Historian: Founders' Memorial Lecture, Girton College* (Cambridge, W Heffer & Sons Ltd, 1956).

Cane, P, 'The Law Commission on Judicial Review' (1993) 56 *MLR* 887.

Cardozo, B, 'A Ministry of Justice' (1921–22) 35 *Harvard Law Review* 113.

Carloway, Lord, 'To "Mend the Laws, That Neids Mendement": A Scottish Perspective on Lawyers as Law Reformers' (speech at the Commonwealth Association of Law Reform Agencies Conference, Edinburgh, 2015).

Carnwath, R, 'Introduction' in M Dyson, J Lee and SW Stark (eds), *Fifty Years of the Law Commissions: The Dynamics of Law Reform* (Oxford, Hart Publishing, 2016) 125–26.

Chalmers, J, Leverick, F and Stark, SW, 'The Process of Criminal Evidence Law Reform in Scotland: What Can We Learn?' in P Duff and P Ferguson (eds), *Current Developments in Scottish Criminal Evidence Law* (Edinburgh, Edinburgh University Press, forthcoming 2017).
Chalmers, MD, 'Codification of Mercantile Law' (1903) 19 *LQR* 10.
Chorley, R and Dworkin, G, 'The Law Commissions Act, 1965' (1965) 28 *MLR* 675.
Clark, L, 'Law Reform and the Work of the Scottish Law Commission' (lecture at the Annual General Meeting of the Scottish Legal Action Group, 2012).
Clive, E, 'The Scottish Civil Code Project' in HL MacQueen, A Vauer and S Espiau Espiau (eds), *Regional Private Laws and Codification in Europe* (Cambridge, Cambridge University Press, 2003) 83–101.
—— 'Codification of the Criminal Law' in J Chalmers, F Leverick and L Farmer (eds), *Essays in Criminal Law in Honour of Sir Gerald Gordon* (Edinburgh, Edinburgh University Press, 2010) 54–69.
—— 'Law Reform and Social Policy' in M Dyson, J Lee and SW Stark (eds), *Fifty Years of the Law Commissions: The Dynamics of Law Reform* (Oxford, Hart Publishing, 2016) 64–72.
Clive, E, Ferguson, P, Gane, C and McCall Smith, A, *A Draft Criminal Code for Scotland with Commentary* (Edinburgh, The Stationery Office, 2003).
Conservative Party, *Protecting Human Rights in the UK: The Conservatives' Proposals for Changing Britain's Human Rights Laws* (2014).
Cooke, E, 'Introduction' in M Dyson, J Lee and SW Stark (eds), *Fifty Years of the Law Commissions: The Dynamics of Law Reform* (Oxford, Hart Publishing, 2016) 339.
Cooke, E and MacQueen, HL, 'Law Reform in a Political Environment: The Work of the Law Commissions' in D Feldman (ed), *Law in Politics, Politics in Law* (Oxford, Hart Publishing, 2013) 141–54.
Cooper, TM, 'The Common and the Civil Law—A Scot's View' (1949–50) 63 *Harvard Law Review* 468.
—— *Selected Papers 1922–1954* (Edinburgh, Oliver and Boyd, 1957).
Cretney, S, 'The Politics of Law Reform—A View from the Inside' (1985) 48 *MLR* 493.
—— 'The Programmes: Milestones or Millstones?' in G Zellick (ed), *The Law Commission and Law Reform* (London, Sweet & Maxwell, 1988) 3–20.
—— 'The Law Commission: True Dawns and False Dawns' (1996) 59 *MLR* 631.
Cronin, K, 'Working on the Larger Canvas—Law Reform in a Federal System: Thoughts on Forty Years of the Australian Law Reform Commission' in M Dyson, J Lee and SW Stark (eds), *Fifty Years of the Law Commissions: The Dynamics of Law Reform* (Oxford, Hart Publishing, 2016) 55–63.
Cross, R, 'The Reports of the Criminal Law Commissioners (1833–1849) and the Abortive Bills of 1853' in PR Glazebrook (ed), *Reshaping the Criminal Law: Essays in Honour of Glanville Williams* (London, Stevens & Sons, 1978) 5–20.
Crossman, R, *The Diaries of a Cabinet Minister*, vol 1 (London, Hamish Hamilton and Jonathan Cape, 1975).
Cusine, DJ, 'Law Reform—Who Cares?' (1993) 38(3) *Journal of the Law Society of Scotland* 101.
—— 'Civil Law Reform: Where are We and Where are We Going?' 2015 *Scots Law Times (News)* 27.
Darbyshire, P, *Sitting in Judgment: The Working Lives of Judges* (Oxford, Hart Publishing, 2011).
Davidson, C, 'Law Reform—Who Cares?' (1992) 37(4) *Journal of the Law Society of Scotland* 130.

Davis, KC, *Discretionary Justice: A Preliminary Inquiry* (Urbana, University of Illinois Press, 1971).

Dempsey, B, 'Law Reform and Devolution: Consultation Processes and Divorce Law in Scotland' (2012) 63 *Northern Ireland Legal Quarterly* 227.

Dennis, I, 'RIP: The Criminal Code (1968–2008)' [2009] *Crim LR* 1.

—— 'The Law Commission and the Criminal Law: Reflections on the Codification Project' in M Dyson, J Lee and SW Stark (eds), *Fifty Years of the Law Commissions: The Dynamics of Law Reform* (Oxford, Hart Publishing, 2016) 108–22.

Devlin, P, 'The Process of Law Reform' (1966) 63 *Law Society's Gazette* 453.

Diamond, A, 'Codification of the Law of Contract' (1968) 31 *MLR* 361.

—— 'The Law Commission and Government Departments' in G Zellick (ed), *The Law Commission and Law Reform* (London, Sweet & Maxwell, 1988) 21–27.

Dickson, B, 'Judicial Activism in the House of Lords 1995–2007' in B Dickson (ed), *Judicial Activism in Common Law Supreme Courts* (Oxford, Oxford University Press, 2007) 363–414.

Drewry, G, 'The Legislative Implementation of Law Reform Proposals' (1986) 7 *Statute Law Review* 161.

Drummond Young, J, 'Introduction' in M Dyson, J Lee and SW Stark (eds), *Fifty Years of the Law Commissions: The Dynamics of Law Reform* (Oxford, Hart Publishing, 2016) 273.

Dunlop, L, 'A Good Name, a Long Game' in M Dyson, J Lee and SW Stark (eds), *Fifty Years of the Law Commissions: The Dynamics of Law Reform* (Oxford, Hart Publishing, 2016) 159–69.

Dworkin, R, *Taking Rights Seriously* (Cambridge MA, Harvard University Press, 1977).

Dyson, M, 'The Future is a Foreign Country, They Do Things Differently There' in M Dyson, J Lee and SW Stark (eds), *Fifty Years of the Law Commissions: The Dynamics of Law Reform* (Oxford, Hart Publishing, 2016) 380–99.

Dyson, M, Lee, J and Stark, SW, 'Introduction' in M Dyson, J Lee and SW Stark (eds), *Fifty Years of the Law Commissions: The Dynamics of Law Reform* (Oxford, Hart Publishing, 2016) 3–16.

Etherton, T, 'Law Reform in England and Wales: A Shattered Dream or Triumph of Political Vision?' (Bar Law Reform Committee Lecture, 2007).

—— 'Memoir of a Reforming Chairman' in M Dyson, J Lee and SW Stark (eds), *Fifty Years of the Law Commissions: The Dynamics of Law Reform* (Oxford, Hart Publishing, 2016) 76–88.

Faris, N, 'Fifty Years of Law Reform—A Note on the Northern Ireland Style' in M Dyson, J Lee and SW Stark (eds), *Fifty Years of the Law Commissions: The Dynamics of Law Reform* (Oxford, Hart Publishing, 2016) 46–54.

Farrar, JH, *Law Reform and the Law Commission* (London, Sweet & Maxwell, 1974).

Gane, CHW, 'Criminal Law Reform in Scotland' (1998) 3 *Scottish Law and Practice Quarterly* 101.

Gardiner, G, 'The Machinery of Law Reform in England' (1953) 69 *LQR* 46.

—— *Capital Punishment as a Deterrent: And the Alternative* (London, Victor Gollancz, 1956).

—— 'Comparative Law Reform' (1966) 52 *American Bar Association Journal* 1021.

—— 'The Trials of a Lord Chancellor', Being the Presidential Address of the Rt Hon Lord Gardiner, Lord Chancellor, President of the Holdsworth Club of the Faculty of Law in the University of Birmingham 1967–68 (Birmingham, Holdsworth Club, 1968).

—— 'Towards the Unity of European Law' [1968] *Nederlands Juristenblad* 5.

——'Law Reform—Not Now?' (1974) 71 *Law Society's Gazette* 1065.
Gardiner, G and Elwyn Jones, F, 'The Administration of Justice' in G Gardiner and A Martin (eds), *Law Reform Now* (London, Victor Gollancz, 1963) 15–23.
Gardiner, G and Martin, A (eds), *Law Reform Now* (London, Victor Gollancz, 1963).
Gardiner, G and Martin, A, 'The Machinery of Law Reform' in G Gardiner and A Martin (eds), *Law Reform Now* (London, Victor Gollancz, 1963) 1–14.
Gibson, P, 'Law Reform Now: The Law Commission 25 Years On' (Denning Lecture, 1991).
Gillan, B, 'Ninth Life' (2014) 59(7) *Journal of the Law Society of Scotland* 18.
Goff, R, 'The Future of the Common Law' (1997) 46 *ICLQ* 745.
Gordon, G, 'New Evidence in Criminal Appeals' 1957 *Scots Law Times (News)* 125.
Gow, N, 'Delay in Divorce Cases' 1958 *Scots Law Times (News)* 125.
Gower, LCB, 'A Comment' (1967) 30 *MLR* 259.
——'Reflections on Law Reform' (1973) 23 *University of Toronto Law Journal* 257.
Gretton, GL, 'The Rational and the National: Thomas Broun Smith' in E Reid and DL Carey Miller (eds), *A Mixed Legal System in Transition: TB Smith and the Progress of Scots Law* (Edinburgh, Edinburgh University Press, 2005) 30–43.
——'Of Law Commissioning' (2013) 17 *Edinburgh Law Review* 119.
——'The Duty to Make the Law More Accessible?: The Two C-Words' in M Dyson, J Lee and SW Stark (eds), *Fifty Years of the Law Commissions: The Dynamics of Law Reform* (Oxford, Hart Publishing, 2016) 89–96.
Hahlo, HR, 'Here Lies the Common Law: Rest in Peace' (1967) 30 *MLR* 241.
Hale, B, 'A Justice of the Supreme Court in Conversation' (JUSTICE Student Human Rights Network Lecture, 16 November 2011) (unpublished attendance notes).
——'Fifty Years of the Law Commissions: The Dynamics of Law Reform Now, Then and Next' in M Dyson, J Lee and SW Stark (eds), *Fifty Years of the Law Commissions: The Dynamics of Law Reform* (Oxford, Hart Publishing, 2016) 17–26.
——'Legislation or Judicial Law Reform: Where Should Judges Fear to Tread?' (Society of Legal Scholars Annual Conference, 2016).
Halliday, J, *Quinquennial Review of the Law Commission* (2003).
Hammond, G, 'The Legislative Implementation of Law Reform Proposals' in M Dyson, J Lee and SW Stark (eds), *Fifty Years of the Law Commissions: The Dynamics of Law Reform* (Oxford, Hart Publishing, 2016) 175–88.
Harpum, C, 'The Refiner's Fire' in M Dyson, J Lee and SW Stark (eds), *Fifty Years of the Law Commissions: The Dynamics of Law Reform* (Oxford, Hart Publishing, 2016) 310–25.
Hodge, P, 'Introduction' in M Dyson, J Lee and SW Stark (eds), *Fifty Years of the Law Commissions: The Dynamics of Law Reform* (Oxford, Hart Publishing, 2016) 29–30.
Hogg, M, 'Codification of Private Law: Scots Law at the Crossroads of Common and Civil Law' in K Barker, K Fairweather and R Grantham (eds), *Private Law in the 21st Century* (Oxford, Hart Publishing, 2017) 107–29.
Home Office, *Rights Brought Home: The Human Rights Bill* (Cm 3782, 1997).
Hope, D, 'Law Reform: Alternative Strategies to Legislation' in *Law Reform: Catching the Eye of Government* (papers from a joint seminar presented by the Law Commission and UCL Faculty of Laws, 2001) 36–44.
——'Do We Still Need a Scottish Law Commission?' (2006) 10 *Edinburgh Law Review* 10.
Horder, J, *Homicide and the Politics of Law Reform* (Oxford, Oxford University Press, 2012).
House of Commons Information Office, *The Success of Private Members' Bills* (2010).

House of Commons Political and Constitutional Reform Committee, *A New Magna Carta?* (2014, HC 463).
House of Commons Select Committee on Procedure, *First Report* (1964–65, HC 149).
House of Lords Procedure Committee, *First Report, Law Commission Bills* (2008, HL 63).
—— *Second Report, Law Commission Bills* (2010, HL 30).
House of Lords Select Committee, *Report from the Select Committee on the Committee Work of the House* (1991–92, HL 35-I).
—— *First Report, Constitutional Reform Bill* (2004, HL 125).
Hunter, J, 'Law Reform: The Meanings and the Methods' in *Proceedings and Papers of the Fifth Commonwealth Law Conference* (Edinburgh, Fifth Commonwealth Law Conference, 1977) 1–7.
—— 'Thomas Broun Smith 1915–1988' (1993) 82 *Proceedings of the British Academy* 455.
Hurlburt, WH, *Law Reform Commissions in the United Kingdom, Australia and Canada* (Edmonton, Juriliber, 1986).
Irvine, D, 'A British Interpretation of Convention Rights' [2012] *PL* 237.
Johnston, D, 'How Law Commissions Work: Some Lessons from the Past' in M Dyson, J Lee and SW Stark (eds), *Fifty Years of the Law Commissions: The Dynamics of Law Reform* (Oxford, Hart Publishing, 2016) 235–44.
Keith, KJ, 'Making Law—Who, How and What?' in M Dyson, J Lee and SW Stark (eds), *Fifty Years of the Law Commissions: The Dynamics of Law Reform* (Oxford, Hart Publishing, 2016) 400–11.
Kerr, M, 'Law Reform in Changing Times' (1980) 96 *LQR* 515.
—— *As Far as I Remember* (Oxford, Hart Publishing, 2006).
Kirby, M, 'Judicial Dissent—Common Law and Civil Law Traditions' (2007) 123 *LQR* 379.
—— 'Forty Years of the Alberta Law Reform Institute—Past, Present, Future' (2008–09) 46 *Alberta Law Review* 831.
Labour Party, *The New Britain* (1964 manifesto).
Langbein, JH, 'Modern Jurisprudence in the House of Lords: The Passing of *London Tramways*' (1967–68) 53 *Cornell Law Review* 807.
Law Commission of India, *The Death Penalty* (Report No 262 (2015)).
Law Reform Commission of Ireland, *Fourth Programme of Law Reform* (LRC 110 (2013)).
Law Reform Commission of Mauritius, *Brief on the Law Reform Commission* (2016).
Law Reform Committee, *Latent Damage* (Cmnd 9390, 1984).
Law Reform Working Group [on the implementation of Scottish Law Commission reports], *Final Report* (2012).
Le Bouthillier, Y, 'The Former Law Commission of Canada: The Road Less Travelled' in M Dyson, J Lee and SW Stark (eds), *Fifty Years of the Law Commissions: The Dynamics of Law Reform* (Oxford, Hart Publishing, 2016) 97–107.
Leach, WB, 'Revisionism in the House of Lords: The Bastion of Rigid Stare Decisis Falls' (1966–67) 80 *Harvard Law Review* 797.
Lee, J, 'The Etiquette of Law Reform' in M Dyson, J Lee and SW Stark (eds), *Fifty Years of the Law Commissions: The Dynamics of Law Reform* (Oxford, Hart Publishing, 2016) 274–96.
Lester, A, 'English Judges as Law Makers' [1993] *PL* 269.
Lewis, S, 'The Bill's Progress' in M Dyson, J Lee and SW Stark (eds), *Fifty Years of the Law Commissions: The Dynamics of Law Reform* (Oxford, Hart Publishing, 2016) 266–69.
Lloyd Jones, D, 'The Law Commission and Law Reform in a Devolved Wales' (Wales Governance Centre Annual Lecture, 2013).

—— 'The Law Commission and the Implementation of Law Reform' (2013) 15 *European Journal of Law Reform* 333.
—— 'Looking to the Future' in M Dyson, J Lee and SW Stark (eds), *Fifty Years of the Law Commissions: The Dynamics of Law Reform* (Oxford, Hart Publishing, 2016) 355–64.
Lord Chancellor's Department, *Proposals for English and Scottish Law Commissions* (Cmnd 2573, 1965).
Lorimer, E, 'Commissioning the Future—A Chief Executive's Perspective' in M Dyson, J Lee and SW Stark (eds), *Fifty Years of the Law Commissions: The Dynamics of Law Reform* (Oxford, Hart Publishing, 2016) 365–68.
Macdonald, HRM, Mullin, JC, Smith, TB and Wallace, JF, *The Laws of Scotland: Stair Memorial Encyclopaedia*, vol 22 (Edinburgh, Law Society of Scotland, 1987).
MacDonald, JW, 'The New York Law Revision Commission' (1965) 28 *MLR* 1.
MacQueen, HL, 'Judicial Reform of Private Law' (1998) 3 *Scottish Law and Practice Quarterly* 134.
—— 'Implementation by Statute: What the Future Holds' in M Dyson, J Lee and SW Stark (eds), *Fifty Years of the Law Commissions: The Dynamics of Law Reform* (Oxford, Hart Publishing, 2016) 201–14.
Maher, G, 'Statutory Interpretation and Scottish Law Commission Reports' 1992 *Scots Law Times (News)* 277.
—— 'Principles and Politics in Law Reform: Sexual Offences in Scots Law' 2013 *Juridical Review* 563.
Malawi Law Commission, *Annual Work Programme* (2012).
Marsh, N, 'Law Reform in the United Kingdom: A New Institutional Approach' (1971) 13 *William & Mary Law Review* 263.
McBryde, WW, 'Law Reform: The Scottish Experience' (1998) 3 *Scottish Law and Practice Quarterly* 86.
McDonald, B, 'Law Reform in Private Law: The Role of Statutes in Supplementing or Supplanting the Common Law' in M Dyson, J Lee and SW Stark (eds), *Fifty Years of the Law Commissions: The Dynamics of Law Reform* (Oxford, Hart Publishing, 2016) 297–309.
McMillan, M, 'The Role of Law Reform in Constitutionalism, Rule of Law and Democratic Governance: Reflections by the Scottish Law Commission' (Association of Law Reform Agencies of Eastern and Southern Africa Lecture, 2011).
—— 'Implementation of Law Reform Reports: Developments in Scotland' in M Dyson, J Lee and SW Stark (eds), *Fifty Years of the Law Commissions: The Dynamics of Law Reform* (Oxford, Hart Publishing, 2016) 369–79.
Miller, K, 'Legal Change: The Social Dimension' (1998) 3 *Scottish Law and Practice Quarterly* 117.
Ministry of Justice, *Report on the Implementation of Law Commission Proposals* (2011, HC 719).
—— *Report on the Implementation of Law Commission Proposals* (2012, HC 1900).
—— *Report on the Implementation of Law Commission Proposals* (2013, HC 908).
—— *Triennial Review: Law Commission, Report of Stage One* (2013).
—— *Triennial Review: Law Commission, Report of Stage Two* (2014).
—— *Report on the Implementation of Law Commission Proposals* (2014, HC 1237).
—— *Report on the Implementation of Law Commission Proposals* (2015, HC 1062).

—— *Responding to Human Rights Judgments: Report to the Joint Committee on Human Rights on the Government's Response to Human Rights Judgments 2014–16* (Cm 9360, 2016).
—— *Report on the Implementation of Law Commission Proposals* (2017, HC 613).
Mitchell, JDB, 'First Principles First' 1959 *Scots Law Times (News)* 1.
Mitchell, P, 'Strategies of the Early Law Commission' in M Dyson, J Lee and SW Stark (eds), *Fifty Years of the Law Commissions: The Dynamics of Law Reform* (Oxford, Hart Publishing, 2016) 31–45.
Munby, J, 'Shaping the Law—The Law Commission at the Crossroads' (Denning Lecture, 2011).
—— 'Introduction' in M Dyson, J Lee and SW Stark (eds), *Fifty Years of the Law Commissions: The Dynamics of Law Reform* (Oxford, Hart Publishing, 2016) 217–18.
Munday, R, '"All for One and One for All": The Rise to Prominence of the Composite Judgment within the Civil Division of the Court of Appeal' (2002) 61 *CLJ* 321.
Neuberger, D, 'General, Equal and Certain: Law Reform Today and Tomorrow' (2012) 33 *Statute Law Review* 323.
New Zealand Law Commission, *A New Interpretation Act: To Avoid 'Prolixity and Tautology'* (NZLC R17 (1990)).
—— *Final Report on Emergencies* (NZLC R22 (1991)).
—— *Justice: The Experiences of Maori Women* (NZLC R53 (1999)).
—— *Evidence* (NZLC R55 (1999)).
—— *Compulsory Treatment for Substance Dependence: A Review of the Alcoholism and Drug Addiction Act 1966* (NZLC R118 (2010)).
North, P, 'Law Reform: Processes and Problems' (1985) 101 *LQR* 338.
Northern Ireland Law Commission, *Annual Report 2015* (2015).
Oerton, RT, *A Lament for the Law Commission* (Chichester, Countrywise Press, 1987).
Office of Public Services Reform and HM Treasury, *Better Government Services: Executive Agencies in the 21st Century* (2002).
Ormerod, D, 'Reflections on the Courts and the Commission' in M Dyson, J Lee and SW Stark (eds), *Fifty Years of the Law Commissions: The Dynamics of Law Reform* (Oxford, Hart Publishing, 2016) 326–35.
Paines, N, 'Reflections on Statutory Implementation in the Law Commission' in M Dyson, J Lee and SW Stark (eds), *Fifty Years of the Law Commissions: The Dynamics of Law Reform* (Oxford, Hart Publishing, 2016) 198–200.
Palmer, G, 'The Law Reform Enterprise: Evaluating the Past and Charting the Future' (2015) 131 *LQR* 402.
Paterson, A, *The Law Lords* (London, Palgrave McMillan, 1982).
—— *Final Judgment: The Last Law Lords and the Supreme Court* (Oxford, Hart Publishing, 2013).
Paterson, A and Paterson, C, *Guarding the Guardians? Towards an Independent, Accountable and Diverse Senior Judiciary* (London, CentreForum, 2012).
Paton, GCH, 'Discere Docendo—III: An Account of the Thirty-ninth Annual General Meeting of the Society of Public Teachers of Law, 17th to 19th September 1953' 1953 *Scots Law Times (News)* 242.
Pentland, Lord, 'The Scottish Law Commission and the Future of Law Reform in Scotland' 2016 *Juridical Review* 169.

—— 'The Scottish Law Commission and the Future of Law Reform in Scotland' in M Dyson, J Lee and SW Stark (eds), *Fifty Years of the Law Commissions: The Dynamics of Law Reform* (Oxford, Hart Publishing, 2016) 340–54.
Phillips, N, 'Constitutional Reform: One Year On' (Judicial Studies Board Annual Lecture, 2007).
Reid, J, 'The Judge as Law Maker' (1972–73) 12 *Journal of the Society of Public Teachers of Law* 22.
Reid, KGC, 'While One Hundred Remain: TB Smith and the Progress of Scots Law' in E Reid and DL Carey Miller (eds), *A Mixed Legal System in Transition: TB Smith and the Progress of Scots Law* (Edinburgh, Edinburgh University Press, 2005) 1–29.
—— 'Smoothing the Rugged Parts of the Passage: Scots Law and its Edinburgh Chair' (2014) 18 *Edinburgh Law Review* 315.
Rodger, A, 'The Codification of Commercial Law in Victorian Britain' (1992) 108 *LQR* 570.
—— 'The Bell of Law Reform' 1993 *Scots Law Times (News)* 339.
Ross, A, Nash, H and Reid, CT, 'The Implementation of EU Environmental Law in Scotland' (2009) 13 *Edinburgh Law Review* 224.
Scarman, L, 'A Code of English Law?' (lecture, University of Hull, 1966).
—— 'Codification and Judge-made Law: A Problem of Co-Existence' (lecture, University of Birmingham, 1966).
—— *Law Reform: The New Pattern (The Lindsay Memorial Lectures)* (London, Routledge & Kegan Paul, 1968).
Schwartz, B and Wade, HWR, *Legal Control of Government: Administrative Law in Britain and the United States* (Oxford, Clarendon Press, 1972).
Scottish Office, *Scotland in the Union: A Partnership for Good* (Cm 2225, 1993).
Scottish Parliamentary Bureau, 'Parliamentary Scrutiny of Bills Arising from Scottish Law Commission Reports' (PB/S3/10/60, March 2010).
Sedley, S, *Lions under the Throne: Essays on the History of English Public Law* (Cambridge, Cambridge University Press, 2015).
Smith, JC, 'Codification of the Criminal Law' (lecture, Inns of Court School of Law, 1986).
Smith, TB, *The Doctrines of Judicial Precedent in Scots Law* (Edinburgh, W Green & Son Ltd, 1952).
—— 'Malice in Murderland' 1957 *Scots Law Times (News)* 129.
—— *British Justice: The Scottish Contribution (The Hamlyn Lectures)* (London, Stevens & Sons Ltd, 1961).
—— 'The Scottish Universities Law Institute: The First Year' 1961 *Scots Law Times (News)* 97.
—— *Studies Critical and Comparative* (Edinburgh, W Green & Son Ltd, 1962).
—— 'Legal Imperialism and Legal Parochialism' 1965 *Juridical Review* 39.
—— 'Unification of Law in Britain: Problems of Co-Ordination' (1965–66) *Acta Juridica* 93.
—— 'Law Reform in a Mixed "Civil Law" and "Common Law" Jurisdiction' (1974–75) 35 *Louisiana Law Review* 927.
South African Law Commission (now the South African Law Reform Commission), *Euthanasia and the Artificial Preservation of Life* (Project 86 (1998)).
Spencer, JR, 'Precedent and Criminal Cases in the House of Lords' (1986) 45 *CLJ* 361.
—— 'The Codification of Criminal Procedure' in J Chalmers, F Leverick and L Farmer (eds), *Essays in Criminal Law in Honour of Sir Gerald Gordon* (Edinburgh, Edinburgh University Press, 2010) 305–25.

Standards, Procedures and Public Appointments Committee of the Scottish Parliament, 'Scottish Law Commission Bill Procedures—Review, Note of Outcome of Review' (2015).

Stark, F, 'Wiping the Slate Clean: Reforming Scots Law's Approach to Evidence of the Accused's Bad Character' (2013) 76 *MLR* 346.

Stark, SW, 'The Longer You Can Look Back, the Further You Can Look Forward: The Origins of the Scottish Law Commission' (2014) 18 *Edinburgh Law Review* 59.

—— 'Promoting Law Reform: By Means of Draft Bills or Otherwise' in M Dyson, J Lee and SW Stark (eds), *Fifty Years of the Law Commissions: The Dynamics of Law Reform* (Oxford, Hart Publishing, 2016) 139–50.

Stark, SW and Faris, N, 'Law Reform in Northern Ireland: Cheshire Cat or Potemkin Commission?' [2016] *PL* 651.

Steven, A, 'Codification: A Perspective from a Scottish Law Commissioner' (Seminar Series on Codification, All Souls College, Oxford, 2014).

Stoddart, C, 'Educating the Judiciary' (2000) 45(6) *Journal of the Law Society of Scotland* 23.

Stott, G, *Lord Advocate's Diary 1961–1966* (Aberdeen, Aberdeen University Press, 1991).

Subordinate Legislation Committee of the Scottish Parliament, 51st Report, 2009 (SL/S3/09/R51).

Sutherland, EE, 'Child and Family Law: Progress and Pusillanimity' in EE Sutherland, KE Goodall, GFM Little and FP Davidson (eds), *Law Making and the Scottish Parliament: The Early Years* (Edinburgh, Edinburgh University Press, 2011) 58–83.

Sutherland, EE, Goodall, KE, Little, GFM and Davidson, FP, 'Law Making and the Scottish Parliament: The Early Years in Context' in EE Sutherland, KE Goodall, GFM Little and FP Davidson (eds), *Law Making and the Scottish Parliament: The Early Years* (Edinburgh, Edinburgh University Press, 2011) 3–8.

Thomas, J, 'Speech Given at the Dinner for Her Majesty's Judges' (Mansion House, 2016).

Topping, MR and Vandenlinden, JPM, '*Ibi Renascit Jus Commune*' (1970) 33 *MLR* 170.

Toulson, R, 'Forty Years On: What Progress in Delivering Accessible and Principled Criminal Law?' (2006) 27 *Statute Law Review* 61.

—— 'Democracy, Law Reform and the Rule of Law' in M Dyson, J Lee and SW Stark (eds), *Fifty Years of the Law Commissions: The Dynamics of Law Reform* (Oxford, Hart Publishing, 2016) 127–38.

Tranter, K, 'Citation Practices of the Australian Law Reform Commission in Final Reports 1992–2012' (2015) 38 *University of New South Wales Law Journal* 323.

United Kingdom Government, Scottish Ministers, Welsh Ministers and Northern Ireland Executive Committee, *Devolution: Memorandum of Understanding and Supplementary Agreements* (2012).

Villiers, C, 'Employees as Creditors: A Challenge for Justice in Insolvency Law' (1999) 20 *Company Lawyer* 222.

Walker, DM, 'Legal Education and Training' 1960 *Scots Law Times (News)* 41.

—— 'The Second Annual Report of the Scottish Law Commission' 1968 *Scots Law Times (News)* 2.

—— 'The Scottish Law Commission under Review' (1987) 8 *Statute Law Review* 115.

Weiss, GA, 'The Enchantment of Codification in the Common-Law World' (2000) 25 *Yale Journal of International Law* 435.

Welsh Government, White Paper, *Renting Homes: A Better Way for Wales* (2013).

—— 'Evidence Submitted by the Welsh Government to the Commission on Devolution in Wales', 18 February 2013.

—— *Report on the Implementation of Law Commission Proposals* (2016).
Williams, G (ed), *The Reform of the Law* (London, Victor Gollancz Ltd, 1951).
—— 'Recklessness Redefined' (1981) 40 *CLJ* 252.
Willock, ID, 'Impressions of Legal Education in the USA' 1959 *Scots Law Times (News)* 71.
Wilson, H, *The Labour Government 1964–70* (Harmondsworth, Penguin Books Ltd, 1974).
Wilson, S, 'Reforming the Law (Commission): A Crisis of Identity?' [2013] *PL* 20.
—— 'Judiciary Diversity: Where Do We Go From Here?' (2013) 2(1) *Cambridge Journal of International and Comparative Law* 7.
Windlesham, Lord, 'The Constitutional Reform Act 2005: Ministers, Judges and Constitutional Change' [2005] *PL* 806.
—— 'The Constitutional Reform Act 2005: The Politics of Constitutional Reform' [2006] *PL* 35.
Wright, R, 'Precedents' (1942–44) 8 *CLJ* 118.
Zander, M, *The Law-Making Process*, 6th edn (Cambridge, Cambridge University Press, 2004).
—— *The Law-Making Process*, 7th edn (Oxford, Hart Publishing, 2015).

INDEX

www.ingramcontent.com/pod-product-compliance
Ingram Content Group UK Ltd.
Pitfield, Milton Keynes, MK11 3LW, UK
UKHW020242290926
15470UKWH00002B/691

9 781509 906918